The American Speakership

The ☆ ☆ ☆ American ☆ Speakership

The Office in Historical Perspective

Second Edition

Ronald M. Peters, Jr.

THE JOHNS HOPKINS UNIVERSITY PRESS   BALTIMORE AND LONDON

The Johns Hopkins University Press
2715 North Charles Street
Baltimore, Maryland 21218-4319
The Johns Hopkins Press Ltd., London

LIBRARY OF CONGRESS CATALOGING-IN-PUBLICATION DATA

Peters, Ronald M.
    The American speakership : the office in historical perspective /
Ronald M. Peters, Jr. — 2nd ed.
        p.   cm.
    Includes bibliographical references and index.
    ISBN 0-8018-5751-1 (alk. paper). — ISBN 0-8018-5758-9 (pbk. : alk. paper)
        1. United States.   Congress.   House—Speaker—History.   I. Title.
JK1411.P48   1997
328.73'0762—dc21   97-16988
                                                                          CIP

A catalog record for this book is available from the British Library.

To Glenda, John, and Julie

Contents

Acknowledgments

Ten years ago I embarked on a study of the speakership of the House of Representatives during the period since the reforms of the early 1970s. My working title was "The Modern Speakership" and my plan was to write an account of the manner in which the speakership had been changed by the reform movement. I planned to write mostly about Carl Albert and Tip O'Neill. The present volume reflects the journey through history upon which I had unwittingly launched myself. At some point along the way I became convinced that the speakership that we witness today cannot be well understood unless we examine how it has evolved in history. Making sense of the way in which the speakership changed over time became the focal point of my thinking and the object of my study.

This study has become a part of my own history in ways that I could not have anticipated. John and Julie Peters were born as this project got under way; neither knows a father who is not working on "the book." Glenda Peters has shared with me the writing of two books and the raising of two children, and she is a part of them and me.

A scholar measures time according to publication schedules, but a teacher measures time in terms of the lives of his students. Several "generations" of graduate and undergraduate students have passed my way during the years of research and writing, and I am indebted to all of them, especially here to those who assisted me in the dogged work that was sometimes required: David Bartlett, Christy Caesar, Gina Carrigan, Ron Grimes, Jon Hale, Bill Hart, Jackie Johnson, Robin LeBlanc, Tony Litherland, Mary McCauley, Cindy Mills, Siobhan Moroney, Mar-

vin Overby, Mary Scribner, Frank Smist, Doc Syers, Joe Theissen, and
Art Vega.

The manuscript underwent sufficient revision to survive two word
processing systems. The mechanics of production were superintended
by Nita Dotson, Toni Evans, Linda Pierce, LaDonna Sullivan, and Betty
Craig. Maryanne Maletz offered valuable advice in editing the first draft
of the manuscript, and Henry Tom of the Johns Hopkins University
Press served as the midwife of several more. Peter Dreyer pruned the
final draft and made sense out of the notes.

Over the years I have benefited from formal and informal interviews
with dozens of members and former members of Congress and those
who worked for them. Except to support specific points of fact, their
contribution to this book is not cited in the text, but my debt to them
is great. I would like especially to thank Congressman Richard Bolling
for the time and insight that he gave me. The entire process was greatly
facilitated by the support of key members of the staffs of speakers Albert
and O'Neill, including Joel Jankowsky, Mike Reed, Charlie Ward, Gary
Hymel, Ari Weiss, Kirk O'Donnell, Chris Mathews, Jack Lew, Steve
Bourke, the late Spencer Smith, and John Barriere. Donald R. Kennon
was just completing *The Speakers of the U.S. House of Representatives:
A Bibliography, 1789–1984* (Baltimore: Johns Hopkins University
Press, 1986) during 1981–82, and he was kind enough to give me the
run of his index cards. This was invaluable to me, and I am greatly
appreciative. The publication of this extensive bibliography has made
a separate bibliography unnecessary in the present volume. Eric
Schwartz provided me with transcripts of Speaker O'Neill's press conferences that contributed greatly to my understanding of his speakership.

Several scholars have offered constructive comments on the manuscript, including David Brady, Tony Champagne, Joe Foote, Larry Hill,
David Levy, Mike Malbin, Bob Peabody, and Ray Smock. In every
respect this book is better for the quality of the advice they gave.

During the early years of the project, the research was supported
by a grant from the National Endowment for the Humanities, for which
I am indebted. Research support provided by the University of Oklahoma Research Council provided the seed money to get the project
started. Data on Speaker Albert's voting record was provided by the
Inter-University Consortium for Political and Social Research.

Finally, I must thank the two persons without whose support this
book would not have been possible. In 1981 and 1982 Speaker Tip
O'Neill took me on as a staff member of the Democratic Steering and
Policy Committee and gave me the opportunity to observe him and his
office at first hand. His staff was always supportive of my efforts and
tolerant of my presence, and the insights that this experience has pro-

vided are imbedded in the interpretation of the speakership that this book offers.

The project would never have been undertaken had not Speaker Albert given it his full endorsement. I do not know how to count my debts to him. Both with respect to the writing of this book and with respect to the founding and nurturing of the congressional studies center that bears his name, he has been a source of support, advice, and inspiration. At the outset of this project, he told me to write a book about the speakership that would explain it to the public. I have tried to do so. In the pages that follow I have tried to write dispassionately of all of the speakers of the House, to let their story unfold here as it did in history; but in this place I may be permitted to rise to a point of personal privilege. In my life I have known no brighter, kinder, or more decent man than Carl Albert. He served as speaker during one of the most difficult periods in American history, and he served his country well. No man can do more.

John Meiers provided able research assistance for the second edition. Thanks to Joanne Allen for her excellent editorial work in preparing the second edition. John Caldwell and the staff of the Carl Albert Center Congressional Archives supported my research in Speaker Albert's papers.

The American Speakership

Prologue: The Speakership in History

So that in the first place, I put for a generall inclination of all mankind, a perpetuall and restlesse desire of Power after power, that Ceaseth onely in Death.   Hobbes, *Leviathan* 1.11

One day in 1923, a Texas congressman named Sam Rayburn said, "I'll tell you what I think. I think that someday a man will be elected who'll bring the speakership into real respectability again. He'll be the real leader of the House. He'll be master around here, and everyone will know it."[1] Rayburn was talking to two powerful members of the House, Nicholas Longworth, a Republican from Ohio, and John Nance Garner, a Democrat from Texas. All three men later became effective speakers of the House, but it was Sam Rayburn who most approximated the "real leader" of which he had spoken. He was a man who lived for the House of Representatives and one who loved power. "I've always wanted responsibility because I want the power responsibility brings," he said when he was elected speaker in 1941. "I hate like hell to be licked. It almost kills me."[2]

The search for "power in the House" is endless. When Congressman Richard Bolling published a book by that name in 1968 and called for a reinvigorated speakership, he echoed Sam Rayburn's sentiment.[3] In our time the standard by which speakers of the House of Representatives most often have been judged is their use of power. Speakers who use it effectively are regarded as "strong" (i.e., good) and those who do not are regarded as "weak" (i.e., bad) leaders. The view that the essence of politics lies in power is essentially Hobbesian and is an artifact of modern political thought. Hobbes transformed the way men thought about themselves and their government. That transformation led eventually to the liberal idea of the state in which freedom and equality are the preferred political values. Locke's application of Hobbesian premises underlies the American Founding. Yet it was not until much later in American history that Hobbesian political science penetrated the American academy. Only at the turn of the century did scholars such as Arthur Bentley and John Dewey articulate the positivist premises of the Hobbesian world-view in which politics is rooted in the pursuit of power.

One scholar who was influenced by the new political orientation was Mary Parker Follett. Her interest was in the speakership of the House of Representatives and her intention was to transform the way in which the office was understood. In 1896 she wrote *The Speaker of the House of Representatives*, in which she sought to reorient the view taken of the office by defining its principal function as political party leadership.[4] Although the speakership, in Follett's view, had at all times been an inherently political office, it had not been perceived in that way. All speakers were political creatures, yet some had been more effective than others. The best speakers were those who stood for something, who had a policy, who commanded the House, and who drove it in the direction of their goals. Henry Clay of Kentucky was the first and greatest of the politically efficacious speakers because he used the speakership as a platform for his policies and national political aspirations. Thomas Brackett Reed of Maine was the greatest speaker among Follett's contemporaries, because he had broken the back of obstructionism in the House and permitted its legislative majority to govern. In a ringing conclusion, Follett called for a strengthened speakership and cooperative governance between the speaker and the president.

Follett's call for the centralization of power in the speakership came just as the office was about to reach its zenith. A decade after her study Joe Cannon was at the peak of his power, but in 1910 the House revolted against Cannon and undermined the powers of the speakership. Sam Rayburn's expressed desire for a strong speaker had come during the tenure of a weak speaker, Frederick H. Gillett of Massachusetts. Rayburn was convinced that the House required strong leadership to function well. Yet history demonstrated that the desire for power was insufficient to bring it about, that the circumstances in which a powerful speakership could thrive might be unusual. Rayburn's conviction was shadowed by an element of doubt.

Rayburn did much to resolve that doubt himself. As speaker, he became a figure of mythic proportions, larger than the office that he held. That myth still shapes expectations of speakers. But an understanding of the speakership that simply looks for a "real leader" of the House, a Sam Rayburn reincarnate, will fail to grasp the essence of the office. For the speakership is more complex than this perspective would suggest. What factors, after all, make it possible for a speaker to command the House? Is "power in the House" the primary goal that speakers should seek? How does the speakership actually present itself to those who come to serve in it? And what forces have served to shape its evolution over time? These questions and others like them form the problem of the present work, which seeks to provide an understanding of the speakership of the House of Representatives. An adequate understanding of the speakership requires a view of the office within the framework of the political system in which it functions, yet that system is constantly undergoing change and the speakership has changed in corresponding ways. In understanding the nature of such change, we may come to have a better grasp of both the office and the polity within which it is embedded.

Contemporary attempts by political scientists to understand party leadership in the House of Representatives have been largely ahistorical. Even where these authors have chosen narrative description, their purpose has been to search for general explanations that transcend time and place. The work of Robert L. Peabody, for example, is characterized by rigorous accounts of party leadership races that, when taken together, form a historical account of leadership transformation across three decades of experience.[5] Yet in drawing conclusions from his studies, Peabody essentially ignores factors subject to historical change, such as the policy agenda, the changing character of the electoral system, and the culture of the House itself. His proximity to the races inside the House leads him to conclude that internal variables are most important in explaining the events he describes. But an account of the internal machinations of the power struggle, itself important, affords an insufficient basis for understanding the forces that have shaped the milieu in which the struggle takes place. Similarly, in her book on party leadership in the House, Barbara Sinclair focuses on the tactics employed by party leaders to build coalitions and maintain internal party harmony, their two presumed primary goals.[6] She recognizes that those tactics have been shaped by the changes that took place in the House during the reform movement of the 1970s, but does not infer from this any theory of how institutional change affects the tasks of party leadership. The result is an excellent descriptive account of the leadership system during the brief period Sinclair studied it, but one that provides little basis for thinking about the system's development.

Joseph Cooper and David Brady evidenced a willingness to come to grips with broader historical forces in their 1981 article comparing speakers Cannon and Rayburn.[7] Their "contextualist" theory argues that the characteristic "style" of a speaker will be shaped by the "institutional context" in which he serves. Effective speakers will be those whose styles are well adapted to the circumstances in which they are called upon to serve. To avoid being tautological (effective speakers are those who are effective), the theory becomes historical. Over time the House of Representatives evolves particular institutional contexts (characterized, say, by centralization or diffusion of power). Within particular institutional contexts, different leaders come to power. Their effectiveness turns on their relative suitability to the context. The contextualist thesis is typically modern. It is both historical and relative. It accepts the criterion of power, but it denies that power can be attained simply by institutional reform or an act of individual will. Instead, the contextualist thesis argues that evolutionary forces set parameters within which the range of human choice is channeled. The House will get a real leader when the circumstances permit it, and the skills that the real leader must possess will depend upon the circumstances.

Cooper and Brady's fundamental premise—that institutional development must be placed within the context of the broader evolution of the political system—is correct. Its capacity to differentiate between the nature and requirements of office during various historical eras yields a much richer understanding of politics than do approaches that emphasize the current behavior of political actors. The contextualist theory is particularly appealing to a generation of scholars of the "postreform" House, whose perspective is largely shaped by an immersion in the reforms of the early 1970s and their effects on the institutional life of the Congress.[8]

The present volume seeks to develop a historical understanding of the speakership of the House of Representatives. It argues that the speakership has undergone several distinct historical transformations, and that these transformations have paralleled and been caused by broad changes in the political system of which the House and the speakership are a part. Each historical period has had a characteristic pattern of party politics, a predominant policy agenda, and in the House of Representatives particular institutional arrangements and a distinct speakership. While the view taken here is essentially compatible with the Cooper-Brady thesis, it is broader. Their concept of a relationship between "institutional context and leadership style" is a product of social science; in seeking a precise focus in studying patterns of historical relationship, Cooper and Brady draw on contemporary organization theory. My view is more broadly historical. The "contexts" that drive the "style" are themselves a part of a pattern of political and social evolution that must be studied in order to understand the speakership. At the same time, within the "contexts," individual actors and events that are not historically or contextually determined will influence the House. An adequate understanding requires narrative description as well as an account of trends.[9]

Attempts often have been made to divide American history into periods designated by some set of theoretically meaningful criteria.[10] Among political scientists, such attempts have most often come from students of political parties and voting behavior.[11] In recent years, attempts have been made to sector American history according to trends in public policy and the development of the administrative state.[12] Inevitably, any such attempt must involve a degree of arbitrariness, since history does not actually come so neatly packaged. Historical periods are analytic constructs, not historical facts, and history proceeds "from day to day, / To the last syllable of recorded time,"[13] without regard to the scribblings of academic writers. Periodization is useful not because it is exact, but because it helps us to think intelligently. By drawing attention to continuities within a span of time and differences between one era and the next, attempts to periodize history serve to clarify our thinking.

Since the subject of this book is the speakership of the United States House of Representatives, the historical scheme around which the discussion is organized draws upon key turning points in the office. These transitions did not occur in a historical vacuum. The changes in the speakership, and the political system more generally, were shaped by broader changes in American life. The rather visible events in the evolution of the speakership that I have used to divide its history serve as interesting markers and draw attention to the broader systemic and environmental changes by which the evolution of the speakership was shaped. Figure 1 illustrates the periods into which the present study is divided.

The first period, treated in chapter 1, is called the "parliamentary speakership." Henry Clay's tenure was its most famous, but its last, that of William Pennington, was in a way its most revealing. During this era the weakness of the Congress and the speakership reflected that of the antebellum state. The speaker's most important function was to preside effectively over a House of Representatives that was often riven by sectional conflict and party schisms. The parliamentary speakership was effective only when the speakers were. Henry Clay was one of America's most influential politicians during his years as speaker, but he was more powerful than the office he held.

The second period, the subject of chapter 2, began with the Civil War and continued until the revolt against Speaker Cannon in 1910. It is called the "partisan speakership," because it was a product of the strong two-party system that evolved in the half-century after the war. Its last and most famous speaker was Uncle Joe Cannon, but the roots of Cannonism lay deep in late nineteenth-century political experience. This was the great era of party politics in the United States, and the

Figure 1 Historical Patterns in the Evolution of the American Speakership

	Parliamentary Speakership	Partisan Speakership	Feudal Speakership	Democratic Speakership
	1789-1860	1861-1910	1910-1961	1961-
Political System	Fragmented Parties Weak Committee System High Turnover	Strong Two-party System Strong Speakership	Decentralized Parties Autonomous Committees Low Turnover	Weak Parties Autonomous Members Fragmented Committee System
Policy Agenda	Federal State Slavery Tariff National Bank	Industrial State Distributive Policies Regulation of Production	Welfare State Redistributive Policies Regulation of Financial System	Regulatory State Regulatory Policies Budget Politics Off-budget Programs
The Speaker:	Presiding Officer	Hierarchical Leader	Broker	Therapist Policy Maker Symbol

Constitutional Regime

speakership became powerful as a position of party leadership. Its character varied though, according to the capacities of individual speakers and the differing tendencies of the two major parties.

Chapter 3 describes the third period in the evolution of the speakership, which began with the revolt against Cannon in 1910 and ended with Sam Rayburn's death in 1961. It is called the "feudal speakership" because of the manner in which the House was shaped by the strength and autonomy of the committee chairmen. Sam Rayburn was its quintessential and last speaker. The main fact of congressional life in this era was the role of the solid South in the Democratic party and the strength of its committee chairmen in the Congress. After 1932 the stability of the New Deal coalition ossified congressional arrangements, and speakers were forced to tread softly lest they step on the toes of the committee barons.

The fourth period began in 1961 and may well have come to an end in 1994. It is described in chapters 4 and 5. Its central tendency is evident in the manner in which power and influence were diffused in the House of Representatives. I have labeled it the "democratic speakership." This appellation does not refer to the fact that the Democrats were in the majority during this period but instead indicates that the trend of the era is toward democracy with a small d in both parties. I trace the development of this trend in the post-Rayburn House and explain the characteristic patterns of its politics. Finally, in chapter 6 I describe the Republican takeover of the House in the 104th Congress and suggest the possibility that it marks the beginning of a new era in the history of the speakership. I analyze the Republican speakership and the role of Speaker Gingrich, and I assess both in relationship to the book's historical and theoretical framework.

The circles in figure 1 are arranged to suggest that these periods are not wholly discrete, but instead overlapping, with each period shading into the next. Within the circles some main features of the political system and policy agenda are indicated. The upper hemispheres describe the political system, denoting the party system above the arrow and the institutional structure of the House below it. The lower hemispheres describe the policy agenda, indicating its general thrust above the arrow and some specific policy issues below it. The long arrow bifurcating the circles is intended to suggest the continuity provided by the constitutional regime. Below the circles the nature of the speakership during each period is indicated.

Of course the periods into which this study of the speakership have been divided are not the only possible or reasonable way in which to analyze American political development, or indeed the office of speaker itself. A study focusing on the party system, on electoral realignment, on the presidency, or on the Supreme Court, for example, might be organized differently. Similarly, a barefootedly empirical tracing of trends in aggregate indicators might suggest that key turning points in American political development occurred at some point before or after the visible changes in the speakership identified here. Defining periods of historical development is an analytic task, and accounts invoking this mode of analysis are analytic histories. Tocqueville's *Democracy in America* is the prototype. Marking with precision where the aristocratic age ended and the democratic age began is not possible, but generations of observers of political life have found Tocqueville's distinction a useful way of thinking about the development of modern political life in America and elsewhere.

Granting that all classificatory schemes are relative to the subject being classified, it is reassuring to notice that there is considerable consensus about the main patterns of American political development. It is commonly accepted, for example, that the antebellum state differed in fundamental ways from that which emerged after the Civil War. Most scholars acknowledge a turning point in the antebellum era during the 1830s. There is a consensus among students of electoral behavior that the decade of the 1890s witnessed a significant electoral realignment, as did the 1930s. Finally, many political scientists believe that the late 1960s and 1970s ushered in a new period in politics and government.[14] These historical divisions relate to, but are not coextensive with, the periods in the development of the speakership into which the present study is divided. If the key transformations in the electoral system took place in the 1830s, 1890s, 1930s, and at some point after the late 1960s, then they are not on all fours with the transformations of the speakership.[15] This does not mean, however, that they are unrelated to the way in which the speakership changed. It appears that something like a "historical lag" takes place between basic changes in the polity, the policy agenda, and the political system, and changes in institutional arrangements. In each of the historical periods in the evolution of the speakership, the transformation has occurred as a result of changes that were embryonic in the preceding era, and only culminated decades after the initial upheaval took place. The most immediate changes that occur as one period ends and the next begins take the form of a reaction against the old order; but underlying the reaction are ongoing changes in the polity that will eventually shape the new system. The seed of the parliamentary speakership was sown in the Constitution; in a divided society half-slave and half-free; and in the transformation of the cotton South after 1815.[16] It ripened in the 1840s and was cut down in the Civil War. The seed of the partisan speakership was sown by the rapid industrial expansion after the Civil War. It ripened in the 1890s and died in 1910. The seed of the feudal speakership was sown by the progressive movement between 1912 and 1932. It evolved even during the Republican hegemony of the Roaring Twenties, and ripened in the 1930s. It was killed by the reforms of the 1960s and 1970s. The seed of the democratic speakership was sown during the liberal surge in the late 1950s, and it ripened during and after the reform movement.

Within these periods in the evolution of the speakership, changes have taken place in the political system, the policy agenda, the partisan alignment, and in the makeup of the House of Representatives. Some might argue that the periods that have been identified here should be divided into ones of shorter duration, and others might question the possibility of periodization entirely on the theory that each decade, Congress, year, month, day, or hour is a period unto itself. But analysis must begin somewhere, and the mode of analysis presented here suggests the utility of distinguishing a few broadly defined periods in the evolution of the speakership. Within these periods significant permutations in the conduct of the office occurred. These permutations are best viewed as variations on a theme, rather than as different songs, because of the continuity of certain key forces shaping the office. Many readers of this book will have their own ideas about how American political history should be divided; some may have a different view of how the speakership developed. To these readers, the present volume constitutes a call to a dialogue that will, I hope, be based upon the premise that a developmental understanding offers the best insight into the nature of the American political system and the speakership of the House of Representatives.

Further elaboration of the book's historical framework may be found in table 1, which arrays the historical periods and some of their characteristics. The table is illustrative and not comprehensive; it is not possible to include all relevant factors affecting historical change in a single table, or indeed, in a single book. But the table provides an overview of the historical analysis that follows. Arrayed horizontally are the periods into which the study is divided. Listed vertically are some of the characteristics of the political system, the policy agenda, and the House of Representatives that have changed from one period to the next. The information is presented in the order suggested by the theoretical perspective. The evolving society shapes its policy agenda, which in turn shapes the political system, the House of Representatives, and the speakership.

The first variable included in table 1 is the policy agenda. During each of these periods the policy agenda has been dominated by issues that have cleaved the polity even as they have been shaped by it. The parliamentary period was dominated by sectional politics.[17] The partisan period was dedicated to growth and marked by distributive policies.[18] The feudal period brought the development of the welfare state and redistributive policies.[19] The democratic period is destined to be dominated by governmental regulation.[20] The electoral cleavages to which the changing policy agenda has given rise have shaped the party system, the major systemic variable the table presents.[21] Throughout its history, the speakership has been importantly defined by its relationship to the presidency. The presidency was weak until the end of the partisan period, when Theodore Roosevelt demonstrated what the "bully pulpit" could do; yet even a popular president like T.R. could not bully Speaker Cannon. The presidency gained in power during the feudal period, as first Woodrow Wilson and later Franklin Roosevelt demonstrated its capacity for strong leadership of the legislature. The institutionally powerful presidency began to develop in the 1920s and 1930s (marked by the creation of the Bureau of the Budget and the Executive Office of the President), and it matured in the late 1960s during the democratic period.

Inside the House, the broad forces of the political system led to variations in institutional arrangements and career patterns that have been captured by the concept of institutionalization in the work of Nelson Polsby.[22] Institutionalization denotes the trend toward stability in the rules and procedures of the House, its mode of organization, and its membership. Turnover is an aspect of institutionalization, but is discretely indicated because of its fundamental importance in understanding the relationship between leaders and members in a legislative body. All of these factors have helped to shape the contours of the speakership during the various stages of its evolution, but their influence does not totally characterize the office at any particular time. The texture of the speakership is an amalgam of all of these things and more; it can only be adequately grasped by immersion in the personalities and events by which its path through history has been marked.

The list of "independent variables" includes the political party system, but does not differentiate between the two major parties. The roles that the Democratic and Republican parties have played in shaping the political system, the House of Representatives, and its speakership, are complicated. The two major parties have differed in persistent and significant ways, and those differences have been reflected in the manner in which each has governed the House. Each of the parties has been marked by a consistency of character that has persisted from one period to the next. The Democratic party has always been representative of the lower end of the economic ladder, egalitarian in its outlook, and

Table 1   The Evolution of the Speakership: Periods and Characteristics

	Periods			
Characteristics	Parliamentary 1789–1859	Partisan 1860–1910	Feudal 1911–1961	Democratic 1962–
Policy agenda[a]	sectional slavery	sectional distributive	redistributive	regulatory
Party system[b]	fragmented	centralized	decentralized	atomistic
Presidency[c]	weak	weak	stronger	strong
Institutionalization[d]	low	moderate	high	moderate
Turnover in House	high	moderate	low	moderate
Powers of speaker[e]	moderate	high	low	moderate
Speakership	presiding	hierarchical	broker[f]	therapeutic/ policy- oriented/ symbolic

[a] The politics of the antebellum state was sectional. After the war the tendency was toward the nationalization of the economy. During the feudal era, the New Deal introduced the welfare state. The Democratic era witnessed an expansion of the welfare state during the Great Society years, but its essential feature proved to be the problem of economic management through regulation.

[b] In the Democratic period the two major parties have been atomized from within due to the autonomy of members.

[c] The presidency was institutionally weak in the nineteenth century, gained in strength during the first half of the twentieth century, and became truly powerful in the 1960s.

[d] Including the ingraining of the committee system, the development of the seniority principle, and the accretion of precedent.

[e] Referring to formal powers under the rules of the House and to powers deriving from party caucus rules. The key powers are over committee appointments and access to the floor.

[f] The term *broker* is preferred to *bargaining*, since speakers of the feudal period more often brokered compromise among barons than bargained with them (although bargaining did, of course, occur). The therapeutic speaker is a broker with a heart. Unlike psychiatrists, therapeutic speakers enter relationships with policy aims of their own.

internally divided between southern and northern wings and among a variety of organized interests (labor, farm, minority). The Republican party always has been representative of the middle and upper economic classes, less egalitarian in its policies, and sociologically more homogeneous, while occasionally divided ideologically. In governing, Democrats have been less cohesive than Republicans, and their speakers have been more accommodating of intraparty factions than have Republican speakers. Republican speakers have been more assertive and more insistent on party loyalty. They have also been the beneficiaries of stable partisan majorities. It is not the differences between the two parties that have driven the process of evolution from one period to the next, however; instead, each party has been influenced in its approach to governance by the underlying social and political forces and issues that shaped the period. While the parties retained distinct identities, they were pushed in the same direction.

Thus the two major American political parties have responded to changes in the environment of American politics in similar ways. During the parliamentary period there were no strong parties and there were no strong speakers except Clay, whose influence did not depend upon his power as speaker. With the development of strong parties during the partisan period, both the Democratic and the Republican parties tended toward centralization, although the tendency was more pronounced in the Republican party. During the feudal period both of the two major parties were dominated by seniority and committee fiefdoms, although the tendency was more pronounced in the Democratic party. During the democratic period, the tendency toward democratization, communication, and policy has been evident in both parties. Interestingly, these tendencies appear to have seized the parties about equally, yet the Democrats still predominate electorally. The continued Democratic hegemony in the House during the past two decades is due in large part to the advantages that have accrued to incumbency, which has effectively shut the Republicans out of power in the House.

The characterizations of the speakership during each of the four periods require some elaboration. The parliamentary speakership is identified with the duties of the chair because the rudimentary state of parliamentary law, the relative lack of institutionalized features of the House, and the deep sectional divisions in the polity all placed great emphasis upon the speaker's capacity to preside effectively. This was a more important function than partisan leadership during the period. Clay's charisma facilitated his role as presiding officer. The partisan speakers were, by contrast, normally the leaders of their parties during a time when party government was often approximated. The more developed state of House rules, procedures, and precedents, and the greater institutional stability by which the House was characterized, meant that the presiding functions of the speakership were more routinized during this period than had been the case before. Still, the powers of the chair contributed importantly to speakers' political roles.

The feudal speakership was partisan, but the parties were less cohesive. The evolution of committee baronies created other centers of power in the House, and the speakers of this period had to deal with committee chairmen as near equals. Often the speakers had to bargain with the chairmen; more often they had to facilitate deals among and between them. The speakership of the democratic period is symbolic, therapeutic and policy-oriented. It is symbolic because in an era dominated by mass media the speakership is more visible to the public eye, and speakers have an opportunity to affect public opinion. It is therapeutic because speakers must now invest themselves extensively in communication with rank-and-file members on matters great and small. It is policy-oriented because of the greater involvement of speakers in developing legislation, a task that during the feudal period was left for the most part to the committees.

The notion of a therapeutic speakership suggests that the culture of the House has become an important force in shaping the speakership. The folkways of the House today are products of certain trends in late twentieth-century American culture. The concept of a therapeutic culture is interestingly developed by Robert N. Bellah and his associates in *Habits of the Heart*. Their description of the therapeutic relationship stresses "that it is a unique combination of closeness and distance . . . a funny combination of business and closeness." The relationship between therapist and client is "tightly regulated by businesslike procedural rules . . . [T]he therapeutic relationship underscores the intersubjective nature of reality. It alerts the participants to discrepant definitions of the situation, stemming from different personal histories."[23] This description of the relationship between psychologist and client shares some important features with the relationship between speaker and member. The latter relationship is a "unique combination of closeness and distance, a funny combination of business and closeness," and among its main results is a sensitivity of each to the differing views of the other arising out of their varying political as well as personal histories.

Bellah and his team of scholars argue that modern culture, especially the middle-class culture that has been such an important source of political recruitment in recent decades, is strongly marked by therapeutic impulses. These impulses have given rise to an emphasis on interpersonal communication as a way of adjusting conflict and an amoral contractarianism as an evaluative standard for assessing conflicting claims. Evidence of this thesis is to be found in the House of Representatives since the mid 1970s. The cultural trend was brought to the House by a new generation of members, and in responding to their demands (needs), party leaders assumed the role of therapist—listening, bringing together, searching for mutual understanding. By the 1990s these practices had become so common in both parties as to be built into the party structure through caucuses, conferences, policy committees, informal groups, retreats, and many other venues. The therapeutic disposition stamped the speakership as well.

The search for general historical tendencies suggested by table 1 should not be permitted to conceal the importance of particular actions and events. It is evident that the historical tendencies indicated in the table are the product of forces that transcend the roles played by individual actors, but history is not ineluctable. The actors and the events in which they participate manifest a role for free will in human affairs.[24] To understand the speakership, one must not only understand the underlying forces that shaped it during various stages of its path through history; one must also learn about the individual speakers and the events of their speakerships.

Because the theoretical framework of the book is explicitly historical, a brief discussion of the presuppositions of such an inquiry may be useful. Since, in human affairs, everything bears some relationship to everything else, analyses that take a particular perspective are likely to ignore as much as they address. Yet without perspective there can be no understanding, since the world of human things would appear as an undecipherable jumble of fact. The writing of history, like the writing of the novel, is necessarily elliptical.[25] Among political scientists, it is common to examine political phenomena with reference to the larger system of which they are a part. In presenting their theory about the speakership, for example, Cooper and Brady use as their point of reference the party system.[26] In explaining the party system, Everett Carll Ladd employs a frame of reference constructed on the policy agenda facing the government, while Richard L. McCormick, in explaining the policy agenda, depends on the party period.[27] Marxist and neo-Marxist explanations of both the policy agenda and the party system are likely to emphasize the manner in which economic forces shape developments in the political sector, and modern sociology is replete with studies in which political phenomena are depicted as dependent variables at the whim of social currents beyond the power of the political system to control.

I assume that the evolution of the political system is shaped by social and economic forces, but the relationship runs both ways; social habits and economic arrangements are shaped by the political system as well. Sorting out the lines of causality in these complex matters is not a part of the present task, but I expect that over time, these commingling forces will produce equilibria that are related to analytically discrete periods of political, economic, and social development. Within these periods, society is marked by particular social patterns and customs, particular economic forces and arrangements, and particular political institutions and policies. When viewed from the prism of a particular institution, the House of Representatives, and a particular office, the speakership of the House, the characteristic patterns, customs, forces, arrangements, institutions, and policies come together to give the institution and the office definition.

In political life, nothing is fixed. Even within reasonably identifiable historical periods, change takes place continuously. The forces and arrangements that predominate at one time operate differently and to different effect at another. Persons come and go, and the roles that they play change with time and circumstance. It is precisely for this reason that it is important to undertake political analysis from an approach that seeks to make sense out of change, to bring analytic order to our understanding of political events. By examining the speakership in successive periods, we open ourselves to a consideration of the factors that have shaped its development in the past and those that may do so in the future. We are encouraged to think of the speakership less in terms of the disembodied concepts of behavioral social science or modern organization theory and instead as a product of American political development.

The developmental dimension of American political experience is evident within as well as across the periods that have been identified. The parliamentary, partisan, and feudal periods each build to a climax, a denouement. The parliamentary speakership struggled against and finally collapsed in the Civil War. The partisan era built toward and collapsed with the revolt against Cannon. The feudal regime accumulated power until broken on the rack of reform. In each case the speakership, the House of Representatives, and the political system evolved incrementally in response to changes in American society and the public agenda. These patterns are clearer to hindsight than to foresight. Observers of the "postreform" House rely on the assumption that its defining features will endure, and are they not right? There is no reason to suppose that television will go away, that national political parties will reassert their control over nominations, that the presidency will become subservient to the Congress, that the states will supplant the federal government on the cutting edge of public policy, that America will withdraw into a new era of isolationism. Yet one thing is less likely than these, and that is that American society, its policy agenda, its political system, the House of Representatives, and the speakership will not change.

Anticipating change, it is important to remember that the Founders bequeathed to us a great common denominator of American political development. The United States Constitution establishes a particular regime for the American polity that gives it definition and continuity.

Since the speakership of the House is an artifact of the American constitutional regime, its character is in many ways shaped by the demands
of its constitutional role. The most important fact about the House of
Representatives is that its members are elected from single-member,
geographically defined districts. The most important fact about the
speakership is that the speaker is elected by the members. The geographic
basis of representation makes the House like the state of nature. There
is little common tie of party philosophy to bind the members, and each
member is free to pursue his interest (i.e., that of his district) as he sees
fit. The result is that the House of Representatives is radically individ-
ualistic. The recent therapeutic tendency is merely modern culture's way
of resolving conflict. The state of war is pacified by communication
rather than force. The speaker's constitutional obligation is to preside
over the House. He embodies its authority, its dignity, and its capacity
to function as a deliberative institution. The constitutional role of the
speakership has lent an element of continuity to its historical development. The speakership that we witness today differs in many important respects from that of a hundred or two hundred years ago; yet
those earlier speakerships are recognizable precisely because the regime
of which they are a part has retained its fundamental character through
time.

   This historical perspective suggests questions that will recur in the
analysis of the speakership in its evolution from one era to the next.
What were the major issues on the national policy agenda, and how
did they cleave the polity? What were the main features of the political
system, and how did they shape the House of Representatives? What
were the internal arrangements of the House, and how did they affect
the relationship between speakers and members? What was the relationship of the speakership to the presidency? What was the nature of
individual speakers' coalitions in the House, and how did their strategic
position affect their conduct? What personal qualities marked the service
of the House's most effective speakers, and what other factors contributed to their success?

   This book does not present an insider's account of the speakership,
but instead is written deliberately at a distance. The goal is to provide
an interpretation of the speakership that will place the office within the
context of its own history and that of the political system of which it
is a part. While the speakership is an important position of leadership
in our constitutional system, it is an important position of *institutional*
leadership. The office's roots are in the legislative body, and it is affected
by the forces that shape the House of Representatives. Yet if one must
understand the House in order to understand the speakership, it is also
true that by understanding the speakership one can understand the

House. For the speakership sits at the center of the House as no other aspect of it does. What it does not control, it affects; what it does not affect, it reflects. This book, then, hopes to offer more than an examination of an office within the House; it aspires to offer an understanding of the House itself, and of the political system of which it is a part. If it succeeds, it will have accomplished something more, for the United States House of Representatives is the most essentially representative body that Western civilization has yet produced.

1 ☆ The Parliamentary Speakership

The Founding of the Speakership

When the Founding Fathers met during the summer of 1787 to draft the Constitution of the United States, they were the beneficiaries of over a century and a half of experience in representative government in the United States and hundreds of years of experience in parliamentary government in England. When they granted to the new House of Representatives the right to choose its own speaker, they simply acknowledged the common legislative practice in America and England. Since the Founders said nothing at all during the Constitutional Convention about the speakership that they created, it is not possible to say with precision what they expected of it. But some inferences can be drawn from the precedents on which they drew and from the theory of government on which the Constitution rests.

Ultimately the American speakership traces its origin to that of the House of Commons. Yet the speakership of the Commons underwent several transformations in the process of its development. At its inception in the thirteenth century, the British speakers were appointed by the Crown. In the fourteenth century the Commons assumed the right of appointment, while the Crown retained a veto. The speakership was subservient to the Crown until well into the seventeenth century when, as a result of the Puritan and Glorious Revolutions, Parliament asserted its independence of, and supremacy over, the monarchy.[1] With the development of constitutional government in England, the speakership became a more political office. During the eighteenth century, British speakers were often partisan. It was not until the great reforms of the nineteenth century brought democracy to the English constitutional system that the speakership of the Commons became the nonpartisan office that we know today. With democracy came a stable party system in which it was vital that the speaker of the House of Commons deal evenhandedly with both the government and opposition parties. In the end, the speakership was shaped by the imperatives of the parliamentary system.

Throughout the three major eras in the development of the British speakership—the royalist, the partisan, and the non-partisan—there was a thread of continuity. From its earliest beginnings, the office was presumed to represent the power and dignity of the House of Commons. Even the royalist speakers of the early period had the responsibility to insist upon the rights and privileges of the Commons to the Crown and Lords. As a symbol of the authority of the Commons, the speakership was bound to be a focal point of dispute between the Crown and Commons during the great conflicts of the sixteenth and seventeenth centuries. Indeed, seven former speakers of the Commons were beheaded by the Tudor kings. During the revolutionary seventeenth century, the speakership was caught in the adversarial relationship between the king and Parliament. One of the most significant events in the history of the English Constitution occurred in 1642 when Charles I, searching for five members whom he suspected of treason, became the first and only English monarch to enter the House of Commons. Speaker William Lenthall refused Charles I's inquiry as to the members' whereabouts, asserting that his obligation to the House was superior to his duty to the King.[2]

It is not surprising that the speakership that was carried to the New World reflected the character of the speakership of the Commons in the seventeenth century, for the century of English revolution was also the century of American colonization. The impressions of parliamentary government brought by the colonists to America were shaped by the English experience from which they came. To the force of English precedent was added that of American circumstance. The new colonies established legislative institutions as an early order of business. The popular branches of their legislatures were chaired by speakers. The colonial speakers sought for their assemblies the rights and privileges of representative institutions against the authority of royally appointed governors. When, in the eighteenth century, conflicts between Crown and colonial interests became more frequent and severe, the colonial speakers were caught up in political struggle. From the outset, then, the colonial speakership was a political office; yet the colonial speakers also had the obligation to preside impartially within their houses.

In the 1760s and 1770s the conflicts between the royal governors and the colonial legislatures came to a head.[3] The governors held the veto, but the legislatures controlled the governors' salaries, which they were often willing to hold hostage to force approval of their enactments. In the early eighteenth century the Massachusetts General Court had a policy of holding up the governor's salary until he had approved all of its enactments. In Pennsylvania the horse-trading was barely concealed; the governor would approve a set of acts and the speaker of the House would issue a warrant on the treasury for his salary. In North Carolina and Virginia, the speaker of the House was also the treasurer of the colony, holding direct control over the colonial pursestrings. Speaker John Robinson of Virginia held both jobs from 1750 to 1775 and was among the most powerful men in the colonies.[4] The generation of American politicians from which the Founding Fathers were drawn had no concept of a nonpartisan speakership.

The other major precedent for the speakership of the House was the president of the Continental Congress. Under the Articles of Confederation these presiding officers had little power, since the national government over which they presided was itself weak. Yet even they were political creatures who were known to reflect state interests. The weakness of these quasi-executive leaders under the Articles was one of the principal counts in the indictment against them, and among the principal aims of the Founders was the creation of a firm and independent presidency.

In examining the experience of the state governments in the 1780s, it was apparent to the Founders that the gravest danger to the country was the paralysis that legislative supremacy often produced. America needed a national government capable of governing, and this entailed an executive clothed with the authority and granted the autonomy to govern well. Yet the specter of monarchy was always before them, and a great challenge to the ingenuity of the Founders was to find a way to balance the need for an energetic executive with a concern to limit the power of the new presidency. They also feared the possibility of a tyrannical legislative branch, and so they balanced the popularly and regularly elected House against the smaller and more select Senate. Following precedent, the Founders designated the speaker as the presiding officer of the House; guided by their complex theory of checks and balances, they named the vice president as the presiding officer of the Senate. The Founders surely expected that both offices would come to be filled by ambitious politicians—their theory of government required it. Yet both the speaker of the House and the president of the Senate had important roles to play in providing for stable and equitable leadership of their respective chambers. The vice president's task would be complicated because of his relationship with the president; the speaker's task would be complicated because of his relationship with his constituents. Once the vice presidency became politically subservient to the presidency, one potential constitutional tension was alleviated. But the speaker of the House remained an independently elected leader of the popular branch of the Congress, and because of his obligations to his constituencies in the House and in his district, he would be placed in direct opposition to the president.

The relationship between the presidency and the speakership has been among the most significant in shaping the character of the latter and has at times affected that of the former. Since both offices derive from a common theoretical foundation in the Constitution, a brief explication of that theory will contribute to an understanding of the role of the speakership as it has evolved in history. The Founding Fathers were guided by two different theories of leadership. The first, most explicitly stated, and most commonly known was Alexander Hamilton's conception of the presidency, in which "energy in the executive branch is a leading character in the definition of good government."[5] The other theory was implicit in Madison's conception of the representative assembly, and derived from the notion of deliberative government. Both Madison and Hamilton believed in a strong executive and in the role of the representative legislature. Both men valued deliberative government, but Hamilton characteristically sought the wisdom and stability that deliberation required from an independent executive, while Madison emphasized the role of the balanced legislature. Hamilton's faith lay in the art of statesmanship; Madison wanted to structure the legislature so that the conditions of deliberative rationality within it were maximized. The Hamiltonian vision of leadership relied upon the capability and vision of the great statesman; the Madisonian vision required the steady and systematic filtering of the best legislators to the top.

Madison feared that a Hamiltonian leader might become a demagogue. Hamilton noted in the first *Federalist* that "Of those men who have overturned the liberties of republics, the greatest number have begun their career by paying an obsequious court to the people: commencing demagogues, and ending tyrants," yet he never explained why his vigorous executive would not become an abusive tyrant.[6] It would seem to demand more in the way of republican virtue than his view of human nature would allow.[7] Madison, recognizing the same problem, had a theory. A demagogue might as easily arise in a numerous popular assembly as in a national electoral arena. As he put it in the fifty-eighth *Federalist*:

> The more numerous the assembly may be, of whatever characters composed, the greater is known to be the ascendancy of passion over reason . . . the larger the number, the greater will be the

proportion of members of limited information and of weak capacities. Now it is precisely on characters of this description that the eloquence and address of the few are known to act with all their force. In the ancient republics, where the whole body of the people assembled in person, a single orator or an artful statesman, was generally seen to rule with as complete a sway as if a scepter had been placed in his single hand.[8]

To avoid this possibility was the principal object of a theory of legislative leadership. Although the Founders never articulated it, such a theory lies at the core of the Constitution's provisions for the House of Representatives. Members of the House are biennially elected; the Founders expected those members to feel a close connection with their constituents' interests. They are to be at least twenty-five years of age, reflecting a more mature judgment than that required to vote or exercise the full rights of adulthood, but a sufficiently young age to open the door of political opportunity to most Americans (women have always been eligible to serve in the House of Representatives). They are to be citizens of the United States and residents of the state from which they are elected; thus they are tied to their country and to their localities, representatives of the state and the nation. And they are to have the power to elect their own leaders, including their speaker.

What kind of legislative leaders will such members require? In explaining the various provisions governing the election of members of the House, Madison indicates several qualities requisite to a deliberative assembly that the qualifications were designed to ensure.[9] The House should be responsive to the American people, to the particular interests of the individual constituencies, knowledgeable, stable, wise, and capable. Merit will be the main factor determining elections to the House and should be the main factor in determining its leadership. It follows that the speaker of the House should be a person of substantial reputation, respected by his peers, capable of representing the House in the government and to the people, a firm and fair moderator of its proceedings, and possessed of political wisdom—the precondition of deliberative rationality. Recognizing that the House would inevitably be marked by conflict of interest, its speaker should have the capacity to reconcile conflict. His ultimate responsibility is to see to it that the House of Representatives can function as a legislative institution; in order to do that, he must be perceived by the members as fair, firm, and in command of the proceedings of the House.

Madison was suspicious of political parties. His concern about the effects of factions in American politics is well known. He must have been aware that a speaker of the House might be the leader of its majority faction. Still, there is no evidence to suggest that the Founders expected the speaker to be a party leader as such. Their desire to foster the conditions of deliberation required that the speaker's first obligation was to manage the House so that deliberation could take place. This duty might well come into conflict with the active leadership of a party caucus. While the speaker, as a representative of his district, would have had the obligation to act politically on behalf of his constituents, it did not follow that he would have had to assume the active leadership of a legislative party. Legislative parties might not have arisen, or someone else might have led them. There is, obviously, potential for conflict between the speaker's parliamentary and representative functions. Madison's theory sets the framework of the problem, but leaves it unresolved.

Just as the speaker's political role is implicitly available, but not specifically defined by the Constitution, so too is his role as a deliberative leader. Madison is clear on the need for deliberative leaders—those "whose wisdom may best discern the true interest of their country."[10] He hoped that all members of the House would be so wise, but his theory required especially leaders who "possess superior talents . . . by frequent reelections become members of long standing . . . [and are] thoroughly the masters of public business."[11] From among such members, presumably, would come the speakers of the House. But would House speakers be lost to the deliberative process by virtue of their role as presiding officers? Again we are confronted with a tension that the Founders created but left unresolved. They knew that much of the deliberation in representative assemblies went on "out-of-doors," as the experience of the Constitutional Convention attests. A speaker need not participate actively in floor debate in order to have an impact on legislation. But George Washington, the great presiding officer of the Grand Convention, remained aloof from the Convention's proceedings indoors and out until the Convention's last day. If speakers followed his example, they would tend toward parliamentary neutrality at the expense of both politics and deliberation, except where the interests of their own constituents were at issue.

The Founders posed more problems for the speakership than they solved by their theory of government. They pointed toward what the government and the House demanded of its leadership, but they could not guarantee that those qualities and practices would be forthcoming. The political system that they created set some clear boundaries around the speakership; its responsibilities in the chair and its dependency upon its two major constituencies, in the district and among the members, were the most significant. But the exact contours of the office were left by the Founders to history, ensuring that the speakership would be shaped by patterns of political development yet to unfold. The result was a certain ambivalence about the office that has characterized it throughout its history, beginning with the First Congress.

The Speakership's First Decade

Frederick Augustus Muhlenberg of Pennsylvania was the first speaker of the United States House of Representatives. Why was he chosen, and what did his colleagues expect of him? The most direct evidence is the duties first imposed by the original rules of the House. The speaker is instructed to preserve order and decorum, to determine who shall speak among those rising simultaneously, to call members to order for violations of the rules, to appoint members to committees, and to rule from the chair on points of order. To assure that the speaker would remain to some extent removed from partisanship, he was not to speak to issues while in the chair and not to vote unless the vote be by ballot or to make or break a tie. In addition, the speaker as presiding officer was to present the public face of the House as an institution, a matter of ceremony.[12]

Why was Frederick Muhlenberg chosen to fill this position in preference to, say, James Madison? He was elected speaker on April 1, 1789, the first day the House attained a quorum of thirty members. His election was decisive, carrying twenty-three of thirty votes.[13] His opposition came primarily from Jonathan Trumbull of Connecticut and Elias Boudinot of New Jersey. Muhlenberg's election was harbingered as early as March 4th, the day he arrived in New York. At that time thirteen representatives had appeared, of whom four were from Pennsylvania.[14] The Pennsylvania House delegation caucused on the matter of the speakership, along with Pennsylvania Senators Robert Morris and William Maclay.[15] Maclay contends that the Pennsylvanians decided that the choice of speaker should hinge upon considerations of merit alone; they would not promote Muhlenberg's candidacy as a state delegation matter. This is hardly believable. It understates the desire of the Pennsylvania delegation to have the speakership and the amount of effort they invested in getting it. The fact that they caucused on the matter at all suggests that they wanted a Pennsylvania speaker. That Muhlenberg was their own clear choice, that he was widely discussed as a prospective speaker, and the importance that they attached to the speakership combine to indicate that his colleagues from Pennsylvania could not have viewed the choice of speaker as a wholly nonpartisan matter.

The choice of Muhlenberg as speaker was brought about in part because of the fact that New York coveted the chief justiceship of the Supreme Court. Virginia and Massachusetts already had claimed the first two constitutional prizes with the election of Washington as president and John Adams as vice president. Two other plums remained, the speakership and the location of the federal government. Southerners wanted the permanent seat of government located to the south (along the banks of the Potomac river). Maryland and New Jersey also offered to receive it. As a middle state, Pennsylvania had a strong claim to consideration as a location for the government. If it could win the speakership, its chances of winning the capital would be enhanced.[16]

These political considerations swirled in the background, but had the choice of speaker been purely nonpolitical, Muhlenberg might still have been selected. As a three-term speaker of the Pennsylvania House and as the presiding officer of its ratifying convention, he had the requisite experience in the chair.[17] His experience in the Continental Congress had exposed him to national issues and had enabled him to get to know representatives from other states. Furthermore, among his colleagues there was no clear alternative. Of the thirty men who gathered on April 1, 1789, to organize the House (assuming that those not present were not considered for the speakership), sixteen had never served in the Continental Congress.[18] Of the fourteen who had, those who had served the longest were Gerry of Massachusetts (ten years), Sherman of Connecticut (eight years), and Madison of Virginia (seven years). These three men were also the only three who had served in the 1787 convention. Yet Gerry was an antifederalist, Sherman was thought to be too old for the chair, and Madison was regarded as too valuable to be lost to debate, an indication that the members did not expect the speaker to be a deliberative leader.[19] Members would presumably also have been reluctant to select a speaker from the same state as the president. Muhlenberg's opponents each had some claim to consideration. Boudinot had served five years in the Continental Congress and had been its president. Trumbull had served nine years as governor of Connecticut. Still, neither offered decisively superior qualifications to those of Muhlenberg. When combined with considerations of geography and large state balance, and with an active group of supporters lobbying a full month on his behalf, he won an easy victory.

As Washington was the model president, Muhlenberg was a model speaker. He was evidently firm and fair in the chair, and he conveyed a sense of institutional dignity to the world out of doors. His personal bearing was "magnificent." While in the chair he remained aloof from partisan debate. Yet Muhlenberg was a politician, and a representative of his state and district. He could not escape playing a political role, one that he exercised out of doors with considerable vigor, and from the chair when the opportunity arose. Muhlenberg was a firm supporter of Pennsylvania's attempt to secure for itself the permanent seat of government. "We as Pennsylvanians are determined, and I think consistent with our duty to have this place," he wrote to Benjamin Rush. His feelings were perhaps animated as much by his aversion to New York as by his allegiance to Pennsylvania. "I need not tell you," he added, "how improper a place New York is in every respect, to be the seat of government."[20] Whatever his motivation, he was willing to match action to words. On May 31, 1790, a motion was made "That a permanent seat for the government of the United States ought to be fixed at some convenient place on the banks of the river Delaware."[21] This motion was objected to on the grounds that it was not in order. Muhlenberg sustained the objection and his decision was appealed. The votes on the appeal were 29 yea and 29 nay. Casting his vote in support of his ruling, Speaker Muhlenberg earned temporary reprieve for Germantown (near Philadelphia) as the seat of government.[22]

Even if the speaker was expected to conduct himself in a partisan way when the occasion demanded it, it does not appear that he was expected to be a strong partisan leader. During its first decade the business of the House was managed by ad hoc committees. While the speaker appointed them, there is no evidence that he was active in their deliberations. The two main protagonists of the First Congress were James Madison, who sat on numerous committees, and Secretary of the Treasury Alexander Hamilton.[23] The *Annals of Congress* confirm that Muhlenberg refrained from partisan debate on the floor of the House. Maclay's journal reveals a good deal about his activities out of doors. Muhlenberg seemed to have taken upon himself the obligation to become a focal point for social activity. In addition to the mandatory rounds of callings, the speaker is frequently mentioned as having invited guests to dinner, having attended social functions, and having met with smaller groups of senators and representatives for breakfast or lunch. Although the environment of New York was by no means as isolated as that of Washington would be after 1800, it was nonetheless far from home. Few members of Congress brought their families with them. Politics was therefore the principal agenda for most, and the breakfasts, lunches, and dinners were often devoted to the discussion of political issues. In these gatherings, it is clear that Muhlenberg felt free to express his views.[24]

The first speakership of the House reflected a tension within the office and a considerable degree of uncertainty about it. It also suggested the direction the office would eventually take, for Muhlenberg's selection as speaker was due in part to his reputation as a supporter of the Constitution. During the First Congress the overriding national issue was the establishment of the government under the Constitution itself. Other deep-seated conflicts were apparent then (over the tariff, for example) that would later come to divide and define the polity. But in selecting their first speaker, those members then present were most concerned to choose a man who was perceived to support the Constitution—in those early days the very definition of federalism. And so Frederick Muhlenberg was, in a sense, selected as the representative of a partisan political point of view on the policy issue by which the polity was cleaved.

The partisan tendencies manifested during the First Congress became more accentuated during the remainder of the eighteenth century. The Federalists were, for the most part, the majority party of the decade, although their majorities were never overwhelming, and party identification itself was ill-defined.[25] From the skirmishes between Federalists and Republicans of the Federalist decade emerged the contours of the first American party system as it was to develop after 1800. Likewise, the struggle between Hamilton and Madison defined two of the principal constitutional issues of American history: the relationship between the federal and state governments and that between the executive and legislative branches of the federal government.

Washington's stature served to protect the new office of president of the United States from legislative encroachment, and lent political credibility to Treasury Secretary Hamilton's legislative program. In spite of Washington's relative aloofness from the Congress, however, Hamilton's active involvement in the legislative struggle alienated many Republicans in the Congress and raised the question of the proper degree of executive influence in legislative affairs. Hamilton's program for the development of the American economic system required the active intervention of the federal government in matters that had historically been the province of the colonial or state governments, if matters of governmental cognizance at all. Hamilton trod upon the prerogatives of the states as well as those of Congress.

Among the dominant issues on the national agenda during the first decade of the Constitution were commerce and international trade. The enactment of the first tariff law and the establishment of the First National Bank in the First Congress laid the basis for a national policy of economic growth. However, the problem of developing America's domestic economy quickly came into conflict with America's relations with France and England and the question of involvement in the war between the two. Federalists tended to favor higher tariffs for the promotion of domestic manufactures, the creation of the national bank to promote investment, and a conciliatory policy toward England, America's most important trading partner. Republicans tended to favor moderate tariffs, to distrust the power of a national bank, and to sympathize with the spirit (if not the form) of the French Revolution. Underlying these differences in policy was a basic difference in outlook. Federalists were more suspicious of democracy and more oriented toward an industrial expansion guided by the hand of capital. Republicans, while no less devoted to private property, were inclined to fear the power of the federal government and gave a far more egalitarian interpretation to the idea of the rights of man. To the Federalists, Republicans were Jacobins in disguise; to the Republicans, Federalists were undisguised monarchists.[26] These differences in policy had assignable political consequences. Among them four are of particular relevance to the problem of the speakership: the political conflicts of the 1790s led to the establishment of an adversarial relationship between Congress and the president; there emerged as a result of these conflicts the rudiments of institutional organization within the Congress; the deliberative aspects of the legislative process became subordinated to political considerations; and the American party system was born.

The adversarial relationship between Congress and the presidency arose in spite of the position of honor accorded George Washington. By the end of his second term, even he was being openly criticized, and when the unfortunate John Adams assumed the presidency, a torrent of calumny was released.[27] The particular character of the disagreement between Federalists and Republicans did much to exacerbate the constitutional tension between the president and Congress. Hamilton and Adams were viewed by many Republicans as monarchists in principle, and attempts to assert executive power by the Federalists were assumed to be an indication of monarchical intent. Hamilton, Adams, and the other Federalists worried most about the need for firm government, which for them meant a firm executive, and attacks by Republicans on Federalist policy were often viewed by the Federalists as an attack on the stability of government itself. The nature of the party divisions that evolved during the first decade of the government increased the tensions arising from the constitutional separation of powers. The speaker of the House and the president of the United States stood on opposite sides of the constitutional divide, and it remained to be seen whether partisan forces could bring them together, rather than driving them further apart.[28]

It was in part due to the separation of powers and the political conflicts between the Federalists and Republicans that the Congress first recognized the necessity of internal organization. Of course, a large legislative body would eventually have had to organize; however, political forces made organization desirable before the growth of government made it necessary. The Republicans in the House of Representatives sought to resist the policies of the Treasury Department by institutionalizing their control over the federal purse strings through the establishment of the committee on Ways and Means. Under the leadership of Albert Gallatan, who "knew the numbers," the Republicans could compete more evenly with the administration.[29] The development of the committee system was not to come full course until Clay became speaker, but the impetus toward it was present from the earliest political struggles between Federalists and Republicans.[30]

The development of the committee system worked at cross-purposes with the deliberative character of the House as the Founders had conceived of it. If deliberation is the application of reason to the process of decision making, specialization fosters conditions of deliberative rationality. However, specialization entails compartmentalization. In the Founders' view, deliberation is a process of discussion undertaken by capable persons; a deliberative assembly is a group of such persons adequately representative of the population being served. During the first few congresses, much of the business of the House was conducted in the Committee of the Whole, on which all members sat. This procedure fostered discussion, but put decision making at risk, since majority rule was liable to be used to advantage by leaders who could exercise the most leverage on members. The decisions made in the deliberative assembly might not be based on the deliberations that occurred there. Madison, who was preeminent in debate, lost some legislative battles to the superior influence of the administration, and in particular to Alexander Hamilton. In order to protect its interests, it is to the advantage of the majority party to exercise political control off of the floor of the chamber in order to ensure that it will retain political control over it. The committee system is a vehicle for control of the legislative process by the party in power. Whether it enhances or diminishes the power of the speaker depends upon the extent of his control over it. In exercising organizational control, the party in power concedes that considerations of political expedience, as well as a concern for legislative efficiency, outweigh any desire to maintain the conditions of deliberation on the floor, among which must certainly be a sense that the deliberations affect the outcome. The gradual process by which organization overcame deliberation (in the Framers' sense) began during the first decade under the Constitution, due in significant part to the Republican Party's attempts to defend its interests and principles against a Federalist Party in control of the executive branch of government.[31]

Control of the institutional processes of the Congress depended upon the control of a majority of its votes, and this could be obtained only at the ballot box. In addition to organizing themselves in the Congress, the Republican and Federalist parties found it necessary to organize themselves for political purposes throughout the country. While the focus of this organization was the presidency, its impetus came from the Congress. John Beckley, the Republican clerk of the House of Representatives, became the nation's first campaign operative, and the Republican strategy for seizing the presidency evolved from within the Congress. National political parties emerged for the first time.[32]

The speakership of the House was caught in the midst of the evolving competition between the executive and the legislature, and between Federalists and Republicans. Frederick Muhlenberg had been selected as the first speaker because he was perceived to be qualified to preside and was known to be loyal to the Constitution. During the First Congress, however, he revealed Republican leanings. The Federalists took note and elected Jonathan Trumbull of Connecticut as speaker of the Second Congress. Trumbull was a faithful, if not an active, Federalist speaker. By the Third Congress, however, Republican strength in the House had increased and Muhlenberg reclaimed the chair. His successor in the Fourth Congress, Jonathan Dayton of New Jersey, was nominally a Federalist, but worked hard to ingratiate himself with Republicans. His election to the speakership was by a coalition of Federalists and Republicans. The first three speakers were not aggressive political leaders. That a more partisan speakership was possible under the circumstances, however, was proven by Theodore Sedgwick's conduct as speaker of the Fifth Congress. An ardent Massachusetts Federalist, Sedgwick's support of administration policy angered the Republicans. This was the Congress that passed the Alien and Sedition Acts and the Naturalization Act, and during which the Republican party in the Congress finally coalesced to present a uniform front of opposition to the Federalists. Sedgwick personified the evils that Republicans found in the Federalist program. At the end of his term, Republicans refused to join in the vote of thanks from the House.

The Speakership during the First Party System

With Jefferson's elevation to the presidency, the nation for the first time found an assertive president at the helm of a government in which his party controlled a majority of the seats in both houses of the Congress. Jefferson had witnessed Hamilton's skill in leading the Congress from out of doors, and the price paid by Adams for his relations with the Congress. As president, he was determined to work effectively with the Congress by asserting his own leadership and by working through and with a coterie of Republican supporters. Jefferson's agents in the House included William Branch Giles of Virginia, Joseph H. Nicholson of Maryland, Caesar A. Rodney of Delaware, Barnabas Bidwell of Massachusetts, and Wilson Carey Nicholas of Virginia.[33] The speaker of the House, Nathaniel Macon of North Carolina, was popular but not illustrious. It is indicative of the role played by the speaker that Macon, a man widely liked and trusted, should have been chosen for the office in preference to one of the more aggressive party leaders used by Jefferson as his floor agents. In Jefferson's shadow, there was little room for Macon to carve an independent leadership role, a role for which he had little inclination in the first place.[34]

Among Speaker Macon's key appointments was John Randolph of Roanoke to the chair of Ways and Means. The mercurial Randolph was combative by nature. Loyal to Jefferson at the outset, he eventually split with the president over the Florida issue in 1805. Randolph was a bothersome administration opponent. For perhaps the first time in American congressional history, a committee chairman launched himself in opposition to the policy of a president of his own party. Randolph lost the immediate legislative battle, but Jefferson suffered the longer-lasting wound—the breakup of his congressional majority. Speaker Macon found himself caught between his close friend Randolph and his sense of obligation to President Jefferson. As speaker, he recognized his obligation to his president; yet Randolph exerted "more influence over Macon's . . . life than any other person ever did, and who was in turn . . . more influenced by him than by any other."[35] In this situation, Macon found himself politically paralyzed, much to the detriment of his reputation. Randolph became more and more obstreperous, alienating many of his fellow Republicans, and dissatisfaction with Macon became more widespread. Eventually, Macon and Randolph broke openly with Jefferson, joining with a handful of other Republican renegades to form a small rump group known as the "Tertium Quids." The Quids became a thorn in the side of the administration, and Macon's leadership of the administration party in the House became more tenuous.[36] Jefferson's efforts to manage the House through his lieutenants and in the face of Randolph's opposition reflected the underlying political dynamic of the period. The Federalists were still sufficiently numerous (numbering about twenty-seven by Jefferson's estimate) to carry weight. The Republicans outnumbered them, but were divided internally. It was the schisms within the House that led to a paralysis of leadership; Randolph's erratic behavior simply compounded the difficulty.[37]

Macon's association with Randolf ultimately claimed his speakership. Joseph Varnum of Massachusetts challenged Macon for the chair in the Ninth Congress and carried the challenge to four ballots. Jefferson was disappointed in Macon's support of Randolph, but he decided to conciliate Macon, supporting him for speaker rather than martyring him to Randolph's cause.[38] Unfortunately, the speaker proceeded to rub salt into the wound that Randolph had opened by reappointing him to the chair of Ways and Means. The Ninth Congress proved difficult for Jefferson because of the bitterness engendered by the Napoleonic Wars and Britain's harassment of American shipping. The struggle over non-importation agreements in 1806 split the Republican party and brought the conflict between Jefferson and Randolph to a head. With the members in open rebellion, and under strong pressure from Jefferson, Macon stripped Randolph of his chairmanship of Ways and Means at the outset of the second session of the Ninth Congress.

In 1807 the House chose Varnum to replace Macon, selecting a man who, while opposed to Randolph in geography and principle, lacked the assertiveness of character to deal with him in practice. Varnum was chosen speaker as the candidate of the northeastern Republicans, those most harmed by Jefferson's policies on foreign trade. His election reflected the decline in Jefferson's support on the Hill. Sectionalism was manifested as the northeastern Republicans rebelled against the southern regime, and especially against the vituperative Randolph.[39] With Varnum in the chair, however, things went from bad to worse for Jefferson. As a lame duck president, his influence was diminished. Distressed by damage to American shipping during the Anglo-French war, Jefferson called for and received from the Congress an embargo on all American shipping to the belligerents—a devastating blow to foreign trade. The consequences were severe and the repercussions strong. Southern planters and New England manufacturers alike had reason to complain.

Disobedience to the law was widespread, requiring Jefferson in 1809 to seek enforcement powers from the Congress. Unfortunately for Jefferson, the Enforcement Act was widely violated. According to Treasury Secretary Gallatin, the embargo was "defeated by open violations, by vessels sailing without any clearance whatsoever."[40] In spite of the numerous violations, the embargo cost the country some $50 million in lost revenues. By 1808 tobacco was almost worthless and wheat prices had dropped from two dollars to seven cents a bushel. The embargo nearly destroyed the Republicans' capacity to govern. In 1807 there was a Republican governor in every New England state except Connecticut; after the elections of 1808, there were none.[41] Politically defeated, personally beaten, and financially drained, Jefferson left the presidency nearly destitute, having to borrow money to get home.[42]

In spite of its sorry conclusion, the Jefferson presidency established the principle of party government and demonstrated that a president who is willing to take the initiative could make it work. The Republicans were a majority party. Jefferson was their leader. They caucused and acted like a party, but their partisan leader in the House was not the speaker. The first instance of party government under the Constitution was characterized by *presidential* rather than *congressional* leadership of the Congress. That Macon was not a forceful party leader is as much a commentary upon the office he held as upon his character, for Macon was selected as speaker as one acceptable to the various factions within the party, rather than as a leader of any one of them. The speaker of the House serves at the pleasure of the members, while the president serves at the pleasure of the public that elects him, and this provides a president with an independent political base. From this base, he may seek to lead the Congress rather than to conciliate its members.

Another lesson is revealed by the manner in which Macon's speakership was driven by regional and factional politics. As a southerner, the speaker was naturally allied to Jefferson. But Jefferson's policies were those of a nationalist president, his personal philosophy of government notwithstanding. This brought him into conflict with Randolph and other conservative defenders of the deep South. Macon, coming from the South and with close personal ties to Randolph, had few natural allies in the northeastern wing of the party. It was only by Jefferson's support that he held the speakership as long as he did; when Jefferson backed away from him, he was beaten by Varnum. In fact, all of these politicians were to some extent carried along by the political currents of the time. The Republicans could remain unified only so long as there was an essential harmony of interest in opposition to the Federalists. When they tried to govern, they discovered that the regional cleavages of the new republic caused divisions within their own ranks.

With Madison's election as president, America found itself with the same dilemma and less accomplished leadership. American trade was widely disrupted, first by the Embargo Act itself, then by its successor, the Non-Importation Act, and finally, due to harassment by English warships. As a congressional leader Madison had fought against Hamilton's intrusion into the affairs of the Congress, and as president he was neither by nature nor by philosophy inclined to exercise strong congressional leadership. In Varnum the House had a leader who, like his president, wished to avoid conflict. The nation was in a crisis and the leadership vacuum was soon filled by the formidable figure of Henry Clay. The election of 1810 brought to the House of Representatives a group of new congressmen, many from the South and West, who were intent upon more active management of affairs of state. Impatient with the temporizing Madison, the "War Hawks" were determined to take the initiative in both foreign and domestic policy. In the former area their policy was war; in the latter, expansion. Their leaders included a band of South Carolinians led by the "Sage of South Carolina," John C. Calhoun, and including William Lowndes, Langdon Cheves, and

David R. Williams; other new members joining them were Felix Grundy
of Tennessee, Richard M. Johnson of Kentucky, and Peter B. Porter of
New York.[43]

Seizing the initiative at the outset of the Twelfth Congress, the
insurgent group of Republicans caucused and selected Henry Clay of
Kentucky, the "Western Star," as their candidate for speaker.[44] Clay
was elected speaker on his first day in the Congress by a resounding
majority, and under his leadership the House of Representatives entered
into a period of national influence that would not be rivaled until the
end of the nineteenth century. At the same time, Clay carved a role for
himself as speaker that would find no imitation in American history.
Clay was the first strong speaker, and in many ways, his speakership
was unique. Clay was elected to the speakership on his first day of
service in the House, yet it is unlikely that he was personally acquainted
with most of those who voted for him. The House over which Frederick
Muhlenberg presided was composed of 65 members, but by the time
Henry Clay became speaker in 1811 it had almost tripled in size. It is
difficult to fix with precision the point beyond which a deliberative body
becomes too large for its leadership to be intimately acquainted with
its members, but clearly Muhlenberg would have had an easier time
getting to know 65 men than Clay would have had in becoming acquainted with 186. Besides, during the early decades of government
under the Constitution, there was a high degree of turnover in the
membership in the House, and circumstances militated against Clay's
intimate acquaintance with many of his fellow members.[45]

Clay was chosen speaker because he was the leader of a political
faction within the Republican party. The "Young Republicans" had
come to Washington to set the nation on a proper course of action
toward Great Britain, the course of war. United on this policy goal,
they did not wish to be divided by a leadership struggle. Within their
own ranks, Clay stood out. He had served a brief stint in the United
States Senate and had been speaker of the Kentucky House of Representatives. He was the most articulate advocate of the policies the group
espoused: internal improvements, a protective tariff, and war. Clay and
the other "War Hawks" believed that America could not fulfill her
destiny unless she developed her economic potential and asserted her
right to be treated as a sovereign nation. The "American System," with
which Clay was identified through four decades of national political
life, embodied these beliefs.

Henry Clay was one of the very few speakers in American history
to have been elected precisely by advocating a comprehensive policy for
the nation. Coming into office at the helm of a political movement, Clay
had to condition his leadership to its demands. Yet his own party was

divided on the great issues of the day. President Madison was the titular leader of the Republican party and he was opposed to the basic elements of the American System. Further complicating the situation were the claims laid upon Clay by the speakership itself. As the leader of the House he had the obligation to deal impartially with members from the chair. He had to balance his ambitions, the claims of his party, his faction's political goals, his president's positions, the rights of the members, and the desires of his constituents. His reelections to the chair were a testimony to his success.

Perhaps the most striking aspect of the House during this era was its fluidity. The committee system was not well developed in 1811.[46] Members received their committee assignments from the speaker, and could be moved from committee to committee at his wish. They had no fixed committee assignments around which to tie their interests. Membership turnover was high, and average seniority was low. Debate has raged about the presence or absence of party structure during the era. In part, such disputes are matters of definition: what, after all, is a political party? In part, they are matters of fact: to what extent did members sharing common interests and views collaborate?[47]

It seems clear that, by 1811, with the Federalist party in decline, the House of Representatives was dominated by a majority of members who identified themselves, and were identified by their opponents, as Republicans. Beginning with Jefferson's last Congress and continuing for two decades thereafter, however, the Republican party was divided from within, partly along regional lines. Therefore, while a party system certainly existed, it was not of the sort that came to characterize American political life after the Civil War. The relative absence of grass-roots party organization around the country precluded strong congressional parties. Clay's own elections to the speakership are an indication of the weakness of the party system, but not a denial of its existence. No speaker since the Civil War could conceivably have been elected time and again by large bipartisan majorities. Yet Clay's bipartisan support was in part a result of the numerical strength of the Republicans. For Federalists the choice was among Republican candidates. The charismatic Clay won their support as the best presiding officer the Republicans could offer.

Although Clay faced a formidable leadership task, he had more room to operate than his modern successors. Even the rudimentary state of parliamentary law worked to his advantage. Henry Clay was not a good parliamentarian. According to another speaker, Robert Winthrop, "[H]e was no painstaking student of parliamentary law, but more frequently found the rules of his governance in his own instinctive sense of what was practicable and proper than in 'Hatsell's Precedents,' or 'Jefferson's

Manual.' "[48] Follett finds it a measure of his ability that none of his decisions were overturned upon appeal, and indeed, Clay made his mark through rulings from the chair. The absence of a long tradition of precedent gave Speaker Clay more latitude in interpretation than was available to those who came after him. His two most famous rebukes of John Randolph both involved innovation in the rules of the House.[49]

But if Clay was ignorant of parliamentary law, while having his greatest successes in presiding over the House, an explanation of his speakership must search for the factors that enabled him to preside effectively. Uniform testimony leaves little doubt that Clay led the House primarily by his personal popularity and skill. Follett's description is based upon conversations with those who knew Clay. Clay had a

> wonderful personal magnetism which few could withstand. His manner in the chair must have been the ideal bearing of a presiding officer. Although prompt, firm, and decisive, his invariable courtesy and geniality prevented offensiveness. All testify to the marvelous charm of his voice and manner, which attracted attention, awakened sympathy, and compelled obedience. He had a bold and commanding spirit, which imposed its will upon those around him. He carried all before him with his imperious nature to give him complete ascendancy over his party, and the easy leadership of the House.[50]

This characterization is supported by many favorable comments on Clay by his contemporaries and by the widespread support he always received for the speakership. Even if it amplifies his personal qualities, it still conveys a sense of the esteem that he commanded. Henry Clay was always more popular than the policies he espoused, and his sustained dominance of the House was clearly due more to personality than to power.[51] In a political environment lacking fixed structure, the only way to lead was by force of character and personal ability.

James Sterling Young, in *The Washington Community*, wonders if Clay was really a strong speaker, but the question seems to miss what is most distinctive about him.[52] Instead of asking if Clay was powerful, one ought rather to inquire why he was so popular. For it is beyond question that his popularity distinguished Henry Clay from all other American speakers. His is the only case in American history in which members continued to support a speaker irrespective of their partisan or factional allegiances, their geographic loyalties, or their views. If we are to accept the testimony of his peers, we must conclude that Clay was reelected time and again because he was a charismatic leader of the House. What other fact can account for his having consistently gained the support of those who opposed his policies? However much Clay may have tried to exercise political influence through the use of his formal powers, his popularity was due to his ability in presiding over the House. He filled, better than had any of his predecessors, the constitutionally prescribed role of the speaker. Thus, according to a Federalist: "The new Speaker is quite popular. He possesses fine talents and presides with dignity." John Adams Harper held him to be "a gentleman who commands respect and esteem, & keeps good order." It was in keeping good order that Clay made his mark immediately. Macon never gained control of John Randolph, but Clay did. It is a measure of the temper of the times that Henry Clay could have won acclaim for keeping Randolph's dogs off of the House floor. His efforts to bring order to the House did not stop with Randolph, however. He "made old Mr. Smilie take his seat, when that gentleman persisted in being out of order, with a polite request that was so firmly stated as to cause the Pennsylvania veteran to drop his spectacles in bewildered surprise."[53] One member was told to wake up or go home. Others were told to remove their feet from the tables. Most of the testimony pertaining to Clay's conduct of the speakership focuses upon such episodes.

Clay was a great orator. The House often debated issues in the Committee of the Whole so as to allow him to participate. His speeches were passionate, rambling, and captivating. Clay's oratorical skill was related to his capacity as a presiding officer. His personality overwhelmed, and it was only an overwhelming personality that could dominate a House that lacked the levers of power requisite to institutional control. For Henry Clay's House was most distinguished by its absence of fixed structure, and it was in this diffuse environment that his charismatic qualities were permitted to have their full effect.

This is not to say that Clay was inattentive to matters of institutional structure. The committee system became firmly established during Clay's speakership, largely as a result of his leadership.[54] In 1811 when he assumed the office, there were a total of nine standing committees provided for by rule, along with several select committees that served the entire Congress. In 1816 six standing committees were added, and in 1822 came an additional four. By 1825, when Clay left the speakership, there were twenty-five standing committees in all. Along with the increase in the number of standing committees came a dramatic increase in the volume of legislation considered by the House. The standing committee system was a monument to Speaker Clay's effort to gain control of the procedures of the House, but his committee chairmen exhibited little voting cohesion. It appears that relatively few issues required chairmen to coalesce around the speaker. During the entire period of Clay's service, from 1811 to 1825, Young is able to identify only seven issues with Clay. In five of these, Clay came up the loser.[55]

The contextual theory of the speakership views successful speakers as chameleons who adapt their style to the institutional context in which they find themselves. Clay's conduct as speaker is held to demonstrate this fact.[56] According to this interpretation, Clay was less a powerful party leader than a clever institutional politician who wove a protective cocoon of committee assignments around an otherwise problematical power base.[57] The institutional context theory assumes more adaptability than speakers are actually able to demonstrate, and, as applied to Clay, is wide of the mark. The traditional view has Clay as a forceful political leader who established and used the committee system to achieve his policy goals. The contextual view holds that Clay was a cautious institutionalist who used his committee appointments to preserve his speakership. Actually, Clay was a charismatic leader who brought order to the House by the force of his personality. The expansion of the committee system was designed to enhance the efficiency of the House rather than to increase the power of the speakership. Clay was most interested in his national stature; in order to sustain it, he sought to be a popular leader of the House. The context permitted him to do so, but his own ability enabled him to succeed.

Clay's ambition was always to be president, and he spent the bulk of his time as speaker after 1815 running for that office.[58] He was an avowed foe of Monroe, and was a constant thorn in the president's side. He turned down the War Department and the Court of St. James, preferring the speakership as a better political platform. He was one of only two speakers in the parliamentary period to have been widely regarded as "presidential timber," and the only one to be a known contender for the presidency while speaker.[59]

> Clay is an eloquent man, with very popular manners and great
> political management. He is, like almost all the eminent men of
> this country, only half-educated. His school has been the world,
> and in that he is a proficient. His morals, public and private, are
> loose, but he has all the virtues indispensable to a popular man
> . . . Clay has large and liberal views of public affairs, and that
> sort of generosity which attaches individuals to his person.[60]

Henry Clay was what James Madison had feared—a demagogue. The term is used descriptively and not pejoratively. He dominated the House by rhetorical arts, even though he lost some major policy battles. The speakership was his, but there was not much that he could do with it during the Era of Good Feelings. The antebellum state was rural, agrarian, and limited, and its limits confined Clay's ambition. The speakership was a platform for a demagogue, but not a seat of governing power. As speaker, Clay was a great national leader; but he was only one national leader, and not the most influential, and that in a government that did not do much. Clay's charisma was bounded by the political system and the political society in which it was permitted expression.

It is imprecise to say that Clay demonstrated the potential of the speakership, as if to imply that other speakers should be judged by the standard he set. Clay demonstrated one potential of the speakership. He was able to turn the office of speaker to his own political purposes, while at the same time serving the institutional needs of the House well. A different man might not have been able to do so; and under different circumstances Clay himself might not have succeeded. Clay's speakership was *a* model, not *the* model, of the speakership. He was a skilled and charismatic leader in a political institution that lacked fixed structure and competing centers of power. It was the lack of institutional and political definition in the House that enabled him to capitalize on his abilities.

Follett's apotheosis of Clay as the first and greatest of political speakers is challenged by Young, who questions if Clay was really as powerful as Follett's account suggests. Both accounts miss the essential feature of his speakership. Clay was a national political figure whose role as speaker was essentially subsumed by his stature. If every American speaker had been as prominent as Clay, the speakership itself would have been diminished. Clay was not great because he was speaker; he was speaker because he was great. As speaker, he was effective because he brought to the speakership a quality of personal leadership that it sorely needed in the absence of stronger institutional power.

Henry Clay's speakership was interrupted twice. In the Thirteenth Congress, Langdon Cheves of South Carolina served as speaker while Clay and John Quincy Adams negotiated the Treaty of Ghent; in the Sixteenth and Seventeenth Congresses, Clay was absent as he attempted to put his financial affairs in order, and John W. Taylor of New York and Philip P. Barbour of Virginia warmed the chair. Clay returned to the House and resumed the speakership for the Eighteenth Congress in 1823, and left it for good in 1825, just as John Quincy Adams's presidency began. The election of 1824 was a milestone in American politics.[61] It was the first closely contested (and disputed) election since 1800 and presented the curiosity of competition among four major candidates of the same party (Crawford, Clay, Jackson, and Adams). In the end, Adams won the presidency and named Clay his secretary of state. This was the last election in which a congressional nominating caucus chose a candidate (William H. Crawford of Georgia). The dominance of the Republican party hid from view serious philosophical and sectional differences within its ranks. These differences led to a paralysis of government under Adams similar to that which had occurred while his father was president. And just as Jefferson had ridden to power at the crest of a new party movement to succeed John Adams, Andrew Jackson rode to power at the crest of a new party movement to succeed John Quincy Adams.

Jackson's election in 1828 was a triumph of democracy. For the first time since Jefferson, America had a president who commanded overwhelming popular support, much of which came from citizens who had never before voted. The "Old Hero" was able to capitalize upon "a very commonplace feat of arms" to gain in 1814 a national reputation that carried him to the pinnacle of national power fourteen years later.[62] Ironically, Henry Clay's war brought his nemesis, Andrew Jackson, to prominence. A man of strong will and violent temperament, Andrew Jackson was one of those rare American presidents who, by the force of character, become the center of gravity for the entire political system.[63] Loved by common people, Jackson was as strongly hated by many among the elite. He was, like his rival Henry Clay, a demagogue, albeit one of a very different stripe. Clay's charisma was personal, reaching out to those around him; Jackson's was symbolic, having a broader appeal to average voters who had never even seen him. Clay was a demagogue on the Greek model, one who could sway an assembly of men by his presence and rhetoric. Jackson was a political phenomenon new to the American scene, a grass-roots politician. He won the presidency because so many Americans loved "Old Hickory."

Andrew Jackson's political revolution must be understood in the context of the political cleavages of the 1830s. Henry Clay's American system had defined an agenda for the national government that the Adams administration had advanced: protective tariffs, internal improvements, and the creation of the second National Bank. The continuity with Hamiltonian Federalist policy is apparent. Jackson lay in the Jeffersonian tradition. He favored the small farmer against the power of northeastern capital. The nascent industries whose interests were served by a high tariff and a federally controlled banking system formed no part of Jackson's political constituency. Andy Jackson was an agrarian populist. In a society that was still overwhelmingly rural and in which politics was still overwhelmingly local, Jackson brought about a transformation in the political system by attracting an expanded suffrage.[64]

The House of Representatives was the most democratic branch of the federal government, and felt the effects of the Jackson revolution more than the Senate. The House was, through Jackson's two terms in office, more sympathetic to him than was the Senate, where Henry Clay led the opposition. During his first administration, Jackson had a narrow working majority in the House. Occasionally a coalition of forces combined to defeat him, as in the case of the rechartering of the second National Bank in 1832, but generally, Jackson had his way in the House. After his landslide defeat of Clay in the election of 1832, the House was safely his. Not only did the House sustain Jackson's principal legislative aims, it also pointedly refused to go along with the resolutions of censure voted by the Senate, where Clay had taken up residence. The explanation for this difference between the two Houses of Congress would appear to lie in their differing constitutional bases. The Senate, with an indirect mode of election and longer term of office, was composed of more anti-administration Republicans than was the House. The House tended more closely to reflect the polls and Jackson's popularity among the voters.

Andrew Jackson's speaker was Andrew Stevenson of Virginia.[65] A former speaker of the Virginia House, Stevenson had come to the Seventeenth Congress in 1821. In 1825 he challenged incumbent John W. Taylor of New York for the speakership. Taylor was backed by the Adams administration and was reelected to the chair. In the Twentieth Congress, in 1827, Stevenson won the speakership. Stevenson was a man of ambition and ability. He was not the charismatic national leader that Speaker Clay had been, but like Clay he was an able and respected legislator with previous experience as a speaker. Of his tenure as speaker of the Virginia House it has been written:

> It is a matter of history, that at that period the Virginia House of Delegates was a model for a deliberative assembly. Order, decorum, . . . the proprieties of debate, courtesy, . . . attention to business observance of rules, characterized their proceedings . . . Most of those things depend upon the impartiality, the dignity, manner, and voice of the speaker, and if these requisites combine, as they did in Mr. Stevenson, order reigns where else is confusion and chaos.[66]

Stevenson had the abilities required of a speaker, but his election was due to factional politics as much as to leadership potential. During Adams's presidency Stevenson associated with the anti-administration faction in the Republican party. He had supported Crawford for president in 1824 and run against Taylor in 1825. By the time of the midterm elections in 1826 the Adams administration had alienated a majority of members in each house of Congress, and Stevenson won a narrow victory over Taylor and Barbour. Stevenson won election by a bare majority on the first ballot, reflecting the shift in power to the anti-administration forces in the House.[67]

Stevenson's is an early clear case of a member who sought the speakership actively and was willing to trade votes to get it, going so far as to promise to constitute the manufacturing committee in favor of a tariff he opposed. With the support of Senator Martin Van Buren and the New York delegation in the House, he was able to put together a cross-sectional coalition of anti-administration forces. As speaker, he proved himself an effective politician. He was described as "a gentleman of fine manners and amiable deportment" by his friends, and as "cunning," "prevaricating," and "arrogant" by his detractors. A contemporary description of Stevenson would fit many American politicians: "He has, by his *blustering* manners, his apparent *frankness* and *independence*, and mixture with mankind . . . acquired great knowledge of mankind, as well as of the facilities of getting over difficulties, and glossing over what he is not prepared to discuss or explain."[68] He was reelected three times to the chair before leaving the House in 1834 to become ambassador to Great Britain. His tenure was secured in large part by his association with President Jackson. Stevenson was of the "Virginia School," which meant that he and Jackson agreed that low tariffs were desirable, internal improvements were the province of the states, and the National Bank was a tool of northeastern capital. However, like many Jeffersonians, Stevenson was appalled by Jackson's use of patronage and offended by the exclusion of Virginians from the president's cabinet. The latter offense was more personally felt, since Stevenson himself aspired to a cabinet seat. In 1831 Jackson revamped his cabinet and once again bypassed Stevenson, perhaps due to the opposition of Van Buren, with whom he had come into conflict. His eye cast upon a government portfolio, Stevenson nearly lost his base of support in the House. The speakership election of 1831 was closely contested, and he won reelection by a bare majority over three other candidates.[69]

The following year supporters of the National Bank pushed its recharter through the House over Stevenson's opposition. With Jackson's veto the recharter bill died, but the battle over the bank continued through the remaining two years of Stevenson's speakership. Stevenson ensured that the Ways and Means Committee had an antibank majority chaired by future speaker and president, James K. Polk. Under the influence of Stevenson and Polk, the House approved a report antagonistic to the bank. This opposition to the bank won Stevenson favor with Jackson but opposition at home in his Virginia district. The Virginia state elections of 1834 swept anti-Jackson forces into power and harbingered trouble for Jacksonians in the congressional elections. As reward for Stevenson's loyalty, Jackson interceded to appoint him American minister to the Court of St. James. Stevenson resigned his speakership and congressional seat in June of 1834, but Jackson's opponents in the Senate delayed approval of Stevenson's nomination for two years.[70]

Stevenson was a Jackson loyalist. "No Speaker, except perhaps Macon," holds Follett, "has been so distinctly the President's man as was Stevenson during Jackson's administration."[71] That Stevenson was a presidential supporter may not seem surprising today, but in the antebellum political order this was not expected. The party system itself was not so firmly established as to define the speaker's role in terms of party obligation. In fact, Stevenson's support of Jackson had relatively little to do with party loyalty; instead it hinged on his personal ambition to be a cabinet or ministerial officer. Stevenson and Jackson had arranged a specific quid pro quo for the Court of St. James.[72] Thus, the two longest serving of the parliamentary speakers (Clay and Stevenson) were both men for whom the speakership was but a way station to another political office. Clay wished to use it as an instrument of national influence leading to the presidency; Stevenson wished to use it to curry favor with President Jackson in order to obtain a higher appointive position.

This contrast in specific aims offers a lesson about the character of the speakership during America's first party system. The basic structure of the American political system did not change radically during the period from 1811 to 1832. The Republican party was the national majority party up until the time it was transformed into the Democratic party in 1832. The basic issues on the national policy agenda during this era were the tariff, the bank, and internal improvements. There was considerable policy continuity during the period from 1812 to 1834, and the positions of the Federalist/National Republicans and the Jeffersonian Republican/Democrats on the policy agenda were very much the same.[73] With the establishment of the standing committee system under Clay, the House assumed a form of organization that did not change in any fundamental way under Stevenson. Under roughly similar circumstances, however, Clay emerged as an independent congressional leader who could resist, if not command, presidents of his own party, while Stevenson settled into the role of congressional spokesman for his party's president. This difference resulted from the unequal political stature of the individuals involved. Clay's ability was simply superior to that of Madison and Monroe, as Jackson's was to Stevenson's. It is not apparent that Clay would have been able to dominate Jefferson or Jackson. Stevenson, while possessing legislative acumen, lacked Clay's ability as a political leader; but he had no room in which to exercise such skill anyway under Jackson. In a situation in which the political environment was held relatively constant, the personal abilities of the individual speakers in relation to the president with whom they served became the primary factors influencing the conduct of the speakership.

The Speakership during the Second Party System

The Jacksonian revolution recast the Democratic party. Before it had been the party of the Virginia aristocracy; now it was the party of small farmers, western settlers, and immigrants. Martin Van Buren rode the general's coattails to a single term in the White House, but by 1836 a new political party, the Whigs, had appeared on the scene and had figured out the rules of the presidential game. Between 1836 and 1852 the Whigs selected retired generals as their party's nominee four times, winning the White House twice. Still, the foundation of the Democratic party was more solid than that of the Whig party, since between 1832 and 1852 the Democrats controlled the House and Senate in nine of eleven congresses respectively.[74] The Whig party included a variety of factions tied together by a common antipathy to Jackson and the egalitarianism of the Democratic party that he shaped. Its choice of name recalled the old English Whigs' fight against the monarchy in the seventeenth century and the new Whigs' resistance to the rising liberal movement in the England of the eighteenth century. The Whigs stood for constitutionalism and legislative supremacy, yet this veneer of common purpose was not undergirded by a stable political constituency. The Whig party was a party able to coalesce to win presidential elections, but it was not successful in establishing a broad base of political support.[75]

The Whig party was from the outset a loose coalition that included the remnants of the Federalist party, disaffected southern Republicans, and national Republicans in the tradition of Henry Clay, along with assorted outriders like the Anti-Masons. It could wrest the presidency from a Democratic party closely identified with Andrew Jackson and his anointed successor, Martin Van Buren, but was not as well designed to govern the nation in the face of the violent sectional controversies that arose over the issue of the extension of slavery into the new territories of the West. The Whig party lacked a firm sectional base or a guiding philosophy, precisely the weakness that led to its demise in the 1850s. During its relatively brief life however, the country was presented with a situation it had not seen before, in which two national parties competed for control of the federal government. The competition between the Whigs and Democrats during the late 1830s and 1840s concealed from immediate view, however, the fact that both parties were amalgams of factions united for electoral purposes but not joined by a philosophy of governance or the glue of common interest.[76]

The Democratic and Whig parties were coalitions designed to wrest control of the national government, especially the presidency. Several aspects of the political system had changed so as to encourage a bipolar party system. Members of Congress were elected exclusively by geographic districts after 1842, nominations were made almost everywhere by conventions rather than caucuses, and elections involved the mobilization of voters. These features of the electoral system required systematic and national organization. The issues confronting the nation during this period—the tariff, the organization of territories and their admission into the Union, and especially the status of slavery in them—required solutions of national scope.[77]

The speakership of the House of Representatives during this period experienced the highest rate of turnover in its history. Stevenson, a Jacksonian Democrat, was succeeded by John Bell of Tennessee, a National Republican who would later come to identify himself with the Whigs. Bell was supplanted by a fellow Tennessean, but a Jacksonian Democrat, James K. Polk, who served two terms. Polk was replaced by Robert M. T. Hunter of Virginia, a coalition candidate selected precisely because of his lack of party position. His successor, John White of Kentucky was a tool of Henry Clay, a Whig. Democrat John W. Jones of Virginia replaced White and Democrat John W. Davis of Indiana replaced Jones. A Whig, Robert C. Winthrop of Massachusetts, succeeded Davis, then Georgia Democrat Howell Cobb replaced Winthrop. In 1851 and 1853 Democrat Linn Boyd of Kentucky was elected to consecutive speakerships and became the first speaker since Polk and the only other speaker since Stevenson to claim the chair in two successive congresses. This rotation in office was due in part to party competition, but one might have expected that as the parties rotated in power, their respective leaders would pass the speakership back and forth. The mix of personalities holding the chair during the 1840s and 1850s suggests not only the lack of domination by any single party, but also the lack of a cohesive majority within either of them. The Whig and Democratic parties of the second party system were but a pale imitation of the strong parties that were to emerge after the Civil War.[78]

These speakers possessed several politically significant powers, including the power of floor recognition, the power of committee appointments, and the dispensation of House patronage. The power of floor recognition was significant generally, but especially in relation to the increasing efforts by antislavery elements in the House to bring forth petitions.[79] The gag rule that had prevented such petitioning was finally overcome by John Quincy Adams in 1844, and much depended upon the discretion of the speaker. The power of committee appointment had been the speaker's major political power since Henry Clay's speakership. However, by the 1840s the speaker's effective use of this power was significantly abridged because of the commitments that candidates for speaker were forced to make, amounting eventually to a practical requirement that aspirants to the chair make their committee lists known in advance. The speakers of the second party system encountered substantial impediments to exercising strong leadership, and none of them did.

If it was difficult for speakers of this period to be strong leaders, at least the House found it possible to choose a speaker prior to 1849 without too much trouble. Between 1849 and 1860 however, there occurred a dramatic and progressive increase in the sectional divisions underlying the second party system, divisions that would in a very short period of time prove fatal to the constitutional system that it served. The compromises that had held American society together for the first sixty years of its existence proved incapable of resolving the differences forced upon the political system by the problem of territorial expansion. More important, the spirit of compromise itself eventually fell prey to the moral force of the slavery issue. For the second American party system was built around the assumption that the differences that separated the South and the North were capable of yielding a practically effective solution, presenting issues upon which citizens would find it reasonable to compromise. But the slavery issue conformed to neither criterion. Instead, it presented the party system with a moral demand that was incapable of being negotiated, and a political situation in which no equitable compromise could be struck.[80] The political system broke asunder, and amid the chaos the speakership of the House became a visible victim of the breakdown. In the process, the vital role that the speakership plays in the American political system was revealed more clearly than at any other time in American history.

During the late 1840s and early 1850s the underlying weakness in the party system came into full view. Political sectionalism and ideological extremism were rampant. According to Potter: "Voters in 1854 . . . faced a stunning array of parties and factions. Along with the old familiar Democrats, Whigs, and Free Soilers, there were also Republicans, People's party men, Anti-Nebraskites, Fusionists, Know-Nothings, Know-Somethings (antislavery nativists), Maine Lawites, Temperance men, Rum Democrats, Silver Gray Whigs, Hindoos, Hard Shell Democrats, Soft Shells, Half Shells, Adopted Citizens, and assorted others."[81] This disintegration in the party system came about for several reasons. The waves of immigration during the 1840s had created a new national issue in the shape of the question of America's policy toward ethnicity and religious diversity. A revival of religious fundamentalism gave impetus to the temperance movement. But more than anything else, it was the slavery issue and the alternative approaches to dealing with it that destroyed the two-party system. In a heterogeneous society, democratic government requires a high degree of tolerance and a spirit of compromise. The slavery issue was morally and politically beyond tolerance and compromise. Once this issue had fragmented the two major parties by the creation of the Know-Nothings, Abolitionists, and Free-Soilers, it was inevitable that further proliferation of fringe parties would follow.[82]

A radical transformation in the party system was bound to have a major effect on the government. An electoral system that could not produce majoritarian political parties clearly could not easily produce legislative majorities in the Congress. Absent legislative majorities, representative government cannot function. This dilemma was plainly manifested in the paralysis that struck the House of Representatives in its attempts to organize for business during the 1850s. At the heart of the conflict lay the choice of its speaker. Some of the speakership contests during this period were of epic proportion. In 1849 Free Soil Democrats and Free Soil Whigs bolted their parties to deny either major party the capacity to elect a speaker. For the first time the House was forced to elect its speaker under the plurality rule. On the sixty-third ballot, Howell Cobb defeated Robert C. Winthrop. By 1855 the Whig party had collapsed and the Republican party was just organizing. The Free Soilers were insistent, and the Know-Nothings were at the peak of their influence. After two months and 129 ballots the House again voted to have recourse to the plurality rule, and on the 133d ballot Nathaniel P. Banks of Massachusetts was elected speaker of the Thirty-fourth Congress. James L. Orr of South Carolina was elected speaker of the Thirty-fifth Congress in 1857.

The final great struggle for the speakership came in 1859 on the eve of the Civil War. Southern Democrats fought a rearguard action to delay the organization of the House by filibustering. Amid extremely hostile invective, William Pennington of New Jersey was selected on the forty-fourth ballot. His election was secured when the Republicans, unable to elect their own candidate, John Sherman of Ohio, threw their support to a total newcomer in the hopes that his very lack of experience would placate enough Democrats to secure election. The tactic was barely successful, Pennington receiving exactly the 117 votes required to win. He thus became the second freshman congressman to have been elected speaker, but unlike Clay, Pennington was chosen in spite of his lack of credentials and avowed policies, and not because of his abilities and views. Whereas Clay was elected at the helm of a party movement that knew where it was going, Pennington was the last resort of a House that did not wish to get where destiny seemed bound to take it.[83]

It was the breakup of the party system that caused the paralysis of government reflected in these contested speakership elections. During the 1850s America had something like an Italian parliamentary system, divided by numerous splinter parties. The choice of speaker was tantamount to a vote to organize the government. Each of the several parties that participated in the effort to organize the House sought advantage in the makeup of the committee lists, in patronage, and other benefits. Under the circumstances, no party could gain a majority, and no coalition of parties adding up to a majority could be formed. The speakership of the House became the center of national political attention. Constitutionally, the House cannot function without a speaker, and the government cannot function without the House. After the inauguration of the president and vice president, the election of the speaker is the next necessary step in organizing the government.

An examination of the debates surrounding the contested speakership elections of the 1850s reveals that it was the underlying regional divisions along with the potential composition of the committee lists that made the choice of speaker particularly vexing.[84] The flow of business to the floor depended upon the composition of the committees. A proslavery composition would keep a lid on the issue; an antislavery composition would likely bring it to the floor. The fate of the new territories, and of the nation, hung in the balance. This basic sectional and factional problem in committee composition exacerbated the perennial problem faced by speakers in trying to satisfy the demands of individual members.[85] While there is little evidence that the speakers of this period had the political power to control the committees in the conduct of their business after they were appointed, the appointments themselves were sufficiently important to paralyze the House. Ironically, the very contentiousness of the appointment power seems to have prevented these speakers from taking political advantage of it.

Maintaining a minimum degree of order in the House was the most a speaker could expect to accomplish. Lacking the ability to unite the House for constructive action, the speakers in the 1850s all sought to prevent it from coming apart. In an environment in which invective drowned out deliberation, the preservation of a minimal sense of fairness was no small achievement. It is apparent that the speakership was politically weak at this time, and as a result there may have been little incentive for aggressive men to seek it. Still, in preserving order and in moderating with a sense of fairness, a speaker could, even in this adverse climate, facilitate the political adjustments necessary to hold the country together. It was, after all, not Pennington's election as speaker but Lincoln's election as president that precipitated the Civil War.

Conclusion

The speakership of the House is to a great extent the victim of circumstances beyond the control of any speaker, and in fact beyond the control of the House itself. It reflects the political composition of the House, which in turn reflects the political composition of the country. The parliamentary speakership was shaped by the constitutional system, the national policy agenda, and the cleavages in the polity. The period from 1789 to 1860 comprises a full third of the history of the republic to the date of this writing. It welcomed three generations of political actors, it witnessed a variety of major political events, was characterized by a number of different policy issues, and at least two distinct party systems. The era was, however, marked by two fundamental features that lent a degree of continuity to American political experience. First, during the antebellum era the federal government did not establish a truly national regime; consequently, the power of its national offices was constrained by the political system in which they functioned. Second, the polity was fundamentally divided between the cotton South and the industrial North, and the slavery question loomed over the national conscience as a dagger ready to fall.

During the first party system (lasting roughly through the mid 1830s), the policy agenda was dominated by issues of economic development. The divisions in the polity arrayed northeastern industrial capital against the agrarian economies of the South and West. These issues were, of course, fundamentally tied to the existence of slavery in the South, but until the 1830s the political system coped with slavery and the political and economic differences associated with it. The speakership of the House developed as a relatively stable institution, it was delegated formal institutional powers, and individual speakers were more or less effective according to their abilities, the force of the presidency, and their strength within the House. Among them only Clay may be said to have been a strong speaker.

After 1840 the speakership went into a steady decline even though the institutional powers of these speakers were not significantly different than those of their predecessors. What changed was not the power of the speakership but the environment in which it functioned. Political and economic forces pressed upon the viability of slavery in the South, and the expansion of the polity into the western territories forced the issue of slavery to the front of the national agenda. The disintegration of the speakership that occurred in the decade prior to the Civil War was, then, a reflection of the general deterioration of the constitutional order. The speakership did not change fundamentally, but it could not function in a political system in which the federal government itself was paralyzed. Slavery divided the nation morally, economically, and geographically. The tariff question, the relationship of northeastern capital to southern and western debt, the issue of internal improvements, the debate over the national bank, and the continuing struggle over the terms of admission of new states to the union were all affected by the existence of slavery. Slavery and the way of life that it supported were destined to pass into history, but would not go peacefully.

The national government of the antebellum era was weak because it could not be strong. A strong national government required a national mission, and there could be no such mission in a nation divided on its fundamental premise. The presidency passed from the generation of statesmen to the generation of warrior chiefs; the former had stood for the principles of republican nationalism, the latter was merely the product of an electoral system in which personality supplanted principle as a bond among men. That the disintegration of government was endemic to the political system and not peculiar to the House of Representatives is confirmed by the fact that the presidents during the two decades prior to the Civil War included several who were among the least distinguished in American history, and none who were among the best. The presidency neither beckoned great men nor permitted average men to govern boldly.

In the House of Representatives, the rudiments of organization slowly evolved. The committee system took root but did not come to dominate the proceedings of the House. Neither did its speakership. The parliamentary speakership was largely a defensive institution. Its powers were insufficient to claim the interest of great men, and the process of electing speakers was such as to largely undermine their capacity to lead. Eventually, it became virtually impossible to elect a speaker, but by then, the political system was itself on its last legs. Speakers could do little to strengthen their own hand or the powers of the office they held. Henry Clay is the notable exception, yet it is clear that Clay's prominence as speaker was due more to his national political stature than to the use to which he put the office. The committee system first evolved under Clay's guiding hand, but it would have evolved under any speaker or set of speakers, since it was an institutional response to the demands of the legislative body, and not simply a device by which Clay sought or achieved personal power. It is striking that during the first seventy years of government under the Constitution, speakers of the House were able to do so little on behalf of the office.

It would be inaccurate and unfair to relegate these men to the ash-heap of history. Follett regards most of the parliamentary speakers as "second-rate men who were yet the best leaders the House afforded."[86] According to her, the best speakers of this era were Clay, Nathaniel Banks, Howell Cobb, and Robert Winthrop. Yet she contends that Cobb's speakership suffered from an excess of sectional influence, leaving only one Kentucky and two Massachusetts Whigs as the roster of outstanding parliamentary speakers. This book's thesis permits a word on behalf of these speakers. The obligation of the speaker is to facilitate the work of the House. In the parliamentary period, this was no easy task. Polk, for example, had continually to deal with pesky John Quincy Adams and other abolitionists, whose numerous anti-slavery petitions led eventually to the adoption of a gag rule against them. That Polk's rulings were often successfully appealed is taken as a mark against his effectiveness as speaker, but might as easily be regarded as a sign of the times. What the House demanded of the parliamentary speakership was stability in the chair. Especially during the fifteen years prior to seccession, speakers had little choice but to sacrifice an ambition for power in order to hold office. By 1860 even an accommodating speakership was not enough to hold the House together.

The year 1860 was the historical nadir of the American speakership, as of the political system of which it is a part. But from the ashes of war there would arise a new and reinvigorated speakership, the product of a new economic and political order. The new economic order emphasized national expansion and the new political order was characterized by a stable, two-party system in which the speakership of the House became an artifact and architect of party government in the United States.

2 ☆ The Partisan Speakership

Party Government Emerges

In 1860 the American polity disintegrated because its internal schism was too deep for republican institutions to contain it. The speakership of the House was a visible casualty of the chaos that reigned just prior to the war. From the ashes of war emerged a new polity, determined to span the continent and dedicated to the proposition that economic development was the national destiny. The nation's passion to consume its space nurtured a new political system in which Republican presidents behaved according to Whig principles, and the Congress dominated federal policy making. From 1860 to 1910, the speakership of the House rose from the impotency of antebellum America to the pinnacle of its power during the tenure of Uncle Joe Cannon. During this period, a stable two-party system developed, while in the House of Representatives there gradually evolved an internal scheme of governance that had at its core an institutionally powerful speakership. Not all of the speakers of this era were czars, but the forces driving the policy agenda and the political system led eventually to the domination of the House by the speakership in a system of party government.

The concept of party government is at odds with the basic structure of the constitutional system established by the Founders. It asserts the right of the majority party to rule without hindrance by the minority. It is not surprising that the majority's claim of omnipotence would cause the minority to demand the right to obstruct. Claims to rights became a gloss for party philosophy. The Republican party was the party of majority rule, while the Democrats adopted the banner of minority rights. In the South, minority rights and states' rights became synonymous, as the region sought to protect its caste society. In the twentieth century, the Republican party would often espouse theories of property and states' rights against the economic intrusions of the New Deal and the welfare state; but in the nineteenth century the Republican party stood for economic and political expansion mediated by the federal government. The positions taken by the two major parties during the last half of the nineteenth century arose naturally from their respective constituencies.

The Civil War had been fought to settle the question of nationhood and federal supremacy. The Republican party was the party of union; the Democratic party the party of states' rights. Even the northern wing of the Democratic party, led by Stephen Douglas of Illinois, was guided by the philosophy of local autonomy. Douglas's famous defense of majority rule applied to the people of the states and territories in severalty, and not to the nation for which Lincoln spoke. After the war the Radical Republicans sought to impose reconstruction on the South and to ensure suffrage for blacks. As before the war, the Republicans were the party of national purpose and the Democrats were the party of states' rights. From this time forward the South would be safely Democratic, affecting the shape of national and congressional politics until the last decades of the twentieth century. Aside from the great Civil War schism, there had always been a distinct policy difference between the party of Hamilton, Clay, and Lincoln and the party of Jefferson, Jackson, and Douglas. The Federalist, Whig, Republican tradition had always stood for national economic expansion protected by high tariffs, funded by national control of capital, and facilitated by a federal program of internal improvements. The Democratic-Republican, Republican, Democratic tradition had always favored local autonomy, states' rights, and low tariffs. The former was the party of northeastern capital, the latter was the party of southern and western agrarianism. With the influx of waves of immigrants in the two decades before the war and the four decades after it, the Democratic party became the party of ethnic and religious diversity and gained a foothold in the big cities of the Northeast. The split between its southern and northern wings arose from the circumstances of the war, and deepened as industrialization fostered economic divisions between North and South.[1]

The political constituencies and policy views of the two major parties dovetailed to produce differing views on the role of the government, and these philosophical differences led to sharpened political conflict in the last years of the nineteenth century. In the House of Representatives, the effective use of tactics of obstruction such as the disappearing quorum and the abuse of roll-call votes by minorities (Democratic and Republican alike) led to a paralysis of government in the 1880s. This paralysis brought about the Reed Reforms of 1890 that established the basis for unimpeded majority rule. The system of majority party governance permitted by the Reed Rules was brought to its culmination under the leadership of Joseph Cannon during the first decade of the twentieth century.

The Republican party dominated the government during and after the war, and the party was united in some policy areas.[2] Lincoln's assertion of presidential power in suspending the right of habeas corpus was sustained by the Congress (although later invalidated by the Supreme Court), and the Congress was quick to provide the administration with the financing needed for the war. Even such controversial items as the first conscription law and the first income tax won quick congressional approval.[3] The Republicans passed laws to foster economic expansion. These included the establishment of the Department of Agriculture, the Homestead Act, the Pacific Railroad Act, the First Anti-Polygamy Act, the Morrill Land-Grant College Act, and the National Bank Act.[4] Evidently, a Republican majority in the Congress was sufficiently united on a broad range of policy aims to govern.

But this consensus was not sustained during the remaining years of the Civil War and the reconstruction period. The Thirty-eighth Congress restricted itself for the most part to financing the war, while the Thirty-ninth and Fortieth Congresses became embroiled in a vicious struggle over reconstruction policy and the control of the national government with President Andrew Johnson. This conflict led to the unsuccessful effort to remove the president, but resulted in the triumph of the Reconstruction program of the radical Republicans. Within the Congress, the Republican party became badly divided between radical, moderate, and conservative factions, and the policy of the party proved in fact to be that of the largest and most vociferous of its factions, the radical Republicans.

The most influential member of the House of Representatives during this period was Thaddeus Stevens of Pennsylvania. Stevens, the chairman of the Ways and Means Committee, was the leader of the radicals, and his influence over the House exceeded that of its speakers. Galusha Grow, the speaker of the Thirty-seventh Congress, was a colleague of Stevens from Pennsylvania and clearly Stevens's man.[5] His successor, Schuyler Colfax of Indiana was an effective party spokesman, but regarded by some as a mouthpiece for Stevens. According to George Rothwell Brown, Colfax "frankly proclaimed the supremacy of Congress to the Executive as a fact, as Clay had proclaimed it in Jackson's day as a principle," but to Hubert Bruce Fuller he "belonged to the class which biologists term invertebrates. He led a gelatinous political existence."[6] To detractors Colfax was a "miserable popinjay, charlatan, and small potato demagogue."[7] Colfax was tactful and charming, but lacked the character to exert forceful political leadership. Stevens provided that.[8] According to Fuller: "Colfax possessed neither will nor mind of his own. Thaddeus Stevens furnished him with these mental attributes. The fact that Stevens permitted him to remain as speaker for six years furnishes the best index of his character. He was the alter ego."[9] Although Stevens served as the chairman of the Ways and Means Committee, his influence rested less on institutional power than on the avid support from his ideological faction and the force of his own character. One-party political systems are often subject to factionalism. Often these factions are oriented around dominant personalities or influential cliques, and politics becomes a game of personal competition in which power itself is the goal.[10]

Among the products of one-party rule during the period after the Civil War was the spoils system. Party organization at the state and local levels lay in the hands of party regulars who controlled patronage. The decade of the 1870s witnessed a reduction of state expenditures (due in large part to restrictions imposed by postwar state constitutional revisions), but a drastic expansion of local expenditures for public works. With the expanded governmental activity came thousands upon thousands of politically controlled jobs and appointments. At the federal level, expenditures for rivers and harbors increased by 1,000 percent in the decade, and the federal government launched a massive program to subsidize the building of the national railroad system.[11] The need for phalanxes of customs officers to collect the duties generated by the protective tariff provided ample scope for federal patronage.

Since the time of Jackson it had been an accepted American practice to treat political patronage as the spoils of a battle won. With the dramatic expansion of the national economy and the dominance of American politics by local, state, and national political organizations, political patronage became a means by which the controlling political party sought to ensure its continuation in office. During the postwar years the national Republican party benefited from the patronage system. The use of patronage and the distribution of political favors to industrial interests supporting parties and candidates was scandalous, but it contributed to the existence of strong and stable party organizations. In the Republican party, those who were the operators and beneficiaries of the system saw little reason to alter it in the name of political reform. The system was, in their view, not only useful to them but good for the country, since through it the party was able to maintain those policies that promised maximum industrial expansion and economic growth.[12]

The corruption of the Gilded Age eventually touched the speakership. Schuyler Colfax and James Gillespie Blaine were implicated in the

Crédit Mobilier scandal for having accepted sweetheart stock deals from the Union Pacific Railroad. Blaine was speaker when the charges were brought, and he commissioned a select House committee to investigate them. He had managed to accumulate considerable wealth during his years of public service and his name had appeared on a list of members receiving stock disbursements, so he was reasonably suspect; but when the committee was able to find no hard evidence to disprove the speaker's claims of innocence, he was exonerated. In 1875, while serving as minority leader, charges of illicit stock dealings with the railroads were again raised. Blaine defended himself by reading aloud the infamous "Mulligan Letters" and won public vindication when the letters contained no incriminating evidence. The controversy was sufficient to deny to Blaine the Republican presidential nomination in 1876, but his career was resurrected by service in the Senate and as secretary of state. He carried the Republican banner in 1884, losing the election to Grover Cleveland. Colfax was not so fortunate. The evidenciary trail proved that he had lied under oath about receiving a payment of $1,200 from the Union Pacific as a dividend for stock that he never purchased. The vice president completed his term, but his public career was at an end.[13]

During his six years as speaker (from 1869 to 1875) Blaine was an effective leader of his party and of the House. His speakership was partisan. He used the speaker's list of those who wished to obtain recognition on the floor, and he was not reluctant to insist that measures be altered to conform to his own preferences before agreeing to grant recognition. As a necessary means of bringing some order to the proceedings of the House, the speaker's list was a precursor of the role that the Rules Committee came to play after 1880 in floor scheduling. Blaine's assertive use of this prerogative was a major step in the accumulating power of the speakership.[14] Yet Blaine was unwilling to curtail obstructionism. On the principle that "you can lead a horse to water but not make him drink," he refused to deal with the problem of the disappearing quorum.[15] Although highly partisan, Blaine respected the rights of the minority. On one highly publicized occasion, Representative Benjamin Butler of Massachusetts, a radical Republican, pressed for House consideration of a bill to force the southern states to permit blacks to vote. The House voted against consideration of Butler's bill, preferring instead to take up an appropriations bill. As the session proceeded into the evening, Speaker Blaine left to attend a formal dinner. With attendance low, Representative Butler and his supporters moved again for consideration of the force bill. The Democrats obstructed this, allowing Blaine time to return to the chair. During a session that extended from 7:30 in the evening until 4:00 the next afternoon, Speaker Blaine presided over the House without respite, as the radical Republicans fought with the conservative Republicans and Democrats for control. Eventually Butler's opponents were able to muster a quorum of their own number, and the struggle ended. Speaker Blaine won the esteem of Republicans and Democrats alike by his commitment to honor the rights of the minority as they were then understood. He accepted the legitimacy of the tactics of obstruction and believed that it was the obligation of the majority party to unify for action or to wait the minority out. When he retired from the chair a week later and was voted the thanks of the House, the applause from both sides of the aisle was thunderous and in waves.[16]

Blaine's impartiality in this instance was displayed in the full knowledge that in the next Congress the Democrats would be in control. By preserving the procedural principles upon which obstruction rested, he ensured his own party's prerogatives to obstruct in the future. As the leader of a partisan majority party, Blaine had made the speakership politically effective, yet had not undertaken to bring about institutional reforms that might have guaranteed majority party governance. With the elections of 1874, the Democratic party returned to power in the House, and the country would see how the party of Jefferson and Jackson conducted its business.

The return of the Democrats to power in the House in 1875 came about largely as a reaction by the public to the scandals that plagued the Republicans during the Grant administration. During Blaine's speakership the chief of the Democratic opposition had been Samuel J. Randall of Pennsylvania, a Philadelphia Democrat possessed of a peculiar strength of character that enabled him to be a strong leader of men. Randall had orchestrated the tactics of the Democrats in opposition to the Reconstruction program of the radical Republicans and was largely responsible for the filibusters that brought about the defeat of civil rights bills, endearing him to the party's southern wing. On one occasion he stood on the floor for seventy consecutive hours in opposition to a force bill.[17] He was practiced in the arts of political obstruction.[18] A product of machine politics, Randall was a thoroughgoing party man yet an ardent supporter of the protective tariff, a Republican policy. Perhaps due to his views on the tariff, he was bypassed for speaker by his party in 1875 in favor of Michael C. Kerr of Indiana, a man of mild temperament and poor physical constitution. Kerr did not survive his term as speaker, and Randall was chosen to succeed him. As chairman of the Appropriations Committee and as a staunch supporter of the southern position on reconstruction, Randall was situated to win the support of a caucus majority in spite of his heretical position on the tariff.

Randall no sooner assumed the chair than he found himself confronted by one of the greatest political crises in American history, arising in the disputed Hayes-Tilden election of 1876. He chaired the proceedings by which the electoral votes for president were taken. His firm and impartial handling of this process won respect from both Republicans and Democrats. Under the terms of the Electoral Commission Act, the rules of the House were temporarily modified to forbid the use of the dilatory tactics to which Randall, as a minority Democrat, had often recurred. His enforcement of the terms of the act was firm and fair, even when it appeared plain that the decision of the Electoral Commission would give the election to the Republicans.[19]

As speaker, Randall was as firmly committed to the preservation of those rules favoring minority obstruction as he had been as a minority floor leader. He would entertain no proposition to count a quorum or to limit dilatory motions. Still, he was a strong leader and he is responsible for several important changes in the procedures of the House that subsequently contributed to the centralization of power within it. He insisted that there could be no appeal to the House from a speaker's decision on floor recognition and initiated the practice of recognizing committee chairmen in preference to other members. In 1879 he commissioned the Rules Committee to recodify the rules of the House, and the reforms of 1880 that resulted did much to simplify the cumbersome code by which the House had been governed since 1789. Perhaps the most significant change instituted by Randall was in the power of the Rules Committee itself. This was made a standing committee of the House, and all propositions affecting House rules and procedures were to be channeled to it. The committee was empowered to bring its resolutions to the floor at any time, paving the way for it to assume the task of gatekeeper of the House. That the first major reforms in the House were undertaken by a Democratic speaker for the purpose of centralizing control over the House agenda indicates that the underlying forces producing them were endemic and not partisan.[20]

A major change that Randall supported was the adoption of the Holman Rule in 1876, named after its author, Congressman William S. Holman of Indiana. As a former chairman of the Appropriations Committee, Randall was not without concern for its prerogatives. Under the reforms of 1880 the appropriating power was centralized in the committee, with only two exceptions. Randall fought to unify the appropriating power, arguing that only by a centralized appropriations mechanism could public expenditures be kept under control. The Holman amendment enhanced the power of the Appropriations Committee by providing that riders to appropriations bills would be in order only when their effect was to reduce public expenditures. The Appropriations Committee was given the power to legislate substantively for the purpose of cutting expenditures, a politically potent power that Randall would later put to good effect when he returned to his post as the chairman of the Appropriations Committee during the tenure of Speaker Carlisle.[21]

Randall's position as a high-tariff Democratic speaker is worth analyzing. The Democrats had been associated with the concept of a "revenue only" tariff since before the Civil War. The return of the party after the war was marked by its resurgence in the South and West, two bastions of low-tariff supporters. How did Randall exercise such effective leadership of the party for so long a period of time while remaining in opposition to its mainstream on the major policy issue of the era? An answer lies in the cleavage between the party's southern and northern wings. The Democrats could not have been led by a southerner at any time soon after the end of the war, and Randall's rise to the leadership seems to have occurred in the same sort of vacuum that characterized Democratic presidential politics of the 1860s and 1870s. By the 1880s tariff reform had become an increasingly important issue and the forces for reform had gained strength within the Democratic Caucus. Randall's opposition to the party position on the tariff issue became increasingly less tenable. Although the Democrats castigated the Republicans in principle for the excesses of spending occasioned by the Republican surpluses, they were not reluctant to seek federal largess for their districts through the Rivers and Harbors appropriations. Randall's tight-fisted ways won no favor among Democrats on this score, and it is no surprise that Rivers and Harbors appropriations were given to the Commerce Committee under Randall's own reforms of 1880.

Six years of Democratic rule were briefly interrupted in 1881 by the election of a Republican House and the choice of J. Warren Keifer of Ohio as speaker. Keifer's speakership was among the less fortunate experiences of the chair. A friendly but weak man, he vacillated in executing the functions of presiding officer and lacked acumen in the political conduct of the office. His committee appointments were not conducive to the success of the party's policies. Worse, he unabashedly engaged in nepotism, appointing his son and two nephews to well-paying House positions (in the case of his son, as secretary to the speaker). Still, the Forty-seventh Congress produced significant legislation, including the Pendleton Act creating the federal civil service, the immigration act of 1882, and the creation of a new commission to review the tariff schedule. These bills suggested that a tide of reform was under way, and the Democrats were better positioned than were the Republicans to ride it. The 1882 elections swept the Democrats back into power, and the speakership was up for grabs.[22]

Randall once again sought the chair, but was opposed by Samuel S. Cox of New York and John G. Carlisle of Kentucky. Randall was confident of victory, but underestimated the strength of sentiment in the party for tariff reform, Carlisle's major issue. It was no longer possible for a high-tariff Democrat to win a majority in the Democratic Caucus, and Carlisle won easily. Carlisle's selection reflected the changing demographic base of the Democratic party and the increasing influence of populist ideals. The party's strength was increasingly centered in the South and the West, and the faction of northeastern protectionists that Randall led had shrunk to barely a quarter of the party's membership. While the party had always been committed in principle to a lowering of the tariff, Carlisle was the first speaker to have sought the office explicitly on the premise that he intended to do something about it.[23]

Unfortunately, Carlisle still had Randall to deal with. Acknowledging Randall's seniority, Carlisle reappointed him to the chair of Appropriations, affording him a power base from which to oppose any general lowering of the tariff. In league with the Republicans, Randall led a group of about forty protectionist Democrats in voting against the Morrison tariff bill of 1884, causing its narrow defeat. Carlisle was helpless in the face of Randall's influence with the swing Democrats. Imbued with the traditional Democratic respect for minority rights, the speaker was unwilling to bring the full powers of his office to bear on behalf of his policy aims. In the elections of 1884 Grover Cleveland became the first postwar Democratic President. Cleveland was elected on a tariff reform platform. With a president and a speaker committed to lowering the tariff, the Forty-ninth Congress afforded a decidedly more optimistic prospect for a tariff bill.[24]

First, however, Carlisle and his supporters had to confront the power of Randall. They introduced a plan for the reform of the committee system that would reduce the number of committees, spreading the power of appropriations among several committees rather than leaving it in the hands of the Appropriations Committee. Randall opposed this plan fiercely, arguing that it would inevitably lead to an increase in public expenditure as each appropriating committee sought to increase its share of federal outlays. Randall's opposition was of no avail; the plan was adopted in just four days with only seventy dissenting votes.[25]

Randall had lost much of the basis of his power as chairman of the Appropriations Committee, but he was still a member of the House, and under its rules was a potent force in opposition to any tariff reform measure to which he did not subscribe. Using the same tactics as a member of the majority in the 1880s that he had used as a member of the minority in the early 1870s, Randall continued his opposition to tariff reform. The Morrison tariff reform bill in the Forty-ninth Congress was more rationally calculated than the across-the-board reductions proposed in the Forty-eighth Congress. A carefully crafted schedule of duties designed to win over enough protection votes to swing the balance was presented to the House. However thirty-five disaffected Democrats joined a united Republican party and voted against a motion to go into the Committee of the Whole for the consideration of the bill, and the tariff reform effort was defeated. In the second session of the Forty-ninth Congress, tariff reform was again undertaken. Again it was moved that the House enter the Committee of the Whole to consider the bill. Again Randall opposed Speaker Carlisle. This time the vote was closer, but the result was the same. On a 148 to 154 vote, with twenty-eight Democrats voting in the negative, the motion was defeated.[26] Thus, during his first two congresses as speaker, John G. Carlisle, widely regarded as a forceful exponent of his party's policy and as a strong speaker, was twice unable to gain floor consideration of the principal piece of legislation upon which his program rested.

Carlisle was a characteristic Democratic speaker. The Democratic party has always been diverse and divided, and there is far greater pressure within the party toward accommodation and conciliation than in the Republican party. This led to a reliance on the seniority principle that compelled Carlisle to appoint his strongest opponent to the second most powerful position in the House. It made both Randall and Carlisle reluctant to use the powers of the speakership to constrain the minority, for they recognized that the minority might well (and often did) include Democrats as well as Republicans. The persistent Democratic tendency to diffuse power in the House arose from the need on the part .of Democrats to allow accommodation among the various wings of their party. John Carlisle was a good speaker, but he was a good Democratic speaker; in consequence, he failed to attain his major legislative objective during his first two terms.[27]

In the Fiftieth Congress the impetus finally quickened for passage of a tariff bill. Carlisle was reelected speaker and promoted the bill in his acceptance speech. At his suggestion, President Cleveland devoted the entirety of his first presidential message to the Congress to the subject. Prior to Congress's convening, the president had stumped the country to promote the policy, tying his reelection prospects to tariff reform. In the House, the mantle of reform was taken up by the new chairman of the Ways and Means Committee, Roger Mills of Texas. The Mills tariff bill was pushed forcefully by Speaker Carlisle. In a House more closely divided than its predecessor (169 Democrats to 152 Republicans), the Mills bill was finally approved with only four dissenting Democratic votes. Randall, lying ill in Philadelphia, was paired against the bill, but the coalition necessary to block tariff reform was finally broken. Yet

Speaker Carlisle's victory proved in the end to be ephemeral; the Republican-controlled Senate killed the tariff bill, and the ultimate goal of his speakership was never attained.[28]

John G. Carlisle's speakership was paradoxical. He had clearly advocated a party program and had vigorously supported it. Fearing that pork barrel spending might blunt the movement for tariff reform, he worked with Randall to limit federal outlays. Concerned that an overcrowded legislative agenda would preempt his own policy goals, he used the power of recognition arbitrarily to deny the floor to many bills. He insisted on the absolute discretion of the speaker in floor recognition. In short, Carlisle was a strong party leader. Still, he was unwilling to undertake any major reform of the House rules to prevent obstructive minority tactics. The Carlisle years were among the most frustrating ever experienced in the post–Civil War House because the political divisions within the Democratic party combined with the obstruction that the rules allowed. The increasing frustration was felt and noted by a rising star in the Republican party, Thomas Brackett Reed of Maine. The natural tendency of the Republican party was toward centralization of power in the party leadership. The Republicans were more cohesive than the Democrats, and had a greater incentive to establish procedural control. Reed's election to the speakership was a declaration of war on obstructionism.

The End of Obstructionism

The Fifty-first Congress was, with two exceptions, the most closely divided in America's post–Civil War history.[29] The Republicans regained control of the House by a bare seven-vote majority, 166 to 159; they controlled the Senate by a two-vote margin; and President Harrison had claimed the White House while trailing Cleveland by eighty thousand popular votes. The Republicans enjoyed less than a clear mandate to govern. In spite of their marginal situation, many in the Republican hierarchy were convinced that the reestablishment of Republican political dominance and sound national policy required that the party prove itself better able to govern than the Democrats. Given the disarray of the government under the previous Democratic regime, this may have seemed an easy task. But the Republicans knew that the same tactics of obstruction by which they had delighted in tormenting Speaker Carlisle would soon return to haunt them in their efforts to run the government. In the months preceding the convening of the Congress, the Republicans met frequently to plan their strategy.

Among the Republican leaders, none was more adamant in his conviction that the rules of the House must be reformed than was the new speaker, Thomas Brackett Reed of Maine. As de facto leader of the Republican minority in the Fiftieth Congress, he had witnessed the chaos that had resulted from Speaker Carlisle's unwillingness to deal effectively with obstruction, especially when, in the waning days of that congress, Congressman James B. Weaver of Iowa tied the House in knots for eight days in order to force a floor vote on the organization of the Oklahoma territory. As speaker, Reed was determined that his own party's program should not fall prey to obstructionist tactics, and he decided to prevail on reform of the rules or resign his speakership.[30]

The two most egregious practices used to obstruct the business of the House were the disappearing quorum and the dilatory motion. The disappearing quorum was possible because a member of the House cannot be compelled to vote, while according to House rules a quorum under the Constitution could only be established by the actual votes of members on a pending question. On closely divided votes, a minority could stall the House merely by refusing to vote, denying it a quorum. Dilatory motions were more diverse, ranging from spurious demands for recorded votes to useless motions for adjournment. The common element of these tactics was that members availed themselves of valid parliamentary rights for the express purpose of preventing business from proceeding.[31]

Reed assaulted both of these bastions of obstructionism straight-forwardly. At his instruction, the Rules Committee withheld its pro-posals for the Fifty-first Congress pending the development of a revised code and the settlement of all cases of contested elections. During the interim, the House operated under the general rules of parliamentary law. Functioning as the presiding officer under general parliamentary law, Speaker Reed consistently refused to accept dilatory motions. Then, on January 19, 1890, the storm broke. The House had under consid-eration the West Virginia election case of Smith v. Jackson. The Dem-ocrats knew that the Republicans would settle disputed cases in favor of Republican candidates, and planned to obstruct the election cases until the Rules Committee brought forward a set of rules acceptable to the minority side. When the Democrats moved against consideration of the election case and called for a recorded vote, the battle was on. The actual record of the vote showed 161 voting aye (for consideration of the case), 2 voting no, and 165 not voting. Calmly, Speaker Reed an-nounced the vote:

THE SPEAKER: On this question the yeas are 161, the nays 2
MR. CRISP: No quorum.
THE SPEAKER: The Chair directs the Clerk to record the follow-ing names of members present and refusing to vote.

[Applause on the Republican side.]

MR. CRISP: I appeal—[applause on the Democratic side]—I appeal from the decision of the Chair.

THE SPEAKER: Mr. Blanchard, Mr. Bland, Mr. Blount, Mr. Breckinridge, of Arkansas, Mr. Breckinridge, of Kentucky.

MR. BRECKINRIDGE, OF KENTUCKY: I deny the power of the Speaker and denounce it as revolutionary. [Applause on the Democratic side of the House, which was renewed several times.]

MR. BLAND: Mr. Speaker—[applause on the Democratic side.]

THE SPEAKER: The House will be in order.

MR. BLAND: Mr. Speaker, I am responsible to my constituents for the way in which I vote, and not to the Speaker of the House. [Applause.]

THE SPEAKER: Mr. Brookshire, Mr. Bullock, Mr. Bynum, Mr. Carlisle, Mr. Chipman, Mr. Clements, Mr. Clunie, Mr. Compton.

MR. COMPTON: I protest against the conduct of the Chair in calling my name.

THE SPEAKER (proceeding): Mr. Covert, Mr. Crisp, Mr. Culberson of Texas [hisses on the Democratic side], Mr. Cummings, Mr. Edmunds, Mr. Enloe, Mr. Fithian, Mr. Goodnight, Mr. Hare, Mr. Hatch, Mr. Hayes.

MR. HAYES: I appeal from any decision, so far as I am concerned.

THE SPEAKER (continuing): Mr. Holman, Mr. Lawler, Mr. Lee, Mr. McAdoo, Mr. McCreary.

MR. McCREARY: I deny your right, Mr. Speaker, to count me as present, and I desire to read from the parliamentary law on that subject.

THE SPEAKER: The Chair is making a statement of the fact that the gentleman from Kentucky is present. Does he deny it? [Laughter and applause on the Republican side.][32]

And so it went over three days of tumultuous debate. In the end, the Democrats had no recourse, since their appeal from the decision of the chair was subject to the same authority from which it had arisen. Without a voting majority to overturn the speaker's decision, there was nothing further that could be done in the way of obstruction.

Within a short time the Rules Committee brought in its revised code, formally enshrining in the rules of the House the principles enforced by Speaker Reed under general parliamentary law. The speaker was now empowered to count a quorum, and to declare dilatory motions out of order. A quorum in the Committee of the Whole was reduced to 100 members, allowing its business to proceed while the rest of the membership attended to other matters. The Committee of the Whole was empowered to close debate on sections and paragraphs of bills under consideration, and the speaker was given greater power over the order of business. The rules increased the power of the speaker but at the same time increased the efficiency of the House. While obstructionism was not wholly precluded, it was made more difficult. With the Reed Rules in place, the Republicans had a chance to govern.[33]

The theoretical issues raised by the struggle for reform are important. Plainly, all parties to the event recognized that the debate over the House rules was not only a matter of party interest, but also a matter of political and constitutional principle. The development of obstructionism in the House posed fundamental questions about its character as a representative body, the role of leadership within it, and its capacity for deliberative action. The basic principles of majority rule and minority rights upon which the Constitution rested, were thrown into conflict with each other and the resolution of this conflict had the effect of shaping the American polity thereafter. The Reed reforms represented more than the triumph of a great speaker or the victory of a political party; they also represented a metamorphosis in American democracy.

Speaker Reed held that the rules of a legislative body must be designed to allow a majority of its members to express its will in enactments. In asserting this simple idea he appealed to "the first principles of democracy and republicanism alike."

> Our government is founded on the doctrine that if 100 citizens think one way and 101 think the other, the 101 are right. It is the old doctrine that the majority must govern. Indeed, you have no choice. If the majority do not govern, the minority will; and if the tyranny of the majority is hard, the tyranny of the minority is simply unendurable. The rules, then, ought to be so arranged as to facilitate the action of the majority.[34]

This expression of the principle of majority rule states succinctly the moral basis of party government. In a representative government the party controlling the majority of seats in the legislative body is entitled to organize the body, and is entitled to adopt rules that facilitate its governing task.

But what of the rights of the minority? Are not the rules of a representative body also intended to protect all members equally in their rights as members, and should they not preserve the rights of members of the minority party to represent the interests of their constituents effectively? In opposition to Speaker Reed's position, the Democrats appealed to the spirit of the Constitution and found there a very different doctrine than that upon which Reed had rested his case. For according to the Democratic view, the Constitution and the political system to which it gave rise were designed primarily to prevent the majority from exercising untrammeled authority over the minority. The Bill of Rights, the provisions for separation of powers and checks and balances, and the practice of judicial review were among the major features of the American political system that demonstrated an intention that the majority rule only under conditions acceptable to significant minorities. The rules of the House of Representatives were a logical extension of this principle. The fixed procedures they specified were the only safeguards available to a minority in a body that, in the end, necessarily responded to the decision of the majority. Freedom of debate, the right of members to make motions procedurally in order, and the right of members to vote or not to vote all were essential requirements of a legislature that would fulfill the Constitution's intent that America be governed by consensus rather than by fiat.[35]

Viewed from this perspective, the activities that fell under the label of obstructionism were merely the legitimate recourse of the minority to express the intensity of its feelings on important matters of public policy. The more responsible advocates of delaying tactics might well have recognized that the system had been abused; but the scope and nature of the abuses that had occurred would not have justified the House abandoning itself to the unrestrained will of the majority. The notion that the business of the House would be conducted by the majority was in and of itself chimerical, since it presupposed that an active, self-conscious, and autonomous majority existed. Instead, the Reed reforms promised to add to the power of an already domineering speakership and place in the hands of a tiny clique of majority party leaders the power to dictate policy, not only to their own party, but to the country as well.

In response to these arguments, Speaker Reed and his supporters drew a sharp line between the Constitution and the rules of the House. The Constitution was indeed intended to protect political minorities, and was in fact the only source by which minority rights could be protected. The Constitution established a democratic system of government and then constrained it by structural provisions designed to impede the process of majority rule. In seeking to protect their rights, minorities should have recourse to the Constitution. But it did not follow from this fact that all procedures adopted under the Constitution should afford to minorities the capacity to frustrate majority will by paralyzing the government. As Madison had put it in the Tenth *Federalist*: "If a faction consists of less than a majority, relief is supplied by the republican principle, which enables the majority to defeat its sinister views by regular vote. It may clog the administration, it may convulse the society; but it will be unable to execute and mask its violence under the forms of the Constitution."[36] The rules of the House had been interpreted so as to allow the minority to clog legislation. Far from being an arrangement demanded by the Constitution, the obstructionist tactics seemed to Reed plainly contrary to the Constitution's express provisions and evident intent. How could it be the case that a Constitution that empowered the House to compel the attendance of its members could permit them to stop its business by merely refusing to answer the roll once inside its doors?

The debates over the Reed rules, especially that which empowered the speaker to count a quorum, seem arcane a hundred years later. A century of experience under the Reed rules has had the effect of making them seem natural, as the previous one hundred years of experience enshrined the earlier rules. As one sorts through the arguments on either side of the question of the quorum count, it is difficult to recapture the seriousness of purpose with which intelligent and experienced persons split hairs in differentiating between the House's power under the Constitution to compel the attendance of its members and its obligation under the Constitution to record the yeas and nays to repass legislation over the president's veto. Still, it is important to understand the underlying political and philosophical issues that gave rise to such hairsplitting.[37]

At issue was not merely a question of power, nor simply a matter of procedure. At stake was the character of the House as a deliberative institution and the nature of the American representative system. In advancing his reforms, Reed directly broached the question of the House's standing as a deliberative body: "The making of laws is the main function of a legislative body. To that end all other things . . . are subordinate . . . In order to make laws wisely the body must be a deliberative body; but deliberation, however necessary or valuable, is only the means to an end; and that end is the right decision whether to make a law or not, and what shape to put it into if made."[38] Deliberation, Reed acknowledged, required debate, but not all debate was deliberative. Constructive debate required the attendance of members prepared to speak as well as that of members prepared to listen. It entailed that dialogue pertain to the topic at hand. And it contemplated action. Debate for its own sake did not constitute deliberation; debate for the purpose of obstruction and delay certainly did not constitute deliberation either. "Deliberation," held Reed, "implies thought, and not necessarily words, except as they are food for thought."[39]

The obstructionists claimed that the Reed rules gave untrammeled

power to the majority to exercise its will irrespective of the views of
the minority. Meaningful debate could occur only within the ranks of
the majority party. Unfortunately, all too little debate occurred there
either. The minority's capacity to avail itself of House procedures was
not designed to deny the majority the right to rule, on this view, but
only to ensure that it gave due attention to the minority's point of view.
By denying the minority the capacity to delay the proceedings of the
House, the Reed rules rendered the minority impotent in debate. A
deliberative assembly, as Reed himself acknowledged, implied listeners
as well as talkers. But the majority was not naturally inclined to listen
to the minority unless coerced.

Where, in this debate, does the truth of the matter lie? Speaker
Reed's basic proposition that the rules of the House should not be
structured so as to prevent its majority from consistently legislating
seems now to be beyond controversy. Less convincing is the contention
that only by facilitating majority rule could the House be deliberative.
The dilatory tactics of the minority were not artifacts of deliberation,
but insofar as they had the effect of forcing the majority to compromise
on legislation, they were not wholly at odds with the deliberative character of the House. It was when obstruction clearly became intended
to prevent action rather than to shape it that it became intolerable. For
most of the history of the House up until 1890, the use of tactics of
obstruction had not been undertaken for the purpose of systematically
stopping business. During that long period of time the rules of the House
had demonstrated forbearance toward the minority. In the end it was
the abuse of procedure by the minority that brought about the need for
reform. In bringing about that reform, however, Speaker Reed seems
to have been more concerned with efficient government than with deliberative government.

The plea of the minority against the Reed reforms must be understood against the backdrop of the other powers available to the speaker
as the presiding officer of the House and as the leader of the majority
party. The ability to count a quorum and to refuse dilatory motions
enabled speakers to move the business of the House along, but did not
enable them to determine what that business would be. All speakers
since Reed have had these powers, but not all have been regarded as
strong leaders. The primary political significance of the Reed reforms
lay not in the powers that they specifically conferred upon the speaker,
but rather in the manner in which they enhanced other powers already
at his disposal. The enlargement of the speaker's power under Blaine,
Randall, and Carlisle had made the office politically potent. In the case
of the Republican party, the cohesiveness of the party's majority often
lent political clout to the office's formal power. In denying the minority

the capacity to obstruct, the Reed rules did not create a majoritarian despotism, but rather eliminated the last barriers to one that was already incipient. In doing so, the reforms of 1890 did not guarantee that legislative despotism would emerge, but they did make it possible.

Thomas B. Reed was a great speaker of the House; that he was willing to risk losing the office itself in order to establish the basis of his power in it is indicative of his character. He was a gregarious man, although not one to form casual friendships. He often gave the impression of being cold and aloof, yet he was a natural leader of men. The secret of his success seems to have been found in his character. He was blunt, straightforward, and possessed an analytical ability that enabled him to cut directly to the heart of an issue. Reed was not a great orator. During his entire career he gave few set political speeches. He was the sort of man whom a legislative party will naturally choose as its leader, one who can keep the opposition on the defensive. But the speakership requires more than ability as a floor leader; it also demands political acumen and the courage to articulate and defend a set of policies. These qualities Reed possessed in abundance. He demonstrated from the outset that rare ability to establish a clear set of legislative priorities and marshal support for them.

Working under the new rules, but with the slimmest of majorities, the Fifty-first House under Speaker Reed's leadership was the most productive since the Civil War. It passed a total of 611 public bills, the largest number in history to that date.[40] Included were several major bills including the Oklahoma Territories Act, the Sherman Anti-Trust Act, the McKinley Tariff, and the Sherman Silver Purchase Act. These bills became law, although other major House-passed legislation, such as the federal elections ("force") bill, died in the Senate. Reed proved himself to be a masterful politician, both in using the powers of the House to foster programs he favored and in using them to frustrate programs he opposed. His handling of the force bill demonstrated his command of the House.[41] Reed supported legislation that would enfranchise blacks in the South. The Republican conference made the measure a party vote, and the rule specified the exact time at which the vote on the bill would be taken. At the appointed hour, the bill was brought up and passed by a party-line vote.[42] The use of the rules by the speaker to pass a measure violently opposed by a minority illustrate the effects of the Reed reforms in eliminating obstructionism. Under the rules of the preceding Congress, the force bill would have been filibustered to death in the House (as it subsequently was in the Senate). Reed's ability to see the bill passed depended upon the rules, his power as speaker, and on the cohesiveness of his majority; still, his own force of will was crucial to his success.

Speaker Reed also used his power in opposition to legislation. A conservative Republican, Reed was by nature opposed to free silver. He believed, as did most Republicans from the East, that the viability of the national credit depended upon the gold standard, and he opposed any effort to dilute it with free silver. Increasingly from the South and West, however, came the cries of small farmers and businessmen whose economic fortunes were tied to eastern capital and whose costs were kept arbitrarily high by the combined effects of the gold standard (which entailed tight money and high interest rates) and the protective tariff (which entailed high prices). The issue divided party loyalties, with many Republicans from the West responding to the pleas of their constituents for free silver.

The issue was broached legislatively in 1890 when the House took up a bill to solace the free silver movement by involving the federal government in the purchase of silver through the issue of treasury notes. The bill represented concessions to the free silver movement, but not enough to satisfy its supporters. Reed regarded it as representing the furthest possible extent of compromise, and brought the bill to the floor under a gag rule that was approved by the narrow margin of 120 to 117. The bill itself passed by the slightly larger margin of 135 to 119. In the Senate, however, it was amended to provide for the free coinage of silver. When the bill came back to the House, a large number of Republicans were absent from Washington. Under ordinary procedure the Senate amendments would have been taken up in the Committee of the Whole, where it appeared that the pro-silver faction could command a majority.[43]

A determined Reed referred the bill to the Committee on Coinage and ordered the clerk to omit reference to the fact when reading the journal on the next day. An objection was raised that the entire journal had not been read, and the speaker's ploy was revealed. Objection was then made to the journal itself, and its approval was defeated, 117 to 105. Evidently, Reed did not command a majority on the question. A resolution was introduced calling for the consideration of the bill as amended by the Senate in the Committee of the Whole. The resolution carried, and the amended journal was passed by the slim margin of 132 to 130. Immediately the bill was called from the speaker's table, but the speaker and his henchmen undertook a protracted effort to delay its consideration until more gold Republicans could return to town, arguing that the bill lay not on the speaker's table, but in the Committee of the Whole. An all-night effort by the leadership produced a voting majority the next day, and the House insisted upon its disagreement with the Senate free silver amendment. The result was the passage of the Sherman Silver Purchase Act as a compromise measure.[44]

The most fateful bill of the Fifty-first Congress was the McKinley Tariff Bill. The bill raised tariffs considerably, creating a widespread and adverse public reaction. A consideration of the size of the federal surpluses that the protective tariff engendered helps explain why it was such a controversial issue. In 1860, the cumulative federal deficit was $64,844,000, and by the end of the Civil War in 1865 it had mushroomed to $2,677,929,000. Between 1866 and 1894, the government ran a string of twenty-eight consecutive years with budget surpluses, which ran as high as $145,544,000 in 1882 and were sustained by both Democratic and Republican majorities. They enabled the government to reduce the deficit to $961,432 by 1882. While the government was enjoying this harvest, the economy was booming as well. The per capita gross national product realized a 73 percent increase (measured in constant dollars) from 1869 to 1892.[45] Yet, due to the tariff and the gold standard, prices and interest rates remained high, a particularly bad situation for small farmers, homesteaders, and silver miners in the West. There arose a demand for free silver and easy money so that debtors in the West could repay creditors in the East with devalued currency. The pressure was on for lower tariff rates as well.

The Republicans tried to maintain the protective tariff by assuaging the opposition. They applied as much of the surplus as was politically feasible toward the reduction of the national debt, and promoted public expenditures for rivers, harbors, post offices, veterans pensions, and other pork barrel projects of interest to constituents. Typical Republican tariff reform sought to diminish the surplus by lowering or eliminating the imposts on consumables such as sugar. The tariff on industrial goods was maintained at a level that effectively prohibited imports (and competition for domestic producers), ensuring high prices. The final step was a modified bimetalism that involved the government in the purchase of virtually the entire national production of silver at a fixed ratio of 16 to 1. Each of these elements of Republican strategy was manifested during the Fifty-first Congress, and the last two were embodied in the McKinley Tariff and the Sherman Silver Purchase Act.[46]

Reed's use of the powers at his disposal to govern the House indicated the potentiality of a strong speakership and a united party majority. The power of floor recognition was backstopped by complete control of the Rules Committee. The two Democratic members of the Rules Committee were former speakers Randall and Carlisle; Reed would summon the two to his office and, with an expansive smile, announce: "Gentlemen, I have called you here to tell you that we have decided to perpetrate the following outrage." But if outrages there were, the Democrats had one recourse at the polls. If the Republican policies were to be rejected by the voters, the Republican party would be as well. The

Republicans rested their fate on the McKinley Tariff, and the voters delivered a knockout punch. In one of the most resounding electoral defeats in American political history, the voters turned the Republicans out of power in the House in the election of 1890; the seven-vote majority upon which Speaker Reed had built his program was obliterated, and the party alignment in the House during the Fifty-second Congress was 231 Democrats to just 88 Republicans, although the Republicans retained control of the nonelected Senate 47–39.

The Democrats could now use the new powers of the speakership to their advantage, but centralized control proved to be too foreign to the culture of the party. Upon gaining control of the House in the Fifty-second Congress, the Democrats elected Charles F. Crisp of Georgia as their speaker and, rejecting the Reed rules, adopted those of the Fiftieth Congress.[47] In the Fifty-third Congress, they did so as well, but Reed, as the leader of the Republican minority, buried obstructionism for good by forcing the Democrats to adopt the practice of counting a quorum. In organizing the Fifty-third Congress the Democrats had incorporated a few of the Reed reforms: the quorum in the Committee of the Whole was set at 100 members, and the Rules Committee was given control over the flow of business to the floor. The Democrats refused to count a quorum, however, and Reed was determined to make them do it. He demonstrated the strength of his convictions, but he had a political motive as well. With Cleveland back in the White House and Democratic majorities in both Houses of the Congress, there could be no excuse for a failure of the Democrats to govern.

Reed repeatedly berated the Democrats for their unwillingness to count, while at the same time organizing Republican filibusters. In November of 1893 Reed delayed the adjournment of the House by denying it a quorum. In February of 1894 he struck at a Democratic attempt to pass a measure allowing for the coinage of silver in the federal Treasury. Reed and his Republican troops imperturbably called roll call after roll call, denying a quorum each time. Although a physical quorum was often present, the House could not act and the Democrats could not produce a quorum from their own ranks in spite of their majority. The struggle lasted over two full months, until finally on April 13th the Democrats surrendered. A quorum-counting rule was presented authorizing the speaker to appoint a teller from each side of the aisle to note those present and not voting, and, on the basis of their report, declare a quorum when in fact a majority of members were physically present. On April 17 the leader of the obstructionists stood vindicated before the House and held that "The House is about to adopt the principle for which we contended under circumstances which show its value to the country. I congratulate it upon the wise decision it is about to make."[48] The rule was adopted and the quorum issue was settled for good.

Since their electoral victory in 1890 had seemed to imply a mandate to do something about the McKinley Tariff, the House Democrats undertook a downward revision in the Fifty-second Congress, but the measure died in the Senate. It was not until Cleveland's second administration in 1893 that the Democrats had sufficient control of the government to legislate. The result was the passage of the Wilson-Gorman Tariff and the repeal of the Sherman Silver Purchase Act. These two steps stamped the Democrats indelibly with the responsibility for the economy, which they came to regret when it turned sour in the panic of 1893. The government's $2 million surplus was quickly transformed into a $60 million deficit, initiating a string of six consecutive years of deficit financing. The gross national product (in constant dollars) fell from $60.4 billion in 1892 to $57.5 billion in 1893 and $55.9 billion in 1894. The Democrats, of course, where hardly more responsible for the conditions leading to the recession than were the Republicans, but they held the mantle of power, and the electorate was quick to visit responsibility for the economic debacle upon them. In the election of 1894 they suffered their worst defeat in two decades, and in the Fifty-fourth Congress the House of Representatives returned to Republican control, with 244 Republicans to 105 Democrats. Tom Reed was once again speaker, and this time he had a large partisan majority with which to work.[49]

With the Republican landslide of 1894, momentum was created for the Grand Old Party to recapture the White House in 1896. The Fifty-fourth Congress saw a large Republican majority in the House and a slim GOP margin in the Senate. With the Democrat Cleveland ensconced in the White House, policy making was at a stalemate, and this Congress proved to be one of the least productive in American history. McKinley's election in 1896 gave the Republicans total control of the government, and they were determined once again to put their stamp upon legislation. Speaker Reed had contested McKinley for the Republican presidential nomination in 1896, but the powerful speaker had lost to his former lieutenant by a wide margin. McKinley and Joe Cannon, the two congressmen who, with Reed, had formed the most powerful Rules Committee in the history of the House in the Fifty-first Congress, had both been defeated in the Democratic wave of 1892, but the ill-fortune that McKinley suffered as the author of the tariff bill was short-lived, and within a year he was elected to the governorship of Ohio. From that safe perch he presented a presidential image that the more capable Reed could not match; in two decades of political life, Reed's caustic wit had opened too many wounds. Still, his is among the few cases in American history of a sitting speaker competing viably for the presidency.[50]

In 1897 the Republicans were determined to act on the economic situation, and McKinley called a special session of the Congress to revise the tariff. Reed stacked the Ways and Means Committee and refused to appoint any others until the business of the session was completed. A colleague of Reed's from Maine, Nelson Dingley, was appointed to the chairmanship of Ways and Means, and, working in tandem with the speaker, Dingley produced the tariff bill of 1897 that bore his name. When the Congress convened in regular session, Reed ruled with an iron hand. In one widely publicized case, Reed killed the Nicaragua Canal Bill in the face of a petition signed by a majority of members seeking its discharge.[51] Reed's power was not without its limits. Although personally opposed to pork barreling, expenditures under the Dingley Tariff were as high as under the McKinley Tariff in 1890. The protective tariff produced a seductive surplus that even tight-fisted Republicans could not resist. Reed was also philosophically opposed to expansionism and to the deepening American involvement overseas that eventually gave rise to the Spanish-American War and the annexation of Hawaii. This brought him into direct conflict with President McKinley, with whom he shared some degree of personal animosity arising out of the 1896 election contest.[52] Yet, in spite of setbacks in foreign policy, Reed was widely recognized as the most powerful man in the government. It is noteworthy, that at the height of his power Reed never engendered as much criticism as his famous successor, Joe Cannon, in spite of the fact that Cannon was by far the more affable and well liked of the two. This fact testifies to the degree of Republican solidarity that Reed enjoyed; the operation of the Republican machine under Reed was less onerous to Republican members than it became under Cannon a decade later, when the progressive wing of the party challenged the regulars on basic policy issues.[53]

Under the leadership of Tom Reed the Republican party laid the basis for an American system of party government in the House of Representatives. In contrast with Democratic Houses of this time, the historical record favors Reed and the Republicans as the party of effective government. The triumph over obstructionism was a historic event, and history has vindicated Speaker Reed. The reason why the Republican party was able to best govern during the partisan era was that its policies were supported by a majority of politically active Americans. Yet we ought not overlook the contentions of the defenders of obstructionism. They viewed the House procedures as the only protection available to the minority in an institution that responded to the principle of majority rule. The Democrats were correct in their concern that the Reed reforms would lead to the unmitigated tyranny of the majority; however, their fear was misdirected. For in the end it was not the quorum count or the rule against dilatory motions that facilitated the centralization of power in the House; instead it was the speaker's control over floor recognition, the committee system, and the Rules Committee. The Reed reforms created a situation in which these vital powers of the speaker could be turned to the ends of legislative tyranny, and it was not long before Uncle Joe Cannon did.

Tyranny

Joseph G. Cannon entered the Congress in 1872 and Thomas B. Reed entered in 1876, but by the mid 1880s Reed had risen to party leadership while Cannon toiled in his shadow as a member of the Appropriations Committee. During Reed's years as speaker, Cannon was elevated to the chairmanship of the Appropriations Committee and appointed to the Rules Committee. Yet, of the powerful and illustrious Rules Committee of the Fifty-first Congress (consisting of four once and future speakers—Reed, Cannon, Randall, and Carlisle—and a future president, McKinley), Cannon alone was a member of the Fifty-sixth Congress. Surprisingly, Cannon was not selected by the Republicans to replace Reed; instead, the party turned to David B. Henderson of Iowa, a former chairman of the Judiciary Committee. Henderson served as a lackluster speaker during the Fifty-sixth and Fifty-seventh Congresses. His election in preference to Cannon was based in part on geographic considerations. He was the first speaker to have come from west of the Mississippi, and drew support from the increasingly sizable western wing of the party. Members may also have had doubts about making Cannon their speaker. For while he had been a loyal lieutenant to Speaker Reed and a tight-fisted chairman of the Appropriations Committee, Cannon had by 1898 served in the House for twenty-two years without having authored so much as a single piece of significant legislation. In fact, Cannon would serve on through four terms as speaker and seven further terms as a member, a total of forty-six years, and never author a major bill.[54]

With Henderson's retirement Cannon at last won the position he had long coveted.[55] When he became speaker, he had already survived two decades of partisan warfare in the House and had witnessed the effective leadership of Blaine and Reed, as well as the frustration of most of the other speakers of his time. He understood from within the system of party government that the Republicans had evolved. Cannon was by nature neither devious nor tyrannical; he was, in fact, among the most popular and colorful members of the House. Yet he was a rock-ribbed conservative from Illinois and a firm believer in party government. Joe Cannon was honest, frank, shrewd, principled, and stubborn. These were the qualities that guided his speakership, and led him gradually but inexorably to turn a system of party government into a system of legislative despotism.

A driving force behind the development of Cannonism was the progressive movement and Cannon's opposition to it. Uncle Joe Cannon was never a tyrant in the classical mold, one who wished to govern in his own interest. He was instead a man whose vision of America was rooted in the experience of his youth in the Midwest, where freedom meant capitalism and progress meant economic growth. Joe Cannon had no personal interest in the great corporations, the trusts, or the big banks. His brother was a small town banker in Danville, Illinois, and Cannon had a significant interest in the bank. Joe Cannon's was the world of the petit bourgeois. It was merely coincidental that in serving the interests of this America he also became the guardian of the American corporate interest. For according to Cannon, what was good for business was indeed good for America, and what was good for business was the protective tariff.[56]

The 1880s and 1890s witnessed the development of various forms of radicalism in American political life. From agrarian movements in the plains to trade unionism in the cities, more and more Americans seemed to be rejecting the faith in free enterprise upon which Cannon believed the country to have been built. In Cannon's view, the Democratic party had been won over by the radical populists and their demagogic leader, William Jennings Bryan. The radicalization of the Democratic party had further fragmented it, leading to its defeats in 1894 and 1896. That the Democrats should have fallen prey to radical notions was understandable to Cannon; that the Republican party evidenced increasing signs of it was intolerable. Yet the same social and economic forces that made populism and progressivism such a strong influence among Democrats in the Southwest soon appeared in the solid Republican territory in the upper Midwest and Great Plains. In Wisconsin, Kansas, Nebraska, Iowa, and the Dakotas, progressive ideas became more widely held. The reason was simple: the homesteaders and farmers were burdened by the high tariff and frustrated by the inability of their representatives to do anything about it.

McKinley's assassination and Teddy Roosevelt's elevation to the presidency was a blow to the Republican establishment. Now, as Senator Mark Hanna of Ohio had put it, "that damn cowboy is in the White House," and the nation had a progressive Republican at its head. Teddy Roosevelt had the power of the presidency and a bully pulpit from which to preach, but Uncle Joe Cannon had the Republican party machinery in the House of Representatives and a firm intention to bar the door to progressive economic policies. It was in the face of a serious division within the Republican ranks that Cannonism evolved, a situation that both stamped its character and sowed the seeds of its demise.[57]

The situation that Cannon faced was very different from that which Reed had encountered. While Reed and McKinley were political rivals, the speaker was not far distant from the president in terms of Republican policy. The gulf between Cannon and Roosevelt was far greater. Since Lincoln's death the Republican presidents had not offered strong leadership to the Congress. The sole Democratic president of the partisan period, Cleveland worked with Speaker Carlisle for tariff reform. It was not until the progressive Roosevelt confronted a conservative Republican establishment in the Congress headed by Cannon and Rhode Island Senator Nelson Aldrich that the partisan speakership came head to head with an assertive presidency. Cannon's situation was complicated further by the serious insurgency within his congressional party. Cannon was hedged on three sides between the Democrats, his president, and the rebels within his congressional party. It was necessary for him to try to gain as much control as possible over the House's machinery in order to control its business. It was out of this political situation that Cannonism grew.

Influenced now by the historical image of Cannon as the overbearing czar of the House, we often forget that his first speakership was characterized by a spirit of good feelings. At the close of the Fifty-eighth Congress, John Sharp Williams, the Democratic leader, praised the speaker in "recognition of kindly services and kindly feeling already extended and already appreciated." Champ Clark, who was to become Williams's successor and under whose leadership the revolt against Cannon was organized, was more effusive: "Historians of our times will record the fact that the Fifty-eighth Congress was celebrated above all its predecessors for all its extraordinary kindness of feeling which prevailed among its Members."[58] Hardly the language of an oppressed people, this! What explains the comity of the Fifty-eighth Congress in light of the enmity of the succeeding ones?

Several factors were involved. Roosevelt was a nonelected president and had an important political incentive to moderate his policies in order to seek election in his own right in 1904. During 1903 and 1904 the president was extremely solicitous of the more conservative congressional leadership, especially Speaker Cannon. Also, Cannon was a very popular man, and his natural kindliness and sense of humor fostered a spirit of amicability that influenced the mood of the House. One of Cannon's first steps as speaker was to permit John Sharp Williams to appoint the Democratic committee lists. Significantly, the Fifty-eighth and Fifty-ninth Congresses did not face the one issue capable of giving rise to great conflict. The House considered a number of regulatory bills, but the one issue capable of actively engaging Cannon's attention was the tariff, and so long as times were good there seemed little reason to tinker with it. Roosevelt favored lower tariff duties, but thought that too much emphasis had been placed upon tariff legislation in the past, and preferred to emphasize regulatory bills designed to extend public controls over the large industrial corporations. In 1904 Roosevelt reached an explicit agreement with Cannon and Senator Nelson Aldrich of Rhode Island, the leader of the Senate Republicans, that the president's railroad reform bill would be passed so long as no attempt were made to alter the tariff.[59]

In fact, a great deal of progressive legislation was passed into law during Cannon's speakership. This included the Elkins Act (1903 — regulating shipping), the Hepburn Act (1905 — putting teeth into the Interstate Commerce Commission's power to set railroad rates), the Meat Inspection Act (1906), the Pure Food and Drug Act (1906), the Mann-Elkins Act (1910 — extending the power of the ICC to telegraph, telephone, cable, and wireless companies), and the Mann Act (1910 — barring the transportation of women across state lines for immoral purposes).[60] Cannon would subsequently respond to the charge that he was a reactionary by citing the volume of progressive legislation that the Congress had passed during his tenure. The passage of the Roosevelt legislative program was due to the fact that it responded to what the country had come to demand, not to the beneficence of Joseph G. Cannon. That it could have been passed suggests both the limits of Cannon's power and the nature of the situation in which he found himself. For Cannon could not unilaterally stand in the way of the majority sentiment in the country without jeopardizing his own position. As powerful as he was, Cannon had to calculate the costs and benefits of opposing the popular Roosevelt and the increasingly progressive mood of the country. He made a conscious choice to accept parts of the Roosevelt regulatory agenda in return for the preservation of the Dingley Tariff rates that had been in effect since 1897. Unilaterally, Cannon held the tariff reformers at bay for the duration of the Roosevelt presidency.[61]

In 1909 the nation had a new and more conservative president, William Howard Taft. During the first year of Taft's presidency the nation undertook a drastic revision of its tax laws. The Congress approved the Sixteenth Amendment to the Constitution, which authorized the collection of the federal income tax. The Payne-Aldrich Tariff Act lowered most duties to 38 percent, while cutting some duties further, and imposed a tax on corporations dealing in interstate commerce. Cannon had staved off tariff reform for as long as he could, and now

he moved to structure the Payne-Aldrich bill to preserve as much protection as possible. In the struggle over the Payne-Aldrich Tariff, the
nature of Cannon's power in the House came into public view, and the
Payne-Aldrich scrap marked the beginning of a battle, of which the
revolt against Cannon was the denouement.[62]

The election of 1908 had hinged in good part on the tariff question.
The government had run an $87 million surplus in 1907, and there was
widespread demand for a downward revision. Cannon was attacked in
his district for his opposition to reducing tariff rates, and for the first
time in years, he was forced to curtail his campaigning on behalf of
other candidates in order to tend the home fires. While Taft won a solid
electoral victory, the Democrats had for the first time since 1892 sensed
the possibility of Republican vulnerability, especially on the tariff question. The 1908 Republican platform committed the party to a prudent
revision of the tariff. The House of Representatives elected to the Sixty-
first Congress consisted of 219 Republicans and 172 Democrats, and
the number of potential insurgent Republicans from the West was sufficient to stimulate an interparty dialogue between Democratic leaders
and Republican renegades over the possibility of limiting Cannon's
power.

Cannon, sensing danger, took unprecedented steps to ensure his
position. His agents, James E. Watson of Indiana and James R. Mann
of Illinois, solicited pledges on his behalf in order to head off any
challenge for the speakership from within the Republican ranks. Since
the chair was out of their reach, the Democrats and insurgent Republicans chose to focus upon the rules and sought to dilute the speaker's
power by expanding the membership of the Rules Committee. Thirty
Republican insurgents signed a letter committing themselves to the rules
fight, and with this support the Democrats proposed to take on the
speaker. In the ordinary manner of procedure it would be moved that
the rules of the preceding House be adopted, and on this motion the
previous question would be moved, closing off debate. If there were to
be any changes in the rules, the previous question would have to be
defeated. On March 15 it was, by a vote of 193 to 189; Speaker Cannon's
power appeared threatened for the first time. Yet it was not enough for
the Democrats and insurgents to defeat the previous question. In order
to win they had to pass an amendment of their own. The Clark resolution, offered by Democratic leader Champ Clark of Missouri, amended
the rules to provide for an expanded Rules Committee of fifteen members, the speaker to be excluded. For Cannon to be defrocked, it was
merely necessary for the coalition to hold together for a second consecutive vote.[63] It did not.

In the vote on the Clark resolution, sixteen Democrats bolted their party's leadership to give Cannon the margin he needed to preserve his power. Then, in a marginal concession to the opposition, a resolution offered by Congressman John Fitzgerald, a Tammany Hall Democrat, was approved with the support of twenty-three Democrats. The Fitzgerald Resolution established a unanimous consent calendar by which the speaker was deprived of his unilateral control over minor legislation, and a strengthened Calendar Wednesday, which provided for a call of the committees that could only be set aside by two-thirds vote. Cannon's support from the traitorous Democrats is easily explained; they had been bought off by the speaker's promises that the impending tariff revision would include provisions desired by their constituents. The New York Democrats did not want the tax on beer raised, and eight of them voted for Cannon's rules. Georgia and Florida Democrats wanted lumber protected; Georgia gave the speaker seven votes, and Florida one. In Louisiana, sugar was the issue, and Cannon received two votes from the bayous. And so it went. In the end, he was able to swing enough Democrats to his banner to offset the defections of insurgent Republicans. Having preserved his power, he turned his attention to the tariff bill itself.[64]

The House Ways and Means Committee, under Chairman Sereno E. Payne of New York, held two full months of public hearings on the tariff in preparation for markup. Their product was a tariff bill that brought about significant reductions in many items. Unfortunately, the Ways and Means Committee was not privy to all of the deals that Cannon had been forced to strike in the rules fight. When Uncle Joe saw that the bill failed to honor some of the commitments he had made, he ordered it recommitted and revised. The new bill that resulted was attacked on the floor of the House and tariff reformers succeeded in making some modifications. Then the bill went to the Senate, and Nelson Aldrich and company did their work.

The Senate reported 847 amendments to the Payne bill, most of which raised the duties in it. The Senate version was more to Cannon's liking than the modified House bill he had extracted from Payne, since the duties were high enough to discourage foreign competitors. It was an easy task for Cannon to stack the conference with members sympathetic to the protectionist cause. The bill as reported by the conference was more protective than the House bill. It also concealed a significant protective provision to allow duties to be raised on products from countries that discriminated against U.S. goods. President Taft wanted a more moderate tariff, but he failed to pursue the Congress vigorously on the issue. The final bill as signed by the president was still protectionist, and Taft's reputation was diminished from the first months of his administration.[65]

The passage of the Payne-Aldrich Tariff was the beginning of the end for Joe Cannon. As the special session drew to its close, he announced his committee list for the Sixty-first Congress, and his vengeance was apparent for all to see. Three insurgent members were stripped of their committee chairmanships. Cannon loyalists were elevated out of seniority order to key chairmanships. An indication of the reaction among the insurgents may be gleaned from Charles N. Fowler's statement to the speaker:

> Do you suppose that I was not aware of your ignorance, prejudice, inordinate conceit, favoritism, putrid preferences, and that like all such characters possessing absolute power, malice is the mainspring of your every action under such circumstances? Do not forget that I chose my course in plain sight of your political guillotine, and the political carcasses of those you had decapitated . . . you revel in a glut of brutal power like Nero to terrorize your subject.[66]

Cannon's action and the insurgents' reaction stemmed from an unalterable political conflict over the role of government in the economy. Although Cannon had acquiesced in some progressive legislation under Roosevelt, he had now indicated how he intended to conduct the government with Taft in the White House. With no champion to lead and protect them, the progressive Republicans had no choice but to confront the need to strip the speaker of his power. The political events of 1909 laid the foundation for the revolt of 1910.

In understanding the revolution against Uncle Joe Cannon, it is important to differentiate the issues from those associated with the adoption of the Reed rules. If one merely compares Cannon's statements of philosophy with Reed's, one will not notice the difference. Cannon grounded his speakership on the principle of majority rule and the practice of party government just as Reed had done:

> The one and only purpose of rules in the House of Representatives is to furnish a method for the legal expression of the will of the majority. There is no rule or combination of rules in the House that can stifle the will of the majority. The rules have been developed through many years to the end that the minority shall be protected in every right, but that a loud, determined, and belligerent minority shall not be able to overturn the will of the majority.[67]

By stating, in effect, Reed's position on the relation between the majority and the minority in a legislative body, Cannon attempted to clothe his own centralized administration of the House in the garments of the

fight against obstructionism. The villain in this fight was not the overbearing majority but a minority prepared to see the government crippled
rather than concede the right of the majority to govern. This had been
the case in the 1880s.

By the first decade of the twentieth century, the situation had
changed. Many who opposed Cannonism were from within the ranks
of his own party. No minority on either side of the aisle threatened to
block public business, but members from both parties suffered at the
hands of a speaker who came to insist upon the prerogative of judging
every legislative initiative. Although Cannon claimed fealty to the principle of party government, the Republican party was divided internally.
The circumstances were not surprising; they were precisely what the
American constitutional system encourages. Yet Cannon would not
acknowledge that the party government for which he had fought for
three decades was simply incompatible with the situation in which his
party now found itself.

The immediate object of the attack on Cannon was his control over
the Rules Committee. Since the reforms of 1880, the Rules Committee
had been used by Republican and Democratic speakers alike for legislative control. Except for privileged bills, bills considered under sus-
pension of the rules, by the unanimous consent of members, or on
Calendar Wednesday, no legislation could be considered by the House
without the approval of the Rules Committee. Often the committee
would bring important business to the floor under a special order that
defined the conditions of debate, its availability to amendments and/or
substitutes, and even the precise time at which a final vote on the measure
would be taken. It was easy for speakers to rig these special orders to
ensure that bills they favored would be difficult to alter or defeat. On
some occasions, such as in the case of the adoption of the conference
report on the Payne-Aldrich Tariff, the special order would even waive
procedural points of order against specific provisions of a bill or the
bill itself. The ability to determine the rules under which legislation
would be considered was a key element of the speaker's power. His
control over the Rules Committee was absolute: he sat as its chairman,
and he appointed its other members. The rules themselves, of course,
were approved by a legislative majority, and even the special orders for
a particular bill required majority approval. Because of the speaker's
other influential powers, especially that of making committee appointments, it was not difficult to gather a voting majority in favor of special
orders; the special orders were written so as to ensure a majority of
votes in adopting them.[68]

The speaker's power over the Rules Committee provided a uniquely
visible and justifiable object of attack. His power of floor recognition,

while often arbitrarily employed, was a necessary artifact of his function as presiding officer. His power over committee appointments was deeply ingrained in the history of the House, and carried more clearly partisan implications. The Rules Committee was the organ of the House that arguably played the greatest role in shaping the conduct of its business. The development of the Rules Committee itself came about because of the need to manage the business of the House efficiently; but it was not assumed that the Rules Committee would be used as an arbitrary instrument of party government. At the outset of the republic, the speaker had much more latitude within which to operate and a greater obligation to function impartially. With the development of party government in the House after the Civil War came a corresponding increase in the extent to which the House managed itself by fixed rules. The debate over Cannonism then, may be viewed as having hinged on the question of whether it was the function of those rules to ensure reasonable conditions of impartiality in the House or to guarantee the speaker's power to control its business.

The challenge to Cannon's control over the Rules Committee was not a last-minute plot hatched in the middle of the night; it was the culmination of several years of vigorous public debate. The Democratic party had excoriated Cannonism in its 1908 platform, and the years 1908 and 1909 saw article after article in the nation's major periodicals and newspapers on the subject. The climate of public opinion was overwhelmingly opposed to Cannon and Cannonism; in fact, public opinion was by far more virulently opposed to Uncle Joe than were the members of the House. Aside from the bitterness felt by those Democrats and insurgent Republicans with whom he had personally contended, most members of the House liked Uncle Joe; yet the public had no way of appreciating the personal qualities by which Cannon took the edge off of his use of power. His enemies in the press were violent in their attacks upon him, and if the occasional polls of newspapers and readers were at all accurate, Cannonism was opposed by both American opinion leaders and the public whose opinion they led.[69]

Cannon's opponents were nurtured by public debate, but they were able to win only because they were organized. The insurgent Republicans had met as early as December of 1908, and throughout the special session in the winter of 1909 they continued to meet regularly to discuss strategy and complain about their situation. These meetings led to the revolt against the rules proposed for the Sixty-first Congress. Throughout the special session the insurgents chafed under Cannon's iron rule. When, in retribution for their lack of support on the Payne-Aldrich bill, he used his power over committee appointments to punish them, they became intent upon launching their attack at the first opportunity.[70]

Ironically, that opportunity was afforded to the rebels under the Fitzgerald amendments. Cannon had supported these amendments in order to diffuse opposition to his control over the Rules Committee. Calendar Wednesday was to be held inviolate as the occasion of the call of committees. On Calendar Wednesday, March 16, 1910, Congressman Edgar Crumpacker (R. Indiana) rose as chairman of the Committee on the Census to call up the census bill, even though his committee was not at the top of the Calendar Wednesday list. His motion was defeated. Seeking to obtain the floor, Crumpacker moved consideration of his bill on the grounds that it was privileged under the Constitution, since the Constitution provided for the taking of the census. Cannon ruled in Crumpacker's favor, Fitzgerald challenged the ruling of the chair, and Cannon was overruled by the House. The next day Crumpacker moved for reconsideration. Unwilling to be overruled again, Cannon referred the matter to the House for its decision. He posed the question for the House in a manner that would have clearly carried implications for the integrity of Calendar Wednesday: "Is the bill called up by the gentleman from Indiana in order as a question of constitutional privilege, the rule prescribing the order of business to the contrary notwithstanding?" A majority of members wished to let Crumpacker have the floor, since the census needed to be taken. However, they did not wish to vote on the question as put by the speaker. Consequently, a substitute motion, stating merely that the Crumpacker resolution would be in order, was moved and passed.

The House thus reversed its decision of the day before, but it did not clearly settle the constitutional question at issue. It made no difference. Accounts vary as to whether Congressman George Norris from Nebraska, a leader of the insurgents, had with him a rumpled envelope upon which he had previously drafted a resolution for the revision of the House rules, or whether he now saw his opportunity and sat down immediately to write one. In any event, upon the disposition of the census business, Norris rose to a question of constitutional privilege, and moved a resolution to amend the House rules to provide for a Rules Committee composed of fifteen members to be elected from grouped states, with nine seats drawn from the majority party and six from the minority. The speaker was to be ineligible, and the committee would elect its own chairman.[71] The basis of his claim to constitutional privilege was the fact that the Constitution charged the House with the responsibility to make its own rules.

It was obvious that Norris had discovered a way to force the issue of rules revision on to the floor of the House. Cannon could rule against Norris, as he no doubt would, but Norris would gain a vote on the ruling; or, the speaker could rule in favor of Norris, allowing the House to take up the resolution itself. In either case, a majority of the House would now have a chance to work its will on a specific proposal to remove the speaker from the Rules Committee. But who was in the majority in the House? This question was not just a question of partisan loyalty or philosophy of governance; it was also a more practical question of who was in town. The vote would undoubtedly be close, but as it happened many of the regular Republicans were not in town, trusting to their czar to control the floor as he had always done in the past while they celebrated St. Patrick's Day at home. The outcome of the struggle, then, would hinge upon the number of insurgents having the courage to defy Cannon and the number of regulars who could be brought back to Washington. Cannon worked both ends of the equation, sending his minions on errands of persuasion and sending telegrams to the troops. In the meantime, he stalled the House by taking under consideration the point of order by Congressman Dalzell that the Norris resolution was out of order.

The battle was protracted for two days while the regulars filtered slowly back into town. Cannon remained in the Capitol the entire time, sleeping on a red couch in his office. Finally on Saturday, March 19, he decided that he could delay no longer. Clean clothes were brought, and looking fresh and in command, Cannon called the House to order. Relying on a precedent set by Democratic Speaker Randall, Cannon sustained Dalzell and ruled the Norris resolution out of order. Norris appealed the ruling of the chair, and on the vote the speaker's decision was overturned 164 to 182. Uncle Joe then calmly presented the Norris resolution to the House for consideration. Norris, seeking to accommodate wavering members on the key vote, offered a substitute to his own resolution calling for a Rules Committee of ten members, six of the majority and four from the minority. The speaker was to be ineligible, and the committee would elect its own chairman. This substitute resolution carried easily.

The battle was over, but the drama had not ended. Speaker Cannon was a man of unquestioned principle, and his principles taught him that the House must be governed by its majority. That, after all, was the basis of his claim to govern. The vote on the Norris resolution seemed to Cannon to indicate that the majority of the House was no longer in sympathy with his leadership. In one of the most dramatic moments in the history of the House of Representatives, Cannon gave leave for a motion to vacate the chair and to proceed to the election of a new speaker. But the leader of the insurgents knew when to quit; Norris perceived quickly that to unseat Cannon would reduce the hard-won

reforms to a battle of personalities rather than of principles.[72] He moved
to adjourn, but the more radical insurgents obtained the floor first and
moved to vacate the chair. With the majority of the insurgents rallying
to support Cannon, the motion was defeated, and Cannon stood re-
confirmed, if not vindicated, as speaker.

The revolt against Cannon was the natural reaction of the political
system to a form of governance that was foreign to it. What is most
surprising is not the fact that it occurred, nor even the fact that it took
so long to occur; it is that Cannonism could have arisen in the first
place. For the system of governance developed by Cannon was not a
natural outgrowth of the Constitution or the Reed reforms, even though
it proved itself to be a possible outcome of both. Cannonism developed
because the way in which the policy agenda cleaved the polity at the
turn of the twentieth century. The Republican "stalwarts," "standpatters"—by whatever name called—were just that: the guardians of an
old order that was passing away. The progressive movement cleaved
the Republican party, causing Cannon to impose his dictatorship and
forcing the insurgents to destroy it.[73] Cannonism and the revolt against
it occurred because of the political circumstance in the Republican party,
because the rules of the House allowed it, and because Uncle Joe Cannon
decided to do it. As Cannon's power in the House grew, his use of it
became increasingly more severe. As he came to feel himself and his
political viewpoint isolated from the currents of American politics, he
became increasingly convinced of his obligation to use his power to
preserve his vision of the public good.[74]

It would be very mistaken to portray Cannon as a mere anachronism.
His speakership was the culmination of a half-century of American
political development. The Civil War established the primacy of the
national government, and the postwar era was the great era of nationalization: the geographic nationalization of the country, the stretch of
its economy from coast to coast, and the primacy of the federal political
system. The era was committed to growth, to progress, to expansion,
to capital. Both political parties were carried along by the historical
tide. The Democratic party, the party of Jefferson and Jackson, was
caught in a conflict between its principles and the changes taking place
around it. The Democrats could not resist the historical tide, but were
not well positioned to lead it. With Grover Cleveland as its standard-
bearer, the Democratic party sought a brand of progressive nationalism
that could reconcile its agrarian roots with the demands of a national
economy. But when the party was commandeered by William Jennings
Bryan, it left to the Republicans the role of party of national destiny.[75]
For so long as a national majority gave priority to economic expansion,
the Republicans would be the natural governing party. It was in response

to the exigencies of the partisan period in American politics that the strong speakership developed. Democratic speakers were affected by the tendency, but it was the Republican speakers for whom it was most natural. The revolt against Cannon was really a revolt against the policies for which he and the Republican's had stood. It signaled the end of the Republican era. A new era lay on the horizon, in which growth would give way to equity as the governing principle of the nation, and in which a polity that now filled the continent would seek stability in a new kind of political order. In that new political order, the Republican party would no longer represent the nation's natural majority.

While the rise and fall of Cannonism were certainly the result of historical trends in American politics that transcended the influence of a single man, those trends might have yielded a different historical outcome had someone other than Joseph G. Cannon come to power. As one contemporary observer put it:

> The Speakership system existed for years without developing its beneficent possibilities. The rules are essentially what they were in the day of Reed, Crisp, and Henderson. It required the combination of the system and the personality, characterize it how one may, of Joseph G. Cannon. It required more. It required the incentive furnished in the social-political crisis which the country is to-day facing.[76]

To understand Cannonism one must grasp the interrelationships among the system, the man whom it produced, and the political issues that stamped it. In the end, Cannonism was at odds with the American constitutional regime. At the pinnacle of his power, Cannon was forced to accommodate to programs he opposed in order to keep his coalition together. At bottom, the fallacy in Cannonism lay in the hypocrisy upon which it rested. While proclaiming authority under the auspices of the majority, Joseph Cannon was in fact a prince who was able to turn a party plurality and the rules of the House to his purposes. In opposition to the claim that centralized governance was required in order for the House to deal with its heavy and complex agenda, stood the fact that Cannon himself determined the issues the Congress would address. Against the claim that a deliberative body demanded party government stood the fact that under Cannon the House had ceased to be a deliberative body at all and instead had become an institution in which deliberation was supplanted by partisan power politics.

Conclusion

The forces driving the national policy agenda during the speakership's partisan era were westward expansion and industrialization.

Among the specific issues were the tariff, regulation of industry, the attempts by the North to force the South to bring black Americans into political participation, and the basis of the currency. In the decades after the Civil War, Alexander Hamilton's vision of America's future was realized, while Thomas Jefferson's faded into a distant past. The robust growth of the economy was accompanied, perhaps driven, by the development of big industry. The American political system sought to promote the development of the industrial colossus, while at the same time striving to control it. The Republican party was the natural majority party of this era, controlling the White House during all but the two Cleveland administrations, the House during seventeen of twenty-five congresses, and the Senate during twenty-three of twenty-five congresses. The Democratic party was stamped by the division between its southern and northern wings. It proved more receptive to the equitable claims of the lower classes than the Republicans, but could not establish a governing majority on the backs of common men.

The political system that emerged during the partisan period was dominated by the two major parties, which were able to control their own nominations and, hence, demand loyalty of their members. This was the great era of the back room, and back-room politics was practiced with as much adeptness in the private salons of rich Republicans as in the saloons frequented by Democratic ward heelers. The control exercised by party bosses in the electoral process naturally suggested the desirability of partisan control in legislative bodies. At the same time, the nationalization of politics carried with it the implication of centralization of political power. That nationalization and centralization were at best uncomfortably set in a political system framed by the Constitution was a historical anomaly.

The evolution of internal House arrangements in the partisan period was marked by a consistent tendency toward centralization of control, one manifested in both parties, but most naturally in the Republican party. The tendency toward centralization evolved in three phases. The first phase was a quest for efficiency in an increasingly large and unwieldy legislative body. The use of the speaker's list and the establishment of the Rules Committee were the two principle steps taken. The Randall reforms of 1880 were the most visible act. The second phase was the attempt to overcome obstructionism in order to permit the legislative majority to govern. The elimination of dilatory motions and the disappearing quorum were the key steps, both accomplished by the Reed reforms of 1890. The final phase was the centralization of power in the speakership. The Randall and Reed reforms had made this possible, but not inevitable. What led to Cannonism were the political circumstances of the early 1900s and Uncle Joe Cannon's unique position and character.

Unlike the parliamentary speakership of the antebellum era, speakers of the partisan period did much to shape the House and the office of speaker. Blaine's use of the speaker's list, the Randall reforms, the Reed reforms, and Cannon's use of power all brought significant changes in the speakership. Is it that these men were simply superior to most of their antebellum predecessors, or does an explanation lie elsewhere? It would appear that the transformation of the speakership from a weak and often paralyzed office prior to the Civil War to the powerful position it became under Cannon occurred not simply because strong-willed speakers sought to bring it about, but because the forces driving America's evolution during the partisan period demanded it. The speakers of the era were the vehicles of historical change, and did not themselves cause it.

During the partisan period the speakership often rivaled the presidency in power. The strongest of the partisan speakers refused subserviency to the presidents with whom they served. This is not surprising. American presidents of the nineteenth century did not possess the institutional powers of their twentieth-century successors. Foreign policy, the clearest prerogative of presidential power, lay fallow during America's prolonged isolation from the world. It was only at the turn of the twentieth century that Theodore Roosevelt suggested the plebiscitary potential of the presidency and America's potential as an imperial power. Yet not even the popular Roosevelt could dictate party position or public policy to Uncle Joe Cannon. Cannon refused to have one of Roosevelt's messages read to the House. The power of the partisan speakers, then, was set against the weakness of the presidency that they confronted.

What explanation can be given for the efficacy of the Republican regime under Blaine, Reed and Cannon, in contrast to the difficulties of the Democrats under Randall, Carlisle, and Crisp? The Republican party was the nation's natural majority party during the partisan period. Its constituency base was, by the 1890s, firmly established in the industrial Northeast and Midwest. It reflected the major currents in the economy. In the half-century after the Civil War, national industrial capacity nearly tripled. The business class dominated the national political agenda, and no organized labor movement existed to compete with it. The agrarian sector worried about the effects of industrialization and urbanization and suffered the consequences of the protective tariffs that supported the rapidly growing economy. Populists and progressives feared the power of big business and pressed for policies such as free silver, lower tariffs, and regulation of industry.[77] The policy alternatives

confronting the government were either to support the national economic expansion or to restrain it in the name of equity. The Democratic
party stood for the principle of equity in an age that did not demand
it. Its policy agenda called America to its agrarian past rather than to
its industrial future.[78] The greater effectiveness of the Republican party
was undergirded by its posture with respect to the national policy
agenda.

Their harmony with the policy drift of the industrial era made it
easier for Republican speakers to lead the House. Blaine enjoyed a
situation in which the Democratic party did not afford a viable political
alternative. Reed faced a competitive two-party situation in which his
own party's ranks reflected a more homogeneous constituency than did
that of the Democratic opposition. The Republican party was also philosophically more cohesive than the Democratic party. This enabled the
Republicans to gather policy consensus when the Democrats could not.
We should also note the political benefits that the Republicans gained
from their economic policies. The protective tariff yielded substantial
budget surpluses that the Republicans were able to put to political use.
The party was able to build a political infrastructure at the state and
county level that was supported by federal largess and federal patronage.
By contrast, the Democratic speakers had to cope with a disunited party,
with a philosophy of decentralized government, and they would not
abide the sort of party governance that the Republicans pursued. Finally,
we cannot overlook the personal element involved in the Republican
success. Randall, Carlisle, and Crisp were good politicians; Blaine, Reed,
and Cannon were better. The considerable skills of individual speakers
were important in bringing about the specific changes that did occur.
It was available to Blaine, Randall, and Carlisle to count a quorum, but
they were unwilling to do so; Reed did. The partisan era witnessed
several of the outstanding American speakerships. This was due to the
character of the times and to the character of the speakers who served
then. Among them, Thomas Brackett Reed distinguished himself as the
most able. Reed put his speakership on the line *before* securing power,
while Cannon put his at risk only after having lost the power that
sustained it.

Cannonism represented a triumph of procedure over substance, of
practice over theory. Its demise represented a triumph of the reverse
order. Just as the Reed reforms had rescued the American constitutional
system from the perversion of obstructionism, the revolt against Cannon
rescued it from legislative despotism. But if the transformation of the
House under Reed created the conditions from which Cannonism arose,
the revolt against Cannon changed the House in a manner that eventually
gave rise to a new system of internal government. The result was neither

a return to despotism nor a return to obstructionism; in fact, it was not a return to any form of governance that the House had witnessed in the past. Instead, the House of Representatives entered a new era in which it most resembled a set of feudal baronies.

3 ☆ The Feudal Speakership

Caucus Government

The demise of Cannonism represented more than just a political coup d'état, for Uncle Joe Cannon was not just a tyrant, but a tyrant who symbolized a conception of America and of its future.[1] The revolt against Speaker Cannon in 1910 did not immediately result in the destruction of the system over which he had presided. The new Rules Committee that was established as a result of the insurgent revolt was controlled by standpat Republicans loyal to the speaker.[2] However, the election of 1910 ushered in a Democratic majority for the first time since 1895, and along with it a new period in the evolution of the House. The empirical data demonstrate conclusively that the trend in institutionalization of the House began in 1911.[3] In considering how they wanted to run the House, the Democrats were guided by a commitment to democratic procedures, by the sectional nature of their coalition, and the personal disposition of their new speaker, Champ Clark of Missouri.

As minority leader during the last years of Cannon's reign, Clark had ample opportunity to develop a strong prejudice against Cannonism, and he was prompted by circumstances to develop a conciliatory approach to leadership. He preferred to leave the business of party management to the floor leader, Oscar Underwood of Alabama. "Although I am going to be Speaker next time," Clark said, "I am going to sacrifice the Speaker's power to change the rules."[4] Clark's attitude toward the speakership was hardly nonpolitical; he frequently participated in debate when not presiding, and his conduct in the chair was partisan within the rules. But Clark allowed Underwood free play in floor scheduling and management of the party caucus, and under the new regime the floor leader and caucus guided the party program.[5]

In organizing the Sixty-second Congress, the Democrats imposed several changes in the rules. Cannonism had rested upon three principal powers: floor recognition, control of the Rules Committee, and the power of committee appointment. Of these, the first two had been limited in the preceding Congress, the first by the establishment of the Unanimous Consent calendar (which removed from the speaker the sole power of approval of minor and private bills), and the second by the revision of the Rules Committee. The Democrats now removed the last of the speaker's major powers, his control over committee appointments. This power was given to the Democratic members of the Ways and Means Committee, who formed a Committee on Committees. This change gave great influence over committee appointments to Underwood, the chairman of the Ways and Means Committee, who was also designated as majority floor leader. The speaker could now influence, but not control, the process of committee assignment.[6]

Other rules changes implemented by the Democrats were less dramatic but consistent with the tenor of the reform movement. The Unanimous Consent calendar was changed to require that bills reported to it lie three days before being called up; the discharge rule was strengthened; the Holman Rule was readopted; and a new rule of germaneness was applied to revenue bills in order to prevent the accumulation of nongermane riders.[7] The most striking feature of these reforms was less the restraint that they placed upon party leadership than the restraint that the majority party placed upon itself. The readoption of the Holman Rule in the appropriations process and the adoption of a germaneness provision for revenue bills gave power from a legislative majority to every individual member under the rules. The Democrats were dedicated to egalitarian principles of internal governance and the party's internal divisions discouraged the centralized legislative control that the Republicans had developed.

The strongly egalitarian character of the Democratic party was apparent in the operation of its caucus. Speaker Cannon had believed that the theory of the American Constitution required party governance, but Cannonism evolved into a system of one-man rule under the aegis of party authority. The insurgent Republicans had challenged Cannon's political philosophy and system of centralized control, while the opposition Democrats had attacked the Republicans. Upon assuming power, the Democrats sought to exercise party governance through a binding party caucus. If the party was to govern, they believed, let it govern by the vote of its majority. Whereas Cannon had sought the authority of his party's majority to govern the House at the time of his election as speaker, Underwood tried to bind his party's majority on individual pieces of legislation. These two approaches to party control had different effects. Whereas Cannon had often exercised control by keeping unwanted legislation off of the floor, Underwood sought to control legislation by ensuring a majority vote on the floor. The result was despotism under two different guises.

In a system of caucus government the dynamics of the caucus are of paramount importance. As the chairman of the Ways and Means Committee and of the Committee on Committees, Underwood had tremendous leverage on rank-and-file Democrats. The caucus was employed when the leadership wanted to bind members in support of a given piece of legislation. Members made general and specific commitments to the leadership in the process of securing committee assignments, district patronage, office clerk hire, and other favors. The caucus rules established a simple majority as a quorum for business, with two-thirds of those members present and voting required to approve a motion to bind. It was not always necessary for the leadership to control two-thirds of the rank and file, but rather some lesser number, ranging down to two-thirds of a quorum. Of 291 Democratic members of the Sixty-third Congress, for example, the number required to bind might have been as few as ninety-eight.[8]

The psychology of a caucus governance is central to its nature. The leadership's aim is to give vent to intraparty differences in a forum that bears no ultimate responsibility for governing. As Underwood put it: "Let 'em talk, let 'em have it all out here. Then there will be no kick afterward."[9] But caucus governance is merely a variation of one-party politics, and in America one-party political systems have had at best a spotty record. The outcome of caucus government is a bitter minority party that feels that the right to participate meaningfully in legislative deliberations has been lost, and a disgruntled faction within the majority party. The Democratic party was divided between its southern and northern wings. Since the southern Democrats constituted a minority in excess of one-third of the caucus, it was protected by the caucus rule requiring two-thirds support for a binding vote. The Republican party was divided between its regular and insurgent wings. Even though the regular Republicans chafed under the drubbing they received from the Democratic caucus, their suffering was less than that of the progressive insurgents, who, having brought the Cannon machine to its knees, now found themselves forced out of the action by the same Democratic party that had previously embraced them so warmly in the revolutionary struggle.

Government by caucus may be efficient, but the debates in a party caucus are not likely to attain the same level of mature deliberation as those that take place upon the floor of a responsible legislative body. It is the essence of deliberation in a legislative body that "various and competing interests" (to cite the tenth *Federalist*) seek accommodation. The distribution of interests represented in a party caucus is not the same as that represented in the legislative body as a whole. Caucus debate ignores the views and interests of a significant sector of the electorate. The secret nature of a party caucus denies to the public knowledge of its representatives' behavior; consequently, the deliberative process is not leavened as it should be by a concern for public opinion. Finally, caucus debates easily descend into squabbles about the best interest of an abstraction—the party—instead of focusing upon the real interests of the constituents who are supposed to be served.[10]

The period of "King Caucus" was relatively brief, and its dominance of legislative affairs can easily be overstated. Underwood served as majority floor leader during the Sixty-second (1911–12) and Sixty-third (1913–14) Congresses. During the Sixty-second Congress, Taft was in the White House and the Republicans controlled the Senate. In the Sixty-third Congress, Underwood used the caucus to pass the Underwood-Simmons Tariff, the Federal Trade Commission Act, the Clayton Anti-Trust Act, and the Federal Reserve Bank Act.[11] With Woodrow Wilson exercising strong leadership from the White House and solid Democratic majorities in both houses of Congress, the Democrats were able to enact the bulk of the president's legislative program. But the party caucus was not invoked for the majority of legislation, and for a fuller understanding of the manner in which the Democratic system operated, it is necessary to consider the effects of other changes brought about by the new regime.

Of these changes, none was more consequential than the independent role played by the new Rules Committee. Under Cannon the Rules Committee had served as the personal fiefdom of the speaker and had supported the speaker's program. The Rules Committee had the power to block floor consideration of any bill that the speaker opposed, and it could structure special rules designed to limit or forbid floor amendments on bills it allowed to go to the floor. One of the most significant reforms undertaken by the Fitzgerald Rules of 1909 was the provision that the Rules Committee could not deny to the minority a motion to recommit any bill with specific instructions for its revision.[12] The revolution of 1910 led to an expanded Rules Committee controlled by the standpat Republicans loyal to Speaker Cannon. When they came to power in 1911, the Democrats further expanded the size of the committee and brought it under the influence of the Democratic leadership. After the Democrats assumed control of both the executive and legislative branches in 1913, the committee was more frequently used by the leadership to control the floor. Having once gained caucus approval of legislation reported by substantive committees, the leadership used the Rules Committee to fashion special rules designed to ensure floor passage. During the period of Democratic control of the House under Speaker Clark, the average number of special orders issued by the Rules Committee doubled from the levels of the Cannon era.[13] In this respect, the Rules Committee operated under the Democrats in a manner quite similar to that in which it came to function in the period after 1973.[14] Notwithstanding the partisan use of the Rules Committee during the reign of King Caucus, the fact remained that the speaker could now influence the committee (and hence the floor agenda), but could not control it. The loss of institutional control over the Rules Committee meant that the actual extent of the speaker's power would depend upon his capacity to influence the committee and its chairman.[15] The establishment of an independent Rules Committee was one of the principal ingredients in the recipe for the feudal speakership. In this, as in other respects, the Democratic experiment in party governance under the Clark-Underwood regime proved a poor harbinger of the future.

Sometimes the changes that take place in an institution conceal from view the pattern of which they are a part. The transformation of the speakership under Clark ushered in a new form of governance in the House, but it did not endure. The Wilson administration has been remembered for the strong party government and progressive domestic policies that it promoted. The use of the caucus and other accoutrements of party governance were undertaken at the same time that the speakership was weakened. Champ Clark chose to have less power than his predecessors in the partisan period. The Democratic interregnum witnessed the disembowelment of the speakership, but did not establish an enduring system of caucus government. Other trends were under way that ultimately brought about a strongly decentralized system. Among the most important of these were the use of seniority as a relatively inviolable rule for career advancement in the House, the tendency toward longevity of service, and the rise of southern influence in the Democratic party.

The seniority principle increased in importance as a direct result of the diffusion of power under the Democratic rules. The Democratic leadership tended to use the committee appointment power to broaden its base of support, and the seniority rule was "safe" in this respect.[16] The trend toward longevity of service (which traced its origins to the middle 1890s) continued, and was especially pronounced among southern members in the Democratic party.[17] These two factors combined to cause the third, the rise of southern influence. Throughout the last two decades of the nineteenth century and the first two decades of the twentieth century, the Democratic leadership in the House had been comprised of a mix of southern (John Sharp Williams of Mississippi;

Charles F. Crisp of Georgia, Oscar Underwood of Alabama), border (John G. Carlisle of Kentucky; Champ Clark of Missouri), and northern (Samuel J. Randall of Pennsylvania) members. After 1912, the leadership of the party increasingly centered in the South. Of fifty-eight standing committees in the Sixty-third Congress, thirty were chaired by southerners, and eight by members from the border South.[18] Of the seven Democratic members of the Rules Committee in that Congress, four were from the South and one from the border. Underwood of Alabama was the party leader. He was succeeded by Claude Kitchen of North Carolina, who was in turn succeeded by Finis Garrett of Tennessee. In 1928, John Nance Garner of Texas gained the party's leadership, and, after a brief interruption by Henry Rainey of Illinois, Joseph Byrns of Tennessee, William Bankhead of Alabama, and Sam Rayburn of Texas led the party until 1961. This trend took root in the second decade of the twentieth century and laid the basis for the system of Democratic governance that was to come to full fruit three decades later under Sam Rayburn. It proved to be contrary to the spirit of party governance advocated and pursued by Wilson and Underwood.[19]

The operation of the caucus system used by the Democrats attained its maximum effectiveness during Wilson's first administration, especially during the Sixty-third Congress while Underwood served as majority leader. It is evident that the effectiveness of the Wilson administration and the system of caucus government in the House resulted from a favorable policy tide. Progressivism had its moment in the sun, and the Democrats were able to govern the nation just so long as the policy consensus kept the party united behind the administration's program. This did not last long, however. In 1915 Underwood went to the Senate, and was succeeded as floor leader and chairman of Ways and Means by Claude Kitchen. Basic differences in political philosophy between Wilson and Kitchen led to a clash of political wills, and they did not work as closely together as had Wilson and Underwood. Because of this, Wilson began using congressman John Nance Garner of Texas as his intermediary to the House.[20] The Democrats had suffered heavy losses in the election of 1914, bringing their congressional majority down from 290 seats to 231. With the growing involvement of the United States in European affairs, Americans became increasingly concerned about the possibility of engagement in a general European war. Running on the theme that he had "kept us out of war," Wilson was reelected in 1916, but the party retained control of the House of Representatives by the narrowest of margins, electing an identical 215 members to the Republicans, and relying upon the support of five independent members to retain organizational control. Wilson did not keep America out the of war, and during his second administration he won congressional support for his war program only at the cost of bitter divisions within the party, which proved fatal in the 1918 congressional elections, when the Republicans swept the Congress.[21] The Republicans had the first opportunity to exercise control over the proceedings of the House since the revolt against Cannon. The country wondered if the Republican party would now return to the principles of the old regime, or accept the reforms that the Democrats had undertaken during the intervening eight years. Behind this question lay a significant question of public policy: would America return to the policies of standpat Republicanism or confirm and extend the progressivism of Roosevelt and Wilson?

The Return to Normalcy

The Republicans accepted and extended the diffusion of power that the Democrats had imposed, but they did not stray far from the conservative fiscal policies of the old standpatters. The terms of the policy debate changed in the 1920s. With the adoption of the federal income tax, the tariff was no longer the primary issue of fiscal policy. Instead, partisan debate focused on the proper rate of progressivity in the tax code. On either side of this debate stood the rhetoricians of old, the Democrats to the left, the Republicans to the right. The principles and the positions of the two parties did not change much. Significantly, while the political philosophy of the Republican party remained very consistent with its tradition, the party did not return the Cannon machine to power. In fact, it was during the Republican hegemony of the Roaring Twenties that the seeds of the bipartisan stability that would later characterize the feudal period were planted.

The old regime did not go to its grave silently. The first decision facing House Republicans was the selection of their speaker. Uncle Joe Cannon's right-hand man, minority floor leader James R. Mann of Illinois, was the presumed favorite. Mann was a master parliamentarian and legislator, and had proven a thorn in the side of the Democrats for the eight years during which they had held power. He had been swept from office in the election of 1912, and had returned in the Sixty-fourth Congress to his old position on the Appropriations Committee and as the Republican floor leader. He had proven himself to be a more formidable legislator than Cannon had ever been, and during the period of his leadership of the minority, he had used his influence over Republican committee appointments to establish a firm power base in the House. With the presumption of election lying in his favor, and with many regular Republicans standing solidly behind him, he appeared a likely choice for the speakership. A measure of Mann's ability comes in this comment from "Cactus" Jack Garner: "The most useful legislator

I ever knew was not a member of my party. His name was James R. Mann, and he was a Republican from Illinois. He was the hardest worker and the most adroit parliamentarian."[22]

But many regular Republicans feared that Mann's close association with Cannon would harm the party in the presidential election of 1920. Mann's opponents called up the specter of Cannonism in seeking to deny him the speakership. They settled upon Frederick H. Gillett of Massachusetts as an alternative to Mann. Gillett was the longest continuing member of the House and second in total service to Joe Cannon. Supporting Gillett was a coalition of insurgents, farm state Republicans, and distrustful regulars led by Nicholas Longworth of Ohio. From outside the House, Democratic National Committee Chairman Will C. Hays and Senator Boise Penrose of Pennsylvania assisted in the anti-Mann movement. By the eve of the conference vote Mann's defeat was inevitable, and when the votes were counted, Gillett had won a solid victory (138 to 69 with 18 scattered) and became the new speaker.[23]

But if Mann's enemies could outvote him, they could not outsmart him. As Republican floor leader, Mann had exercised unilateral power over the party's committee assignments, especially in the Sixty-fifth Congress, during which he obtained conference approval for a rule making his slate of committee nominations nondivisible. On the same day that he was defeated by Gillett for the speakership, Mann pulled a political coup that placed him in a unique position of influence within the party anyway. Rather than return the power of committee appointments to the speaker, as had been the case under Cannon, the Republicans voted to create their own Committee on Committees. Instead of following the Democratic precedent of placing this power in the hands of the Ways and Means Republicans, they decided to form an entirely new committee composed of a small number of members selected by the leadership and confirmed by the conference.

Rising in opposition, Mann successfully proposed a larger committee upon which each state delegation would be represented by a single member, but entitled to one vote for each Republican member in the delegation. By this arrangement, the Committee on Committees was dominated by the representatives of the larger states from which the most Republican members had been elected. Mann took advantage of the reformist impulse toward diffusion of power and equity in order to wrest the power of committee assignments from the hands of the newly elected leadership. As calculated by one observer, the Gillett forces controlled twenty states to Mann's twelve, but the Mann forces controlled the committee's votes 124 to 92. Mann was himself selected as the committee member from the state of Illinois, and by combining control of a large block of votes with the intimate knowledge of the

Republican members he had gained over two decades of involvement in committee appointments (first as Cannon's lieutenant and then as floor leader), Mann was able to win a position of influence in the House that its speaker, Gillett, could not match.[24]

And so there occurred under the Republicans an affirmation of the Democratic system (the Republican-controlled Sixty-sixth Congress adopted the rules of the Democratic-controlled Sixty-fifth Congress) and an extension of its principle.[25] Just as under Speaker Clark the effective leadership of the party lay with floor leader Underwood, now under Speaker Gillett the actual leadership of the party lay in the hands of James Mann. Even the party's elected floor leader, Frank Mondell of Wyoming, was under Mann's influence. In addition to Mann and Mondell, the leadership of the party included Phillip P. Campbell of Kansas, the chairman of the Rules Committee, Martin B. Madden of Illinois, who was subsequently vaulted to the chair of the Appropriations Committee by Mann, and Samuel E. Winslow of Massachusetts. Returning to his ancient position on the Appropriations Committee was Uncle Joe Cannon himself, until his retirement in 1922. Notably, there was not a southerner or border state member among them, although both the eastern and western wings of the Republican party were represented. Of these men James R. Mann was preeminent during the remainder of his period of service in the House (until his death in 1922) in spite of the fact that he never attained the speakership.[26] The extent of Mann's influence may be gathered from this plaintive statement by Nicholas Longworth, the leader of the Gillett faction:

> The performance of the Republican Committee on Committees of its most important duty, that of selecting the Steering Committee, the Floor Leader and the Whip, was exactly what ought to have been expected from the men and under the methods controlling. Its net results was [sic] to make Mr. James R. Mann the dominating figure in the next House of Representatives. It is the most complete sort of triumph for reactionism. Even the final effort of some of us to enlarge and liberalize the Steering Committee, so as to secure representation upon it of the progressive sentiment of the West, of the states on the southern border, which substantially contributed to the Republican majority, and of labor, was defeated by the usual vote. If it had been deliberately planned to restore the conditions existing in the House ten years ago, as a result of which the Republican majority became a minority, the plan could not have been more successfully consummated. Then the leadership was held by Mr. Cannon, and assisted by Mr. Mann of Illinois, Mr. Dalzell of Pennsylvania and Mr. Tawney of

Minnesota, together with Mr. Payne of New York acting as chairman of the Ways and Means Committee. Under today's arrangement the real leadership is held by Mr. Mann, assisted by Mr.
Cannon of Illinois, Mr. Mondell of Wyoming and Mr. Moore of
Pennsylvania, together with Mr. Fordney of Michigan acting as
chairman of the Ways and Means Committee.

As I gaze upon these two pictures, I find it impossible to differentiate between them. If there is any real difference it might lie
in the views of the two chairmen of the Ways and Means Committee. After service on that committee with both for a good
many years I am inclined to think that, as compared with Mr.
Fordney, Mr. Payne was a rather advanced tariff reformer.[27]

In differentiating between the curious influence exercised by Mann
and the more enduring leadership system to which the Republicans
became committed, we see that the model of House governance developed by the Republicans was essentially one in which the party, and
hence the House, was governed by a party committee. In the Sixty-fifth
Congress the Republican minority had created a Steering Committee
composed of five members and chaired by the floor leader. Mann held
all of the strings of power in the party at that time. With Gillett's defeat
of Mann for the speakership in 1919, it was evident that Mann could
not serve effectively either as floor leader or as chairman of the Steering
Committee. With the revision of the Committee on Committees, the
chairmanship of that committee was lost to him as well. Mann managed
to retain influence through his role on the Committee on Committees,
and the formal apparatus of party leadership fell into the hands of a
Steering Committee selected by the Committee on Committees that was
chaired by Mondell but led by Mann. Mann's influence on the Committee on Committees was greater than Mondell's. While Speaker Gillett
was not formally a member of the Steering Committee, he was invited
by Mondell to attend its meetings and eventually the Committee came
to meet in the speaker's office.[28]

The actual control exercised by the Mann circle concealed from view
the extent to which the Republicans were dedicated to the diffusion of
power. One indication of this was the fact that the chairmen of standing
committees and members of the Rules Committee were excluded from
the Steering Committee. This was a far cry from the days in which the
speaker chaired a Rules Committee controlled by himself and the chairmen of the Ways and Means and Appropriations Committees. The
formal diffusion of power created the necessity for informal collusion
among those members of the party in a position to exercise actual
influence. Mann's influence on the Committee on Committees was ac-

tually enhanced, since in an environment in which power was diffused, his own assumed more importance.[29]

The tension between a system that was in form diffuse, but in fact centralized, was lessened by the general ideological cohesiveness of the party. While insurgency remained a factor in Republican party politics throughout the 1920s, the insurgents steadily lost ground. Several factors account for this decline. With the exception of the Sixty-eighth Congress (1923–24), the Republican majorities in the House were too large for the insurgent faction to hold the balance of power. In the Sixty-eighth Congress the Republican margin fell to eighteen votes. The insurgents were active in their attempts to frustrate the program of the Coolidge administration and in fact helped the Democrats in their attempts to alter administration tax bills. In the presidential election of 1924, thirteen insurgents bolted the party to support the La Follette ticket. With the return of a sizable 247–183 majority in the Sixty-ninth Congress (1925–26), these insurgents were politically weakened.

Also undermining the insurgents' influence was the fact that the Democratic party had, under Wilson's leadership, claimed much of the insurgent agenda for its own. This factor was related to a third, the loss of Theodore Roosevelt as the national leader of the progressive Republicans in 1919. Roosevelt's legacy lay in the fact that the mainstream of the Republican party had accepted much of the basic thrust of the new nationalism. While still very conservative in fiscal policy, the Republicans in the 1920s embraced such progressive notions as the regulation of the meat industry, provision for maternal and infant care, control of child labor, and regulation of federal election practices. Just as in the days of Cannonism, the standpat Republicans of the 1920s accepted reform legislation compatible with their economic principles. They were willing to abide progressive legislation so long as the tariffs were high, taxes were low, and government expenditures were reduced. Finally, the strength of insurgency was weakened by the very diffusion of power for which the 1910 insurgents had fought. Under Cannon, the insurgents could justify their rebellion on the grounds that they had been excluded from the party's decision-making system. Under the more open rules of the 1920s, however, they could only cavil at their lack of influence upon their Republican colleagues. Thus, a relatively homogeneous Republican party governed the House during the 1920s, a party that could afford the luxury of a diffuse power structure because of its internal harmony on policy. Although Gillett was not generally regarded as a strong speaker, the party was able to enact the majority of its legislative program under the cooperative leadership of Mann, Mondell, and their colleagues.

When, in 1925, Nicholas Longworth of Ohio succeeded Gillett in the speakership, it appeared that the House might have its first strong speaker since Cannon. Longworth had led the fight against Mann, and he was determined to be as strong a party leader as Mann had been. He enunciated a philosophy of party government reminiscent of Cannon's: "In this country, in order to have effective legislation, it must be obtained by responsible party government. That's what we are going to have in the next Congress."[30] Matching action to words, Longworth disciplined the thirteen progressives who had bolted the party in 1924 by barring them from the Republican conference and stripping them of their committee assignments. In a move to ensure his majority's control of the floor, Longworth pushed through an increase in the number of signatures required for a discharge petition from 150 to 218.

However reminiscent of Cannon Longworth's actions may have seemed, in fact Longworth espoused a theory of party government for which he was ill clothed by the powers of the speakership. Yet he became known as a powerful and effective speaker, the first assertive speaker since Cannon. If Longworth possessed some of Cannon's reputation while lacking most of his authority, an explanation of his speakership will have to look elsewhere than to his formal power. Lacking the powers available to Reed and Cannon, Nicholas Longworth led the House by force of his character. For all of the lip service that he paid to the principle of party government, the essence of Longworth's speakership lay in his personality. "There will never be another Reed or another Cannon, another Carlisle or Crisp," said a contemporary commentary, but there was presented to Longworth the opportunity to "create a new kind of greatness for that exalted office. The old order has gone but no new order has definitely come." Longworth could be a "guiding and inspiring Speaker."[31]

Nick Longworth was at one and the same time the most popular and most aristocratic of twentieth-century speakers. His manner was dashing and his charm always on display. He had "the human affection of the House of Representatives as really no other Speaker [had]." He was a man with "no personal hatreds, no personal resentments, no political bigotries, no political alarms."[32] As a member of the Ways and Means Committee for over two decades, Longworth had played a major role in the great tariff and taxation battles of the first quarter of the twentieth century. Yet his commitment in life was not just to the legislative institution of the House of Representatives. The heir to an Ohio fortune, married to Alice Roosevelt, an accomplished violinist, and a man of culture and breeding, Nick Longworth had many interests in life, and he pursued them avidly. "Former Speakers, being older men and conscientious, lunched horridly on crackers and the well reputed apple. The able Mr. Mann, who once ruled the House as floor leader, was too busy to eat at all. Not so the present Speaker. He never misses a day at the Round Table in the members' restaurant, and at gay parties he is regularly the last to leave."[33] A raconteur, a card shark, a bon vivant—Nicholas Longworth was in these respects the most dashing speaker since the days of the dueling Henry Clay. Longworth's unabashedly elitist lifestyle alienated some members of Congress while enthralling others. He was advised to tone down his image if he wanted to be speaker, but refused to do so. After he became speaker, his spats, his cravats, and his rakish hats became assets. Members of the House appreciate a speaker who enhances its image. The boldness of Henry Clay, the eloquence of James Blaine, the commanding presence of Tom Reed, the homespun humor of Joe Cannon, the fierce intensity of Sam Rayburn, the Irish gregariousness of Tip O'Neill—in these various personas, influential speakers have filled the contours of office. Nicholas Longworth, like these others, lay claim on the House by imposing his personality on it.

Longworth's style was more collegial than autocratic. He worked with the Republican steering committee and especially with a group of lieutenants that included John Q. Tilson of Connecticut, Bertrand Snell of New York, and James Begg of Ohio.[34] The "big four" were the center of gravity in a Republican party that enjoyed a comfortable majority. Since he commanded the Republicans, Longworth could afford good relations with the Democrats. "He has been so fair to the Democrats," said one observer, "that many good Republicans have protested."[35] Longworth's fairness was undergirded by substantial majorities. During his three terms in the chair he never enjoyed less than a 42-seat majority. Having dealt decisively with the insurgents at the outset, he faced little opposition within the party. The Roaring Twenties were a time of political consolidation, and the Republican party was well suited to preside over the kind of government the majority of citizens wanted. If the previous decade's progressive policy trend had been favorable to governance by the Democrats, the decade of the twenties marked a return, if not to normalcy, at least to stability. While the Longworth congresses witnessed their share of partisan conflict, it was not until the last year of his speakership that the stock market crash took its toll on the Republican party's ability to govern. Longworth's leadership of the House stood for the most part untested against the demands of a deeply divided party or a narrow party majority.

Longworth was a generalist and a compromiser. He had gained expertise in tax and tariff legislation during his career, but as speaker he preferred to remain aloof from the details of legislation. Although he was a staunch Republican, he was neither so rigid nor so foolish as to sacrifice that which was attainable for that which was not. He was "a conservative who in order to save some of conservatism would never hesitate to abandon some of it."[36] He was willing to work with Democrats when it was warranted. In company with Democratic floor leader and close personal friend, John Nance Garner, Longworth initiated "the Board of Education," the drinking hideaway later made famous by Speaker Rayburn. The "Board" enabled the leaders of the two parties to reach a working accord during a period in which the Republican party predominated.[37]

Longworth's impartiality derived partly from the changes in the rules of the House that had been imposed by the Democrats in 1911 and retained by the Republicans in 1919. The rules were themselves fairer than they had been under the old regime, and any speaker who enforced the rules was ipso facto fairer than Uncle Joe Cannon had been. One indication of the extent to which the rules of the House had become formalized was the appointment by Longworth of Lewis Deschler as the first official parliamentarian in 1925. Previously the clerk at the speaker's desk had performed this function. Deschler, a Republican, became the personification of the nonpartisanship of the rules, and through long service became an influential figure in the affairs of the House until his retirement in 1975. There remained within the purview of the rules some latitude for the partisan use of the chair. But if Speaker Longworth treated the Democrats fairly, it was at least in part because he could afford to; his majorities were large enough to sustain him under the rules and with a nod toward the minority.

It may seem surprising that a speaker as verbally committed to the principle of party governance as Longworth was would establish techniques of bipartisanship. The difference between Longworth's association with Garner and Cannon's association with John Sharp Williams lay in Longworth's willingness to deal with the Democrats on many issues. Whereas Cannon had exercised arbitrary control over the schedule of the House, Longworth was willing to work with Garner in determining the order of business. His solid legislative majorities made such cooperation possible and his pragmatic nature made it seem desirable. In working with Garner rather than rolling over him, Longworth demonstrated that a sense of bipartisan comity was not incompatible with assertive leadership; indeed, in establishing a working relationship with the Democratic leadership, Speaker Longworth proved that an assertive speaker must, in a diffuse legislative environment, seek on all fronts to further his own legislative aims. A speaker who in the end lacks the power to compel allegiance within his own party profits little from the abusive treatment of the minority party. Nicholas Longworth realized that his own best interests as a party leader were served by a legislative environment that was not embittered by partisan use of the rules. Together, he and Cactus Jack Garner established the foundation of bipartisan accommodation that lay at the heart of the speakership during the feudal era. In the end, Longworth's speakership was far different from the rhetoric of Reed and Cannon. The defeat of his party in 1930, and his death soon thereafter, came as the full force of the Depression took hold of America. The Democratic party became the House's natural majority party, and America greeted the New Deal.

The New Deal and the Congress

The 1930s witnessed a dramatic transformation in the nation's political agenda. A new Democratic electoral coalition emerged that dominated American politics for forty years.[38] The New Deal created a new relationship between the federal government and substantial organized interests in society. In the old game, the federal government supported favored industries by imposing protective tariffs. In the New Deal game the federal government took steps to prop up the economy in other ways. For example, the New Deal agricultural policy attempted to stabilize farm prices by introducing the principle of acreage allotments to reduce supply in order to drive up price. The policy responded to the demands of the organized farm lobby. In the industrial sector the combined effects of the Depression and New Deal policies created the conditions under which modern trade unionism arose. Roosevelt accepted the principle of federal relief for the needy and the many New Deal programs designed to put people back to work served a widespread constituency among the poor. Federal public works projects contributed to state and local governments. The Tennessee Valley Authority involved the federal government in regional economic development. Social security introduced the basic principle of federal responsibility for citizen welfare. The National Youth Administration and the Civilian Conservation Corps served young people. The New Deal, in sum, launched the redistributive state. It is not surprising that the more egalitarian of the two major parties was the governmental vehicle and political beneficiary of the new order.

These federal programs served widespread, enduring, and organized interests in American society. The political coalition to which they gave rise lent definition to American political life, and the consequences were felt in the Congress. The tendency toward stability was already present, especially within the Democratic party, and the seniority system had entrenched the power of southern Democrats. The newcomers who came to town in 1933 and 1935 did not upset it; instead, those who stayed on enlisted themselves in its long apprenticeship. By cooperating with those at the top of the power structure, those at the bottom served their own interests and those of their constituents. This was a game ideally suited to the character and temperament of the Democratic party, a party marked by diversity and devoted to logrolling. From the Roosevelt administration, to the oligopoly on Capitol Hill, through the growing bureaucracy, to the congressional constituencies, everyone found something to gain. The forces that shaped the new policy agenda sprang from trends in American life that predated the Depression and New Deal and would have in time made themselves felt anyway. The farm crisis was created by increased productivity caused by scientific and technological advancement. Trade unionism was the product of mass production, an artifact of economic and technological development. The increasing federal role in the economy was the result of the economy's growth, and not the result of its failure in the Depression. In the early part of the twentieth century, America became a modern industrial society and its central government was bound to play a greater role in the nation's affairs. Ironically, while for most of its history the Democratic party had stood against the nationalization of politics and for most of its history the Republican party had stood in favor of it, in the twentieth century those roles became reversed. By the 1930s the stage was set for public acceptance of a greater federal role, and the Depression triggered it. As it happened, the Democrats were positioned to reap the political rewards. The public accepted the Democratic view of the role of government and propelled the Democrats into power for four decades. A new political equilibrium arose in the nation and a new power structure developed in the House.

That power structure was centered in the Congress. Historians of the presidency regard Franklin Roosevelt as having finally established the ascendancy of presidential power in the American constitutional system, yet Roosevelt was careful to defer to the Democratic barons in the Congress on the control of federal spending. This is best seen in the development of the federal public works projects for which the New Deal is best known. Roosevelt could not shake himself from the idea that a person who receives federal welfare ought to be willing to work. Of all the New Deal welfare programs, social security is conspicuous by its generosity—the federal government simply hands out the checks. The other New Deal programs, such as the Works Progress Administration, the Public Works Administration, the Civilian Conservation Corps, and the National Youth Administration, all had work requirements.

Once it was decided to tie federal money to human labor, it became necessary to find objects upon which the labor could be visited. Under a general welfare scheme, all that is required are accountants and caseworkers. When welfare is funded through public works projects, someone has to decide where the projects will be located. The question of relief can no longer be separated from the distributional issue of district work projects. Members of Congress fought to bring home the bacon to their districts; the impact was felt in all parts of the country, but was especially strong in the South, where the Depression had hit the hardest. The evolution of the main New Deal spending programs went hand in hand with the emergence of the conservative coalition that was to be New Deal liberalism's greatest nemesis. Southern Democrats were always more conservative and tight-fisted than their northern brethren, except where the federal pork barrel was concerned; there they were among the first to get their snouts in the trough. Wielding great power in the committees, the southerners used it to good effect in the distributional fights. Conservative southern opposition to Roosevelt remained quiescent until the court-packing episode of 1937, which triggered the development of the conservative coalition in the Congress. Roosevelt's decision to purge the Congress of southern Democrats who had opposed his reelection in 1936 sealed many southerners in opposition to him.

When the administration came forward with a $1.5 billion request for the WPA in 1937, the Congress earmarked a third of the money for specific district projects. Roosevelt offered a compromise: if the WPA funding would be unearmarked, the president would support earmarking in other areas of the budget.[39] This compromise indicated that the Democrats in the Congress would not allow the New Deal to establish the hegemony of the Roosevelt administration; instead, the New Deal would be a district-oriented, congressionally controlled system of federal largess. When, fifteen years later, the Democrats lost control of the White House, the New Deal remained embedded in the congressional committee rooms, and the essence of the New Deal persisted long after the New Dealers passed from the scene. That essence lay not in the force of an overpowering executive, but in the slow accretion of power by the committee chairmen. In the post–World War II period, the Republican Party controlled the White House more often than not, often by landslide margins. But during the entire period from 1932 to 1989, the Republicans controlled the Senate during only five congresses, the House during only two. Franklin Roosevelt's New Deal was, in the end, a congressional phenomenon.

This is not to deny that the presidency was fundamentally transformed by the New Deal. It was. Since FDR, the public's expectations of the presidency have been different than they were before. The public expects leadership from the president, and it is the president who sets the basic elements of the national political agenda. But if the president can and must set the major items on the agenda, he cannot enact them by himself. Instead, he must seek to persuade the Congress to follow his leadership. This led to a strengthening of the link between the presidency and the speakership. On occasion speakers had been supporters of presidents, but there existed no norm that demanded it prior to the New Deal. Since the New Deal speakers, especially Democratic speakers, have viewed it as their obligation to support presidents of their own party. Thus, the New Deal had the ironic effect of solidifying congressional power in the committee system, which the speaker could influence but not control, and of imposing on the speaker the duty of supporting a president of his own party. From 1932 forward, speakers would be caught in a crossfire between the congressional power structure and their obligation to the White House.

It is not possible to overstate the impact of the dominance of the conservative southern wing of the Democratic party in shaping the House of Representatives during its feudal era. As a practical political matter, the program of the radical Republicans to force white southerners into line in the nineteenth century ensured that the South would remain solidly in Democratic hands for so long as it was controlled by the heirs of the cotton kingdom. When, in the middle of the twentieth century the Republicans allied with the conservative southerners in opposing the civil rights revolution, the party accomplished the seemingly impossible task of alienating white and black southerners alike. The conservative coalition that emerged in 1937 and remained a fact of congressional life through the 1970s was bottomed on southern conservative control of the committee system in the Democratic party. While the nation was enjoying the Roaring Twenties under Republican governance, the Democratic party in the House continued to become increasingly dominated by its southern faction. In the first session of the Sixty-fifth Congress (1917–18), southerners controlled twenty-eight of fifty-nine chairmanships, with border states controlling another eleven. The twelve years of Republican control from 1920 to 1931 saw a continuation of the same trend within the Democratic party. In 1931 the southern Democrats controlled twenty-seven of forty-seven chairmanships and, for the first time since Crisp, the speakership of the House.[40]

The evolution of the system of committee baronies was perhaps not inevitable, but it was clearly a likely outcome of the revolt against Cannon. Once the decision had been made to dismantle the central power of the speakership, power was bound to flow somewhere, and the committee chairmanships were likely venues. After the speaker was stripped of his power to appoint the committees and their chairmen, the alternatives were constant dogfights or seniority. The seniority principle, which had evolved under the czars as a means of avoiding intraparty disputes, now assumed more significance than before and became the predominant route to power in the Democratic caucus. At the same time, the average length of service of members was on the rise. It had wavered between 1.54 and 2.79 terms from the Second Congress (1791–92) through the end of the nineteenth century. The Fifty-seventh Congress (1901–02) saw the average term rise above 3.0 (at 3.11) for the first time, and it rose steadily thereafter. In the Seventieth Congress (1927–28) it rose to 4.26, and from 1941 (Sam Rayburn's first full year as speaker) to 1961 (his last) the average term of service rose from 4.24 to 5.65.[41] As the average seniority of members rose, so too did that of the committee chairmen, especially of the major committees. In 1913 the average member had served 3.14 terms and the chairmen of the major committees had served on average 7.88 terms. By 1931 the average tenure of members had increased to 4.48 terms and that of the chairmen of the major committees to 9.11 terms.[42]

When the Democrats recaptured the House in 1931, power in the party was centered in the Texas delegation. The speaker, John Nance Garner of Texas, had been a leading force in the party since the Wilson administration. Surrounding him was an inner circle of power brokers that included several from Texas: J. Marvin Jones, the chairman of the Agriculture Committee (whose sister, Metze, was married to Sam Rayburn for a few months in 1927); James P. Buchanan, second-ranking member of the Appropriations Committee; Sam Rayburn, chairman of the Interstate and Foreign Commerce Committee; Hatten Sumners, chairman of the Judiciary Committee; and Joseph Mansfield, chairman of the Rivers and Harbors Committee. In addition to these Texans, the power structure included Joseph Byrns of Tennessee, chairman of the Appropriations Committee; John McDuffie of Alabama, second-ranking member of the Rivers and Harbors Committee; the dean of the House, Edward Pou of North Carolina, who was the cousin of James P. Buchanan; the chairman of the Rules Committee, William Bankhead of Alabama; John Collier of Mississippi, chairman of the Ways and Means Committee; and Charles R. Crisp of Georgia (the son of the former speaker), second-ranking member of the Ways and Means Committee.

This group of southern power brokers was formidable, but constrained in its control of the House. Speaker Garner and his protégés held one of the narrowest legislative majorities in the history of the Congress, a mere three-vote margin. The southern oligarchy encountered the opposition of northern and liberal Democrats, who felt systematically excluded from the centers of party decision making. The White House was still in the hands of Herbert Hoover, while the Senate was controlled by Republicans. As a practical matter the Democratic House leadership had little leeway in developing its own program for reconstruction; the leadership provided by John Nance Garner was of crucial importance in enabling the House Democrats to function effectively.

"Cactus" Jack Garner was a conservative Texan who was a master of the legislative process. As a member of the Ways and Means Committee, he had proven himself a potent force on tax legislation even in the face of sizable Republican majorities. In 1924 he guided the House to the adoption of a substitute tax package in place of the highly regressive proposal of Coolidge's Treasury Secretary, Andrew Mellon. In 1926 the Republicans attempted to repeal the federal estate tax, but under Garner's leadership the House knocked the repealer provision from the tax bill and in conference coerced the Senate to recede by threatening to sink the entire bill. Garner was never one to push legislation of his own. During his thirty-year House career he sponsored only four bills. From the time of his association with President Wilson, however, he was a major force in legislation in the House, and was reputed to be the most skillful politician in that body. Garner, said one contemporary observer, "does not excel in any one quality—except, perhaps that of being the best politician on either side. But he has more of the qualities that go to make the ideal member than anyone who has been in the House since Uncle Joe Cannon was in his prime."[43]

As speaker during the Depression, Garner's politics were economically conventional. Like many Democrats from the South, he was a fiscal conservative who believed that the first essential for economic recovery was a balanced federal budget. At the same time, he was unwilling to abide President Hoover's apparent lack of concern for the suffering of the American people, and looked with favor upon direct federal relief for the poor, to be financed by such taxes as necessary to pay for it, with a balanced budget. In 1932 Garner sponsored, as his fourth and last piece of legislation, a public works jobs bill that passed the Congress but was vetoed by Hoover. Garner's commitment to the balanced federal budget reflected the mainstream economic thinking of the times.[44] His philosophy was that of a Jefferson/Jackson Democrat— egalitarian, rural, states' rights oriented, and populist. He was a part of the Democratic party's past, and not of its future. As the nation's leading elected Democrat during the Seventy-first Congress, Garner's views became a focal point for Democratic policy.

Jack Garner was one of the more colorful characters in American political history. He was a frequent poker player and known to take a drink. Later, when Garner was vice president, John L. Lewis would create a stir by calling him a "labor-baiting, poker-playing, whiskey-drinking, evil old man." Culturally, he was the antithesis of his predecessor, Longworth. Longworth was lionized by the newspapers, although he never held a press conference; Garner held daily press conferences, yet he otherwise shied away from the press. In his press conferences he was taciturn in responding to questions. "You can speculate all you want to," he would say; "[I] have nothing to say."[45] During his career in the House, Garner pursued his business interests at home. In time he accumulated substantial wealth, but never wore it on his sleeve as Longworth had.

Garner continued the institution of the Board of Education. The new Republican leader, Bertrand Snell of New York was a frequent visitor to the Board room, but he and Garner did not share the same close personal friendship as had Garner and Longworth.[46] Garner's control of the House hung by the barest thread, and he could not afford to be as accommodating to the Republicans as Longworth had been to the Democrats. The exigencies of the Depression made bipartisan cooperation extremely difficult. Had there existed a public consensus in favor of strong governmental action to stem the Depression's tide, the groundwork would have been laid for cooperative action by the Republican administration and Senate and the Democratically controlled House of Representatives. However, President Hoover was determined to see the crisis through with a minimum of federal intervention, while the Democrats were for both philosophical and political purposes committed to strong federal action. The results of the 1930 election should have provided a sufficient indication to Hoover that public sentiment was in favor of more positive action. But when the Congress passed the major public works bill authored by Garner in 1932, Hoover vetoed the bill as a pork-barrel extravagance and the essential difference between the Republican and Democratic approach to economic recovery and Depression relief was clarified in the public mind.

A major defeat for Garner in the Seventy-first Congress was the Revenue Act of 1932. The one policy favored by both the administration and the Democratic leadership was that of a balanced federal budget.[47] With the decline in revenues caused by economic collapse and increased spending for the Reconstruction Finance Corporation and various agricultural subsidies, the need for new revenues was widely accepted. The Republicans favored the imposition of a manufacturers' sales tax as the most expeditious means of raising revenue quickly. Garner was opposed to a sales tax because it was regressive. On the Ways and Means Committee, Charles R. Crisp of Georgia supported the sales tax on practical grounds, and convinced Garner that it was the only means of gaining a permanent increase in the tax base. When the bill was brought to the Committee of the Whole House, northern Democrats bolted the leadership and prepared to vote against it if the sales tax remained its principal feature. Garner took the floor to appeal for support, and in a dramatic gesture that indicated as well as anything could the conventionality of the economic thinking of the time, asked all members who supported a balanced budget to rise in place. Everyone stood, but in the end, the House proceeded to vote down the sales tax and adopt in its stead a catchall measure that produced about the same amount of revenue.[48]

Garner's leadership of the Democratic party in the House brought to him great public visibility. As the nation's leading elected Democrat and as the leader of the influential Texas delegation in the Congress, Garner had ample political assets to enable him to contend for the presidency in 1932. His major liability was the fact that he was from the South; no southerner had been seriously considered for the presidency since the Civil War, and the South was so heavily Democratic in its leanings that a legitimate question arose as to the ability of a southerner to govern the entire nation. The Garner flag was, however, picked up by William Randolph Hearst and his powerful chain of newspapers, and this support was sufficient to propel the speaker into contention for the nomination.[49] With Hearst's editorial support, Garner won the California primary over Franklin Roosevelt and Al Smith and entered the convention with a solid core of support in the Texas and California delegations. The convention deadlocked through its first three ballots, with FDR lying just 110 votes short of nomination. Garner then threw his support to Roosevelt and was unanimously selected as the vice-presidential nominee, and the Democratic ticket went on to victory in the fall election. Garner thus became the only speaker ever elected on a national ticket.[50]

Upon the election of Franklin D. Roosevelt to the presidency and John Nance Garner to the vice presidency, the speakership of the House of Representatives fell to Garner's majority leader, Henry T. Rainey of Illinois. Although generally not well known, Rainey's story is one of the most interesting in the history of the speakership. Henry T. Rainey was the only speaker in the twentieth century to have won his way to party leadership over the opposition of his party's establishment. As a northerner and a liberal, Rainey represented a wing of the Democratic party that would ultimately come to control it; but Rainey was thirty years ahead of his time both politically and institutionally. His speakership offers a fleeting moment of progressivism in a congressional party that was destined to be dominated by a southern oligarchy for thirty years. And his technique of leadership as "the legislative marshal of the New Deal" would not take effective root in the House until the 1970s.[51]

Rainey came to the House in 1903 and served until defeated for reelection in the Republican sweep of 1920. In the election of 1922 he reclaimed his seat. During his first nine terms in office, he established a reputation as a maverick progressive (often called the "Illinois La Follette"), and became known for his outspoken views in favor of low tariffs and progressive taxation.[52] By 1920 he had climbed to eleventh on the seniority ladder and was the tenth-ranking member of the Ways and Means Committee. With his return to the House in the Sixty-seventh Congress, he was placed as the second-ranking Democrat on the Agriculture Committee. In the following Congress he moved back to his old seat on Ways and Means as the eighth-ranking member. In each of the ensuing three Congresses, he advanced a notch on the Ways and Means Committee, until by the Seventy-first Congress he had arrived at the number five seniority position. In the Seventy-second Congress (1931–33), he advanced to the third spot and was elected majority leader. His political return from electoral defeat was a remarkable accomplishment, undertaken as it was in the face of the opposition of the party establishment. As a downstate Illinois member, Rainey was able to capitalize on the support of northerners who did not trust Tammany Hall and western progressives who shared his outlook. Rainey was also second in seniority among House Democrats to the venerable Edward Pou of North Carolina. In an institution that rewarded seniority, this was not an insignificant claim.

Rainey's election as majority leader in 1931 revealed the divisions within the Democratic caucus. The establishment candidate was John McDuffie of Alabama, the majority whip. The machine candidate was John J. O'Conner of New York and Tammany Hall. Garner had a firm grip on the speakership, and it was apparent that the South would control virtually all of the key committee chairmanships. The demand of northern members for a role in the leadership was equitable. McDuffie's withdrawal at Garner's request indicated that the southern establishment wanted to unify the party. O'Conner, as the Tammany Hall candidate, did not fit the bill but Rainey, as a maverick midwesterner, did. Thus, Rainey was elected with a coalition of southern and northern support.[53] In spite of his election, he was never able to win acceptance within the establishment. He did not frequent the Board of Education, and his relationship with Speaker Garner was strained. Garner, in fact, was unwilling to relinquish to Rainey many prerogatives that had been exercised by Democratic floor leaders under Speaker Clark. Rainey was not disloyal to Garner, but was often too outspoken to satisfy the sense of propriety of the tight-lipped speaker. He joined with Garner in sponsoring the public works bill of 1932 and defended the sales tax provision of the Revenue Act of 1932, the latter with extreme distaste. Still, he remained very much an outrider in a leadership structure that was dominated by the southern oligarchy.[54]

Consequently, Rainey's election to the speakership in 1933 appeared problematical at the end of 1932. Within a few weeks after the 1932 election, no fewer than four candidates had declared for the speakership, including Rainey, Byrns of Tennessee, McDuffie of Alabama, and Rankin of Mississippi. Bankhead of Alabama was also mentioned as a possibility. McDuffie was once again the candidate of Garner and the establishment. The southern oligarchy was riven, however, as can be seen in the number of southern candidates. When Congressman Thomas H. Cullen of New York, the Tammany Hall candidate, joined the field the party suffered a complete geographic split, with candidates from each of its major regions. As the second-longest-serving member and as the majority leader of the party, Rainey's claims were substantial. In addition, he benefited from the desire of the northern machine delegations to wrest power from the southern oligarchs. His campaign manager was Albert Sabath of Chicago's Cook County machine. In a caucus held on March 2, 1933, Rainey was elected speaker in a three-way deal that saw Byrns receive the majority leader's position, Tammany's Cullen elected to the new position of assistant leader, and Arthur H. Greenwood of Indiana bump McDuffie as the party whip. The Texas delegation was assuaged with six key committee chairmanships, including the advancement of Buchanan to the head of the Appropriations Committee.[55]

As much as this arrangement smacked of back-room politics, Rainey's election was ensured by the election of 129 new Democrats; of these, ninety-five were from the North, twelve from border states, and seventeen from the South. The state electing the most new Democratic members was Illinois, with eleven. Contiguous states elected forty-one others. These new members were politically tied to President Roosevelt's commitment to political action. Rainey had for several years advocated a diffusion of the power structure in the House through the creation of a party steering and policy committee similar to that employed by the Republicans. In 1933 he made this proposal a key element in his campaign platform for the speakership. The concept of a party steering committee had been strongly opposed by Garner, who favored the management of the House by the speaker and the committee chairmen. But the idea was very attractive to new members, who could have no hope of influence under the leadership of the old guard. So compelling was the political need to reach out to the new Democrats, that even McDuffie was led to endorse the steering committee concept in announcing for the speakership.[56] Rainey became the first speaker since Champ Clark to come to the office committed to reform, and like Clark he was committed to decentralizing reforms.

The deal that made Rainey speaker revealed deep divisions within the Democratic party in the House. McDuffie was the establishment candidate, supported by Garner. Rainey was the liberal candidate, Cullen the Tammany machine candidate, and Byrns the candidate of the border south. The situation was very unstable. Over a hundred new Democratic members held the balance of power in a congressional party that had enjoyed extreme stability for almost three decades. The seniority system was threatened by the presence of so many new members, whose personal interest could not have been immediately served by it. Since the seniority principle lay clearly in favor of the South, the southerners were particularly threatened by the reform tendencies of the new northern members. The seniority rule had become the foundation of the Democratic congressional party, and for the phalanx of new members to have usurped it would have threatened the underlying coalition upon which the Democratic House majority had been built. In these circumstances the election of Rainey as speaker served both to assuage the new members and to preserve the seniority principle.[57]

The changes wrought in the committee system by Speaker Rainey were slight. For the most part the Democrats remained bound by seniority. Among forty-five standing committee chairmen of the House there were no uncompensated violations of seniority.[58] McDuffie of Alabama, twice frustrated in his bid for the speakership, was rewarded by the chairmanship of the Insular Affairs Committee in spite of the fact that he had not been a member of it in the preceding Congress. Major committee assignments were denied to freshman members: Rules, Ways and Means, and Appropriations received no freshman appointees. In the case of the Rules Committee, two southerners from the Seventy-second Congress, Garett of Texas and McMillan of South Carolina, were replaced by two other southerners, Howard Smith of Virginia and William J. Driver of Arkansas. In the case of Ways and Means, a clear geographical shift took place. The departing members from the Seventy-second Congress included three southerners and one member from the North; the new appointees in the Seventy-third Congress consisted of three northerners, one member from the border, and one member from the South. The only southern appointee, Jere Cooper of Tennessee, came from a district contiguous with that of the majority leader, Joseph Byrns. His appointment, along with those of Charles F. West of Ohio and John W. Boehne, Jr., of Indiana, violated the seniority principle, as Cooper was a third-termer and West and Boehne were in their second terms. The makeup of other legislative committees was naturally heavily influenced by the appointment of new northern Democrats. Banking and Currency received five new Democrats, all from the North; Education, seven—five from the North, two from the South; Civil Service, nine—seven North, one border, one South; Foreign Affairs, nine—seven North, one border, one South; Rivers and Harbors, six—four North, one border, one South; and Interstate and Foreign Commerce, four—all northern.[59]

With such a heavy infusion of new northern members into the Democratic party, it might have been reasonable to expect that the continued adherence to the seniority principle would eventually have led to the rise of northern influence in the House. Instead, there were a number of southern and border Democrats already serving who later rose to positions of great influence: Howard W. Smith of Virginia served from 1931 to 1967 and was a dominant chairman of the Rules Committee in the 1950s and 1960s; Wright Patman of Texas, a relatively liberal southerner, served from 1929 to 1976, and became chairman of the Banking and Currency Committee; Clarence Cannon of Missouri served from 1923 to 1964, and was the longest-serving chairman of the Appropriations Committee; Carl Vinson of Georgia served from 1914 to 1965 and dominated the Naval and Armed Services committees for decades; and Sam Rayburn of Texas served from 1913 to 1961 and became chairman of the Interstate and Foreign Commerce Committee, majority leader, and the longest-serving speaker. Of the class of 1933, William M. Colmer of Mississippi served until 1973 and became chairman of the Rules Committee. Perhaps the most influential northern member of that class was Thomas J. O'Brien of Illinois, who for decades spoke for the votes of the Cook County delegation in the House. Other northerners did not serve long enough to rise to the top of the committee system.

Speaker Rainey's commitment to diffuse power in the House ran head-on into the presidency of Franklin Roosevelt and his first hundred days. However much the speaker and his supporters might have wanted collegial decision making, the country demanded immediate action that could only come about by firm control of the House. Rainey did appoint a steering and policy committee for the Democrats, and created a variety of special committees designed to involve members in the canvassing of opinion. But the real business of the House was being done at the other end of Pennsylvania Avenue, and Speaker Rainey's job was primarily to see to it that the president's program was expedited. In order to accomplish this, the speaker held up the appointment of most committees during the special session called by Roosevelt to deal with the crisis. He appointed a special committee to deal with the Economy Act, a budget-cutting measure that gave broad power to the president to cut federal expenditures, and he used the Rules Committee to bring the New Deal legislation to the House under special orders that severely limited the capacity of the membership to amend the bills as reported by committees.

In a crisis atmosphere and with firm leadership by the White House, Speaker Rainey acted as though he had real power, but he actually had little. Rainey lacked Garner's force of character, and his powers under the rules and his political leverage were extremely limited. Although he enjoyed a vast majority in comparison with Garner, that fact turned against him. Garner could appeal for party loyalty in a situation where every vote counted, but Rainey always had to fight the assumption that marginal votes were not needed. Under a Republican administration, Garner controlled such patronage as was available to the Democrats; but under Roosevelt all federal patronage was controlled by Postmaster General and Democratic National Committee Chairman James Farley. Thus, Rainey was a speaker who lacked both the resources and disposition to be a strong party leader.[60]

The support that President Roosevelt received from the Congress in 1933 facilitated cooperation between the White House and the Democratic leadership in the House of Representatives, and appeared to presage a productive 1934. But the president's relations with the Congress suffered a downturn in 1934 that fostered poor relations between the president, Speaker Rainey, and Majority Leader Byrns. Among the solutions advanced for the nation's economic crisis was the old Bryanite program of free silver. Rainey, an old Bryanite himself, favored the plan in spite of Roosevelt's opposition. When in early 1934 the president vetoed an economy bill that he regarded as involving excessive expenditures, the House voted overwhelmingly to override the veto and Rainey was faulted for inadequate leadership. The president's frustrations in dealing with the Congress soon gave rise to rumors that he intended to see Rainey replaced in the next congress, but any intention that he might have had was rendered moot by Rainey's death in August of 1934.[61]

The death of the speaker opened the door for the New Dealers to place their own man at the helm of the House. Sam Rayburn of Texas, the chairman of the House Interstate and Foreign Commerce Committee, was the favored candidate of the Brain-trust. Two factors militated against Rayburn's selection. Majority Leader Byrns was the heir apparent. The deal that had made Rainey speaker and Byrns majority leader was bottomed on a coalition of northeastern, border, and midwestern Democrats that still held a majority in the Democratic caucus. Also, many members were concerned about the power of the Texas delegation. Texas would control six major chairmanships in the next congress in any case, and John Nance Garner of Texas presided over the Senate. To have both the House and Senate led by persons from the same state was not without precedent: in the Harding administration the vice president has been Coolidge and the speaker had been Gillett, both of Massachusetts. But the influence of Texas under a Garner-Rayburn arrangement would have been even more powerful due to the number of committee chairmanships controlled by the state. In the face of all of these factors Sam Rayburn came to the evident conclusion: "I cannot," he said, "be elected."[62]

Rayburn's withdrawal left the field to Byrns, and with the support of the Pennsylvania delegation voting en bloc he won an easy victory. As their new majority leader the Democrats selected William B. Bankhead of Alabama, who had supported McDuffie in 1933 and was associated with the old Garner faction of the party. In Byrns and Bankhead the Democrats selected men known more for gentility than forcefulness. Joseph Byrns enjoyed likening himself to Uncle Joe Cannon, but age and demeanor were the only Cannon-like qualities he possessed.[63] Byrns's election was in part a result of his work as chairman of the congressional campaign committee. With his help the Democrats had actually increased their representation in the House in the off-year election of 1934. Many members felt themselves indebted to him. Still, it is a striking fact that, having a clear majority of members and having with Rainey's election broken the grip of the southern establishment for the first time, the northerners would acquiesce in a return of the speakership to the South. Byrns's support by Pennsylvania was mirrored by the support in Illinois and Michigan that ensured Bankhead's election as floor leader. There was no paucity of northern candidates in either case. In the last seriously contested speakership election in the twentieth century, Byrns was challenged by McCormack of Massachusetts, Greenwood of Indiana, and O'Conner and Mead of New York. Bankhead was challenged by McCormack, Mead, and O'Conner. The acquiescence of the North in the leadership of the South is hard to explain; perhaps the power of the southern committee chairmen was such as to influence northern votes. The newer members from the North either had to bind together and sweep the slate clean, abolishing the seniority principle along the way, or seek their respective advantages individually under the seniority rule. Evidently a sufficient number chose the latter.

Like his two immediate predecessors, William Bankhead was also destined for attenuated service in the speakership. He had sought the majority leadership in 1932 with little hope of attaining it, since McDuffie, a principal contender for the speakership, was also from Alabama. Bankhead instead took the chair of the Rules Committee, which had became a powerful and independent post. Upon Rainey's death Bankhead emerged as the establishment candidate for majority leader, and this time McDuffie no longer stood in the way. Sam Rayburn's aspirations were once again thwarted by Garner's position as vice president and the numerous positions held by the Texas delegation, and so Bankhead became the floor leader for the Democrats under Speaker Byrns. With Byrns's untimely death in 1935, Bankhead became speaker.

Speaker Bankhead was also beset by health problems. He had suffered his first major heart attack as early as 1932, and another followed in 1935. He labored with a weak heart during the remainder of his life, and this condition seriously impeded his ability to provide effective leadership for the Democrats. A distinguished man from a very well known family (his father and brother were U.S. senators and his daughter Tallulah was a famous actress), Bankhead was an adept parliamentarian and presided over the House with dignity if not with vigor. Although he was a loyal supporter of the New Deal, he was less than forceful. "His way of rule was not the harsh tsarism of Joe Cannon, the rough and tumble domination of Nick Longworth," said one account at the time of his death. "Partly from natural bent, partly of necessity, he used the gentler arts of persuasion, parliamentary device, friendship."[64] The combination of a gentle manner and a poor physical constitution seriously inhibited Bankhead's ability to lead. The House was not without leadership, however, for the real direction of its affairs during Bankhead's reign lay in the hands of its majority leader, Sam Rayburn, who had in 1936 finally overcome his liabilities and been elected floor leader with the support of the White House. Working in close cooperation with the administration, Sam Rayburn provided the strength that Bankhead lacked. When, in 1940, Bankhead succumbed to his third heart attack, Rayburn assumed the formal title to go along with the power that he had exercised since 1937, that of the speaker of the House.

Sam Rayburn

Sam Rayburn had come to Congress in 1913 just as the Democratic party was taking control of the government. Contrary to his later advice to young members, Rayburn was unwilling to take a back seat to the House establishment, and spoke out for populist causes, particularly the regulation of railroads and public utilities. During the era of King Caucus there was little enough that a new member from Texas could do to pass legislation, but within a few years Rayburn became a protégé of the influential John Nance Garner and a favorite at the Wilson White House. So stubborn was he in the pursuit of his causes, however, that in time he came to be at odds with President Wilson over his aggressive support of reformist legislation. By the end of the decade Rayburn found himself roadblocked within his own party and then, in 1919, sealed off by the return of the Republican party to power. During the long period "in the wilderness," as it has been called, Garner and Rayburn worked to establish influence in the House Democratic party.[65] Garner led in opposing Secretary Mellon's tax policies, while Rayburn labored in the shadows, slowly earning respect and influence among his peers. By the steady operation of the seniority principle, he rose to become the ranking member of the Interstate and Foreign Commerce Committee, and with the Democrats' return to control of the House in 1931, he became its chairman.

Rayburn now had his chance to show what he could do, and the record of accomplishment is remarkable. No speaker has matched Rayburn's record of legislative accomplishment as chairman of the Interstate and Foreign Commerce Committees between 1933 and 1936. It was, to be sure, a period of legislative activism, and Rayburn's success was due in part to the influence of the Roosevelt White House and the size of the Democratic majorities. Still, commentators uniformly stress the substantial nature of his accomplishments, and they credit them to Rayburn himself. Enacted under Rayburn's leadership were the Securities Act of 1933 (establishing the Securities and Exchange Commission), the Railroad Holding Company Act of 1933, the Stock Exchange Act of 1934, the Public Utilities Holding Act of 1935, the Rural Electrification Administration Act of 1936, and the Federal Communications Act of 1934 (establishing the Federal Communications Commission). Rayburn achieved within three short years all that he had aspired for in 1913 and had failed to achieve in the intervening time. Just as important, he succeeded in establishing his reputation as a man who could make the legislative process work. By 1936 his reputation and alliances were made, and he awaited his opportunity to ascend to the party leadership. Speaker Byrns's death in 1936 opened the door for Rayburn, and Speaker Bankhead's death four years later closed it behind him; Sam Rayburn, in 1940, became the leader of the House Democratic party and was to remain so until his death in 1961.[66]

Rayburn was a product of the system that he was chosen to lead. A southerner, he could speak for and to the South. A former committee chairman, he could address the committee barons as first among equals. A party leader, he could articulate and symbolize the principles for which the party stood. A New Deal loyalist, he could present the administration's positions to the House. And, a disciple of the Garner-Longworth Board of Education, he could reach across the aisle to work with the Republican leadership.[67] If the situation into which he fell was complex, his own complexities were the mirror image of it. He had his chance to provide for the House of Representatives the sort of strong leadership to which he had long aspired. But even with his long years of service, his proven record as a committee chairman and party leader, and his personal determination to assert himself, it was by no means apparent that he would become the legendary figure he later did. "Neither his history nor his personality affords a reliable clue to the future," so astute an observer as Joseph Alsop could say in 1941.[68] Rayburn's future would be shaped as much by the nature of the House of Representatives as an institution as by the capacities of Sam Rayburn the man. It remained to be seen what impact the man might have upon the institution he was called upon to lead.

The contextual theory of leadership argues that congressional leaders must adapt their personal styles to the institutional context; successful leaders do so, unsuccessful leaders do not.[69] According to this view, Sam Rayburn was a successful speaker because he was able to adapt his style to the institutional context in which he found himself. Obviously, successful party leaders must adapt themselves to circumstances that change over time; however, congressional leaders also have personal and political backgrounds that shape their characters and affect their "styles." The process of achieving a leadership position involves the making of commitments to persons, to positions, and to beliefs. When a person arrives at the leadership level, he cannot easily divest himself of the influences that have molded his character. In 1940, after twenty-seven years of service in the House, Sam Rayburn was a wholly formed man whose capacity to adapt his style to circumstances was limited. Recognizing this, persons who worked with Rayburn have expressed doubt about his capacity to have led the House under the circumstances of the 1970s and 1980s.[70]

The contextual thesis also gives insufficient attention to the manner in which a leader can shape the institutional context within which he is called upon to lead. Certainly a speaker cannot ordinarily affect the broad environmental factors that shape the House; he cannot easily go out and form a new political party for example. Yet a speaker can have a significant impact upon the attitudes of the members of the House. The norms that shape legislative behavior are amenable to the influence of the speaker as a power wielder and as a role-model. Sam Rayburn spent decades telling new members that "to get along, go along." Might we not presume that many of the thousands of members whom he advised believed him? In fact, the character of the House of Representatives in the 1940s and 1950s was greatly reflective of Sam Rayburn's character and values. Comity, fair-dealing, honesty, diligence, and devotion to the House were the norms that shaped the midcentury House as a legislative institution. It is not merely coincidental that they were the precise values for which Sam Rayburn stood. If the contextualist thesis tends to overstate the capacity of a speaker to vary his style according to circumstances, it also tends to understate the effect that a leader can have in molding the institution he is called upon to lead.

The character of Sam Rayburn's speakership varied according to two major factors: the presidents with whom he served and the ideological divisions within the two parties, the latter a reflection of the changing policy agenda. Four distinct periods are discernible in the Rayburn speakership. The first three correspond generally to the administrations of Franklin Roosevelt, Harry Truman, and Dwight Eisenhower. The last period began in approximately 1957 and concluded with Rayburn's death. These four periods are made distinct because of the different circumstances in which Rayburn was called upon to lead. Rayburn did not change significantly as a man or as a party leader. Nor did the institutional context of the House of Representatives change significantly during the twenty-one years of Rayburn's leadership. But the issue agenda of American national politics did change fundamentally during Rayburn's tenure. The changing policy agenda was accompanied by turnover in administrations and in partisan control of the Congress, and in the late 1950s by an influx of liberal Democratic members.

Sam Rayburn was a New Dealer, but as the 1940 election approached he was ambivalent about the prospects of a third term as president for FDR. John Nance Garner was staunchly opposed to three-term presidencies and stood to benefit if the anti-Roosevelt forces in the party settled upon a draft-Garner movement as the best way to head off a Roosevelt run. The Garner candidacy put Rayburn in a difficult spot, since he was loyal to Roosevelt. Eventually, Rayburn endorsed Garner on the premise that the president would not seek a third term. When Roosevelt decided to run again and Garner withdrew, Rayburn's support went to the president. From 1940 onward, Rayburn was committed to Roosevelt, and became his most powerful ally on the Hill.

By the time that Sam Rayburn became speaker in 1941, his relationship with Roosevelt was cemented. From the outset of the New Deal the president had relied on Rayburn's support as chairman of the House Interstate and Foreign Commerce Committee in enacting some of the most controversial New Deal legislation. During the period from 1937 to 1941, while Bankhead was speaker, Rayburn had carried the burden of defending the Roosevelt program during the most difficult period of FDR's presidency. The Court-packing scheme of 1937 had triggered the rise of the conservative coalition in the Congress, and isolationists were opposed to any American involvement in a second world war. Anti-Roosevelt sentiment was strong in Texas, and Roosevelt understood that Rayburn's support was often given at the risk of some political danger at home.

In 1941, however, Roosevelt was in a far stronger position after his 1940 reelection than he had been before, and Rayburn was widely regarded as a more forceful leader than Bankhead had been. The policy agenda was driven by conditions abroad. The war in Europe and the Pacific grew steadily more serious, and while isolationist sentiment was still strong it became increasingly possible to argue from the point of view of the national interest. In leading the administration's fight for Lend-Lease and the extension of the draft, Rayburn was able to win the support of most House Democrats. During these early years of his speakership, he was an aggressive right arm for administration policy. His efforts were marked as much by horse-trading as by appeals to conscience.[71] When Roosevelt sought funding for Lend-Lease, Rayburn informed him that it could not pass unless the spending was to flow through the normal House appropriations process, where logrolling was a way of life.[72] In 1937 Majority Leader Rayburn had traded district projects for support of the WPA and the Fair Labor Standards Act, and in 1941 Speaker Rayburn logrolled to make America the arsenal of democracy. Sam Rayburn's pattern of brokering was firmly set; he became the quintessential Democratic speaker. It should not be inferred, however, that Rayburn's service as a wartime speaker was without difficulty. The strength of anti-Roosevelt and antiwar sentiment in the country was evidenced in the results of the 1942 election, which saw the Democratic majority in the House decline from a robust 268–162 to a bare 218–208 margin. It was perhaps propitious that this, the narrowest of Rayburn's majorities, was brought to him after the war was under way, since the demands of war and a wartime economy lent leverage to presidential and congressional leadership.

Later Rayburn was proud of professing his equality with the presidents with whom he had served. "I have served under no president," he would say, "but I have served with eight of them."[73] Just as with the aphorism "To get along, go along," this famous Rayburn saying is a coloration of the truth. For in fact, Sam Rayburn always viewed it as his obligation to support a president of his own party, and in the area of foreign affairs, a president of the opposite party. As much as any other person, Rayburn helped establish the traditions of legislative deference to the presidency, and of bipartisanship in foreign policy. Rayburn was willing to caution Roosevelt in private, but once FDR had made up his mind, Rayburn felt obligated to support the president.[74] Although of dramatically different backgrounds and temperaments, Rayburn and Roosevelt were able to forge an effective working partnership. Rayburn's first period as speaker was therefore defined by his relationship with Roosevelt and wartime circumstances. Roosevelt was neither a normal president nor a president functioning in a normal situation. He was an overwhelmingly popular president leading his country in time of great danger. Rayburn's role as the president's right arm in the House was only one of the roles that he was eventually to play as speaker.

In FDR, Rayburn worked with a strong-willed and popular president during wartime. Left unanswered was the question of whether Rayburn would assume a more independent posture under a less powerful president or a president of the opposite party. As it turned out, Rayburn was given a chance to try his hand in both sets of circumstances. Harry Truman was in a decidedly weak position during 1945–48. In contrast to Roosevelt, Truman was little known and less appreciated. Truman and Rayburn were established friends by 1945, and Truman was with Rayburn in the Board of Education when news of Roosevelt's death reached him. Rayburn believed that Roosevelt had been a great president, but his bond of friendship to Truman was a strong cement, and from the outset Rayburn was Truman's staunchest ally on the Hill.[75] While Truman enjoyed the honeymoon naturally accorded a new president under trying circumstances, he did not quickly win the respect of the Washington community or the country. He needed the support of a powerful speaker, and Rayburn was willing to help.

Truman's twenty-one point program was an attempt to establish an agenda for his presidency distinct from the New Deal and the aura of Franklin Roosevelt, but it was too sweeping in its scope and insufficiently considered in detail. As a purely political matter Rayburn felt that the twenty-one points were too much too soon. As a loyal Democrat and a friend of Truman's, though, he accepted his obligation to support the president's program when he could do so without jeopardizing his district. In 1946 the Truman administration had some significant successes, including the Full Employment Act, the National School Lunch Act, and the Atomic Energy Act. Still, most of the twenty-one point program died in the Congress, much of it in the committee rooms. Rayburn could help Truman on the floor, but he could not budge the barons if they did not want to be moved.

Truman's most serious defeats came at the hands of the "do-nothing" Eightieth Congress in 1947–48. This was the first congress controlled by the Republicans since 1930, and was led by Speaker Joseph W. Martin of Massachusetts. It is interesting to consider the manner in which the Republicans governed the House after such a long period out of power. To those persons for whom consistency is an intrinsic good, Republican principles of political economy, and the policies that typically flow from them, must seem things of great beauty. During a time when the federal government was funded by tariff revenues, the Republicans stood consistently for high tariffs. Once the Democrats had launched the federal income tax as a major source of revenue for the government, the Republicans established tax cutting as the basis of their economic program, and they have rarely deviated from that principle. In the 1920s, Secretary of the Treasury Andrew Mellon led a tenacious Republican attack on income tax rates, and Democratic adversaries such as John Nance Garner and Wright Patman established the enduring Democratic complaint that Republican tax cuts returned more money to the rich than to the poor. The Republicans countered by arguing that tax cuts would spawn economic growth to everyone's advantage, and that the regressivity of the Republican tax cuts was in direct proportion to the progressivity of the Democratic tax code.

The New Deal and World War II had led to a dramatic expansion of the federal share of GNP, just as the New Freedom and World War I had done.[76] The federal share always increased during Democratic administrations and the Republicans always fought to restrain federal spending and cut taxes. In 1947, H.R. 1 under Speaker Martin was an income tax bill that reduced tax rates across the rate schedule by amounts ranging from 30 percent at the bottom to 10 percent at the top.[77] While the percentage cuts were progressive, the aggregate savings were regressive: the rich saved more dollars than the poor. The Democrats alleged the program to be unfair while the Republicans pointed out that this result was due to Democratic policies previously established. The situation in 1948 was a rerun of the battle between Mellon and Garner in the 1920s. Along with tax cuts, the Republicans proposed to cut spending. Led by the conservative chairman of the Appropriations Committee, John "Meat Axe" Taber of New York, the Republicans drafted a bill calling for an across the board reduction in expenditures.[78] The Democrats objected on the grounds that some priorities should be established for spending cuts. The Democrats wanted to preserve both the programmatic aspects of the policies to which they had become wedded, and the logrolling politics that had given rise to those policies in the first place. Democrats like to bargain and trade favors; their politics is that of coalition building. Republicans like to do things across the board; theirs is the politics of economic principle. Democrats are not without principles, nor are Republicans immune to deals. But when either party has been positioned to govern, it has governed according to its own inclinations. Joe Martin's task as leader of a Republican party with a solid majority was far different than that which usually confronted Sam Rayburn. Rayburn always had to worry about the delicate relationship of his southern and northern wings, and in fact often had to reach across the aisle to pick up votes that were not available to him within his own party. His technique was most often classical Democratic logrolling. Martin could appeal to the natural tendency of his party. When H.R. 1 hit the floor of the House, Martin lost only three Republican votes.[79]

Joe Martin had been a member of the House since 1925 and had served as minority leader for the Republicans since 1939. He was a product of the Longworth machine and renewed the leadership mechanisms put in place by the Longworth faction when it unseated James

R. Mann in 1919. Policy matters were taken first to the Republican Steering Committee where general guidelines were established. The legislative committees would then draft bills in general conformity with the approach sanctioned by the Steering Committee.[80] Martin's task was to enunciate forcefully the principles of traditional Republicanism, and it was possible for him to rally a nearly unanimous majority because his policy views were almost universally shared by Republicans. Martin has been described as "a thoroughly uncomplicated Republican partisan," and at the outset of the Eightieth Congress this approach seemed to suffice.[81]

A second key to Martin's success lay in the well-considered decision to limit the focus of the party's legislative program to those areas where there was a sufficient consensus within the party to assure passage. Other principal areas of legislation broached by the Republicans were labor law reform, leading eventually to the passage of the Taft-Hartley Act; a limitation on terms of office for presidents; and the lifting of wartime economic restrictions. These were all areas in which the party had widespread agreement. There was some Republican sentiment, mostly in the Senate, for innovation. A group of Republicans led by Senator Taft had legislative ambitions that outstripped those of the more cautious House. Initiatives from that quarter led to rifts within the Republican party.[82] Truman was able to cause trouble within Republican ranks by proposing legislation that had a constituency among the more liberal Republicans. The record of the Eightieth Congress was, therefore, not entirely one of harmonious Republicanism, and as that Congress wore on, it became increasingly difficult for the liberal and conservative wings of the party to reconcile. Considering the modest legislative ambitions of the conservative Republicans and the partisan division of the government, it is little surprise that the Eightieth Congress could be effectively characterized as having done nothing.

The Republican-controlled Eightieth Congress could not attain its policy goals by fiat, because Harry Truman was no pushover and the powers at his disposal were considerable. He moved quickly to ensure that the Republicans would get no help from the lower echelons of the administration, he used his patronage powers to maximum effect, and he stood prepared to wield the veto when necessary.[83] In the House of Representatives, Truman had the support of the still influential Rayburn, but now Rayburn found himself in an uncomfortable position. Having for years relied upon his close relationship with Joe Martin, it illbehooved him to treat Martin less well than Martin had treated him. The relatively monolithic character of the Republican majority afforded few options for useful interparty coalition building except in foreign policy, and it was not in Rayburn's nature to engage in a partisan dispute with Martin. Nor was it in his interest; Sam Rayburn expected to be speaker again.

Truman's strategy in dealing with the Republicans made Rayburn's situation more difficult. The president wished to assert a progressive program of his own, protect the fundamental elements of the New Deal, and establish a record upon which to run for election in 1948. He planned to use the Republican leadership in the Congress as a public whipping boy. At the same time, Truman wanted to foster a spirit of bipartisanship in foreign policy that would enable him to pursue a constructive role in rebuilding Europe and in creating a new postwar international order. Under these circumstances Rayburn served as his bridge to Martin, and while Truman was largely unsuccessful in passing his domestic program, he was successful in attaining his other goals. The fundamental elements of the New Deal were preserved, bipartisanship in foreign policy was maintained, and a record was established that led to his eventual election in 1948.[84]

Truman's hand was naturally stronger after his victory in 1948, but the circumstances were still difficult. The Congress was now back in the hands of the Democrats, but this only served to raise expectations in the face of a conservative coalition that seemed to emerge into public visibility only when the Democrats were in power. Truman's second administration was marked by conflict throughout. He battled the unions, the steel companies, the Koreans, and General MacArthur. His major legislative accomplishments were in the area of foreign policy, while only some parts of his Fair Deal were enacted into law.[85] The Fair Deal was even more sweeping in its scope than had been the twenty-one points of Truman's first administration. It addressed such divisive issues as civil rights, the elimination of the oil depletion allowance, the federalization of offshore oil, and the revision of the Taft-Hartley labor law. On many Fair Deal issues the House was controlled by the conservative coalition. Rayburn, whose personal and political ties to the coalition were strong, made an agreement with the president: if his Fair Deal bills cleared the committees they would get their day on the floor.[86] However, many bills were killed in committee, and on the floor they were vulnerable to conservative coalition substitutes. Many of these issues were politically difficult for Rayburn at home. He preferred to maintain a very low profile on civil rights issues, and while he had opposed Taft-Hartley, he was unwilling to take a strong stand in favor of liberalizing the labor law. On the federalization of the Tidelands offshore oil area and the elimination of the oil depletion allowance, he was directly opposed to Truman.[87] To assist Truman, Rayburn pushed through the Democratic caucus a "twenty-one day rule" that allowed committees to bring to the floor bills that the Rules Committee had blocked for twenty-one days; but the rule was invoked only twice in the Eighty-first Congress and eight times in the Eighty-second Congress.[88] As Truman's popularity ebbed due to the Korean War, the steel seizure, and the natural atrophy of a lame duck presidency, Rayburn became more cautious in supporting the president. The speaker's commitment to support Truman was constrained by the power of the committee barons and the political ramifications of the president's policy agenda in his district.

With the election of Eisenhower and a Republican Congress in 1952, Rayburn found himself once again the minority leader. This time, Eisenhower was in the White House and Lyndon Baines Johnson had been elected as the Senate minority leader. These two men, their character and their ambitions, did much to shape the remainder of Sam Rayburn's years as speaker. Dwight Eisenhower was a natural electoral politician, a seasoned diplomat, and, as recent scholarship has indicated, a shrewder backroom dealer than his political adversaries realized.[89] He had won the nomination of the Republican party over Robert Taft, the ideological favorite of traditional Republicans, and Ike recognized the need to work with the Democratic leadership in the Congress, since conservative Republicans would be likely to oppose many of his moderate proposals. In the Congress he found in Sam Rayburn and Lyndon Johnson men who had reasons for wanting to work with him. As always, upon assuming office the Republicans sought to lower taxes and cut expenditures. In spite of a recession, conservative Republicans in the Congress proposed tax cuts in the face of higher governmental outlays. When Eisenhower submitted his first tax proposals in 1953, they were opposed by Chairman Daniel Reed of the House Ways and Means Committee. It became necessary for Speaker Martin to throw the full weight of the leadership against Reed in order to head off a fight. In a brazen move, Speaker Martin called a meeting of the Republican members of the Ways and Means Committee and invited the chairman to attend. Rejoicing in the Republicans' difficulties, Rayburn called for a hands-off policy toward the Republican squabbles. He knew that with friends like Reed, Eisenhower would eventually need the support of congressional Democrats.[90]

Rayburn and Johnson enunciated a policy of bipartisan support for administration proposals that were consistent with traditional Democratic aims. Democrats would not oppose for the sake of opposition, but would offer constructive support wherever possible. This strategy was an acknowledgment of Eisenhower's popularity, but also reflected the moderate tendencies of Johnson and Rayburn. That the cooperative approach had payoffs for the Texans became immediately apparent.

While they had opposed Truman's policy of federalizing Tideland oil property, they were pleased to support the Eisenhower policy of giving to the states control over their coastlines (in the case of Texas, up to one hundred miles out). Eisenhower's first bill-signing ceremony as president was for the Holland bill to return the Tideland oil lands to the states, and there standing smiling beside him was Minority Leader Sam Rayburn.[91] Ironically, this occurred at precisely the same time that Speaker Martin was doing battle with Chairman Reed over the president's tax bill. In pursuing a bipartisan legislative strategy, Eisenhower found it easier to work with Rayburn than with Johnson. Ike had been born in Denison, Texas, in Rayburn's district, and while the president had never lived there for any length of time, the fact lent to their relationship a sense of common experience. The two men also shared many of the same values. Eisenhower's relationship with Rayburn was closer than his relationship with Johnson. Whereas in Rayburn, Eisenhower found a man noted for fidelity to his word, Johnson was perceived by Eisenhower to be publicly cooperative but privately obstructive. In some cases Eisenhower found it necessary to take extraordinary measures to pressure Johnson.[92]

The combined effects of the recession and the Republicans' inability to cope with it led to the election of a Democratic Congress in 1954. Instead of merely waiting for a Republican government to act, the Democrats now were bound to play a more active role. The question confronting the Democratic leadership in the Congress was, should they seek accommodation with Eisenhower or should they confront him with programs of their own design? In choosing the former policy, Rayburn and Johnson pursued centrist politics with which both they and the president could live. In this policy, however, lay the seeds of intraparty conflict among the Democrats that would break open during Eisenhower's second administration. In understanding why the Democrats pursued accommodation rather than confrontation with Eisenhower, it is necessary to consider the unique relationship between Lyndon Johnson and Sam Rayburn.

Lyndon Johnson had come to Washington in 1931 as a congressional secretary, and Sam Rayburn had taken him under his wing. Later, Rayburn would become known as the mentor of many young congressmen, but Lyndon Johnson was the first and the closest. Over the next two decades Rayburn assisted Johnson as his career blossomed. With Rayburn's assistance, Johnson was appointed by Roosevelt as the Texas director of the National Youth Administration. In 1938 LBJ was elected to the Congress. A decade later he won a narrow election to the Senate. In 1953 he won the post of Senate minority leader, and when the Democrats regained their congressional majority in 1955, he became the majority leader. Now the two Texans, mentor and protégé, held the two highest legislative posts in the land. Rayburn was in the twilight of his career, but for Johnson, there were higher rungs to climb. Both men understood that the presidency would be within Johnson's reach, and much would depend upon the manner in which they approached their task as the leaders of Congress.[93] They settled on a policy of constructive opposition to Eisenhower.[94] So long as the president did not attempt to undo the essentials of the New Deal and Fair Deal, Rayburn and Johnson would work to pass his program. Often this entailed compromise on the part of the Democrats, but as often it required the administration to accommodate Democratic policies. In the House of Representatives, Rayburn was able to hide behind the conservative coalition and the strength of southern committee chairmen. His firm policy of supporting the chairmen was in large part rooted in the fact that moderate-to-conservative policies would result. This accommodating approach served both Johnson and Rayburn well—the one wanted national influence and the other wanted domestic tranquility in the House. But it did not so well serve the interests and ambitions of the liberal wing of the Democratic party, which was becoming more restless in the Congress and in the national party. In recounting this part of the story, the balance of Sam Rayburn's speakership may be placed in clearer perspective.

In 1954, when the Democrats returned to power in the Congress and Lyndon Johnson became Senate majority leader, Paul Butler, a lawyer from South Bend, Indiana, was chosen as the chairman of the Democratic National Committee.[95] Butler was a staunch liberal and a supporter of Adlai Stevenson. His election was a harbinger of Stevenson's nomination in 1956, as well as an indication of the increasing strength of the liberal wing of the Democratic party. As opposed to the Rayburn-Johnson strategy of accommodation and compromise, Butler believed that the best strategy for the Democrats lay in drawing clear lines between their policies and those of the Republicans. The task of the Democratic Congress in 1954 was to build a record upon which to elect a Democratic president. Rayburn and Johnson recognized the threat to Johnson's ambitions and Rayburn's leadership in the House in the selection of the new national committee chairman. Rayburn traveled to New Orleans to attend the meeting of the committee in an attempt to head off the Butler appointment, but by the time he arrived the choice had been made.[96] With the Stevenson forces now in control of the national party apparatus, all the two Texans could do was to preserve their own influence in the Congress.

Adlai Stevenson's two presidential campaigns caused a serious rift in the Texas Democratic party, with popular governor Allan Shivers leading the conservative faction of the party that opposed Stevenson. The "Shivercrat" revolt made life difficult for Johnson and Rayburn, who as the leaders of the Congress had to support the Democratic party's nominee. At times, Texas politics put a strain on the relationship between the two congressional leaders. But looming larger was the problem created by Paul Butler and the Democratic National Committee. After Stevenson's devastating loss to Eisenhower in 1956, Butler called for the establishment of a national Democratic Advisory Committee, paraphrasing the name of a group with whom Rayburn had been allied in Texas in the fight against Shivers. The DAC was to be composed of seventeen nationally prominent Democrats, including Stevenson, Truman, and, from the Congress, Rayburn and Johnson. It was to be chaired by Butler and its function was to plan policy for the Democrats. Rayburn and Johnson emphatically declined to participate on Butler's committee. Their public statements emphasized their roles as elected officers of the government. "We believe," said Rayburn, "it would be a mistake . . . and respectfully decline . . . In the House of Representatives we have 233 Democratic members. I fear if we took a position on an outside committee a great majority would feel we were consulting with somebody else . . . not them."[97] This reason was no doubt sufficient, but it conveniently obscured the underlying political motivation: Rayburn and Johnson had no intention of placing themselves in a subordinate position to the liberals on the DAC. Butler and the DAC proved a consistent thorn in the sides of the two Texans. The committee was not reluctant to take public positions on legislative issues even when they placed it at odds with the party leadership in the Congress. The fact that the membership of the committee was composed of every other major presidential candidate, including John F. Kennedy of Massachusetts, Hubert H. Humphrey of Minnesota, and Stuart Symington of Missouri, prevented Johnson from portraying himself as the national spokesman of the Democrats. The fact that all of the other presidential candidates were more liberal than either Johnson or Rayburn made it difficult for the two Texans to assert national leadership.[98]

Within the Congress liberal sentiment was also growing stronger. In 1957 a group of eighty liberal congressmen read into the Congressional Record a "liberal manifesto" that asserted the need for strong Democratic leadership in passing a party program. While such a program would face the likelihood of Eisenhower vetoes, the House liberals shared Butler's view that it was important to establish a record upon which to challenge the Republicans in 1958 and 1960. Many liberal members of the House had come to chafe under Rayburn's conservative leadership. They began to hold him to account for a legislative system that shut them out of positions of influence. Majority Leader John W.

McCormack and Minority Whip Carl Albert, in line of succession to the speakership, did not sign the manifesto. Interestingly, staunchly liberal Thomas P. "Tip" O'Neill, Jr., of Massachusetts, an obscure member of the Rules Committee, and Richard Bolling of Missouri, a known aspirant to the throne, did not sign it either.[99]

The liberals began to meet on a regular basis in the office of Congressman Eugene McCarthy of Minnesota, and became known as McCarthy's Mavericks. Staff was shared on an informal basis. In 1959 they moved to formalize the alliance, and the Democratic Study Group was formed.[100] Rayburn opposed the establishment of the DSG in concept and in execution, recognizing in it a threat to his own leadership in the House. Rayburn's success as speaker had resided largely in his ability to arrange informal coalitions of southern conservatives and northern liberals. This process of coalition forming had usually been accomplished on a person-to-person, case-by-case basis. The formalization of the liberal bloc would lead to intraparty bargaining little conducive to the kind of leadership that Sam Rayburn could provide. Finally, there was a simple substantive ground for objecting to the DSG: it was too liberal for Mr. Sam.

Rayburn's reservations about the DSG proved well-founded. During the second Eisenhower administration, the liberal reformers pressed for House consideration of major legislative initiatives in housing, education, civil rights, and labor. The DSG was not alone responsible for creating the pressure for legislative action; major interest groups brought pressure to bear upon the government and even the Republican administration felt the need to respond to the entreaties of civil rights groups, labor reformers, and urban mayors. Still, the liberal tide pressed Speaker Rayburn between the rock of southern conservative influence in the House (especially among the committee chairmen) and the hard place of rising liberal expectations. His response is instructive.[101]

The first major initiative of the liberals was voting rights legislation. The bill was heavily opposed in the South, and the key to successful passage lay in breaking the back of the anticipated southern filibuster in the Senate. In the House, a combination of liberal Democrats and Republicans held the balance of power, provided that the control of the Rules Committee could be broken. With Speaker Rayburn's tacit support, the civil rights bill moved through the House in 1956 toward final passage. However, nobody was anxious to bring the issue to a head in an election year. Both Republicans and Democrats were wary of the political fallout no matter what the legislation actually accomplished. Consequently, the House Democratic leadership decided to delay floor consideration until late enough in the legislative session to preclude Senate consideration. When the House-approved bill was finally sent over to the Senate, Senate Majority Leader Lyndon Johnson sent it to its deathbed in the Judiciary Committee, chaired by conservative southerner James O. Eastland of Mississippi.

The following year afforded better prospects. With a new Congress in full bloom, there was little excuse for delay. Once again the House passed a civil rights bill designed to lend teeth to federal enforcement of black voting rights in the South. The key issue lay in the disposition of criminal charges against persons found guilty of obstructing voting rights. Southerners wanted jury trials in the expectation that white southern juries would enforce the law leniently; civil rights groups wanted federal judges to hand out the penalties, hoping that the judges would take a sterner view of the law. In the end, the House bill provided for the trials to be held before the judges. When the House bill reached the Senate, the pitfall of the Judiciary Committee was avoided by holding the bill at the Senate president's desk. Its immediate floor consideration was moved, bypassing Eastland's committee. The Senate debate was prolonged by a filibuster culminating in South Carolina Senator Strom Thurmond's record-setting 24-hour speech.[102] In the end, cloture was invoked and the Senate passed the bill with a weak jury trial provision. As a result of a compromise struck by Speaker Rayburn, Minority Leader Joe Martin, Senate Majority Leader Johnson, and Senate Minority Leader William Knowland of California, the jury trial provision was retained in conference, and the bill was passed into law.

Speaker Rayburn's support of the Civil Rights Act of 1957 has been taken to indicate his firm commitment to the cause of American blacks. If so, a lesson about his speakership is demonstrated by the muted fashion in which this support was manifested. Rayburn refrained from interjecting himself publicly into the debate over the bill. His silence was dictated by a concern for his district and by a concern for his relationships with senior southern committee chairmen. According to the account of then majority whip Carl Albert, Speaker Rayburn sought Majority Leader McCormack's leadership when the bill came to the floor since civil rights was too tough an issue in Rayburn's Texas district.[103] Congressman Richard Bolling of Missouri, who was one of Rayburn's agents on this issue, indicates that the House was well into floor consideration of the bill before he became convinced that the speaker in fact supported it. However strong his personal commitment to the cause of civil rights, Speaker Rayburn was forced to maneuver behind the scenes.[104]

A second example of Rayburn's cautious approach to the liberal agenda came in the area of labor reform.[105] The McClellen Senate investigations, spearheaded by counsel Robert F. Kennedy, had turned up widespread evidence of corruption in some labor unions. There was a clamor for a labor reform bill and the public outcry made the passage of some kind of bill inevitable. There were, however, two thrusts to the reform movement. On one side were those who supported trade unionism but wanted to see the unions cleaned up; on the other side, were those who were hostile to trade unionism itself, mostly Republicans and southern Democrats. The goal of House liberals was to produce a bill that would address the issue of corruption while leaving trade unionism intact. The goal of the administration, House Republicans, and some southern Democrats, was to strike blows at the power of the trade unions. Sam Rayburn had one influential union in his district and had supported union issues during the Roosevelt administration. Still, his district was basically anti-union, and Rayburn tried to maintain a low profile on labor issues. Yet, as a national leader of the Democratic party, he was a supporter of working men and women, many of whom belonged to unions.

Since trade unionism was opposed by many of his constituents, whereas trade union support for the national Democratic party was vital, Rayburn needed a safety valve. Fortunately, one was provided by the unions themselves when they insisted upon a very pro-union bill that accepted reporting requirements but otherwise gutted the Taft-Hartley Act. With the support of Congressmen Stewart Udall of Arizona, Frank Thompson of New Jersey, Lee Metcalf of Montana, and Congresswoman Edith Green of Oregon, a compromise bill was introduced by Congressman Carl Elliot of Alabama. This bill provided for disclosure measures to combat corruption and also included limitations on some union practices. It was supported by leading liberals and by Speaker Rayburn. The introduction of the union-sponsored alternative enabled Rayburn to endorse the Elliot bill publicly as a compromise measure that was fair to the trade union movement. President Eisenhower supported a third and tougher version, the Landrum-Griffin Bill, and went so far as to speak on national television on its behalf. Rayburn sought time to respond from the networks, but was turned down by all except a single radio network.[106] When the day of the vote on the labor bills arrived, the Elliot bill was defeated by fifteen votes and Rayburn had suffered a major legislative defeat. Interestingly, all but four of the large Texas delegation voted against the speaker, leading to allegations that Rayburn was not fully in support of the bill. Congressman Bolling attributed the lack of Texas support to a different factor: Senate Majority Leader Lyndon Johnson, also from Texas, persuaded Texas members that a tough anti-union vote would serve them well at home. If so, Johnson paid a price when organized labor jumped on the Kennedy bandwagon in 1960.[107]

The Landrum-Griffin bill, like the civil rights bills of 1956 and 1957, demonstrated all of the features of Rayburn's deteriorating situation in the House. Caught between northern liberals (now represented in increasing numbers), southern conservatives (constituting a diminishing percentage of Democrats, but seated atop the committee system), and Republicans, Rayburn had to avoid open combat as a matter of survival. Even when he put his prestige on the line, as he did with the Elliot bill, he had no assurance of winning, and losses damaged his reputation. The extent to which the speaker was a true believer in the liberal causes he is said to have supported privately but avoided publicly will never be known. But it is clear that the rising liberal tide threatened Speaker Rayburn.

Another factor affecting Rayburn's speakership in the late 1950s was the role of Judge Howard Smith, the chairman of the House Rules Committee. Rayburn had enjoyed a close relationship with Eugene Cox of Georgia, who would usually support a request by the speaker for a rule. Judge Smith was a mild-mannered southern gentleman whose natural inclination was to accommodate Rayburn as well. But as the policy agenda turned to the left, it became increasingly difficult for Smith to support Rayburn. In the Eighty-sixth Congress, Rayburn staved off liberal attempts to rein in the Rules Committee by promising that he would persuade Smith to bring liberal bills to the floor. In the end, this was a promise that Rayburn could not keep.[108]

A major factor affecting the situation on the Rules Committee had been the cooperative relationship between Rayburn and Republican leader Joe Martin. Often Martin would help Rayburn by producing a few moderate Republican votes. When in 1959 the Republicans, in a surprise move supported by Eisenhower, unseated Joe Martin as their floor leader in favor of Charles Halleck of Indiana, the speaker suffered another blow. Halleck was an abrasive street fighter and more conservative than Martin. He and Rayburn had less than cordial relations and Rayburn was cut off from the Republican support he often needed to pass legislation. In fact, Halleck and Smith formed an overt coalition designed to control the House through the Rules Committee. While as late as 1957 Rayburn still had the power to bully Smith into submission when absolutely necessary, after 1959 the Rules Committee was effectively out of Rayburn's control.[109]

The Rayburn-Johnson strategy of demonstrating strong congressional leadership backfired on Lyndon Johnson's quest for the 1960 Democratic presidential nomination. Trying to demonstrate his leadership in the Senate, LBJ chose not to run in the primary elections. This proved to be a fatal mistake, as the primary field was dominated by liberal candidates such as John F. Kennedy, Hubert H. Humphrey, and

Stuart Symington. In the end, Kennedy's campaign was the best managed and best funded, and he won a first-ballot victory at the Los Angeles convention. In a move to unify the party, he offered the vice-presidential nomination to Johnson. Overcoming Rayburn's serious reservations as well as his own reluctance, Johnson accepted the offer and the Democratic ticket went on to a narrow victory in November. Kennedy's election harbingered an assertive liberal agenda, and the problem of the House Rules Committee was brought to the cusp.

As the Eighty-seventh Congress convened in 1961, the liberals were on the warpath for reform of the Rules Committee, and this time they had the support of a new Democratic administration that could ill afford to be roadblocked by Judge Smith and Charlie Halleck. And so, in the last year of his life, Sam Rayburn took on his last and greatest battle as speaker of the House. In a meeting held at the Kennedy estate in Palm Beach, Florida, Speaker Rayburn agreed to "take care" of the Rules Committee, and asked the president-elect to stay out of the fight.[110] As the day of the Democratic organizational caucus approached, Rayburn contemplated two alternative strategies in dealing with Judge Smith. One was to purge Congressman William Colmer from the committee. Colmer had made himself vulnerable by supporting Vice President Nixon during the election, and a purge would have been easily attainable in the caucus. The second alternative was to pack the committee by adding to it three new members, two Democrats and one Republican. The two Democrats would be appointed by the leadership and the balance of power on the committee would have swung away from Smith and to Rayburn. The purge strategy had certainty on its side, but it was contrary to precedents Rayburn had established at the time of the Dixiecrat revolt of 1948 and after Adam Clayton Powell had bolted the party in 1956. In both instances Rayburn had refused to purge a member for actions taken outside the House. Besides, Colmer was an influential member of the southern wing of the party and a purge of him would have alienated southerners for the life of the Eighty-seventh Congress if not for the entire Kennedy administration. Finally, several other southerners had supported Nixon, and in fairness they would have had to be punished too. Rayburn therefore settled upon the packing plan.[111]

Judge Smith realized that his defeat in the caucus was certain since it was controlled by a large majority of liberals. He sought to strike a deal with Rayburn whereby the Rules Committee would give up its power over conference reports and would agree to permit five major administration bills to come to the floor of the House. This offer was not acceptable to Rayburn; the administration's program was far too sweeping in prospect for these terms, and to have accepted such an offer from Smith would have been to acknowledge his own inability to control the committee and the House. Consequently, the caucus was asked to approve the packing scheme, which it proceeded to do, and the battle moved to the House floor. There, Rayburn faced the conservative coalition of southern Democrats and Republicans. In this case the natural strength of the coalition was augmented by the full support of the Republican leadership. Halleck brought the Rules Committee issue before the Republican conference and established opposition to the Rayburn plan as a party position. A livid Rayburn called Halleck to task for what he regarded as an unreasonable lack of comity, but Halleck was not Joe Martin and remained determined to defeat Rayburn.

Fortunately for Rayburn, Joe Martin still had influence among congressional Republicans. Martin promised to support Rayburn and, in the end, Republican votes from the northeast (including seven Republicans from Massachusetts) proved to be the margin of victory for Rayburn. Martin himself was paired for the Rayburn plan. The battle for southern Democratic support proved brutal. Carl Vinson of Georgia, the venerable chairman of the Armed Services Committee, took the lead on behalf of the Rayburn plan, alternatively appealing for support of the new Democratic administration and threatening poor committee assignments. Richard Bolling of Missouri, Rayburn's principal lieutenant on the committee, was the speaker's chief vote counter in the campaign. More so than on any other issue in his career, Rayburn placed his own reputation on the line. "Boys," he said, "are you with me or with Judge Smith?" With all of this effort, the estimates indicated the speaker was shy of the needed votes as the day of the House vote approached. Facing reality, Rayburn postponed the vote for a week and the Kennedys were called in for support. This led to a heavy-handed attempt to swing votes with district pork. It worked, as in several instances southern Democrats traded support for favors. When the final vote was in Rayburn had won 217–212; he lost sixty-four southern Democrats and was saved by twenty-two northeastern Republicans.[112]

Rayburn's victory over Judge Smith and the conservative coalition was to be his last major legislative conquest. By the fall of 1961 his health had deteriorated significantly, and complaining of a case of lumbago, he took his departure from Washington before the end of the congressional session to return to Bonham. It was apparent to everyone that only a very serious condition would draw Sam Rayburn away from his duties, and indeed, Rayburn was in the final stages of an incurable cancer that finally claimed his life in December of 1961. Thus ended one of the most illustrious careers in American politics.

Sam Rayburn was the prototypical speaker of the feudal era. He was nurtured in it, he helped shape it, and he benefited from it. At his death he had become a mythical figure, and like all mythical figures, his reputation was a mixture of fact and embellishment. Precisely because his image looms so large over the House that he left behind, it is important to place his speakership in some perspective. Newspaper accounts hailed Rayburn as the most powerful man in the Congress, the most powerful speaker since Cannon, the second most powerful man in the government, and the nation's leading Democrat. There was an element of truth in each of these characterizations. Yet Sam Rayburn's actual power was not as great as the commentaries would suggest, which may be seen by reviewing the factors that served to limit it. Any analysis of congressional power must begin with the districts, and Sam Rayburn was often threatened, especially in the 1940s. Of the eleven elections during the time that he served as speaker or minority leader, he was challenged six times in the Democratic primary, losing from 25 to 43 percent of the vote within his own party. His opposition came from the political right and was often well financed. The positions that Rayburn was led to take as a national Democratic leader on such issues as labor and civil rights were not supported by most of his constituents. Whereas in Washington Rayburn was perceived as a southern compromiser, in Bonham he was perceived by many as a liberal. This tension led Rayburn to adopt a district "style" designed to deflect attention from the positions he took as speaker. Whereas in Washington Rayburn was known as a stern leader, at home he presented himself as a friendly local rancher whose front porch was always open to passers-by.[113]

The same conflict between liberalism and conservatism marked his efforts in Washington. There, the strength of the conservative coalition was arrayed against the demands of the liberal wing of the party. To favor the liberals was to ensure defeat on the floor; to favor the conservatives was to jeopardize his standing as speaker. The situation was exacerbated as the size of the Democratic majorities diminished, and they were often small while Rayburn was speaker. The number of southern Democrats was typically about a hundred. In the nine congresses during which Rayburn was speaker, his majorities were 105, 13, 53, 92, 35, 29, 33, 130, and 87. Rayburn often lacked effective majority control of the House.

The strength of the conservative coalition was enhanced by the power of southern committee chairmen. That Rayburn found it necessary to bargain to get bills through the Rules Committee is one indication of the weakness of his position; another is the fact that he needed the help of the Rules Committee to kill bills that the northerners wanted but he opposed. But if the power of Judge Smith was the most visible aspect of the system by which the House was run, it was paralleled in other areas of legislation: Chairman Clarence Cannon of the Appropriations

Committee, Chairman Carl Vinson of Armed Services, Chairman Jere Cooper of Ways and Means, Chairman Harold D. Cooley of Agriculture—these men formed the backbone of the House. Their committees met at the call of the chair, and without the support of the chairman, legislation could not pass. Rayburn could deal with these men but he could not dictate to them.

To the limits imposed upon Rayburn by his district, the size of his majorities, and the committee system were added limitations that derived from his own character. Rayburn was a product of the nineteenth century. He traveled outside of the United States only once, he usually traveled by car or train rather than by plane, and he rarely socialized. His view of the world was that of a conservative prairie populist. The difference between Rayburn's conservatism and that of his mentor, Jack Garner, is indicated by the fact that Garner became a wealthy man, whereas Rayburn never did. Rayburn refused to accept free rides on the railroads; Garner rode for free in a private car. Rayburn's populist streak was compatible with the egalitarian thrust of the New Deal. But Rayburn was slow to accept the civil rights movement, the labor movement, and 1950s liberalism. Rayburn was not a reactionary, but he had achieved his populist legislative ambitions by 1935. Thereafter, he was a cautious supporter of progressive Democratic presidents.

Rayburn's personal influence was in certain respects a myth. His reputation for holding a hundred conferences a day conveyed the image of a speaker who liked to pal around with the members. In fact, admission to the Rayburn inner circle was always highly prized and sparingly bestowed, and the vast majority of members never felt personally close to the speaker, especially during the last three congresses he led. Unlike the persuasive, cajoling, majority leader of the FDR era, the Sam Rayburn of the latter 1950s was an aloof man who left the politicking to subalterns. The notion, therefore, that Rayburn typically swung votes by direct persuasion was truer of his early years as speaker than it was of his later years, and was never a wholly accurate depiction of his approach.[114]

Sam Rayburn was a man carved for the role he played, yet he was also a shrewd politician who was able to create a political labyrinth in which his own skills would prove most effective. His success lay less in his ability to swing large numbers of votes than in avoiding situations in which that would be necessary. When he wanted legislation stopped, he let others stop it; when he wanted legislation passed, he worked with the committee chairman to get bills that could command a floor majority. Rayburn had few close friends even among the older members. He cultivated younger members, generation after generation of them; to him, these protégés were surrogate sons. It was through these younger members, such as Lyndon Johnson, Hale Boggs, Carl Albert, and Richard Bolling, that Rayburn worked to influence the legislative process. Rayburn was a man of strong will and iron integrity. He was no pushover. But neither was he the dominating force in the House of Representatives that legend suggests.

Sam Rayburn's speakership may be viewed as theme and variation through four distinct periods. It was marked by elements of continuity arising from the underlying constitutional stability of the system, the entrenchment of the internal organization of the House, and Rayburn's character. The major factor beyond Rayburn's control was the independent constituencies served by his members. The conservative coalition, by any standard the most severe impediment to Democratic party leadership in the House, was and is an artifact of independent congressional districts. Lacking the capacity or desire to influence the districts, Speaker Rayburn was limited in his ability to influence the members those districts produced.

The internal structure of the House was firmly ingrained by 1940. The metamorphosis that had begun with the revolt against Cannon in 1910 had produced an oligarchy in the Democratic party that was nurtured by John Nance Garner and inherited by Sam Rayburn. The strength and stability lent to the House by the domination of the oligarchy weakened the institution of the speakership (in comparison with that of the partisan period) but served to strengthen the hand of a speaker who was a part of the power structure, a speaker like Sam Rayburn.

Sam Rayburn was a product of natural selection. He was not a man who adapted himself to his environment; he was a man who was nurtured by the environment around him. His success lay primarily in his ability to preserve an environment in which his own leadership qualities could prove effective. The mystique deriving from his age and long service, his baleful stare from the chair, his hundred "conferences" a day, his "boys"—these were the techniques by which he shaped his own image and the attitude of those he was called upon to lead. Similarly, the Rayburn emphasis upon the virtue of honesty and his reputation for fairness in dealing with members contributed to the creation of an atmosphere of comity in the House that facilitated his leadership. Some accounts of Rayburn's speakership imply that he led by force of character and strength of will.[115] This is not entirely true. He did not win votes by staring people down; instead, he established a set of expectations about behavior that enabled him to deal for votes when necessary. A significant aspect of this technique was the manner in which Rayburn himself would remain aloof from the trading, often leaving that task to others. In this manner he maintained his own image of fairness and preserved his own political capital for those occasions when it was most needed. The entrenchment of the rules of the House under its precedents assisted Rayburn in this respect. At his side was Longworth's parliamentarian, Lewis Deschler, a man whose stature in the House was unique in its own right. Rayburn did not want to alter the rules of the House in order to attain his own goals as party leader. His ability lay in his deliberate attempt to impose his own values upon the House rather than to adapt his behavior to the circumstances.

As against these elements of stability were three principal sources of change: the personality and program of the presidents with whom Rayburn served; the proportion of Democrats and Republicans in the House; and the nature of the issues on the national agenda. The speakership has, since 1932, been essentially reactive to the presidency. Uncle Joe Cannon conducted the business of the House with a great degree of independence of the White House even when the popular Theodore Roosevelt was president. He was able to do so because he controlled the business of the House under its rules; no speaker since Cannon has been able to do so. After the revolt against Cannon, the speakership lay prostrate; after the election of Roosevelt, the presidency assumed new influence. Since the New Deal, speakers have been subordinate and/or reactive to the presidents with whom they have served. When the president and the speaker have been of the same party, the subordination has been voluntary; when the president and the speaker have been of opposite parties, the subordination has been reactive. But in all cases it has occurred.

If Rayburn's deference to the presidency helps explain the policies he supported, the variation in the partisan makeup of the House affected his strategy. When the Democrats were thrown into the minority, Rayburn allowed the Republicans to stew in their own juices and come to him when the time was ripe to cut a deal. Thornier was the more common situation when the Democrats were in at least nominal control of the House. This case had three variations. When the Democratic majority was large, as in the Seventy-seventh and Eighty-sixth Congresses, the appeal to party loyalty lost its natural force. While the conservative coalition was less likely to hold the balance of power, the centrifugal tendency of the members was much greater. When the Democrats held a slim margin, the conservative coalition actually held the balance of power in the House, as in the Seventy-eighth, Eighty-second, Eighty-fourth, and Eighty-fifth Congresses. While Rayburn was able to appeal to party loyalty just as Garner had done in the Seventy-second Congress in 1931, his efforts were not as successful since the coalition had not materialized in Garner's time. Consequently, the ideal balance from Rayburn's point of view lay in the middle zone in which the balance was close enough to encourage a sense of party loyalty while large enough to provide a cushion against the power of the coalition. Rayburn's best situation was one in which he could win votes by appealing to a modest number of southerners on a personal or pork-barrel basis. He was precise about the number: "You never," he would say, "want more than 269 members."[116]

But more than anything else, Rayburn's speakership varied according to the issues that confronted it. Roosevelt's New Deal coalition provided a stable basis for Democratic party governance in the House during the 1940s. The war carried FDR and Rayburn through the first period of his speakership, and after the war the Truman administration set a new policy agenda for the country that was a precursor of the liberal outlook that would come to prevail from 1958 to 1968. The Eisenhower years were marked by accommodation and compromise. In a way, Rayburn's position was similar to Joe Cannon's in 1908. Each was a powerful speaker who reflected the prevailing values of his time but who had come to outlive the policy consensus on which his power had been based. Rayburn was too conservative for the liberal tide that would sweep the country in the 1960s, and could not have functioned effectively in the reformed House that the 1970s produced.

Conclusion

The feudal speakership was the culmination of trends that took root after the revolt against Speaker Cannon in 1910, and culminated with Sam Rayburn's death in 1961, a fifty-year period. This half-century of American political experience witnessed two world wars, the Great Depression, dramatic changes in American life, four Democratic and five Republican administrations, and the service of eight speakers. This array of historical happenings presents an obvious challenge to the notion that the span of time covered by the present chapter may be usefully viewed as encompassing a particular variation of the speakership. In concluding the discussion of the feudal speakership, then, it is important that we analyze it from the general theoretical perspective that has guided the analysis, explaining the continuity in the development of the office in relationship to the many significant changes that took place in American society along the way.

The national policy agenda in the first half of the twentieth century was more complex than the agenda that shaped the development of the political system during the last half of the nineteenth century or of that which defined the antebellum polity. The quest for equity is more complicated than that for freedom and growth, and the politics of the twentieth century has been essentially a quest for equity. In the period prior to the Civil War, the antebellum state searched for its identity. During the fifty years after the war, the American nation sought economic expansion. In the fifty years that began when the progressive movement brought down Uncle Joe Cannon, the nation's quest was for social justice. Woodrow Wilson's New Freedom involved a lowering of the tariff and the initiation of the progressive income tax that would eventually replace it as the government's primary source of revenue. The Federal Reserve Act established public control over the nation's monetary system. The Clayton Anti-Trust Act lent teeth to the government's power to regulate big business. Regulation of child labor, workplace conditions, and other aspects of the nation's economic life were central to the Democratic vision. From this perspective, the "return to normalcy" was a historical anachronism. By the time the Depression brought about the final decline of congressional Republicanism, the nation's commitments were already to a program of economic redistribution and social reform that would last through the 1960s and the Great Society. The Eisenhower administration and the brief Republican congressional interludes in the late 1940s and early 1950s did not alter the fundamental character of the nation's policy commitments.

What, then, is the connection between the national commitment to the politics of redistribution and reform and the development of the feudal speakership? Among many relevant factors, three are central. The first is that a redistributive national policy agenda is designed for incumbent advantage. When the government is taking from the few and giving to the many, then the many have every reason to support those who are doing the redistributing. Progressivism was at first a movement of intellectuals and have-nots. The Depression transformed it into a movement in which the average working American found it sensible to enlist. Once the principle of redistribution became accepted by a national majority, which was certainly the case after 1932, the power structure that controlled the redistribution became entrenched.

The second and connected factor was that the Democratic party was positioned correctly to reap the benefits of the shift in the policy agenda. It had always spoken for the poor man; now it could speak for the majority. The hegemony of the Democratic party shaped the speakership into a feudal institution because of the nature of the party's coalition and its culture. The sectional divisions within the party led to the reliance on seniority as an exclusive rule of career advancement. The attractiveness of a congressional career to members, along with their ability to win renomination in districts that were often dominated by one party, led to lengthened tenure, with those serving the longest rising the highest. This is what led to the creation of the committee baronies.

Third, and finally, the House nurtured those who became the feudal speakers. Clark, Gillett, and Longworth were products of the previous era; Garner, Rainey, Byrns, Bankhead, and Rayburn were products of the feudal system. They had been nurtured in it, believed in it, and had come to power in it. They had no reason to change it. The feudal speakership did not spring full-blown upon the House. It developed during the twenty-year period after the revolt against Cannon, and became entrenched by the New Deal and the emergence of the conservative coalition. By 1937 the feudal system was in place, and the men who were to control it had been shaped by it.

The implication of the emphasis that this discussion has given to Sam Rayburn can be made explicit: he was the great feudal speaker. The evolution of the House from Cannon forward prepared the ground for Rayburn's speakership. During the three decades from 1911 to 1941, the House evolved its feudal system and nurtured Rayburn in it. In 1941 the man and the moment met. But having said as much on Rayburn's behalf, it must be pointed out that Rayburn was far from being a transformative speaker. To the contrary, his own interest and inclination lay in opposing change. The reason was simple: any change would have derogated from his unique position of influence in the House. For Rayburn's power lay in his relationship with the barons. To have undermined their power would have undermined his influence. For so long as he lived, Sam Rayburn was the great feudal leader; but by living so long, he eventually became a formidable obstacle in the path of political reform. His death came just as the tide of reform broke over the House he loved.

Sam Rayburn's passing unleashed forces of change, just as had occurred when Cannon was stripped of his power in 1910. But the changes in the House that were brought about by the revolt against Cannon came quickly because of a turnover in partisan control. The changes in the House that came in the wake of Rayburn's death were much slower in coming about. In fact, the speakerships of Rayburn's two successors, John W. McCormack of Massachusetts and Carl Albert of Oklahoma, marked a transition in the House during which a new period in the history of the House and of its speakership would emerge.

4 ☆ Emergence of the Democratic Speakership

The Reform Movement Begins

The pressure for reform of the House of Representatives had been held at bay by Sam Rayburn until the last year of his life. His death left a gaping hole in the House Democratic leadership and opened the floodgates to a wave of reform that would last for fifteen years and leave the House of Representatives a very different institution than Rayburn had known. After his death there emerged a new leadership system in the House that was more open and participatory. The feudal system did not go immediately to the grave with its leader. The influence of seniority and the southern wing of the party remained strong through the 1960s. But the social and political changes that occurred during that decade brought with them dramatic changes in the House. The speakerships of John W. McCormack of Massachusetts and Carl B. Albert of Oklahoma were fundamentally defined by an upheaval in American politics and the reform movement in the House of Representatives. The character of the House and of the speakership were greatly changed, and a new period in the evolution of the speakership began.

The defining characteristic of the democratic speakership is the diffusion of power among relatively equal members. The diffusion of power was caused by a transformation of the political system from one dominated by political parties to one in which autonomous members sustained independent electoral bases in their districts. The underlying cultural foundations of the new era stressed openness, participation, and equality. It is not coincidental that the opening of the political system went hand in hand with the culmination of the liberal political agenda in the 1960s and early 1970s. The liberal policy agenda and the democratic reform agenda were conceptually and politically related.

Their effects, however, were independent of each other. The new political structure that the reform movement put in place survived the completion of the policy agenda that went along with it. By the late 1970s the policy winds blew in a conservative direction, even in the context of the more open and participatory environment that the reform movement created.

The speakers of the democratic era confronted the House as a more open institution than Rayburn had known. The first two men to occupy the democratic speakership were products of the old regime: McCormack, Rayburn's majority leader, and Albert, his whip. McCormack and Albert were fated to preside over a rapidly changing House of Representatives, and their speakerships were essentially transitional. Their successors, Thomas P. O'Neill, Jr., of Massachusetts, James C. Wright, Jr., of Texas, and Thomas S. Foley of Washington State, came into office after the reform movement had crested, and were less beholden to the old order. By the time that they inherited power, however, American politics had taken a turn to the right. The analysis of the democratic speakership must begin with the reform movement in the House of Representatives and the two speakers who confronted it.

John W. McCormack served in the Democratic leadership in the House longer than any other man, including Rayburn. From 1941, when he became Rayburn's majority leader, until his retirement in 1970, McCormack was a fixture among Democratic leaders. A tall, thin, Irishman from Boston, McCormack was as dedicated to the House as Rayburn had been, and was comfortable in the feudal milieu. Yet he differed from Rayburn in several respects. His district was urban and Catholic, while Rayburn had represented Protestant farmers, mostly Baptists. McCormack's policy views were more liberal than Rayburn's too, although McCormack always preferred to call himself a progressive rather than a liberal. His personality was as outgoing as Rayburn's was reserved. McCormack loved to be around people, loved to debate, and was happiest when surrounded by a throng.[1]

McCormack's outgoing personality was well suited for the new leadership system that developed during his speakership. The groundswell of liberal demands could only be met by opening up the process of leadership deliberation, and meeting with people was something that the speaker liked to do. The Democratic leadership system that emerged in the 1960s was essentially collegial.[2] The Democratic leaders began taking formal positions on important party bills and used the whip system more assertively to round up votes. The party whip organization, which had been first created by Oscar Underwood during the days of King Caucus, had remained fairly stable until the mid 1950s. In 1955 Whip Carl Albert increased the number of whip zones and elaborated and extended the group's function.[3] Instead of merely counting the votes, the whips were now more often asked to persuade members. The whip counts became more frequent, and occurred earlier in the legislative process. A study of counts in 1963 found them over 90 percent accurate.[4]

Knowing how the members planned to vote was, of course, not enough. Convincing wavering members to vote the leadership's way was the key problem. The common story about Sam Rayburn had focused on the number of "pocket" votes he had at hand on the big issues. The Democratic leaders under the new system also rounded up "if needed" votes, but they did it as a team. Giving most of their attention to the swing votes, appeals would be made on the basis of party allegiance, philosophy, personal favors, or, more rarely, substantial preferments such as committee assignments, district projects, or support for favored legislation. Explicit quid pro quos were not usually involved, and the imposition of sanctions was even scarcer. McCormack, Albert, and party whip Hale Boggs of Louisiana were much more likely to persuade than threaten, and they did not have much to threaten members with.[5] Much of the academic literature on the House of Representatives has stressed the effects of the reforms of the 1970s. These reforms were important, and the speakership of the reformed House was affected by them. But the change to a more open and participatory leadership system antedated the reform movement and was prerequisite to it. The democratic speakership began to develop after Rayburn's death and the reform movement was an important step in its evolution.

As the new era in American politics dawned, the political agenda of the liberal wing of the Democratic Party became the agenda for the nation. John McCormack and John Kennedy had been political rivals in Massachusetts politics, but McCormack did not question his obligation to support the president's program. During the Kennedy administration the House Democratic leadership struggled to pass administration initiatives in education, tax revision, and civil rights. Facing strong southern opposition within their own ranks, and working with a president who had yet to establish his influence on the Hill, the going was difficult. All of this changed when, after President Kennedy's death in November of 1963, Lyndon Johnson pushed hard to enact the administration's major initiatives. During the balance of Kennedy's term Johnson pushed through major education, tax, and civil rights laws. When Johnson's landslide victory in 1964 carried huge congressional majorities for the Democrats, the way was clear for the enactment of the Great Society program.

Lyndon Johnson's prowess changed the game for the House Democratic leadership. With a forceful president and large majorities, the leaders' task was a lot easier. The heart of the Great Society came from the Education and Labor, and Judiciary Committees where the liberals were in firm control. Threatened by the reimposition of the 21-day rule, the Rules Committee was unable to put up strong resistance, and the way was cleared for speedy enactment of Johnson's program. But the nature of that program itself harbored trouble for Speaker McCormack, for the essence of the Great Society was on social and political reform, on openness, fairness, and participation. The policy agenda of the 1960s reflected the political culture of the times, and led to increasing unrest among newer, younger, and more liberal members of the House who felt shut out by a seniority system that subordinated them to the will of the standing committee chairmen. In the midst of his party's greatest legislative triumphs since the New Deal, John McCormack came under more frequent and more open attacks by House Democrats. McCormack was widely liked but rarely feared. To many younger liberals, he seemed to lack the organizational ability and persuasive force to marshal Democratic majorities.

The best-known indictment of McCormack came from Congressman Richard Bolling of Missouri. Bolling had considered challenging McCormack for the speakership in 1961, but instead chose to mount a challenge to Carl Albert for the majority leadership. Bolling withdrew from the race when he concluded that he could not win. In a 1965 book, *House Out of Order*, Bolling attacked the institutional weakness of the speakership under the rules of the Democratic caucus.[6] By 1968 he was willing to address McCormack's perceived weaknesses more directly. In *Power in the House*, he presented a detailed critique of McCormack's leadership.[7] Bolling charged McCormack with a lack of regularity in scheduling, an unwillingness to move decisively to take control of the major committees by appointing program Democrats to a majority of seats, an inability to anticipate trouble before it was too late to do anything about it, and a lack of effective and forceful leadership on behalf of liberal legislation. Dropping all restraint, he called for McCormack to step down and urged Majority Leader Albert as his successor.

On McCormack's behalf it might be noted that caution in dealing with committee chairmen and a reluctance to challenge the southern wing of the party were hallmarks of the speakership of Sam Rayburn. Bolling believed that a Democratic speaker in the 1960s could undertake a confrontational approach to the "crunchers" (as he called the southerners) and survive. Yet the potential for southern conservatives to bolt to the Republican party was far greater in a decade in which Republican Barry Goldwater had carried the deep South than it had been before. Bolling's insistence that the House needed more consistency in scheduling no doubt reflected a concern shared by many members. Still, it seems incongruous to for him to have criticized McCormack for a failure to assert power while at the same time urging a regularity in programming that would limit his use of one of the major powers at his disposal, floor scheduling.

Bolling's criticisms were in part valid, but they reveal a great deal about the circumstances of McCormack's speakership. With the exception of the years of World War II, Speaker Rayburn never dealt with an activist president of his own party who enjoyed broad popular support. One has to go back to the early days of the New Deal to find a parallel to the Great Society years. There, we find that speakers Rainey, Byrns, and Bankhead were also regarded as weak. The underlying truth is that during the feudal period, the speakership had been gutted and the presidency had become more powerful. Rayburn's unique stature was tied to his relationships with the committee chairmen and the presidents with whom he served. McCormack lacked Rayburn's stature and many of his leadership qualities, but it would have been difficult for any speaker to have upstaged Lyndon Johnson. And Rayburn never had to deal with an aggressive Republican like Richard Nixon.

In the early 1960s the center of American politics moved leftward, and the center of the House of Representatives moved along with it. A new generation of younger, more liberal, and less patient members came to the House. One of the last members to take his initial oath of office from Sam Rayburn, Morris Udall of Arizona, chose to run against McCormack in 1968. The reform-minded Udall had chafed with his fellow liberals under McCormack's leadership. Udall favored an "issue-oriented" speakership, a speakership devoted to the issues that the liberals wanted to address.[8] Udall's challenge was intended to be symbolic. He announced that if he were to win he would vacate the nomination and insist upon a new election in which other candidates could participate. That he was able to win 58 votes to McCormack's 178 indicated a large element of discontent with McCormack's leadership, but the numbers were less significant than the fact of the challenge.[9]

In the end, the cause of the liberal members' discontent was not the performance of their speaker, but the frustration they experienced in witnessing the political tide turn against their policy positions. The 1968 election brought Republican Richard M. Nixon to the White House. Nixon and southern conservative George C. Wallace of Alabama carried 60 percent of the vote against Hubert H. Humphrey, a Democrat who stood for the best impulses of the liberal mood. Nixon was a tough politician, and congressional Democrats were forced to deal with a phenomenon that was new in their lifetime, an assertive, conservative Republican president. Amid the bitter invective of the Vietnam War and the civil rights movement, gentle John McCormack was ill placed. In

1969 Speaker McCormack, hounded by a scandal surrounding one of his aides, saddened by the deteriorating health of his wife, and approaching eighty years of age, announced his intention to retire at the end of the Ninety-first Congress. To the end, McCormack resisted the reform of the House. With his retirement in view, the current of reform against which he had stood was unleashed, and the House of Representatives embarked upon a period of change unlike anything witnessed since the revolt against Joe Cannon.

The story of congressional reform has been well and often told.[10] Here the focus is on the role of the speakership in the reform movement and the consequences of the reforms for the speakership. The reform movement in the House was marked by two conflicting tendencies.[11] Many reforms were designed to democratize the House, either by opening its procedures to public scrutiny or by diffusing power among its members. But other reforms were designed to strengthen the power of the party leadership, especially the speakership. Among the democratizing reforms were rules requiring open committee meetings, recorded committee votes, recorded votes in the Committee of the Whole, the proliferation and distribution of subcommittee chairmanships, automatic caucus votes to confirm committee chairmanships, and the adoption of the bill of rights giving subcommittees more autonomy from their parent committees. Among the reforms designed to enhance the power of the speakership were the revival of the Steering and Policy Committee, granting to it the power of making committee assignments, giving the speaker increased flexibility in bill referral, granting to him the right to nominate Democratic members of the Rules Committee, and granting to the Steering and Policy Committee the right to nominate all standing committee chairmen for Caucus ratification.[12] There was a reciprocal relationship between these two sets of reforms. The main target was the power of the committee chairmen. It was not possible simply to strip them of power, however, because the House would be left rudderless. The strengthening of the speakership was the logical concomitant of the attack on the chairmen.

The consensus among students of congressional reform has been that the decentralizing tendencies of the reform movement were more consequential than the centralizing tendencies.[13] This is not surprising, because the impetus for reform came about as a reaction to the perception that power had become too concentrated in the hands of the feudal oligarchy. The reformers wanted to undo an oligarchic despotism, not create a tyrannical one. After all, they were from the liberal wing of the party, and the policy goals that they sought to achieve were being roadblocked by conservative southern chairmen, not by Speaker McCormack. If the rap against McCormack was that he lacked force, there were two solutions at hand: either get rid of McCormack and get a new speaker with more power, or else undermine the power of those who would stand in the path of liberal social legislation by changes in the rules. The reformers sought to change the rules, but the reforms that were to strengthen the speakership did not immediately offset the fragmentation that flowed from the decentralizing reforms.

In the end, the reform movement came about because the power structure was conservative and the new issue agenda was liberal. The reforms were part and parcel of a broad shift in national policy most visibly illustrated by the Great Society. Liberal Democrats wanted to push aside the power structure in order to pass liberal legislation. Moderate Republicans wanted to put forward an active Republican alternative to the Democratic program. Since they had no responsibility to govern, and had no power to change the rules of the game, they could only accommodate by changing leadership. In 1966 they unseated Charles Halleck as minority leader and elected Gerald Ford of Michigan in his place. Ford advanced a new issue agenda for the Republicans, dissociated himself from the old conservative coalition, and brought younger and more moderate Republicans into positions of influence within the House Republican conference.

For the liberal reformers in the Democratic caucus the task was more difficult. They wanted to legislate, but could not do so if opposed by the old-line committee chairmen who ran the system. They decided that in order to achieve their policy goals, they would have to change the system. Morris Udall's challenge to Speaker McCormack in 1968 raised the liberal banner; in 1969 the liberals attacked. The locus of the movement was in the Democratic Study Group, the liberal organization that had been spawned a decade before in an attempt to push a liberal agenda on Speaker Rayburn and the southern barons. Led by liberals such as Jamie O'Hara of Michigan, Frank Thompson of New Jersey, Phillip Burton and Chet Holifield of California, and Don Fraser of Michigan, the DSG launched an assault on the southern bastion of privilege. DSG staff director Richard Conlon was actively involved in the planning and played a major role in the reform movement.

The reformers first step was to revive the Democratic caucus, which had been dormant for fifty years and normally met only once at the beginning of each Congress for organizational purposes. Yet within the party's rules lay tremendous power for the caucus, power not exercised since the days of Champ Clark and Oscar Underwood. The caucus retained power over Democratic committee nominations, could instruct Democratic members to vote the party's position on the floor (except when in doing so the member would violate a commitment to his nominating authority), and could adopt other rules on House governance.

With a liberal majority in the caucus, the potential to use these powers was always a threat to the conservative southern committee chairmen. But the liberals had to recognize that by overplaying their hand they might drive the conservatives into the hands of the Republicans. In 1969, far from trying to overplay their hand, it was enough to try and win a regular monthly caucus meeting with an accessible agenda.[14]

An indication of the distance that the speakership had come during the feudal era was the reluctance of Speakers Rayburn and McCormack to have the caucus meet. Both opposed the DSG and were against providing the liberals with a regular forum in which to press their policy agenda and demands for institutional reform. The major factor causing the change from King Caucus to no caucus was the emergence of the conservative coalition.[15] The conservatives enjoyed a working majority on the floor of the House in most congresses, and dominated the committee system. Rayburn and McCormack had to broker compromise and this required a certain amount of maneuvering room, which could best be maintained by allowing the Byzantine world of the committee system to work in its mysterious ways. The caucus is a forum that is designed to enable a party majority to have its way, but Rayburn and McCormack did not want to get run over by liberals.

Speaker McCormack resisted the revitalization of the caucus until his last congress, when he was prevailed upon to support a regular monthly caucus meeting provided that it was brought forward as his own proposal. Majority Leader Carl Albert found himself in a different position. While McCormack was facing the end of his career, Albert looked forward to inheriting the speakership in 1971. He expressed his support for the general aims of the reformers, but did not want to be too closely associated with their specific proposals. He was sympathetic to the need for reform, but was loyal to McCormack. He recognized that he would have to work with conservatives as well as liberals, and chose to lend quiet support to the reformers, providing them with a room in which to meet. Albert suggested to McCormack that a monthly caucus might be a good place for the speaker to meet with his members.[16] Albert knew that McCormack loved to be around people.

The monthly meetings of the Democratic caucus in 1969 led to the formation of a special caucus committee on "Organization, Study, and Review," chaired by Congresswoman Judith Butler Hansen of Washington. The committee proved to be the catalyst for the adoption of the Legislative Reform Act of 1970, which embodied a number of major institutional reforms. For the first time recorded votes in committees were to be made public. In the Committee of the Whole House, recorded votes could now be triggered by a vote of one-fifth of quorum, or as few as twenty members. No longer was it possible for a member to support or oppose a proposition in committee or in the Committee of the Whole, and then turn around and publicly take the opposite position when the matter was before the House. Liberal Democrats, believing that the public was supportive of the thrust of their program, wanted to ensure that conservative Democrats and Republicans would not be able to hide their legislative record from public view. They also knew that some liberal Democrats had a habit of missing key votes, and sought to pressure them to show up and vote. Committee hearings and markups would now routinely be open to the public, and the light of day would shine into the dark halls of the Congress.[17]

It is interesting to analyze the adoption of the recorded vote reform from the point of view of the party leadership. The key amendment was offered on behalf of the reformers by Massachusetts Congressman Thomas P. O'Neill, Jr., a liberal member of the House Rules Committee who had not been a part of the core reform group, and who was a protégé of Speaker McCormack's. He was an ideal bridge between the leadership and the reformers, and he favored the adoption of the recorded vote in the Committee of the Whole. Yet this reform was very problematical from the point of view of party leadership, and Speaker McCormack and Majority Leader Albert were less enthusiastic about it. While it is desirable for members to have all of their votes recorded so that their constituents can know what they have done, the opening up of the process was purchased at a price in terms of the leadership's ability to swing votes. Often, the speaker could appeal to individual members for difficult votes while emphasizing the fact that the vote would go unrecorded. The use of the unrecorded teller vote in the Committee of the Whole was particularly valuable, since no formal tally of an individual member's votes was taken. While a perspicacious observer in the House gallery might notice in which teller line individual members stood, it was generally difficult to keep track of the voting patterns of all members. The adoption of the recorded vote altered the pattern of logrolling, since members were forced to be much more cautious in casting votes.[18]

With the adoption of the recorded vote, it became possible for the Democrats to smoke out Republicans on some major issues (for example, votes against jobs programs during recessionary periods), but it was more frequently the case that the Republicans could make life difficult for Democrats on issues such as school busing, school prayer, and abortion. The legislative atmosphere became more polemical and both sides became adept at framing amendments designed to cause political embarrassment for the opposition. The Democratic leadership often found that the margin of votes needed to pass program legislation lay among southern conservatives. Often, these members would be willing to support the leadership so long as they could do so without causing too much of a stir at home. It is not surprising then that the leadership did not lead the fight for this reform.[19]

But the recorded teller vote was not merely an attempt to open up the legislative process to the public; it was also aimed at curbing the power of committee chairmen. The leadership had more latitude to swing votes when the votes were unrecorded, but so too did the chairmen. Sometimes, the chairmen had more influence at their disposal than the leadership did. In order to truly open up the process, it was necessary to take the legs out from under the committee barons as well. The Legislative Reform Act sought to give some measure of power to the majorities of legislative committees by allowing them to schedule meetings without the consent of the chairman, and by permitting committee members to call up bills that had been cleared by the committee, but upon which the chairman had taken no action. Both of these steps were intended to limit the power of a committee chairman to kill a bill by refusing to hold a meeting or by refusing to bring a committee-passed bill to the floor, both common practices in the past.[20]

It was in part because the reform movement was aimed so directly at the chairmen that Majority Leader Albert was reluctant to take a lead in it. Albert was caught in a dilemma. If the reform movement succeeded in limiting the power of the chairmen, the speakership might not necessarily benefit correspondingly; instead, power might flow to committee majorities or to subcommittee chairmen. If the reformers failed to curb the power of the barons, they would be able to cause a lot of trouble for a prospective speaker who had tried to undermine them. Had it been possible for Albert to sweep into power on the crest of a reform movement that rendered the committee system subservient to his will, then it would have made sense for a majority leader to have led it. But such a sweeping set of reforms was not in prospect, and Albert did not want it. However much he may have wished to see some of the chairmen curtailed, Albert believed in the committee system and did not think that it could be effective if the powers of its leaders were too severely limited. From his own point of view, the existence of a set of power brokers independent of the leadership was useful, for it provided additional places for political pressure and responsibility to fall. In this complex situation, Albert kept his own counsel, provided tacit support for the reformers, and sought to maintain his alliances with the committee chairmen with whom he would, in the end, have to work.

Carl Bert Albert became the forty-sixth speaker of the House of Representatives in January 1971, at the beginning of the Ninety-second Congress, amid high expectations. "Carl Albert will put more power in the House to build a 'Democratic alternative,'" proclaimed one periodical, while another acknowledged that his "intellectual capacity, education, and understanding of national issues [is] immeasurably superior to McCormack's."[21] *Time* magazine correspondent Neil McNeil called Albert a man "with iron in his backbone." But contrasting to these statements was a trace of doubt in others. *Time* noted that members had "long admired but rarely feared Albert's gentle nature."[22] *Business Week* remarked that Albert had "built his power by courting the conservative House establishment, especially the powerful committee chairmen," and wondered if Albert would be able to shake free of his commitments to the establishment to lead the House effectively.[23]

These comments captured both the man and his situation. In 1971, the House was poised to go through a remarkable transition from the old order to the new, and it was Carl Albert's lot to guide the passage. With his ties to the old order and his sympathies for the new, he was in many respects ideally suited to the task. But he found it necessary to walk a fine line in maintaining his relationships with the senior committee chairmen and providing the kind of forceful party leadership that many younger members would demand. Albert's situation is strikingly illustrated in comparing his relative seniority vis-à-vis the committee chairmen with his predecessors and successors. Sam Rayburn and John W. McCormack had outlived most of their peers to lead the seniority lists when they became speaker. Tip O'Neill and Jim Wright came into power after a wholesale turnover had brought more junior members to the head of the committee lists. But most of the chairmen that Carl Albert confronted were more senior than he (see table 2). Indeed, the House reached its peak of seniority in 1971 when Albert became speaker.[24]

Albert had built his career in service to the establishment of Sam Rayburn and John McCormack. A Rhodes Scholar and national oratorical champion as a youth, Albert came to the House in 1947 with bright prospects and a low profile. Although his first election was narrow, his district was safely Democratic, and he was never seriously challenged at home thereafter. This enabled him to pursue his national aims by practicing the Rayburn ethic: work hard, go along, and get along. His excellent memory served him in good stead as he frequented the House floor, memorizing the names of all of the members, especially the Democrats. In listening to the members speak and in visiting with them on the floor, Albert came to realize that in time he could predict how they would vote. He developed a feel for the House and many friendships among the members.[25]

When in 1955 the Democrats resumed control of the House and the position of party whip became available, Speaker Rayburn tapped Albert for the job. In just his fourth term, the "Little Giant from Little Dixie"

Table 2 The Speakers and Chairmen: Relative Seniority

	Chairmen with the same or less seniority		Chairmen with more seniority	
	N	%	N	%
Sam Rayburn (1941) 47 chairmen	44	94%	3	6%
John W. McCormack (1962) 20 chairmen	17	85	3	15
Carl B. Albert (1971) 21 chairmen	8	38	13	62
Thomas P. O'Neill, Jr. (1977) 22 chairmen	12	55	10	45
James C. Wright, Jr. (1987) 22 chairmen	18	82	4	18
Thomas S. Foley (1989) 22 chairmen	14	64	8	36
Newt Gingrich (1995) 20 chairmen	9	45	11	55

was on the leadership ladder. Rayburn's selection of Albert was a natural one. Their districts were contiguous, their backgrounds comparable, their politics similar, and their devotion to the House shared. But there were other more practical reasons why Albert was selected. He offered acceptable geographic balance to the leadership. The other southern/border protégé of Rayburn's who was considered, Hale Boggs of Louisiana, was a Catholic, and Rayburn was leery of having two Roman Catholics on his leadership team. In recognition of Boggs's close ties with Rayburn, a new position of chief deputy whip was created for him. Most of all, Albert was selected because he possessed exactly the right personal qualities. He was smart, loyal, hard-working, friendly, and had a nose for the House.

The appointment as whip brought the speakership into view for Carl Albert, but the path was not automatic. No majority whip of either party had ever become speaker, and Albert knew that he would have to earn his way. Albert took advantage of the opportunities that the position offered to win many friends and few enemies within the Democratic caucus. Since the whip's job was to count and not to coerce, he rarely had to offend. But he was a central cog in the information network and was in a position to do many favors for members. He was especially effective in bridging the generation gap for Rayburn and McCormack.

By the time of Rayburn's death in 1961, Albert was in a strong position to succeed McCormack as majority leader. A challenge to him by Missouri Congressman Richard Bolling was predicated on the need for a majority leader who would actively push the liberal agenda. Albert was perceived by some to be too closely tied to the committee chairmen. But Albert's years of service as whip stood him in good stead, and Bolling was forced to withdraw before the caucus met to vote.[26]

During the years of the New Frontier and Great Society, Albert was a key figure in the House leadership. He carried much of the organizational load for Speaker McCormack, yet never sought to upstage him. He played a major role in the passage of the Great Society, accepting a position on the Education and Labor Committee through which much of the most controversial legislation passed. As he followed the path to power, Albert's political persona was molded and his perceptions shaped. As speaker, Albert was committed to an ethic of hard work. His normal working days were twelve hours long and would remain so through his speakership years. He accepted Rayburn's conception of the speaker as a House insider who operated within the system to make it work. Quiet persuasion, rather than public declamation, was Albert's preferred method. Albert believed in the committee system and the role of seniority in it. He respected the legitimate prerogatives of the committee chairmen, and believed that the committee system and the House could not function effectively unless those in positions of responsibility had sufficient power. The speaker's role was to work with the committee, and not to run around or over them. Above all else, Albert respected the members themselves, and believed that they were entitled to be treated by their speaker with dignity and fairness. And Albert recognized the nature of his own political base, in his district and in the House. He knew that much of his support in the House came from among conservative southern members who would support a progressive leader who was sensitive to their concerns. Carl Albert calculated his own interest in each decision that he made.

Albert's new leadership team included Majority Leader Hale Boggs of Louisiana and Whip Thomas P. O'Neill, Jr., of Massachusetts. Boggs had won the majority leadership in a hotly contested election and O'Neill had swung a key group of northeastern members into the Boggs column.[27] Boggs's preference for majority whip was Dan Rostenkowski of Illinois, the chairman of the Democratic caucus. But Rostenkowski had earned Albert's disfavor by withholding the pledge of the Illinois delegation to the Oklahoman in the speakership election, and Albert retaliated by knocking Rostenkowski's name off of the list.[28] In a surprise move, Texas Congressman Olin (Tiger) Teague defeated Rostenkowski for the caucus chairmanship.[29] The Democratic House leadership had a distinctly southwestern flavor as it set to do battle with Richard Nixon.

The Politics of Opposition

At the outset of the Ninety-second Congress, the Democratic caucus made further changes in its rules. In a direct attack on the committee chairmen, the new caucus rules specified that seniority need not be observed in the nomination of committee chairmen by the Democratic Committee on Committees (still comprised of the Democratic members of the Ways and Means Committee). The caucus also stipulated that a separate vote on any individual nominee for a committee chairmanship could be obtained by the demand of ten members. Spreading the power around, the caucus required that no member could serve on more than one major committee, and that no member could chair more than one legislative subcommittee.[30] These changes indicated that the pressure to diffuse power in the House would continue to be strong, even with new leadership in place. The leadership's task was to forge a Democratic consensus on policy in a changing legislative environment. The aim was to provide an alternative to the program of the Nixon administration.

This would not be an easy thing to accomplish. Speaker Albert's strategic situation was defined by the institutional structure of the House and the political divisions within his congressional party. Institutionally, the speaker sat between the old order represented by the committee chairmen and a new generation of younger and more liberal members; politically, his party was fundamentally divided on two issues, the Vietnam War and school busing. These institutional and political issues tended to cleave the House in the same way. The committee chairmen and other senior members were disproportionately from the South and were hawkish on the war and opposed to busing. Younger and more liberal members were disproportionately from the North and opposed the war while supporting desegregation. Speaker Albert supported the war and school busing, and, as speaker, had to find a way of working with both wings of the party. It is not surprising, therefore, that the Democratic leadership looked to economic issues in search of a party consensus. Here, the economic situation and Republican policy proclivities provided targets of opportunity.

In 1971 President Nixon unveiled his six-point "American Revolution," which was billed as a dramatic change in public policy. In fact, the Nixon program was less a blueprint for reform than a plan to maneuver around the margins of existing public policy. The six points in his program—revenue sharing, welfare reform, executive reorganization, expanded health care, environmental protection, and economic prosperity—were all variations on the postwar policy agenda.[31] Revenue sharing was intended to send resources back to the states, but it was politically marketable only as an addition to the categoric programs to which Congress was wedded. The cornerstone of Nixon's welfare reform proposal was a "family assistance plan" that called for a minimum family income, a traditionally Democratic idea. Executive reorganization was a way to get around a bureaucracy bloated by career civil servants who were for the most part Democrats. It was not a plan to dismantle the administrative state. The effort to preserve the environment was a Nixon step to preempt an increasingly popular issue.

Why did a conservative Republican president choose to trim the sails of the Great Society rather than to sink the ship? The answer lies in politics. Nixon's primary goal was to be reelected in 1972. It was by no means clear in 1971 that the electorate was ready to reject the redistributive policies that the Democrats had put in place. Nixon sought to placate traditionally Democratic constituencies while redirecting some of the federal largess to Republican constituencies in the states, localities, and business community. He opposed school busing in an effort to win over the George Wallace constituency. The Nixon foreign policy was sweeping. He sought to end the Vietnam War on terms acceptable to the United States, and worked toward rapprochement with Russia and China. If he could simply break even in domestic politics, he would most likely be reelected.

Nixon's strategy put the Democratic congressional leadership in a bind. In foreign policy and on the school busing question, Nixon could count on support from southern Democrats. Speaker Albert, in fact, supported the administration's foreign policy, while Senate Majority Leader Mike Mansfield of Montana was a strong opponent. In the House of Representatives the new and accessible monthly caucus agenda was tailormade for conflict on these issues. The liberal wing of the Democratic caucus wanted to bring the Vietnam War question before the caucus; conservatives, such as Congressman Joe Waggonner of Louisiana, wanted to bring antibusing resolutions up. Speaker Albert was caught in the middle, opposed to the conservatives on the busing question and opposed to the liberals on the war. It was easy for Albert to see why Rayburn and McCormack did not want the caucus to meet.

In April of 1972, in a step that would have been unthinkable when Sam Rayburn was speaker, Whip Thomas P. O'Neill, Jr., brought before the caucus a resolution instructing the House Foreign Affairs Committee to bring to the floor a resolution calling for American withdrawal from Vietnam. Over Albert's opposition, the resolution was passed by the caucus, but several members of the Foreign Affairs and Rules committees refused to be bound by it. The amendment was defeated in the Foreign Affairs Committee by a single vote in favor of a Republican-sponsored substitute.[32] The school busing issue came before the caucus twice. In 1972 a resolution by Joe Waggonner called for an end to forced school busing and was defeated after Speaker Albert spoke strongly against it. In 1975 Waggonner brought to the caucus a constitutional amendment to prohibit forced busing, and once again Albert successfully led the opposition.[33] These cases indicate the difficulty of the caucus as a forum for party policy formation. It is easily availed by ideological factions that are more interested in making headlines than in making law. They also indicate the very difficult circumstances in which Albert operated. His caucus was deeply divided, and even his own whip was not with him on foreign policy matters. Faced with these conflicts, Albert's search for a party consensus turned to economic policy.

Since the New Deal and the emergence of the conservative coalition in 1937, the Democratic party had been united only in the area of economic policy. Even in this area southern conservatives had often been allied with Republican budget-cutting efforts. But on bread-and-butter economic matters Democrats differed from Republicans in their willingness to promote interventionist policies aiming at full employment and welfare relief for poor people. The Depression had hit hardest in the South, and many southerners looked upon government spending programs as the legitimate legacy of the New Deal's response to economic crisis. In the early 1970s Democrats proposed federally supported jobs programs, standby wage and price controls, an increase in the minimum wage, broader federal support for education, federal housing and community development programs, federally supported mass transit programs, more generous benefits for transfer programs, higher spending for public works, and a dramatic expansion of public regulatory authority. Liberal Democrats were in the vanguard of the environmental movement, pushed the Equal Rights Amendment, and proposed national health insurance. The House leadership recognized, however, that by making the bread-and-butter issues the core of its party program, it stood the best chance of winning votes on the floor.

Speaker Albert's mission was to translate a traditional set of Democratic policies into bills that could pass in the House. He sought to articulate and advance the economic philosophy of his party. The primary focus was to be on the problem of unemployment, and the primary Democratic goal was to create new jobs. The emphasis upon job creation had become a centerpiece of Democratic policy during the previous decade. It emanated from a belief that government's proper role in a modern industrial economy was to serve as an employer of last resort for the most marginal workers in society. The first postwar federal jobs program was enacted in 1957 as a modern-day variant of the New Deal Public Works Administration. It focused upon major capital projects. During the Kennedy administration, a major Manpower Training and Development Act was passed. Support for these jobs programs was always reluctant and was tied to two premises: either the program had to support the building of needed public works projects, or it had to provide training intended to make the worker more employable. There was no general consensus at first in favor of programs to provide jobs merely for the sake of providing jobs. During the years of the Great Society, however, liberal Democrats broadened their vision of the public role. The War on Poverty brought with it a commitment to provide jobs through the Jobs Corp and the Office of Economic Opportunity, and in the Congress, liberal Democrats for the first time advanced major public service employment bills that had no other purpose than putting people to work. They succeeded in passing a large-scale jobs bill in 1970, but it was vetoed by President Nixon, and the veto was sustained by the Senate. The 1970 bill provided a precedent for the efforts of the Democratic leadership in the 1970s, as public service jobs became the party's primary vehicle for fighting unemployment and the Republicans.[34]

In 1971, working in cooperation with key committee chairmen, Speaker Albert decided to push three specific pieces of legislation as the basis of his party's economic program: an accelerated public works bill, an emergency public service employment bill, and a minimum wage bill. Each bill was within the modern tradition of the Democratic party and evinced the party's willingness to involve the government in a reallocation of private resources to reduce unemployment, increase wages, and encourage economic growth. These bills were selected because they promised to have broad support in the Democratic caucus. Speaker Albert did not conceive of his task in terms of developing new programs; instead, he sought to advance traditional Democratic legislative alternatives to Republican policies, alternatives that had long germinated in the committees. The legislation had the support of the majority of Democrats; but many felt that the Democratic leadership had been lax in supporting it during the Ninety-first Congress.

In response to the demand for more assertive leadership, Albert called a press conference with the chairmen of the committees and subcommittees to which each bill would be referred in order to heighten press and public awareness of the problem of unemployment, to lay the blame for it at the feet of the administration, and to convey to the country the determination of the Democratic party to do something about it. Albert demonstrated that he intended to lead the fight against the administration in a publicly visible way. The technique was one that he would use often during his speakership. It represented an acknowl-edgement that the modern speaker could not be only a House insider, but must also be a public spokesman for his party. Later, Albert would be criticized for being insufficiently aggressive in speaking for the party; but he went much further than either of his two immediate predecessors in publicizing his party's program.

It is informative to consider the genesis of these bills, for they each tell a different story and reveal the speakership in a different aspect. The introduction of the public service employment bill came as a simple extension of the 1970 effort. The leading supporters of public jobs were still around, and the Democrats had learned from their previous ex-perience how to diffuse some of the internal opposition. There was also, at the outset of the Albert speakership, a sense of renewed mission among Democrats that led to greater party solidarity. Consequently, it was a relatively easy task to get the bill through the House. In an attempt to defeat the bill, House Republicans offered an administration-backed substitute that would have replaced the federal jobs program favored by the Democrats with a manpower revenue sharing bill that would have distributed less money to the states. This proposal was defeated on the House floor, as was a subsequent Republican attempt to recommit the Democratic bill. On each vote the Democrats were able to hold the line within their own party and win with minimal Republican support. Speaker Albert was directly involved in persuading a large number of southern Democrats to support the jobs bill. In the end, only twenty-three Democrats voted against the leadership position, and on final passage the Democratic leadership carried the bill by a comfortable 246–142 margin.[35] President Nixon realized that the jobs bill had con-siderable support and planned to veto the public works bill that the Congress was expected to pass at about the same time. So Nixon agreed to negotiate a compromise jobs bill. The compromise emerged from the conference deliberations with the administration's support, and on the adoption of the conference report the Democrats were joined by most Republicans, as the bill was passed by a 343–14 margin. This vote was in stark contrast to the 1970 public jobs struggle, when the adoption of the conference report was opposed by Republicans and barely passed the House, 177–159. Republican members clearly wanted to go on record in favor of a public jobs program.[36]

Albert was involved with the passage of the jobs bill from start to finish, although the primary venue of the action was in the Education and Labor Committee, whose chairman, Carl Perkins of Kentucky, strongly supported it. The key to the passage of the bill lay in diffusing Democratic opposition and marshaling external support. The former was accomplished by paring the 1970 bill down, removing all extraneous provisions. The latter was accomplished by bringing together representatives of various interest groups to organize a concerted lobbying effort. In a pattern that became characteristic of Democratic leadership, representatives of organized labor, municipal, and environmental groups were brought together by the speaker's staff. A preliminary head-count produced a list of Republican and Democratic doubtfuls, and each name on the list was assigned to one of the groups present. It was agreed that Republican votes would be difficult to obtain as long as the vote looked close, and that the most concerted effort should focus on southern Democrats. As the time of floor consideration of the bill approached, the speaker's staff continued to meet with interest-group representatives.[37] In early May the Democratic Steering and Policy Committee met to discuss the bill and to hear an appeal for party cohesion by the speaker. A whip count was conducted, and Speaker Albert was asked to speak to several members whose votes were thought critical.[38] The whip count was supplemented by the reports of the interest-group coalition. By the time the bill reached the floor of the House, the leadership was confident of the votes needed for passage.[39] In the end this projection proved correct. Whereas southern Democrats had come close to defeating the 1970 bill, most of them supported their own party in 1971 and provided fifty-five votes against the Republican substitute on the key vote. This result was no accident. The speaker and Majority Leader Hale Boggs both "made the rounds" of southern offices, garnering pledges of support.[40] Ways and Means Chairman Wilbur Mills also assisted in the effort.[41]

The public service employment bill presented all of the ingredients of successful political management. The bill was a straightforward party bill. It had received a dry run in the previous congress, and the danger of loading the bill with extraneous provisions had been avoided. Albert was behind the bill early, often, and publicly. Organized interests were enlisted in lobbying, and the party machinery was in high gear. The leadership was able to rely on a renewed sense of party solidarity. As a border state Democrat, Speaker Albert was in a particularly good position to appeal to the swing members from the South. Economic conditions made the concept of public service employment attractive. And the Democrats were itching for a victory. In the end, President Nixon decided not to risk having his veto overridden. Here was a prescription for success. Unfortunately for Speaker Albert and the House Democrats, it was not to be repeated as the other elements of the Democratic economic program moved through the Ninety-second Congress.

The concept of a major public works program originated in the Depression-era Public Works Administration. A major federal public works program had been adopted in 1962, and while the idea of a public works bill was a bit rusty, it was very much the kind of bill that Democrats liked to support. It would provide jobs and public works projects in the districts, and if President Nixon chose to veto it, the Democrats could attack him. The Democratic leadership decided to revive the Accelerated Public Works Act of 1962, funded at $2 billion. The aim of the 1962 act had been to stimulate jobs by providing federal support for local water and sewage projects. Now a revived accelerated public works program was to be joined to a renewal of the 1965 Public Works and Economic Development Act, funded at $550 million annually through 1973, which would emphasize long-range economic development of areas with chronically high unemployment. The 1971 bill also included an extension of the Appalachian Regional Development Act of 1965, funded at $6 billion through 1975, and designed to provide special help in transportation and other public facilities in that economically depressed area. Including other more minor provisions, the entire package came to more than $10 billion over a period of four fiscal years.[42]

A bill with this much in district project money was bound to be attractive, even to Republicans, and the measure swept through the House, 319–67. The Senate bill was more conservative than the House's, and passed easily, 77–3. The leadership's strategy was to get to conference, where the Senate receded to the House. The conference report was adopted by a nearly straight party-line vote of 45–33 in the Senate and 275–104 in the House. The margin of victory in the Senate made it clear that a Nixon veto could be sustained. As the public works bill was brought forward just prior to the passage of the public service employment bill, Nixon was able to veto the first while seeking a compromise on the second. His veto of the public works bill was sustained in the Senate. Later in 1971, a smaller, $3.9 billion version was passed into law. It incorporated the Appalachian and public works titles at a much reduced rate of support, while deleting the accelerated public works title entirely.[43]

The fact that the president chose to exercise his veto on the public works bill and not on the jobs bill reflected the underlying dynamics of the situation. The accelerated public works bill passed the House *more easily* than had the public service employment bill. There was, in this case, no concerted Republican effort to defeat the bill, and in fact most of the Republicans voted for it on final passage. This was because of the way that the two bills interacted politically. Since both were brought forward at approximately the same time, and both were clearly labeled as components of the Democratic program, the Republicans could develop a posture toward both bills. Since it was widely expected that the

president would veto the public works bill, there was little incentive for
House Republicans to fight it. The Democratic margin was narrower
in the Senate than in the House (the Democrats controlled 55 percent
of the Senate seats and 58 percent of the House seats), and the Senate
offered a more secure venue for a veto battle than the House. When
the veto of the public works bill was coupled to administration endorsement of the jobs bill, the political heat was absorbed from the
issue.

A possible remedy for the problem that ailed the public works bill
might have been to distance it from the jobs bill, denying the Republicans
the opportunity of voting for one while opposing the other. However,
other political considerations argued against this strategy. From the
outset, the Democratic leadership aimed at bringing forward a *package*
of bills that could be labeled a party program. Albert wanted to advance
these bills as quickly as possible. He recognized that fast action was
essential for establishing the tone and direction of his leadership; and,
the Democrats were anxious to create political conflict with the administration on their own terms. For the Democratic leadership, there
were always two goals in view: one was to enact laws creating employment opportunities; the other was to clarify the differences between
Republican and Democratic approaches to the management of the economy. In the end the Democrats got a half a loaf of jobs and two full
loaves of political credit among those voters who looked to government
for unemployment relief. A similar pattern emerged on the issue of the
minimum wage, but with less success.

The support of increases in the federal minimum wage had been a
staple of liberal Democratic politics for years. In 1966 the Congress
passed a major extension of the coverage of the minimum wage law,
and had increased the minimum to $1.60 per hour.[44] Although the
minimum wage had never been as popular among southern Democrats
as among northern Democrats, in early 1971 Wilbur Mills of Arkansas,
chairman of the House Ways and Means Committee, proposed to increase the minimum wage to $2 per hour beginning in 1972.[45] Mills
reached beyond the jurisdiction of his committee to invade the turf of
the Education and Labor Committee, and challenged Albert's leadership.
The speaker wanted to have his own imprimatur on major pieces of
party economic legislation. Mills had presidential ambitions, and wanted
to carve a role for himself in employment legislation. His aspirations
threatened the speaker, since his position on the minimum wage was
essentially that of a southern conservative, closer to the Republicans
than to Albert, the liberal wing of the party, and the AFL-CIO.

Labor unions wanted an increased minimum wage and extended
coverage. They opposed a subminimum youth wage. Southern cities

opposed the extension of coverage to their employees because it would force them to increase taxes. Service industries opposed extended coverage, although if they were going to have to swallow it they wanted a youth wage. And agricultural interests opposed increases in the agricultural minimum wage. The minimum wage was a classic conservative coalition issue, since the southern and agriculturally based Democrats were allied with the Republican business interests. Here lay the political danger in Mills's initiative. Any bill sponsored by Mills would be bound to reflect the coalition's outlook. If Mills were allowed to get out on front for the Democrats, it would be more difficult to pass a bill that reflected the position of the national party.

To head Mills off, Albert sought a leadership-backed minimum wage bill from the Education and Labor Committee. Congressman John B. Dent of Pennsylvania, the chairman of the committee's subcommittee on labor, took the lead. Dent was an expert on labor legislation and had supported an increase in the minimum wage in previous years. With the concurrence of full committee chairman Carl D. Perkins of Kentucky, Dent agreed to launch hearings immediately, and aimed toward the early passage of a Democratic leadership bill. On March 4, 1971, Speaker Albert, Dent, and Perkins conducted a joint press conference to announce the initiative.[46] Thus was begun one of the most frustrating odysseys of the Albert years, a four-year struggle to enact a bill that at the outset the leadership had hoped to pass in three months.

Initially, it appeared that the contending forces within the Democratic party would reach an agreement. By April 29 the Dent subcommittee was on the verge of completing its hearings on the Mills and Dent versions of the bill, and moving to markup. The subcommittee bill extended coverage to municipal employees and overtime provisions to an additional seven million workers. But it also made concessions to the Mills version, as Mills's earlier effective date for the increase in the minimum wage was included. The Dent subcommittee took the most liberal provisions of each bill and sent them forward.[47] At that time leadership staff anticipated House passage of a bill by Memorial Day, little more than a month away. As it developed, the House did not pass a bill until a year later. Everything that could go wrong, did.

To begin with, there was the irritating problem of Wilbur Mills. In the Ninety-second Congress, Mills's fingerprints were to be found wherever the legislative process was at work, as he sought to increase his power and influence in the House. His role as the chairman of the Ways and Means Committee and of the Democratic Committee on Committees gave him a tremendous power base, and he used it to good effect. In early 1971 he tried to lift the interest lid on certain long-term government bonds. This move brought a vigorous protest from Wright

Patman, chairman of the Banking and Commerce Committee, an old-style Texas populist and a long-time foe of high interest rates. Albert joined Patman in the fight against Mills, and in the first use of the recorded teller vote in the House, Mills prevailed over Albert and Patman 212–180.[48] Mills engaged in a major struggle in October of 1972 with Appropriations Committee Chairman George Mahon to impose a debt ceiling on the federal government. In the process he joined with Republicans to grant to President Nixon a congressional authorization to impound funds in order to stay under the ceiling. This was vigorously opposed by Mahon and Albert as a violation of congressional prerogatives.[49] During the same period of time, Mills proposed a 20 percent increase in social security benefits and the indexing of the benefits to inflation.[50]

With his grasp of and hold over federal tax law, Mills could range widely over the terrain of federal policy. For example, in 1971 he stood in the path of a bill placing import quotas on confectionery products in order to support the sugar industry. Speaker Albert was asked to intercede with Mills by Oklahoma peanut growers, who wanted to win the support of sugar growers for limits on imported peanuts.[51] With Mills abstaining, the sugar bill passed with the quotas intact. In another case, Mills was center-stage in the Democrats' efforts to enact federal campaign reform legislation. The financing provisions of the plan had to pass through the Ways and Means Committee and the Senate Finance Committee. The support of both Russell Long, chairman of the Senate committee, and Wilbur Mills was needed if campaign financing were to pass. There was disagreement as to the best legislative strategy, and disagreement as to the substance of the financing provisions. Given the importance of the bill to the national party and the House leadership, Albert found it expedient to consult with Mills on the strategy choice.[52] In 1972 Mills came forward with a Ways and Means proposal to create an "educational trust fund" along with tax credits to families for each child in school (a boon to parents of children in parochial schools). The proposal elicited a harsh response from George Mahon, who wrote to Speaker Albert that Mills was out "to launch a new and indefensible attack on the Committee system" which Mahon intended to "oppose to the limit of my ability."[53] These examples illustrate clearly the extent of Mills's involvement in various areas of legislation. In Albert's first term as speaker, he found himself joined in battle against Mills in many instances, and even with such powerful southern chairmen as George Mahon, Wright Patman, W. R. Poage, and Carl Perkins on Albert's side, Mills often carried the day.

Mills's record may not have been entirely consistent in substance, but it demonstrated a persistent political pattern: his presidential aspirations required him to build bridges on his left and right, to have a hand in as many decisions as possible. For years a consensus politician, he became an unsettling force within the House Democratic party. His role explains, in part, why the minimum wage bill did not move forward as quickly as it appeared destined to do in April 1971. Mills was not yet ready to play ball. The position that he had established at the outset of the legislative struggle on the minimum wage had served to define the view of conservative southern Democrats—raise the minimum, but do not extend the coverage.

If Mills and the southerners were not always synchronized with Albert's timetable, neither were President Nixon and House Republicans. Faced with the Democratic initiative, the Nixon White House brought forward its own minimum wage plan, which House Republicans overwhelmingly supported. Led by respected, conservative Illinois Congressman John Erlenborn, the Republicans on the Education and Labor Committee fought a pitched battle against the Democratic bill in any of its variations. In a move that provided the Republicans with a target of opportunity, the Education and Labor Democrats added more extended coverage to the bill. This enabled the Nixon administration to step into the breach by accepting higher minimum wage provisions while opposing the extended coverage and other less significant features of the Democratic bill. Allied with conservative southern Democrats, the Republicans would pose a considerable challenge once the bill came to the House floor. While the Senate lagged behind in its consideration of a companion measure, and with other major pieces of legislation occupying its floor agenda, the House dragged its feet on the minimum wage. In July the Dent subcommittee attempted to reach a final agreement with the Mills forces, but by the end of September, they were still at it.[54] In October the bill finally arrived at the full committee, which passed it by a substantial majority of 26–7. The Democrats voted 22–0 for the bill and the Republicans opposed it 4–7.[55] With the end of the first session of the Ninety-second Congress in sight, the bill went to the Rules Committee in October 1971, where it encountered the formidable opposition of Chairman William Colmer. There it lay dormant for five months.[56]

The stalling of the minimum wage bill was the last great expression of the independent power of the House Rules Committee and its chairman. From its creation in 1880 until the revolt against Cannon, the committee had served as an arm of the leadership. During the feudal period, it acquired independent power under the seniority system. After Rayburn defeated Smith in the fight to pack the committee in 1961, the liberal Democratic majority had program control in principle but not in practice. Smith and his successor, Colmer, could still control the committee on most occasions. Colmer's opposition to the minimum wage bill illustrated his autonomy and provides an indication of the limits that had been reached by 1971. With the support of committee Republicans, Colmer refused to move on the minimum wage bill. Colmer opposed minimum wages because he believed that they were inherently inflationary. Yet he did not act by fiat; he had a majority of his committee behind him so long as the pressure was not applied from the leadership. Richard Bolling, on Speaker Albert's behalf, worked to persuade his Democratic colleagues to overrule the chairman, but the votes were not there.

On November 17, 1971, John Dent discussed the legislative situation on the Rules Committee with Speaker Albert. Colmer had announced that in view of the lateness in the session, only "emergency" new legislation would be cleared by Rules for floor action. Albert asked Dent to write a letter characterizing the minimum wage bill as an emergency measure and requesting the speaker's support in obtaining a rule for the bill.[57] Dent thought that the opposition to the bill had been "dissipated" and the time was ripe for floor passage; indeed, the timing appeared to be the emergency—either the bill would pass now or not at all. Such an appeal was bound to be less than persuasive to one who was opposed to the bill in the first place, as Colmer was. Responding to Dent's request, Albert wrote to Colmer calling the measure an emergency and requesting a rule.[58] Colmer's response evoked the old power of the Rules Committee as it expressed itself at its denouement:

> I have your letter of November 17 suggesting that my Rules Committee conduct hearings on H.R. 7130, the so-called Minimum Wage Act. Of course, you recall our previous conversations on this matter, and my strong opposition to the enactment of such legislation at this time . . . Mr. Speaker, I think you will agree that the Committee has been most cooperative with you. In fact, I told you and our good friend, former Speaker McCormack, when I became Chairman of this committee that I would cooperate to the best of my ability with the Leadership, except in those instances where, in my opinion, such cooperation would be a violation of my principles. This is such a case."[59]

Colmer's opposition stalled the bill for the duration of the first session of the Ninety-second Congress. Finally, in the spring of 1972, Albert resolved to break the jam and force the bill out of committee. He demanded that committee Democrats support the bill or else face the leadership's disfavor. Albert's action forced Colmer's hand, since the chairman did not want to be overturned by his committee. He promised to hold hearings on the bill in April 1972. He did so on May 9, and the Rules Committee reported the bill under an open rule according to which an anticipated Republican substitute would be in order.[60]

Having surmounted Wilbur Mills and William Colmer, the minimum wage bill may have seemed destined to become law. However, it faced two more formidable hurdles, the conservative coalition and the Nixon administration. On the House floor the Republican substitute was offered by John Erlenborn of Illinois, with the support of Democrat Don Fuqua of Florida. Fuqua's involvement indicated that the conservative coalition was afoot. Under normal House procedure, the substitute amendment was considered first. In a key move, liberal Republican John B. Anderson of Illinois offered an amendment that liberalized the increases in the minimum wage as presented by Erlenborn. This brought to the substitute the support of several liberal Republicans from the industrial belt.[61] Generally, the Erlenborn bill narrowed the coverage of the minimum wage law as compared to the Dent bill, and stretched out the increases in the minimum wage over several more years. A youth wage provision was added, and the overtime pay provisions were scaled back. In addition, the Erlenborn bill dropped import restrictions that had been placed in the Dent version to protect some domestic industries. On May 11, 1972, the House adopted the Erlenborn substitute by a 217–191 vote, with 63 southern Democrats defecting to the Republican side. This vote was a major defeat for Speaker Albert, but he was not done fighting yet.[62]

A clue to his strategy lay in the vote on final passage, when most liberals jumped on the Erlenborn bill and passed it by an overwhelming margin of 330–78. Under the rules and precedents of the House, the speaker has the power to appoint House conferees on all bills; by custom, the speaker defers to the recommendation of the chairman of the committee from which the bill emanates. House rules provide that a majority of the House conferees must have supported the bill as it passed the House. But what does it mean to have supported a bill?[63] The most elementary measure is the final passage vote; if a member votes for the bill on final passage, he has supported it. In this instance, Chairman Perkins recommended to Speaker Albert a slate of ten Democratic nominees from the Education and Labor Committee who had voted against the Erlenborn substitute but for the bill on final passage. He could scarcely have done otherwise; only one committee Democrat had supported Erlenborn, and Perkins was not about to abandon the conference to members from other committees. But of course he did not intend that a majority of the House conferees should support the House bill. It was widely anticipated that the Senate would produce a bill even more liberal than the original Dent bill, and it was openly planned that the House conferees would recede to key Senate provisions of the bill.

This more liberal conference version of the bill would then come before the House and it would not be open to substitute or amendment. At that point a member who wished to be on record in favor of an increase in the minimum wage would have no choice but to support the Democratic bill.

It was a clever strategy, but it ran into an obstacle. The only way that the House could get to conference on the bill was by unanimous consent or by a majority vote. On July 27 Perkins asked for unanimous consent, but Erlenborn objected. On August 1 Perkins moved that the House go to conference. Normally, the dynamics of a vote such as this are different to those of a vote on the substance of a bill, since the majority party has a vested interest in its power to control conferences. Such a vote is similar to the procedural votes on organizing the House that are central to majority party control. While the prerogatives of the speaker and standing committee chairmen are not ordinarily at issue on substantive votes, they were at issue on this motion to go to conference. Albert and Perkins, both with strong ties to the southern wing of the party, had reason to hope that they would prevail on this procedural vote. If so, they were wrong. The leadership lost the August 1 vote by 190–198. Two months later, on October 3, they tried again, with similar results, 188–196. In August, 47 southern Democrats defected; in October, the number was up to 58. While the southern defections were related to policy, it is hard to doubt that Wilbur Mills and William Colmer, two powerful and spurned southern barons, had a hand in the defeat of their border state colleagues, Carl Albert and Carl Perkins.[64]

Albert and Perkins did not give up, and the battle was not over. Minimum wage legislation was killed in the Ninety-second Congress but was revived in the Ninety-third. In 1973 the Congress passed a bill that was similar to the 1971 Dent bill, and President Nixon vetoed it.[65] The Congress passed an essentially similar bill in 1974 by an overwhelming margin, and this time a Watergate-weakened Nixon signed it.[66] The 1973 and 1974 bills did make some concessions to business interests, but they were for the most part true to the aims of the leadership's 1971 bill. The increases in wage levels and coverage came later, were phased in more slowly, and, because of inflation, were worth less; but the Democratic Congress in the end prevailed. The explanation for Albert's eventual success was owing in part to tenacity, in part to changing economic circumstances (since inflation had rendered the $1.60 minimum wage less adequate by 1974), and in part to clever politics. The leadership traded concessions on the 1973 agriculture bill in return for southern Democratic support on the minimum wage.[67]

In pressing for enactment of his party's basic economic program in the Ninety-second Congress, Albert worked in cooperation with some senior committee chairmen (such as Carl Perkins and Wright Patman) and in competition with others (such as Wilbur Mills and William Colmer), but he could rely on a solid base of Democratic support for each bill. Across the entire legislative spectrum, however, the party was less united. In areas such as agriculture, education, and the environment there was no clear party consensus, and on the school busing and Vietnam War issues the Democratic caucus was badly divided. It is unsurprising, therefore, that Speaker Albert chose to define his party's program on issues around which the party could coalesce. An analysis of Albert's voting record during the Ninety-second Congress reveals a lot about his position.[68] When support for the speaker among Democrats is measured across several issue areas, it becomes clear that his party was much more likely to support him on economic and social welfare matters than on issues of agriculture, education, and the environment. On these latter issues, Democratic votes tended to disperse, there being no clear party consensus or position.

An interesting feature of Albert's voting record is the fact that in a number of cases (about 20 percent) he voted against a majority of his own party; when he did, he voted on the winning side over 80 percent of the time. Most of these votes were on foreign policy. The deep rift within the House Democratic party over foreign policy in general and the Vietnam War in particular fractured it, and Speaker Albert was on one side of the fissure. While the Democratic party was relatively well united on economic issues, on foreign policy the conservative coalition was still often in control, and Albert was a member of it. He had been a loyal supporter of the Johnson administration and its Vietnam policy. He had served as the chairman of the platform committee at the 1964 Democratic convention and as the full chairman of the 1968 convention. At the latter, he had been personally embarrassed by the antiwar demonstrators who were the advance guard of the McGovern wing of the party. Himself a product of postwar internationalism, Albert took the threat of international communism seriously.

On the Vietnam question, then, and in attitude toward the Russians generally, Carl Albert was a hawk. In 1971 especially, the speaker was instrumental in defeating repeated attempts in the Democratic caucus and on the House floor to pass withdrawal resolutions. In 1972 Albert shifted his ground and supported the final version of a caucus-passed withdrawal resolution after having voted against it at first. Albert and Majority Leader Hale Boggs finally joined Majority Whip Tip O'Neill in supporting American withdrawal. By then, of course, there were few troops left to withdraw, but Albert's shift indicated that he had concluded that a continuation of the war could serve no useful purpose.[69]

With the end of the war, some of the divisiveness that it had caused was also ended. But the Vietnam War brought about a resurgence of congressional involvement in foreign policy that had an important effect on the speakership of the House. Carl Albert was the first postwar speaker to play an important role in foreign policy. He was the first to travel abroad and meet with foreign leaders. In the 1970s the speaker of the House became a player on the international scene.

Carl Albert's first term as speaker served to clarify his strategic location among House Democrats. He was not in the middle, so much as he was astride two different coalitions, one in domestic policy and one in foreign affairs. On foreign policy matters, he became an important congressional supporter of President Nixon, the more so due to Senate Majority Leader Mike Mansfield's unbridled antiwar posture. In domestic affairs, he supported a traditionally democratic economic program. Instead of being the leader of a cohesive majority, Albert had to satisfy both wings of his party. Many of Albert's critics were liberal. They failed to appreciate the fact that the speaker's association with conservative and southern Democrats on foreign policy was valuable to him. In fact, Albert's position was squarely at the center of the Democratic party that stood for internationalism abroad and distributive benefits at home. Unfortunately, that party was on the way to extinction. Carl Albert performed a balancing act as speaker; that he was able to do so in a manner consistent with his own values and his constituents' preferences is one important reason why he became, and remained, speaker.

The Ninety-second Congress demonstrated what some political scientists would call "normal policy making." While the Vietnam War was an abnormal historical event, the Republican control of the White House, Democratic control of the Congress, the fundamental differences in partisan approaches to the economy, and the rift between the southern and northern wings of the Democratic caucus all reflected common experiences of post–World War II American politics. The House Democratic leadership had functioned according to the normal pattern that had developed after Rayburn's death. Indeed, the leadership machine under Speaker Albert was brought to new levels of efficiency in legislative management.

Yet, by the end of 1972, some criticisms of Speaker Albert had emerged. His support of House reforms was acknowledged by some, but not widely understood. The improvements in the management of the legislative process that he had brought about were appreciated by members, but not much known by the press and public. Albert was widely regarded as fair, and he was well liked by most members. But an undercurrent of doubt was frequently expressed in the media. Some said that Albert had not sufficiently asserted himself as a party leader. Others felt that he was too deferential to the committee chairmen. A common theme stressed Albert's desire to avoid conflict with members and his insufficiently forceful posture toward the administration.[70]

These comments bore an element of truth. Carl Albert preferred working with people to running over them. He was a private man who did not seek the public eye. His conception of his role as speaker did entail a certain deference to the committee chairmen and a fair-minded treatment of all members. Because these orientations sometimes prevented him from dealing forcefully with members and the press, his reputation suffered. Of course, Albert understood his strategic position better than his critics did. The conservative coalition was still the essential feature of policy making in the House, and the power of senior southern committee chairmen was still a force with which to be reckoned. Speaker Albert's goal was to legislate a Democratic program. In order to do this, it was necessary to work with the committees rather than against their leadership. In contrast to McCormack, Albert was very attentive to the management of the House. Often Albert's critics seemed oblivious to the real improvements in the conduct of House business that he imposed. If one compares the operation of the House under Albert with Richard Bolling's critique of McCormack, for example, the extent of the improvement is clear. Still, the criticisms of Speaker Albert suggested that his reputation and success would depend as much upon the way in which he was perceived as upon the objective accomplishments of his speakership. The democratic speakership would come to depend heavily upon the speaker's capacity for managing his public image and professional reputation. Democratic speakers would require some of the abilities of Neustadt's presidents.[71] As Speaker Albert looked forward to 1973 and the dawn of the Ninety-third Congress, he faced the prospect of an ongoing struggle with a Republican president whose power was enhanced by one of the largest landslide victories in American history. Little could he have suspected that instead of politics as usual, the Ninety-third Congress was to bring him to the vortex of the greatest constitutional crisis since the Civil War.

Constitutional Crisis

Early in 1973 Richard Nixon proposed the most radical change in the direction of governmental policy in the United States since the first New Deal. Fresh from one of the largest electoral victories in American history, on the verge of ending America's most unpopular war, and riding high in the public opinion polls, Nixon undertook a radical transformation in governmental priorities, going well beyond the innovations of his 1971 six-point plan. Nixon, who had been willing to accommodate some Democratic spending programs rather than jeopardize his reelection prospects, was now relieved of the burden of electoral politics and free to pursue "his most basic ideological convictions."[72]

Those convictions called for a dramatic reduction in many federal programs, especially the categoric grant programs that had originated in the Great Society. Calling for a historic turnaround in the direction of government, Nixon proposed to hold the size of government constant by cutting sufficiently in discretionary programs to allow mandated increases in transfer programs, avoiding tax increases.[73] He threw down the gauntlet to the Democrat-controlled Congress, the response of which was "explosively negative, setting the stage for a knockdown fight that may well dominate the next two years of American politics." In a nationwide radio address, Nixon called upon a "new American majority" to back him in his attempts to reverse the direction of public policy. "On both sides of the burgeoning debate, there was immediate recognition . . . that the stakes in the battle go beyond the fate of specific programs to the whole direction of American domestic policy and the identity of the party that will control it in the years ahead."[74]

Speaker Albert recognized the threat to his party and its programs inherent in the Nixon proposals. From the perspective of the House leadership, more was at stake than policy preferences or even than political realignment. The Nixon White House had launched a wholesale attack on the constitutional separation of powers through the impoundment of lawfully appropriated funds and the assertion of executive privilege. Faced by this fundamental challenge, Albert went on national radio and the Sunday talk shows to attack the Nixon budget. He vigorously pursued anti-impoundment legislation in the House, pressed for adoption of congressional budget reform, worked to revive and advance several economic bills (such as the minimum wage bill and a new public service/manpower bill), and launched the most comprehensive review of the House committee structure since 1946. Albert's aim was threefold. He wanted to reassert the Democratic economic program as an alternative to that of the Republicans; he wanted to improve the efficiency of the Congress and its image as a governing institution entitled to respect equal to that of the executive; and he wanted to portray Nixon as an imperial president, a man obsessed with the pursuit of raw power for whom the restraints of the Constitution stood as no barrier to the fulfillment of personal ambition. Albert had to accommodate further the reform tendency within the House, marshal majorities behind Democratic legislation, and undertake a public relations offensive against the president. With the newness of his speakership worn thin by two years of legislative struggle and with increasingly open criticism of his leadership emerging from within the ranks, Albert faced no mean task. All of the leverage seemed to lie on Nixon's side. No one could have predicted that by the end of the Ninety-third Congress Nixon would be driven from office and Albert would stand twice in direct line of succession to the presidency.

At the outset of the Ninety-third Congress, the Democratic caucus strengthened the speaker's hand. William Colmer's fight against the minimum wage bill was the last for him and for "his" Rules Committee. Colmer retired in 1972 and in organizing the Ninety-third Congress in 1973 the caucus gave to the speaker the right to nominate the chairman and all of the Democratic members of the Rules Committee. This reform, which Speaker Albert regarded as the most significant political reform of his speakership, effectively made the Rules Committee an arm of the speaker.[75] The conservative coalition could still vote its interest on the House floor, but it would not be able to prevent legislation from getting there. The battle between Judge Smith and Sam Rayburn was finally over. Still, Speaker Albert resisted a move to give to him the right to unilaterally call bills from the Rules Committee to the floor. Albert realized that the Rules Committee would be a useful buffer against member demands. With its membership within his nominating control, he would likely be able to get legislation out of it when he really wanted to; he did not want to have to turn down the large number of requests that would inevitably come to him if he had power to overrule the committee, and he preferred to see the committee blamed when it killed a bill to which he was opposed.

Other steps taken in 1973 to strengthen the leadership were the appointment of the speaker, majority leader, and whip to the Democratic Committee on Committees, an automatic caucus vote to approve all committee chairmen, and the creation of Democratic committee caucuses empowered to form subcommittees and select their chairmen (taking these powers from the committee chairmen). A subcommittee "bill of rights" was adopted that ensured the autonomy of the subcommittees from the chairmen of the full committees and guaranteed to each subcommittee an adequate staff and budget. The Democratic Steering and Policy Committee was given a larger staff, and the speaker was made its chairman. It was intended that the Steering and Policy Committee would become a vehicle for party policy formation and that its staff would develop a capacity for issue analysis. The Committee would serve as a sounding board for members, since one-half of its membership would consist of representatives elected by geographic zones; but the speaker was given sufficient at-large appointments to ensure control. Rayburn and McCormack, of course, had opposed having a steering committee. Speaker Albert accepted its new role, but did not actively use it in the Ninety-third Congress. The committee's staff, however, was active on a wide variety of legislation on the speaker's behalf, and became an extension of the speaker's office.[76]

These new powers would be needed, because the policy agenda of the Ninety-third Congress promised to be more difficult than that of the Ninety-second had been due to the president's overwhelming electoral victory in 1972. The economy was the major focus. With inflation increasing and unemployment rising, the Democrats pressed for legislation to spur the economy. Public service jobs, public works, and the minimum wage were all a part of their program once again. However, with Nixon's efforts to trim the budget of many basic Great Society programs, the Democrats had to pursue rearguard action rather than a frontal attack. In the spring of 1973 the leadership was involved in legislation affecting public works and economic development, public service employment, the minimum wage, wage and price controls, and mass transit. In every area, the congressional Democrats proposed to spend more money and Nixon threatened vetoes. The appropriations committees were faced with veto threats of any bills that exceeded the Nixon budget. The battle lines were clearly drawn. The economic issues formed the heart of the leadership's program, while other major legislation percolated in the committees. The tension between rural and urban lawmakers was evident in the debate over mass transit and farm bills; the division between fiscal conservatives and liberals was central to the consideration of standby wage and price authority; the conservative coalition was involved in the elementary and secondary school aid bill, where school busing was again at issue.

These "normal" policy conflicts were soon pushed to the back burner as congressional attention became preoccupied with reform and impeachment. Speaker Albert cared deeply about the deliberative capacity and constitutional prerogatives of the Congress. He initiated two major efforts to reform House procedure: the impoundment and budget control bill and the Bolling select committee on reform of the committee system. Albert was convinced that both good politics and good constitutional construction required Congress to assert its authority vis-à-vis the president and he saw a historic opportunity to strengthen Congress's control over the federal budget.[77] Both Albert and Republican Leader Gerald R. Ford of Michigan supported the committee reform bill because they were convinced that the House's capacity to function depended upon bringing order to a committee system that had grown chaotic.[78] Albert supported these institutional reform efforts because he appreciated his responsibility as speaker to defend the prerogatives of the House and attend to the health of its internal system of governance.

The budget reforms were adopted in response to President Nixon's numerous impoundments and his charge that the Democratic Congress could not control federal spending on its own. Nixon dramatically stepped up the pace and dollar amount of impoundments after winning reelection in late 1972.[79] Congressional Democrats were enraged and many constitutional scholars appalled, but there is little evidence that the public was as upset. Nixon's approval rating jumped from 50 percent to 68 percent between November 1972 and January 1973, the busiest period of impoundment.[80] Nixon had convinced the public that the Democratic congressional majority was responsible for excessive federal spending and rising inflation. Turning public opinion against Nixon on this matter would be no easy task. Liberal interest groups joined in the effort, but their constituencies often felt less strongly than did their leaders. As long as the Congress was perceived to be fiscally irresponsible, it was difficult to rally the public against the president.

The charge of fiscal irresponsibility brought about the coupling of the impoundment control bill with the budget act, enabling the Democrats to claim that they had set their own house in order before restricting the president. The passage of the Budget Reform and Impoundment Control Act of 1974 was one of the most significant institutional reforms in history, and demonstrated the determination of the Congress to defend its own prerogatives against the claims of an over-reaching executive branch. The process by which Congress had passed its appropriations and revenue bills was very fragmented, and within the Congress no mechanism existed for reconciling budget outlays with income. Taxes were typically raised with great reluctance, while spending increases were often brought about automatically by trends in the economy. The Nixon administration succeeded in turning the spending issue to the advantage of the Republican party, while in the Congress Republicans rejoiced in voting against the increases in the debt ceiling required by the continued deficits. When in October of 1972 the government faced paralysis because of the struggle over the debt-ceiling increase, the Congress moved to create the bipartisan Joint Study Committee on Budget Control, whose charge was to come up with a plan for a congressional budget process.[81]

While the Joint Committee worked on the development of a long-range plan to deal with the budget, President Nixon raised the stakes in his ongoing contest with the Congress on federal spending by increasing the number and scope of impoundments. Federal law and practice dating back to the Anti-Deficiency Act of 1905 had permitted presidents to withhold the spending of funds in order to achieve efficiency in government (as, for example, when appropriated funds were no longer needed or when a delay in spending might achieve savings to the government). President Nixon asserted a broad prerogative to impound funds across the entire range of discretionary federal spending in the name of fiscal responsibility. Naturally, Nixon picked on programs that he opposed. By 1973 the level of presidential impoundments reached $18 billion, and there was an angry reaction in the Congress.[82] While the House Democratic leadership was gravely concerned about the Congress's capacity to control spending without a budget process of its own, Speaker Albert recognized that the resolution of this aspect of the problem would need to be cautiously undertaken, since any effective budget process would affect the autonomy of the Ways and Means and Appropriations Committees. His support for the Joint Study Committee was based upon a belief that the only possible avenue to reform lay in a comprehensive solution embraced by both chambers, both parties, and both the taxing and spending committees of each chamber.

The impoundment issue was another matter entirely. In this case the constitutional authority of the Congress was under challenge by the executive branch, and the speaker was sworn to defend the powers and prerogatives of the House of Representatives. Besides, the objects of attack were mostly programs that he supported. At the outset of the Ninety-third Congress a dozen anti-impoundment bills were introduced in the House of Representatives; by the end of March 1973, 137 members had joined as sponsors or co-sponsors of anti-impoundment legislation.[83] Faced with a crisis that was at once constitutional, political, and institutional, Speaker Albert acted quickly to control the issue before the Senate got the jump on the House.

At Albert's request the Steering and Policy Committee staff, with other leadership staff members, drafted a resolution limiting presidential impoundments to a period of thirty days without the concurrent approval of both houses of the Congress. The leadership draft was reviewed within days by representatives of key Democratic constituencies in education, labor, and agriculture.[84] The powerful statement against impoundment embodied by the House draft (which in effect automatically disallowed all presidential impoundments by the mere inaction of one house of the Congress) was slightly more stringent than the approach taken in the Senate by Sam Ervin of North Carolina, whose bill would have required concurrent action by both houses of Congress within sixty days in order to approve an impoundment.

The problem with both the Albert and Ervin approaches was quickly pointed out by Professor Arthur Maass of Harvard University in a letter to Senator Ervin.[85] By requiring the Congress to affirm each and every presidential impoundment, the Congress would be forced to legislate each time a president held up the expenditure of funds for reasons of fiscal management. While most of the aggregate dollars in dispute in the impoundment debate involved a relatively small number of large ticket items, there were scores of cases in which a president might reasonably use the powers available to him under the old Anti-Deficiency Act and the more recent Budget and Accounting Procedures Act of 1950 to delay the expenditure of funds. Did the Congress wish to act on every case?

Because of this difficulty, thinking in the House leadership on the anti-impoundment question turned to a congressional veto, with variations involving the amount of time allowed to each impoundment and whether an action of one or both houses of the Congress would be required to disapprove impoundments. A second major issue related to the committee to which impoundments should be referred for action. The two choices in the House were Government Operations and Appropriations. Speaker Albert preferred the Appropriations Committee.[86] After the preliminary staff discussions, Albert approached Chairman George Mahon (D., Texas) of the Appropriations Committee and sought his sponsorship of an anti-impoundment resolution. Mahon's willingness to author the anti-impoundment bill was crucial to its success. The expenditure of public funds was of primary concern to the appropriations committees in the House and Senate, and Mahon could speak responsibly on behalf of that interest. As a southern conservative with a long record of fiscal responsibility, Mahon could credibly offer the anti-impoundment bill without being vulnerable to the charge that the support of an anti-impoundment measure was a step toward profligate federal spending.

During February 1973 the leadership and Appropriations Committee staffs hammered out several draft versions of the anti-impoundment resolution. On March 5, 1973, Speaker Albert and Chairman Mahon conducted a joint press conference to announce the introduction of the bill into the House. On the speaker's orders the bill was referred to the House Rules Committee, where it was assured strong support by Congressman Richard Bolling of Missouri, one of Albert's closest allies. At the same time, the speaker's staff set out to marshal authoritative opinion and public support behind the proposal. At Albert's request, noted scholars were asked to submit their views on the impoundment question to the Rules Committee, and special hearings were planned in order to highlight a consensus of scholarly opinion on the unconstitutionality of the Nixon impoundments. The speaker sent personal letters of invitation to these scholars, and on his behalf freshman Oklahoma Congressman James R. Jones contacted the scholars personally to solicit their responses. Albert also contributed an editorial statement to the *New York Times* on the issue.[87]

In spite of this concerted effort, the anti-impoundment bill faced a rocky road. The entire question of budget reform was the subject of widespread disagreement among House Democrats. Liberal Democrats were against any reforms that would constrain spending on social welfare programs; they liked the anti-impoundment bill but disliked the budget reforms. Conservative Democrats took the opposite view, favoring budget reform but worrying that support of anti-impoundment legislation would appear irresponsible to their constituents. The key to success lay in weaving the two issues together into a fabric that would involve both budget control and an anti-impoundment provision.

In order to move the anti-impoundment bill from dead center, the leadership determined to modify the approach taken by the Mahon bill. Although the first bill had been partially drafted by his own staff, Albert had a second anti-impoundment bill introduced that combined the features of the Mahon bill and those of a bill introduced in the Senate by Edmund S. Muskie of Maine. The new bill differentiated between permanent impoundments (called recisions) and temporary impoundments (called deferrals), and provided that impoundments would be automatically disallowed unless both Houses of the Congress approved, while specifying that deferrals could be overridden only by an affirmative vote of both Houses of the Congress. This would permit the president to use the deferral power for the purpose of attaining efficiency in government while guarding against permanent policy impoundments. The bill also incorporated an expenditure ceiling for fiscal year 1974 in order to attract conservative support.[88]

This compromise version appeared to have a strong chance at passage, but at the last minute a complication arose.[89] Liberal senators continued to support the concurrent approval approach for all recisions and deferrals that the House (following Professor Maass's suggestion) had rejected. In June 1973 the Congress faced the need to raise the debt ceiling. Senator Abraham Ribicoff of Connecticut saw the passage of the debt ceiling as an opportunity to attach the Ervin version of the anti-impoundment bill to the debt-ceiling bill, which would have to pass. Since the House had passed the debt-ceiling bill first and sent it to the Senate, there would be no opportunity to kill the provision in the House, and the matter would have to be taken up in conference. From Speaker Albert's point of view, the Ribicoff bill was double jeopardy. The addition of the anti-impoundment bill would make the debt ceiling increase appear to be an irresponsible act, and Albert's preferred version of the anti-impoundment bill would be preempted.

Albert sought to head off the Ribicoff amendment in the Senate, while asking the House conferees on the debt ceiling to refuse to accept any Senate anti-impoundment bill. Senate Majority Leader Mike Mansfield shared Albert's view of the matter, and with the support of Senators

Walter Mondale of Minnesota and Sam Ervin managed to defeat the anti-impoundment amendment provision in the Senate. This left a clear field in the House for the leadership anti-impoundment bill, which passed in July 1973. The following year the provisions of the House anti-impoundment bill were attached to the larger budget reform bill, and the entire package was enacted into law as the Budget Reform and Impoundment Control Act of 1974, regarded by Speaker Albert as his "cardinal" legislative achievement.[90]

The passage of the budget and impoundment reforms were major accomplishments for the speaker. However, Albert might not have succeeded had not the Watergate hearings in the Senate during the summer of 1973 undermined the public's confidence in President Nixon. The Democrats were able to raise the stakes by associating the impoundments with other abuses of presidential power, characterizing Nixon as a president steeped in the abuse of his authority. The monthly Gallup poll of presidential approval showed Nixon at a five-year peak in the fall of 1972 and winter of 1973 after his reelection and the announcement of the Vietnam peace agreement. In February of 1973 he rode the crest of a 68 percent approval rating. Beginning in March of 1973 and continuing through the summer, Nixon's approval ratings fell steadily, reaching a low of 27 percent after the Saturday Night Massacre in October. It was only after Nixon lost popularity that the Democratic Congress was able to pass its major initiatives. In July of 1974, the president signed the Budget Reform and Impoundment Control Act into law just four weeks prior to resigning from office. The Budget Act and the War Powers Resolution, two main steps in the "resurgence" of the Congress, both were affected by the undermining of Nixon's political strength by the Watergate affair.[91]

The other major reform effort undertaken by Speaker Albert designed to improve House efficiency was the Select Committee to Review the House Committee System, chaired by Richard Bolling. This initiative came directly from Albert. He created the committee, placed his most trusted colleague in charge of it, and testified as its first witness. This was the first time that a speaker had testified before a House committee in over a hundred years.[92] That the committee system needed a once-over was undeniable. Problems of overlapping jurisdiction, multiple subcommittee hearings, nonfunctioning committees and subcommittees, and cumbersome committee processes impeded the legislative process. However, the recognition of the problem was more widespread than the enthusiasm for reform. Every change in committee membership or jurisdiction implied a gain in power for one member at the expense of another. A reform scheme that would satisfy everyone was unimaginable; one that might gather a majority of Democrats and Republicans was possible. Whatever its specific shape, it was essential that the reform plan be pitted against only one alternative, the status quo.

Unfortunately for Speaker Albert's reform goals, the plan that emerged from the Bolling committee was too sweeping to be easily digested by House members. In addition to a wide-ranging reallocation of committee jurisdictions, it would have required a large number of committee position sacrifices by members. The plan also struck at sacred cows by proposing to divide the Education and Labor Committee and to abolish the Merchant Marine and Fisheries Committee. Unsurprisingly, opposition to the Bolling committee proposal developed within the Democratic caucus. The opponents were able to force the issue before the caucus's established vehicle of reform, the Hansen committee on organization. The Hansen committee reported an alternative to the Bolling plan that was palatable to more Democrats. With the Democrats divided, the Republicans advanced their own proposal, and the House was eventually confronted with three plans among which to choose. The supporters of the Hansen plan offered enough carrots to the Republicans to hold a sufficient number of them in line, and it was passed by the full House.[93]

This was a major defeat for Speaker Albert. He had placed his prestige on the line from the beginning, and in the end he chose not to invest the full weight of his office in support of the bill. Albert tried to round up votes, but supporters of the Bolling plan felt that his efforts were only halfhearted. Yet Albert's failure to invoke the power of his office was not the main reason why the Bolling plan was rejected; the key decision lay in allowing the Hansen committee to propose an alternative. While it would have angered opponents of the Bolling plan, Speaker Albert would have been on reasonable ground in demanding a straightforward vote on a proposal as long in the making as this one was, especially since it was Albert's idea in the first place. In a straight up or down vote the Bolling proposal might have lost anyway, but its chances of passage would have been enhanced because it would have borne the mantel of reform at a time when reform was in vogue. Albert's decision to permit the Hansen substitute was due to his own doubts about the wisdom of accepting the Bolling plan. He felt that he had permitted Bolling to go too far, and that the task of implementing something as complicated as the Bolling proposal would be too much for the House to swallow. He also knew that the next few years would likely witness the implementation of a new budget process, and feared that the House's circuits would be overloaded. Bolling himself shared these reservations.[94] Besides, Albert felt that it was fair to permit opponents a chance to come up with their own plan. To have shut out the alternatives would have seemed an arbitrary imposition of the speaker's will to many opponents of the Bolling plan. These were reasonable judgments, but they did not offset the negative political impression that the defeat of the Bolling proposal fostered.

A third major reform of the Ninety-third Congress was the passage of the War Powers Resolution, which harbingered a new role for the speaker in foreign policy, formally and politically. Unlike the budget and committee reform efforts, the attack on the president's power to involve American troops abroad was not a leadership initiative. In fact, Speaker Albert had always accepted the president's preeminent role in foreign policy, and had stood by Johnson and Nixon on the Vietnam War. Nevertheless, the passage of the resolution enhanced the power of the speakership. The speaker was now to be notified whenever an American president sent American troops into combat, and the Congress would be likely to take a more active posture in the shaping of the country's foreign policy. The passage of the War Powers Resolution, like that of the Budget and Impoundment Act, came about as a result of Nixon's weakened political position. Congressional doves had never been able to muster more than a third of the House in favor of any end-the-war resolution, and they seemed no more powerful early in 1973 than they had in the past. Yet by November 1973, one month after the launching of the impeachment inquiry, the Congress overrode Nixon's veto of the war powers bill easily.

The passage of the War Powers Resolution gave to the speaker a formal role in foreign policy making, as it required the president to notify the speaker and other congressional leaders prior to sending U.S. troops into combat. In this respect, however, the law simply codified the increasingly active role that the speaker was coming to play in foreign policy. Sitting at the center of House politics, the speakership could not remain immune to foreign policy issues, and between 1973 and his retirement in 1976, Albert was to become increasingly active in foreign affairs. Throughout his speakership he met intermittently with National Security Advisor and Secretary of State Henry Kissinger to discuss foreign policy matters. Because his foreign policy views were often closer to those of the administration than to the liberal majority in the Democratic caucus, Albert's foreign policy role was often low profile; but his involvement presaged a more active foreign policy orientation for his successors.

As we have seen, the tumult in the House over the budget, committee, and war powers reforms cannot be understood except in the context of President Nixon's weakened position due to the Watergate scandal. The Ninety-third Congress will be remembered most for the impeachment of President Nixon and the resignation of Vice President Spiro Agnew. In December 1973 Speaker Albert issued a major statement on the legislative accomplishments of the year. "The First Session of the 93rd Congress," said Albert, "has been of tremendous significance for the American people."[95] Yet the *Congressional Quarterly Almanac*, in its review of the first session, held that 1973 was, "not a year of landmark decisions for the standard issues of domestic politics."[96] These statements are not incompatible. Albert's list of accomplishments was heavily dominated by the major reforms enacted or considered by the House during 1973. On the other items on the congressional agenda, to which "the lion's share of our attention has been directed . . . some progress has been made, but a good deal of our effort has been expended merely to retain valuable existing programs which we once were able to take for granted."[97] Albert's frank acknowledgment states the fact: 1973, which had dawned as the year of the Nixon realignment, had dissolved into a legislative stalemate because of the Watergate investigation. Nixon was unable to impose his will on the Congress, but the Congress was unable to pass major legislation in the face of his threat to veto.

This impasse was broken dramatically in late September and October of 1973 by the two major events that combined to place Carl Albert on the cusp of the constitutional separation of powers. The first was Spiro Agnew's request for a House impeachment investigation; the second was Richard Nixon's firing of Attorney General Elliot Richardson and Deputy Attorney General William Ruckelshaus from the Justice Department. These two events catapulted Albert into direct line of succession to the presidency, and brought about the impeachment inquiry of President Nixon. The Democratic party had been on the defensive against Nixon for four years. The Republican president had won a sweeping victory in 1972, and many Democrats were anxious to seize upon the opportunity provided by the Watergate scandal to win back the presidency. Speaker Albert felt that it was imperative to avoid the public perception that he as an individual was attempting to win the presidency by nefarious means, and he believed that it was improper for the Democrats to take the presidency away from the party that had carried all but one state of the union in the 1972 election.[98]

Speaker Albert recognized that the political situation was still volatile and could turn in Nixon's favor if the Democrats were perceived by the public as proceeding unfairly. To rush to judgment on Nixon while the vice presidency was vacant would lend the appearance of being a railroad job, would indeed be a railroad job, since due process could not be served on short notice. And so Albert proceeded cautiously toward the crisis. The situation was extremely delicate. Under the rules of the House, an impeachment resolution is privileged business.[99] Many liberal Democrats were eager to act, and if they had insisted upon an impeachment resolution, they could have forced a floor vote. A precipitous floor vote would probably have lacked the majority needed to impeach. Having failed once on an impeachment vote, the political opportunity to try again would most likely never arise. Speaker Albert did not seek the presidency for himself, believing that the Republicans were entitled to it. He believed that the House had the constitutional obligation to treat Nixon and Agnew fairly. But if an impeachment vote were to come, Albert did not want it to be premature.

The Agnew affair arose in the fall of 1973. On September 25, 1973, Agnew, who was about to be brought for indictment on charges of accepting bribes while governor of Maryland, sought a meeting with the speaker and requested a House impeachment investigation, relying on the precedent of John C. Calhoun, who had sought and received an impeachment investigation when charges of bribery were brought against him in 1826. Albert called other members of the Democratic and Republican leadership to the office, along with the chairman of the Judiciary Committee, Peter Rodino of New Jersey, and its ranking Republican, Edward Hutchinson of California. Republican Leader Gerald Ford spoke in favor of the request, while Majority Leader Tip O'Neill opposed it. Eventually, the Democrats asked the Republicans to excuse themselves, and consulted among themselves. Albert ordered House parliamentarian Lewis Deschler to prepare a recommendation, and the group adjourned until the next morning. Later that day Albert received a phone call from Attorney General Elliot Richardson in which Richardson confirmed the details of the Agnew indictment. Richardson also led Albert to believe that the evidence against Agnew was sufficient to convict.[100]

The next day Albert called Democratic leaders into the speaker's office to reach a decision. Deschler recommended that the House proceed on Agnew's request, but Tip O'Neill, entering the meeting a half-hour late, argued forcefully that it was not up to the House Democrats to bail Agnew out of the situation.[101] Sentiment in the House was moving toward an impeachment investigation of Nixon, and it would be less likely to occur if Agnew were also being investigated. O'Neill had emerged as one of the strongest advocates of presidential impeachment and he did not want a little fish to get in the way of the prize catch. O'Neill wanted to let the courts indict Agnew, letting the cards fall where they may. Speaker Albert was in the end persuaded by the political rather than the parliamentary view of the situation, and announced on the afternoon of the 26th that Agnew's request was being denied.[102] On October 10, 1973, Agnew pleaded nolo contendere to a single charge of income tax evasion and resigned the vice presidency. On October 12 President Nixon, acting in part on Speaker Albert's recommendation, nominated House Republican leader Gerald Ford as Agnew's successor.

Ford was confirmed by the Congress and took the oath of office on December 6, 1973, after a two-month congressional consideration of his nomination.

The difference between Carl Albert's reaction to the Agnew request and Tip O'Neill's has provoked comment and is indicative of the very different orientations of the two party leaders.[103] It is clear that Albert and Lewis Deschler undertook a serious consideration of Agnew's constitutional right to a House impeachment investigation. O'Neill, by contrast, seems at all times to have viewed the problem from a political point of view. While Albert weighed the prerogatives of a sitting vice president, O'Neill tried to recall what he knew of Maryland politics, Agnew, and the Baltimore prosecutor who was on his heels, George Beall. "They were all together in Maryland politics, the Bealls and Agnew, O'Neill reminded himself. He does this all the time, goes over the players. He is a man who likes a scorecard at all times."[104] While from a constitutional point of view, it was unclear whether a sitting vice president could be indicted, from a political point of view Agnew's case could not be isolated from Nixon's, thus creating a personal complication for Albert that O'Neill did not face. Albert's own future was tied to Agnew's if Nixon was driven or removed from office. Deschler's voice carried great weight with Speaker Albert in this case, involving House precedent and constitutional interpretation. Deschler, of course, had been appointed to his office forty-eight years previously by a Republican speaker, Nicholas Longworth. While officially nonpartisan, he was known to be institutionally, instinctively, and politically conservative.[105] When the meeting commenced, Deschler made a lengthy presentation in favor of granting Agnew's request, based upon precedent. Albert wanted to be fair to Agnew and wanted to act consistently with House precedent.

O'Neill saw the problem in political terms. He had been pressing for some time for a House impeachment investigation of President Nixon. In September of 1973, with the special prosecutor breathing down Nixon's neck for release of Watergate tapes, it was evident that a formal step to launch an impeachment inquiry was imminent. The first discussions of it had taken place between Chairman Rodino and the House Democratic leadership early in that month.[106] If the House chose to launch an investigation of Agnew, it would be very unlikely to proceed with a concurrent investigation of Nixon. Agnew's request threatened to bog down the House while diverting public attention from Nixon to Agnew. O'Neill's perception was conditioned by political instinct. As Breslin has him saying to aide Leo Diehl:

> You know, Leo, if the guy [Agnew] would've said to us, "Look, I've got a family. I'm afraid of going to the can." Geez, that's all

you have to tell me. I don't want to see any man go to jail. I don't have it in me. Maybe something could have been done for him. Give him some kind of hearing so he could kill a little time and then disappear. But the way the sonofabitch lied to us. And he acted as if it was our duty to believe him. He's got to be kidding. I don't like to be played for a sucker.[107]

Here O'Neill revealed less of a sense of constitutional propriety than an instinctual political feel for the situation. O'Neill saw Agnew, not as one constitutional officer appealing to another, but instead as an embattled politician seeking a way out of the criminal justice system. In the end, Speaker Albert accepted this view.

Albert's decision to deny Agnew's request proved for the best. To have granted it would likely have prolonged the Watergate affair. Within two weeks of Albert's action, Agnew resigned from office. Ten days later, President Nixon fired Archibald Cox, the Watergate special prosecutor, in reaction to which Attorney General Elliot Richardson and Assistant Attorney General William D. Ruckelshaus resigned from office. In the furor that ensued, a formal House impeachment inquiry of Nixon was launched on October 22, 1973. If a month earlier the House had committed itself to an investigation of Agnew, the Democratic Congress would have threatened impeachment of both the president and vice president of the United States simultaneously. To have proceeded impartially and with public confidence would have been extremely difficult. While O'Neill's more overtly political orientation was not inherently preferable to Albert's more cautious constitutionalism, we may say that in the larger historical view, Albert's decision to deny Agnew's request was the best course of action that he could have taken. In other circumstances, the political orientation could have led to disastrous results. We need look no further than the Nixon case to find evidence of this.

Much has been made of Albert's putative reluctance to assume the presidency.[108] Albert always denied this charge, going so far, a decade later, as to release a memorandum from Theodore Sorensen in which a plan for succession was outlined, replete with themes and organizational steps.[109] The Sorensen letter to Albert was one of many communications that Albert had at the time with such experienced Democratic leaders as Joseph Califano, Robert Strauss, Lawrence O'Brien, and Clark Clifford. There can be no doubt that Albert would have been able to draw upon the governing class of the Democratic party if he had become president. But in Albert's view, the country would have been torn apart had the twenty-fifth amendment been used for the first time to take the presidency from the Republicans and give it to the

Democrats. The "impeachment hawks" in the House were oblivious to this concern. They were divided into two factions. The more radical members, typified by Bella Abzug, wanted the presidency outright and were willing to take it. Their threat to take impeachment directly to the House floor was sincere and made real by the privileged status of an impeachment resolution under the rules of the House. A more moderate faction, represented by Tip O'Neill, opposed the more direct tactic, but wanted the Judiciary Committee to conduct its investigation as rapidly as possible. O'Neill consistently badgered Chairman Peter Rodino to move quickly.[110]

The difference between Albert's guarded neutrality and O'Neill's aggressive partisanship was illustrated by their respective floor statements on October 23, 1973, following the firing of Cox. According to O'Neill: "No other President in the history of this nation has brought the highest office in the land into such low repute. His conduct must bring shame upon us all . . . Mr. Speaker, many people are demanding impeachment . . . he has left the people no choice. They have had enough double-dealing . . . the case must be referred to the Judiciary Committee for speedy and expeditious consideration. The House must act with determined leadership and strength."[111] In contrast, Speaker Albert's statement was of a more moderate and impartial tone: "In my opinion, the president's action Saturday was unfortunate. It seems to me to contribute to divisiveness among the American people . . . Resolutions calling for impeachment or investigation that might possibly lead to charges of impeachment will be introduced in the House . . . The House must perform its constitutional function in an orderly and responsible manner under the Rules of the House, completely free of personal or political considerations."[112] The differing tone of these two statements reflected the relative perspectives of a party majority leader and a constitutional speaker, but it also revealed the obvious difference between Albert's constitutional orientation and O'Neill's political orientation toward the impeachment crisis.

The initial choice facing Albert, once the decision to go forward with impeachment was taken, was to determine the appropriate committee. The choice lay between the Judiciary Committee or a select committee. Historical precedent favored a select committee; in the 1860s the radical Republicans had appointed a select committee to go after Andrew Johnson. Advocates of a select committee in 1973 came from among the House liberals who wanted a committee stacked against Nixon and Republicans who expected to use their prerogative of naming the minority members to load their side of the committee in the president's favor. Albert was convinced that a polarized select committee would only create further controversy. The Senate select committee had performed responsibly, but its investigation had developed into a media event, and its members had become public personages. Albert did not want a formal constitutional inquiry into the impeachment of the president to degenerate into a media happening and decided that the proper course of action was to refer the resolution of impeachment to the Judiciary Committee. The committee was not a major committee, and its membership was on average younger and more liberal than most House committees. Albert felt that it was essential that the public see a standing House committee proceeding responsibly, and believe that its investigation was impartial and fair.[113]

Having referred the impeachment question to the Judiciary Committee, Albert determined to stay out of its way. For the party leadership to have been perceived as placing pressure on the committee would have called the impartiality of the proceedings into question. Albert understood the great constitutional significance in impeaching a president. Only one previous president had been impeached, and none had ever been removed from office. It was essential to the integrity of the Constitution that the House of Representatives proceed thoroughly and fairly in its consideration of the charges against Nixon. To do so would require time. The paralysis of government that would attend a protracted impeachment inquiry was, in Albert's view, a necessary price to pay for the public's eventual acceptance of the probable outcome of the process—Nixon's impeachment and removal from office. The period from October 22, 1973, when the House impeachment investigation was launched, through August 9, 1974, when President Nixon resigned, was marked by careful deliberation on the part of the House Judiciary Committee. It took the committee over two months to appoint its counsel, John Doar. The investigation conducted by Doar and his staff carried through the spring of 1974, leading to committee hearings in the summer. In the meantime, the Congress approved Gerald Ford's nomination as vice president, placing a well-liked Republican in direct line of succession to the presidency.[114] The caution exercised by Albert and Rodino proved well advised. While the committee plodded along in its investigation, a legal battle was fought in the courts as President Nixon attempted to protect the privilege of his tape-recorded conversations from subpoena by the Watergate special prosecutor's office. When in July 1974 the Supreme Court ruled that Nixon's claim of executive privilege had to give way to the demands of a legally constituted criminal investigation, Nixon, on August 5, was forced to hand over to the special prosecutor and courts the "smoking gun" tapes of his June 23, 1972, conversations with his chief of staff, H. R. Haldeman, during which the coverup of the Watergate break-in was initiated. In the face of this revelation Nixon acknowledged the certainty of House impeachment charges. When, two days later, he was informed that Senate affirmation of the impeachment charges was assured, he decided to announce his August 9 resignation. Had the House moved more precipitously than it did, there is no assurance that the Senate would have removed Nixon from office. At the very least, the constitutional crisis would have been heightened. The instinctive caution that characterized much of Speaker Albert's conduct served both him and the nation well in the most significant constitutional crisis of the twentieth century.

The downfall of Richard Nixon paid big dividends for congressional Democrats legislatively and politically. Bills that had been frozen by the Watergate crisis or threats of a Nixon veto were now passed into law. On July 25, 1974, the Congress established the Legal Services Corporation, which Nixon had knocked out of earlier antipoverty legislation by his veto. In August 1974 the controversial Elementary and Secondary Education Act was enacted, as was the Housing and Community Development Act. In September the pension reform bill became law; in October the Campaign Finance Act, including for the first time public financing of campaigns, became law; in November the mass transit bill that Nixon had held up by veto threat was enacted; in December the two-year struggle for a strip mining bill culminated in congressional passage and a pocket veto by new President Gerald Ford.

Things were going well for Speaker Albert and his party. In November 1974 the voters handed him an increase in his congressional majority from 242 to 291. His principal nemesis, Richard Nixon, had been driven from office. Legislation for which he had struggled for four years was now enacted or on the way to it. In December the House Democratic caucus dramatically enhanced the speaker's power in the next Congress. The power of making committee nominations was taken from the Ways and Means Committee and given to the Steering and Policy Committee, chaired by the speaker. The Ways and Means Committee was itself enlarged from twenty-five to thirty-seven members, giving the speaker an additional group of appointments to distribute. All committee ratios were altered to reflect the new partisan alignment in the House. At the same time, the autonomy of the Appropriations Committee was greatly abridged when the caucus required that all thirteen chairmen of its subcommittees be approved by caucus vote.

A driving force behind these changes was the Democratic freshman caucus of the Ninety-fourth Congress, the seventy-four "Watergate Babies" who came to Washington determined to have an immediate and positive impact on the image of the Congress and its system of governance. Under the rules of the caucus the Steering Committee's nominees for committee chairmen were subject to an automatic vote. The large freshman class demanded that the nominees come before them to defend their candidacies. Some refused to do so, and a combination of liberal and freshmen members unseated three senior southern chairmen, F. Edward Hebert of Armed Services, W. R. Poage of Agriculture, and Wright Patman of Banking and Currency. Wayne Hays of Ohio narrowly avoided rejection as chairman of the House Administration Committee. This revolution indicated that committee chairmen would now be held accountable by the caucus and signaled a new ethos in the House. These new members, and their ways, would contribute to the circumstances that were to make the Ninety-fourth Congress, Speaker Albert's last, a difficult one indeed.

The Veto War

As 1975 dawned, two men who had shared a quarter-century of experience in national legislative politics confronted each other across a void physically no greater than the Washington Mall but as wide politically as the staunchest advocates of the constitutional separation of powers could have wished. Gerald R. Ford, the unelected Republican president, wanted to win election to the presidency in his own right in November 1976; Carl Albert, the Democratic speaker of the House, sought the return of the White House to the Democratic party. The economic circumstances in which this struggle was to take place were severe. The economy had sunk into its worst recession since the Great Depression. In part due to the actions of the Arab oil cartel, energy costs had skyrocketed, bringing in train higher inflation. For the first time in its history, the nation experienced a combination of high inflation and high unemployment. The major questions on the national agenda were energy and the economy, the two issues that would come to dominate politics for the balance of the decade.

In confronting these major issues, Ford and Albert, and their respective parties, sat on opposite sides of an ideological gulf paralleling the partisan division of the government. Ford stood for a traditional Republican conservatism that emphasized free enterprise and reduced government; Albert stood for traditional Democratic liberalism, with its emphasis on governmental intervention. At stake was the control of the government and the direction of public policy. Personal ambition, party aspirations, and the public interest intermeshed in a series of political conflicts. The politics of the Ninety-fourth Congress marked a resumption of the pattern that had been defined in the Ninety-second Congress. A conservative Republican president was aligned against a liberal Democratic Congress on basic economic issues. However, the balance of power seemed to have shifted decisively to the Democrats. Instead of the pre-Watergate Nixon, the Democrats in Congress faced a president whom they knew too well to fear. The size of the Democrats' majorities in the Congress had been sharply increased. The powers of the speakership had been enhanced. And public opinion seemed to have drifted in the direction of the Democratic party.

Ironically, the improved situation harbored dangers for the speaker. While his position in the House was strengthened and his party's majority enlarged, expectations had risen as much or more. Among the most valuable assets a politician can have is a set of good excuses for losing. Sam Rayburn could always blame the committee chairmen when things went wrong, and later Tip O'Neill would make excuses for losing by blaming the president. Carl Albert's best excuses had been taken from underneath him, yet he still had to deal with that rambunctious outfit, the Democratic caucus, recently infused with a large group of younger members whose culture would settle only uneasily upon the congressional party.

Speaker Albert was fully aware of the opportunities of the moment, the difficulties that he faced, and the implications of the struggle. In a December 1974 interview with columnist David Broder, he acknowledged the pressure on the congressional Democrats to produce legislation in energy and economics that would set the country on the road to prosperity and prove the ability of the Democratic party to govern the nation. "We have to have a credible record on energy and the economy by midsummer or we'll look terrible," said Albert. "That's the test of my leadership."[115] Albert recognized that the record of the Democratic Congress would affect the party's prospects in the 1976 election, but knew that he would enjoy at best a relatively brief "honeymoon" period with new Democratic members. The enlarged House Democratic majority, the enhanced power of the speaker, and the enthusiasm of the seventy-five freshmen Democrats boded well for Albert's prospects, but lying beneath the surface were more basic conflicts that would in the end disappoint both Albert and his Democratic members.

Three factors combined to cause 1975 to be "a most frustrating year for Speaker Albert."[116] They were the intractability of the energy and economic issues, the level of expectations fostered by the size of the Democratic majorities, and President Ford's vetoes. The complexity of the issues was formidable. America was for the first time made aware that its powerful economic system was not immune to pressure from international events. Dependence on foreign oil, increasing competition in international trade, and inefficient business practices at home all combined to wreak havoc on an American economy grown accustomed to insularity. The effect was to divide the nation economically, geographically, and politically. These divisions were reflected in the House of Representatives, where members sought to protect the interests of their states and districts.

The situation was exacerbated by the level of expectations that had been aroused by the 1974 elections. Among liberal Democrats generally, but especially among the members of the freshman class of 1974, a belief developed that with Nixon vanquished the national policy agenda was theirs for the asking. With a two-thirds majority in the House and Senate, the Democrats had a "veto-proof" Congress that would be able to sweep by President Ford and enact a Democratic economic program. It was as if the freshmen believed that it was easy to get Democrats to agree, as if they had never heard of the conservative coalition. The coalition could not hope to defeat legislation on the floor of the House and Senate because the liberal majorities were too large. But it could hope to sustain Ford vetoes where only one-third plus one was needed. Recognizing that fact and calculating his own best electoral strategy, Ford settled upon a political course that combined the vetoing tendencies of Grover Cleveland with the pugnacious anticongressionalism of Harry S Truman. He would count upon the traditional incapacity of the Democrats to agree, veto Democratic bills, and castigate the Congress for incompetency, laziness, and fiscal irresponsibility. Lacking a Democratic presidential nominee upon whom to focus, Ford would use the Democratic Congress as his whipping boy.

In response, a Steering and Policy Committee task force chaired by Deputy Whip Jim Wright of Texas recommended a seven-point economic program that Albert endorsed. It included such Democratic staples as increased unemployment compensation, and emergency jobs measures. Albert launched the task force recommendations at a January 13, 1975, press conference. His goal was to have major Democratic economic legislation passed through the House by the middle of the summer. Significantly, the task force's recommendations would not be brought before the Democratic caucus, but delivered directly to the legislative committees.[117] This demonstrated Albert's traditional orientation toward committee prerogatives and suggested that the Democratic party was unlikely to unite behind the proposals. The agenda included public service jobs, public works, agricultural price supports, increasing the money supply, lower interest rates, emergency housing aid, tax cuts for low-income families, and selective price controls.[118] These were old Democratic ideas. In some cases, such as the public works bill and the public service employment bill, the Democrats simply dusted off previous legislation and sent it forward. There was no essential difference between the jobs/public works battles of the Ninety-second and Ninety-fourth Congresses, but this time the Democrats were careful to force

President Ford to confront the two bills separately so that he could not veto one at the expense of accepting the other, as Nixon had done in 1971.

Speaker Albert had said that it was imperative for Congress to enact economic legislation with a Democratic stamp by the summer of 1975. The confrontation between Albert and Ford came to a head that summer, although not with the results that Albert had sought. In May and June of 1975 the Congress passed three separate bills directly related to the Democratic party program. The first was an emergency jobs bill that formed the cornerstone of the Democrats' antirecession effort. The second was an emergency farm bill designed to provide relief for the agricultural sector. The third was a strip-mining bill aimed at preserving the environment from the excesses of commercial mining companies. The Ford administration opposed all three bills in degree. Ford was against public service jobs in principle, but willing to settle for a modest public service program to enhance Republican congressional election prospects. He believed that the farm bill was excessive and inflationary, but was willing to see a more modest farm program put in place. He thought that the Democratic strip-mining bill went too far in restricting commercial mining during a period of energy shortages, but favored some limits on what the mining companies could do to the environment. Ford's policy positions were those of a moderate Republican, and his goal was to modify the Democratic program. His political situation was in one sense similar to Nixon's in 1972: Ford had no reason to antagonize middle-of-the-road voters. By using his veto with one hand and accepting scaled-down legislation with the other, he could hope to play both sides against the middle.

Ford's political position dovetailed nicely with his policy preferences. By vetoing the Democratic bills, Ford could force the Congress to trim the legislation and establish his own reputation as an effective counterforce to the liberal Democratic congressional majority. In fact, the prospect of more moderate subsequent legislation was openly discussed by all participants in the veto battles, and it placed the Democratic leadership in a real dilemma. If the Democrats moderated the legislation in order to make it more palatable to moderate and conservative Democrats and Republicans, Ford could always shift his ground further to the right in promising to support future legislation. If the Democrats moved far enough toward the center to hold it against a Ford move to the right, then they would have lost the political issues that they were deliberately trying to create.[119] Ford would have merely accepted the bills and proclaimed his effectiveness as a bipartisan leader. The best strategy for the Democratic leadership was to hold fast to relatively liberal positions. They would retain the support of the liberal majority within the Democratic caucus and put Ford on the political defensive on the issues of jobs, farms, and the environment. Albert pressed these issues in the full knowledge that Ford would be likely to sustain his vetoes in a showdown.

Unfortunately, no one told the freshmen Democrats that they were supposed to lose the override votes, and they looked forward confidently to decisive victories over the Republicans. When first the farm bill override attempt and then the jobs bill override vote were lost, the freshmen were shocked. On June 6, 1975, William Brodhead of Michigan, the freshman representative on the Steering and Policy Committee, wrote to Speaker Albert in reaction to the failure of the House to override Ford's veto of the jobs bill:

> I, like many other members, am greatly disturbed by our failure to override the President's veto of H.R. 4481, the Emergency Employment Appropriation Act of 1975 . . . As the representative of the Class of 1974 on the Steering and Policy Committee, I request you call a meeting of the Steering and Policy Committee to discuss this matter as soon as possible. I would suggest the following topics for discussion at that meeting. First, was every possible effort made to secure the votes needed to override? Second, what changes need to be made to prevent a repetition of this debacle? I anxiously await your reply.[120]

Four days later, Ford's veto of the strip-mining bill was sustained by the House and the freshmen congressmen (freshperson congresspersons, as one leadership wag put it) were further enraged. On June 17, 1975, they caucused and developed a six-point program for the more effective leadership of the House. They recommended the establishment of a clear Democratic program, better communications between the leadership and members, a strengthened whip structure, the selection of designated party spokesmen on national issues, the specification of party position roll calls, and the imposition of an "inviolate" five-day work week. Armed with this manifesto, the freshmen demanded and received an audience with Speaker Albert that night.[121]

It is difficult to retrieve a sense of the intensity of the feelings of the freshmen Democrats, nor is it easy to recall just how different they were from their more senior colleagues. Ideologically liberal, policy-oriented, and often lacking in previous legislative experience, they wanted to have an impact on the policies of the federal government at once, not later. They were the politically conscious component of a "therapeutic generation" whose members believed effective communication to be the solution to most human problems.[122] The therapeutic culture is ideally suited to the congressional milieu, where members avoid making moral judgments about each other but find it necessary to "understand" each other's problems in order to reach mutual accord. In the old days this took the form of logrolling, involving raw calculations of self-interest. Eschewing such naked contractarianism, the new member found it important to empathize with a colleague before cutting a deal. Where an older generation of members was drawn to the barrooms and backrooms of urban political conventions, the class of 1974 sought the comfortable confines of the Airlie House resort for a weekend retreat. There they held small group discussions on such shared concerns as "are we as individual members meeting our congressional responsibilities?" and "the future role of new members in the 94th Congress."[123]

We may imagine the consternation of hard-bitten Hill veterans regarding a group of lawmakers who would spend a weekend discussing "what do we still have in common?" It appears to have been equally as difficult for the new members to understand the established ways of the House. To take one example, the major complaint of the freshmen Democrats was the lack of a clear Democratic program. Now, the Democratic leadership did have a program—or at least Speaker Albert thought so. But the major pieces of economic legislation that formed the basis of that program (jobs, public works, minimum wage, farm supports, etc.) appeared to freshmen members as a mere grab bag of spending bills. According to one of the most vocal freshmen, Bob Carr of Michigan, the party needed and lacked "a coherent, well recognized, feeling, sensitive program that we can all identify with. Not a laundry list of legislation that we hope to get passed this year, but a real vision."[124] Leaving aside the therapeutic language in which the point is "couched," we may assume that all Democrats, indeed all politicians, would appreciate a coherent party program. But the fact remained that the Democratic party was not a coherent party precisely because its various elements did not agree in philosophy. Lacking a common philosophy, the party has often resorted to consensus on economic legislation. The legislation on which Speaker Albert tried to frame a Democratic program included public service jobs, public works, and an increased minimum wage. These bills represented the lowest common denominator of Democratic interests, policies upon which northern liberals and southern conservatives could for the most part agree. They were the bread and butter of the Democratic party, and had been since 1932; but bread and butter was not enough for the class of 1974.

In addition to the demand for a clear program, the freshmen Democrats wanted an articulate national spokesman. Speaker Albert was accurately perceived as a reluctant participant in the publicity war. While he recognized the need for visible public leadership, he had never sought the role of party spokesman. In the Ninety-fourth Congress, he decided to do so more frequently, but his capacity to be an effective party spokesman depended upon more than a willingness to try. It required unified party, a clear consensus on party goals, and a public platform. The freshmen were correct in seeing the need for the speaker to play this role; however, they failed to perceive that their own public criticisms made it all the more difficult for Albert to do what they wanted him to do.

From the leadership's point of view, the freshmen's complaints were largely derived from a traditional concern of first-term members—the desire to get reelected. As a staff memorandum to the speaker put it, "the basic underlying fear of the Freshmen Democrats is that they will be defeated for reelection."[125] This fear was not without historical foundation. The Democrats had swept to major victories in 1948 (75 seat pickup), 1958 (49), and 1964 (38), and in each case in the ensuing election had suffered substantial losses (1950:29, 1960:20, and 1966:47). It was natural, therefore, that the freshmen Democrats of 1974, many of whom had won in previously Republican districts, would be very worried about a tough reelection campaign in 1976. Whatever their motives, the leadership regarded some of their perceptions as naive and uninformed. The three veto override votes had been "worked" by the leadership according to normal practice. Whip counts were made, lobbying organizations assisted in counting Republican votes, and uncertain votes received special attention. According to an analysis done for the speaker: "In each instance, the House leadership knew with almost exact precision which Democrats would vote for or against the bill and who would be absent. The maximum number possible was mustered to vote to override. The unknown factor was the behavior of the Republicans."[126]

The facts confirm this characterization. On the jobs bill, the veto of which created the most heat, the whip projected total attendance for the override vote at 423; 422 members voted. Of the 22 Democrats who voted no (to sustain), 15 were reported no, 4 were undecided, and 2 were yes or leaning yes. Only one Democratic vote was uncounted. Virtually all of the defectors were from the South. While the 5-vote margin made the override vote appear close, the leadership knew that Ford had at least 20 if-needed votes on the Republican side. It would have been necessary for the Democrats to have had perfect attendance and complete unanimity to override the veto. The southern votes against the leadership on the jobs bill were in part precipitated by the earlier failure of the override vote on the farm bill. Included among the 71 Democrats who voted to sustain that veto were 54 from the North, including 17 freshmen. In fact, a full third of the freshmen had voted against the leadership on one or more veto override votes. While the

average support for the leadership among freshmen was higher than
among more senior members, their record was, as a leadership memorandum put it, "hardly so unblemished as to allow the Freshmen to
point an accusing finger at Senior Democrats."[127]

If the leadership conducted an effective operation and the freshmen
complained nevertheless, their grievances might have been allayed
through better communications. This, at least, is what many freshmen
seem to have felt. Members who had indicated an intention to support
the leadership on initial whip counts, for example, were not subsequently
contacted. This apparently led many freshmen to believe that the leadership was not doing anything. An improved whip organization with
greater freshmen involvement was among the six points in the freshmen
program. Yet how much could one improve upon a whip function that
was over 99 percent accurate and produced 92 percent unanimity on
the jobs bill vote that was the central object of complaint? Effectiveness
was apparently less important than participation in assuaging the freshmen's frustration. Speaker Albert felt that the leadership's efforts to
communicate were the most extensive in the history of the House, one
of "the greatest achievements of my speakership."[128] Albert was the first
speaker to hold regular meetings with all committee chairmen, the first
to hold regular meetings of a representative party steering committee,
the first to regularly attend the weekly whip meetings, the first to support
monthly caucus meetings, and the first to have reached out beyond the
House to establish regular lines of communication with the Senate Democratic leadership and the Democratic National Committee. In comparison with McCormack and Rayburn, Albert's was a very open speakership. This is not surprising. The essence of the speakership in the
democratic period lies in greater openness, communication, and member
involvement. Albert went further in responding to these imperatives
than had any of his predecessors, and, from his point of view, as far as
a speaker needed to go.

Yet in spite of the greater openness of the party leadership, freshmen
Democrats felt excluded from the action. The freshmen wanted a sense
of involvement and a leader who could command both the attention of
the country and a working majority in the House. Albert had a working
majority in the House, but he could not easily compete with the public
prestige of the president in the veto override battles. In demanding a
larger role in the House and in seeking more assertive leadership, the
new members did not perceive a conflict in their aims. They assumed
that an active leader would be able to enlist them in useful ways in
forging a party program. Yet that kind of activism is compatible with
assertive leadership only when there is a broad basis of agreement within
a party caucus. The vision of a strong leader led many young Democrats

to weaken the leadership they already had. In contrast to their amorphous ideal, Albert seemed to them insufficiently willing to speak out on behalf of the congressional party and insufficiently available to the members. Their concept of communications implied to the freshmen Democrats an approach to leadership that was different from Albert's. To Albert, effective communications meant working within the existing framework of the House, meeting with the committee leaders and consulting with other elected and appointed party officials; to the freshmen, communication implied a visible public leader who would actively seek their involvement. Albert and the freshmen Democrats talked past each other as if they were speaking in different dialects. Speaker Albert knew several foreign languages, but not the language of the class of 1974.

The June 17 meeting proved less than conclusive. Some of the freshmen Democrats seemed mollified. Paul Tsongas, a freshman member from Massachusetts, announced that the speaker had accepted the six-point program, while Albert would only commit to its spirit, calling it a constructive proposal. Although one freshman emerged from the meeting to call once again for Albert's resignation, others spoke on behalf of the speaker. Albert told the press that he sensed no personal criticism of his leadership in the freshmen complaints. On all sides, there was a rhetorical emphasis on evils of the Ford administration and the injustice of the Ford vetoes and the one-third plus one rule that sustained them.[129] Thus, a temporary truce was reached in the hope that, for a time, Democrats might stop fighting each other and turn a united front toward the Republican enemy. This they were able to do in some measure. During the remainder of the Ninety-fourth Congress, the Democrats enacted five additional jobs bills, including a summer youth employment act, a $2.3 billion jobs package smuggled into law in a continuing spending resolution, a local public works capital and development act, a public service jobs title hidden in a supplemental spending bill, and a $3.95 billion construction jobs bill. Of these, Ford vetoed two, the local public works bill and the public service jobs bill. His veto of the public works bill was sustained by the Senate, while the Congress overrode his veto the public service jobs bill. The net outlay for public jobs was only about half of that passed by the House, but still the Democrats could claim that in the end their policy preferences had been enacted into law over Ford's vetoes.[130] In addition to these policy victories, the Democrats created a record upon which Democratic candidates could run on in the 1976 elections.

In the energy area, the Democrats had no such luck. President Ford recognized that a positive energy program was needed. He could veto congressional spending bills, but he could not address the energy crisis by wielding the veto alone. He needed to put a program in place and

he would have to get it through the Democratic Congress. With the
Congress stacked two to one against him, the prospects for passing a
Ford Republican energy package were not good. Still, it was necessary
that something be put forward as a signal of the seriousness of his
intention. Ford's solution was politically shrewd. In January of 1975
he sent to the Congress a combined tax/energy program designed to
put congressional Democrats on the defensive. By using existing presidential authority he moved to impose an oil import fee and at the same
time deregulate "old" oil (constituting at that time an estimated 60
percent of domestic production). The profits that would accrue to the
oil companies by virtue of deregulation would be partly passed on to
the taxpayers by a windfall profits tax, the proceeds from which would
be passed on again to various categories of needy consumers by various
devices. These major steps were combined with a number of minor steps
designed to increase domestic production and reduce consumption.[131]

The Ford program was politically problematic. Democrats from the
Northeast and the Midwest opposed deregulation since it meant more
money from consumers would go to southwestern oil companies. But
by putting the proposal on the table, Ford forced a reluctant Congress
to face its own internal divisions. How could a badly divided Democratic
majority produce an energy program that could be enacted into law?
With jurisdiction over energy spread across a dozen or more subcommittees, the House lacked any effective instrument for developing a
comprehensive energy package. Yet if it failed to do so, Ford would lay
the blame for the energy situation squarely on congressional shoulders,
holding that the Congress would neither enact his program nor one of
its own design. For Speaker Albert, the energy issue was particularly
sensitive, since Oklahoma is one of the largest oil-producing states in
the country. Considering retirement and residing in a very safe district,
Albert had no direct reason to fear the oil lobby; but as an Oklahoman
he recognized that the interests of his own state and region were at stake
in any move to decontrol oil prices.

Some Democrats pressed Speaker Albert for a select committee to
forge an energy bill. The need for a committee to address the energy
question comprehensively had been a major impetus behind the Bolling
committee reform effort; however, the committee on energy and environment that the Bolling committee had proposed was scotched in the
Hansen substitute. Now the same forces that had preserved the old
hegemonies in 1974 rallied against any new select committee that would
have the power to bypass their domains. Albert, who favored the select
committee approach, reluctantly abandoned it when it became clear
that committee chairmen such as John Dingell, Al Ullman, and Phil
Burton would oppose it. The struggle to set up the committee would

sap congressional energy better invested in drafting the legislation itself, Albert reasoned.[132] In place of the select committee, Albert formed a special task force whose job it was to produce a Democratic alternative by synthesizing several initiatives then under consideration by House committees. These included major bills by John Dingell of the Energy and Commerce Committee and Al Ullman of the Ways and Means Committee. The task force had no formal congressional power—it could neither draft nor report legislation—but it was intended to serve as a vehicle for effecting compromise between the various bills then under consideration. The resort to a task force by Speaker Albert was an indication of the changes that had been wrought in the House by the reform movement. Prior to the early 1970s the concept of a legislative structure outside of the committee system would have been anathema to party leaders. With the power of the committee chairmen undermined, and with the proliferation of overlapping subcommittee jurisdictions, the leadership had no effective recourse but to add a layer of legislative bureaucracy on top of that provided by the committee system. At the same time, the committees were still potent enough to resist any direct encroachment on their domains.[133]

In pressing for a bill in 1975, congressional Democrats ran the risk of handing to Ford, the Republicans, and the oil interests more in the way of price concessions than many Democrats would have liked. In fact, the party was divided between the newer, technocratic members who were firmly committed to find a solution to the energy crisis, and politically oriented old timers like Majority Leader O'Neill who were willing to sit tight and await the election of a Democratic president in 1976 before taking a major step toward energy legislation. O'Neill himself could look forward to the possibility that the speakership would be his in 1977, enabling him to stamp the nation's energy policy with his own brand of northeastern liberalism.[134] Obviously, the balance of power on the decontrol issue would shift significantly if O'Neill were to replace Albert as speaker. The end result of this confusion was the passage in the Ninety-fourth Congress of a series of minor energy bills aimed at increasing production, decreasing consumption, and advancing research. The House disapproved Ford's decontrol plan but passed a natural gas decontrol bill of its own that died in the Senate. Other bills were enacted into law, including overrides of President Ford's vetoes of bills relating to coal leasing and electric vehicle research, and an extension of the Federal Energy Administration authorization. These bills addressed various aspects of the energy problem, but they added up to less than a comprehensive policy. By mid 1976 it was clear that Congress and the president would be unable to agree on energy policy, and that positive steps would have to await the results of a 1976 election that would either unite the government in the hands of the Democrats or else convince the congressional Democrats that they had no choice but to work with President Ford. Consequently, energy policy was laid to rest until the results of the presidential election were known.[135]

If 1975 was a year of frustration for Speaker Albert, 1976 was a year of considerable accomplishment. In the battle for public opinion, the tide turned in favor of the Congressional Democrats. The result was a series of legislative victories. Ford stuck to his strategy of tight fiscal policy enforced by the heavy use of the veto. In 1976, however, the House consistently overrode his vetoes. By August 10, 1976 Majority Whip John McFall could claim that the House had succeeded in six of seven override attempts. Included among the six successful overrides were two major public works bills.[136] Looking toward an early adjournment for the 1976 elections, the House set a record pace for the number of days in session, session length, and votes.[137] Since the new budget process impinged upon the normal appropriations process and involved a necessary amount of tension between the new Budget Committee and the Appropriations Committee, it was important that its first use involve as little conflict as possible. It was a credit to those involved that the House was able to implement the new process and clear all but two appropriations bills by July of 1976, the first year the process was used. From the perspective of later experience, it seems amazing that a process that would prove so difficult to manage worked so well during the first year of its existence in the highly charged political circumstances of 1976.

Beyond these legislative successes, the Democrats accomplished the political task of undermining public confidence in the Ford administration. It had been the avowed intent of the leadership to foster public dissatisfaction with the administration by forcing the president to veto Democratic spending bills. Speaker Albert and his advisers knew that Ford would in most cases have his vetoes sustained, but they calculated that the political fallout from the veto battles would redound to the benefit of their party. In this they seem to have been proven correct. The public came to perceive that the constant bickering between the Republican administration and the Democratic Congress was preventing the government from moving forward with the nation's business. The Democrats sought to use their control of the Congress to challenge the policies of the Ford administration in order to defeat Ford at the polls. The legislative politics of the Ninety-fourth Congress cannot be correctly understood apart from this consideration. A platform committee task force appointed by Speaker Albert and chaired by Majority Leader O'Neill presented to the party's convention a vigorous blueprint for a Democratic administration.[138] Much of the rhetorical emphasis of the

House Democrats' statement and many of its policy recommendations were later incorporated into the Democratic platform. In part as a result, the summer and fall of 1976 saw the Democrats relatively well united legislatively and politically behind the candidacy of Georgia Governor Jimmy Carter. By the time the party managed to cohere, however, Speaker Albert had already announced his intention to retire from the House at the end of the Ninety-fourth Congress. Wearied by six years in the speakership, Albert resolved to "return to the scenes of my youth."[139]

As he returned to Oklahoma, Speaker Albert could feel a sense of satisfaction in what he had accomplished. He knew that many observers would say that he had been insufficiently forceful; but he also realized that his speakership had accomplished historic change in the House of Representatives and in the office of speaker. Under Carl Albert the speakership accumulated more institutional power than at any time since 1910. The Congress asserted its role in the government in a way that had not been witnessed for decades. The reigning in of the Rules Committee; the establishment of the Steering and Policy Committee as the Democratic Committee on Committees; the power of multiple referral; the use of select committees; the use of leadership task forces; the enactment and implementation of the budget process; the passage of the War Powers Resolution—these were among the historic achievements of Carl Albert's speakership. Historical and institutional forces that transcended the speakership caused the tide of reform, but Albert was in important respects ideally suited to facilitate the transition. He was a trusted product of the old order who grasped the inevitability of the new. And in the most serious constitutional crisis of the twentieth century, the Watergate crisis, the Constitution, in Senator Hugh Scott's words, "worked." It worked because its officers made it work, and the speaker of the House was the constitutional officer who was primarily responsible.

Carl Albert's speakership was the most difficult in the twentieth century. The Vietnam crisis scarred the polity as had no other event since the Great Depression. School busing divided whites and blacks. The reforms that took place in the House were unparalleled. The Watergate scandal was the most serious constitutional crisis since the Civil War. Through it all, Speaker Albert was never to serve with a president of his own party. Yet although the House coped with these cataclysmic events under his leadership, Albert did not escape criticism from some members and in the press. A lesson of his speakership is that a speaker in the democratic period must not only lead wisely, he must appear to be in command. Impression management has become as important to the speakership as to the presidency. A record of accomplishment is

often insufficient to offset the impression that can be created by critical
members and a caustic press corps. Presidents have a large press staff
devoted to the task of putting the best "spin" on events. Modern speakers
must recognize that one of the best ways to influence members is by
shaping a positive image. Speaker Albert was, in this respect, of the
Rayburn school. Rayburn disdained the press and carved his role as a
man of the House. The impression that his members and the public had
of him was shaped by his great longevity of service and the conformity
of his natural manner to his circumstances. What Rayburn had by
nature, democratic speakers must nurture. They have no choice but to
develop an offensive strategy of impression management. This lesson
was not lost on Albert's successor, Thomas P. O'Neill, Jr., of Massachusetts.

Conclusion

Sometimes history comes neatly packaged. Sam Rayburn's death,
following closely on the heels of the fight to pack the Rules Committee,
marks a clear beginning of the move to reform the House. By the end
of Carl Albert's speakership, the impetus behind the reform movement
was spent. The fifteen years from 1961 to 1976 witnessed the emergence
of the democratic speakership. It is useful to conclude the present chapter
by analyzing the conditions in the political culture, the political system,
and the policy agenda, that spawned the new rendition of the speakership, and the manner in which speakers McCormack and Albert responded to them. The transformation of the House came about because
a new generation of Americans came into active participation in American public life, bringing with them a policy agenda that was anathema
to the old order. It was the development of the liberal movement in the
Congress in the late 1950s that harbingered the institutional changes
that took place there in the 1960s and 1970s. The Democratic Study
Group was the main vehicle of those changes. But the new policy agenda
went hand in hand with a new political culture that was born in the
1960s and matured in the 1970s and 1980s. This was the generation
raised on Dr. Spock, nurtured at Woodstock, and called to politics by
the Kennedys, Eugene McCarthy, and later on, Ronald Reagan.

This new political culture was not just a movement on the political
left. A stress on interpersonal communication, mutual understanding,
clarification of values, and other manifestations of the new culture
permeated academia, the corporate world, and even the military. A new
generation of American leaders was shaped by such beliefs. In the Congress the most visible infusion of the new culture occurred with the
election of the class of 1974, a predominantly Democratic group. But

the 1978 and 1980 elections brought new Republicans to Washington who demonstrated the same tendencies as their Democratic counterparts.

The liberal policy agenda and the new political culture were helped along by changes in the political system. John Kennedy's election marked the beginning of the end for the strength of the two major political parties. Kennedy demonstrated what campaign organization could do in a system dominated by primary elections. In the decade thereafter, television became the primary medium for communication between candidate and voter. The new electoral system produced a generation of political entrepreneurs who would master the art of securing a safe district. The autonomy of members, combined with the diffusion of power within the House due to the reforms, created a legislative environment in which strong leadership was both needed and feared, both sought and rejected.

In these circumstances the tasks facing Speakers McCormack and Albert were difficult. Products of an *ancien régime*, they were called upon to lead a House that was in revolution against the old order. McCormack was past seventy by the time he became speaker, and resisted the reform impulse. Albert was a younger man and had closer connections to the younger and more liberal members who were in the vanguard of the reform movement. Yet Speaker Albert was also closely tied to the committee system and the barons who led it. He needed them to pass a legislative program, and was unwilling to lead a movement to undermine their power. Albert's natural inclination and best strategy lay in providing latent rather than overt support for the reform movement.

Both McCormack and Albert served long enough for their tenures to have been marked by considerable change. In McCormack's case, the transition from the Kennedy to the Johnson administration brought about greatly different circumstances. The Democratic landslide of 1964 created a unique legislative environment in which a deluge of legislation was passed in a short period of time. President Nixon's election in 1968 turned the cards against McCormack, and it was the frustration of liberal Democrats in dealing with Nixon that more than anything else turned them against their speaker. McCormack did not evidence much adaptability. He remained very much true to himself and his sense of his role as speaker. This served him adequately for so long as the Democratic majorities were large and President Johnson popular; but was insufficient in dealing with the more challenging circumstances of his last Congress.

Very little was normal about Speaker Albert's tenure. Albert was a man carved for a speakership unlike that which he was destined to hold.

As a bridge between the old and new generations, and as a political and parliamentary leader, Albert's intelligence, knowledge, and decency served him well. His fate was to serve at precisely the point when the new generation turned against the old and the party became riven from within. Had Albert been able to serve with a Democratic president such as Hubert Humphrey, his role would have been very different. A master of parliamentary and legislative mechanics, Albert would have been able to assist a president of his own party in winning consensus among Democrats. Instead, he was forced to play the role of leader of the opposition at a time when the Democratic party and the House of Representatives were undergoing the most sweeping changes in seventy years. During Albert's tenure the country was caught between war abroad and constitutional crisis at home. Albert demonstrated considerably more adaptability to changing circumstances than McCormack had. He had a sense of where he wanted his party to go, and a strategy designed to get the party there while surviving as speaker in a turbulent time. Albert understood that the members of the House want and have a right to expect honesty and fairness from their speaker; yet this very understanding led him on occasion to place his concern for members above his own power stakes. Carl Albert deserves great credit for the manner in which he handled the Watergate crisis and the reform movement. During his tenure the government weathered the most trying times since the Civil War. The speakership Albert left to his successors was a far stronger office than that which he inherited. Had Speaker Albert been more overtly engaged in the reform effort, his own reputation might have profited; but had he not led wisely and with a clear head, the country would not have survived the tumult so well. His speakership marked the transition from the feudal order to a new and more democratic speakership, one that would require many congresses to mature.

5 ☆ The Democratic Speakership in the Postreform House

The Postreform House

The movement to reform the House of Representatives that began in 1961 when Sam Rayburn led the fight against the power of the Rules Committee, ended in the Ninety-fourth Congress when the power of the old committee barons was finally broken and three of them were unseated. The reform of the rules of the House coincided with an underlying transformation in the political system, as the power of political parties to control congressional nominations gave way entirely to an open electoral arena in which autonomous and sometimes inexperienced politicians won nomination through direct primaries. These new politicians were of a different breed than their predecessors. They were better educated, more oriented toward public policy, and unwilling to take a back seat to their more senior colleagues. The result of these changes was to introduce a new era in the history of the House of Representatives, in which its predominant characteristics were equality of members' rights, diffusion of power, and a more open process of deliberation. The power of the speakership was greater than at any time since the revolt against Cannon in 1910, but the institutional and political context affected the ways in which the speaker's formal powers could be used. The speakership became a more democratic institution, more sensitive to the mood of members and to the vicissitudes of public opinion. The challenge of the office in the democratic period was to find ways to make the more unruly House of Representatives function as an effective legislative body. Speakers could seek to develop consensus or to take the lead in policy development; but the speaker's obligation was to make the House function well while attending to the interests of his party.

The third speaker in the democratic period was Thomas P. "Tip" O'Neill, Jr., of Massachusetts, an Irish politician educated in the old school of party politics. O'Neill served as speaker for five congresses, making his the longest consecutive tenure in the history of the office. So large did O'Neill loom over the House of Representatives that it was easy for commentators to assume that his speakership was prototypical of the office in the last part of the twentieth century. This view was shared by those who thought that O'Neill himself had defined the new rendition of the speakership, and by those who saw the new speakership as largely shaped by institutional forces beyond any speaker's control.[1] Neither explanation is adequate. Tip O'Neill's speakership was shaped by his reaction to the varying circumstances in which he was placed. By the time he became speaker O'Neill was a wholly formed man, as were all of his predecessors. His persona, his geo-political base, and his orientation toward party leadership were fixed commodities. But in the democratic period a speaker can ill afford the luxury of trying to govern according to his own preferences; instead, he must carefully gauge his own best path amid the confluence of events and personalities that surround him. A strategic understanding of the O'Neill speakership requires an explanation of the manner in which the office varied even as the character of the man and the characteristics of the period remained the same.

Jim Wright of Texas became the fourth speaker of the democratic period in 1987. Wright served as O'Neill's majority leader for ten years, and often appeared anxious to hold the reigns of power in his own hands. By the time he became speaker, the Reagan administration had been weakened by the return of the Senate to Democratic control, and by the controversy surrounding the Iran-Contra scandal. Wright soon established himself as an aggressive, policy-oriented leader, and for the first time House Democrats got that which the reformers had sought since their movement began, a policy-making speaker operating in a legislative environment in which the speakership was the principal center of power. Jim Wright pressed the powers of the speakership to their limit in pursuit of his party's legislative program. His emphatic leadership caused considerable disaffection among congressional Republicans, and in the summer of 1989, two and a half years into his speakership, Wright was forced to resign as a result of alleged violations of the House ethics code on charges brought by his Republican adversaries. He was succeeded in the speakership by the Democratic majority leader, Thomas S. Foley of Washington. This chapter will focus upon Speakers O'Neill and Wright, and their conduct of the chair in the postreform House.

The reforms, as we have seen, were largely the product of a liberal movement that began in the 1950s and culminated in the early 1970s. It is ironic that the policies that this movement produced led to a public reaction against the liberals who had produced them. Contrary to the expectations of the liberal reformers, the opening of the legislative process did not lead to an expansion of the positive state. Instead, the major expansion of the positive state in the Great Society preceded the adoption of most of the institutional reforms. By the time that the reform movement had crested, the public's appetite for the positive state had been sated, and the federal government entered a new period of retrenchment. With the election of Jimmy Carter to the presidency in 1976, the Democrats were once again ensconced in power, but the underlying direction of American policy proved to be running against the positive programs for which the party had stood since the New Deal. A government united under the Democrats gave way, after a single presidential term, to an era in which the division of power between the two parties became a normal circumstance. During the speakership's parliamentary period, power resided largely in the states. In the partisan period, power resided in the congressional party leadership. In the feudal period, power resided in the congressional committee system. In the democratic period, power became divided as an institutionally powerful presidency confronted a Congress usually controlled wholly or in part by the opposite party.

Yet, at first, it did not seem that way. In 1977, many Democrats believed, and many Republicans feared, that the 1976 election had brought about a return to normalcy, with the government once again lodged safely in the hands of the Democratic party. Neither the hidden majority nor the real majority had materialized in support of the Republicans, and a Democratic president would be working with substantial Democratic majorities in both Houses of a reformed Congress. The reform movement had broken down the barriers to the liberal policy agenda, and most of the senior, conservative chairmen had retired. In both chambers new men promised to bring new energy to the task of party leadership, and the Carter administration promised a sweeping policy program that included the reform of governmental organization, tax and welfare reform, deregulation, and a national energy policy. Democratic liberals could look forward to a real opportunity to shape the nation's policy agenda. At their helm in the House of Representatives stood white-maned Speaker Tip O'Neill, a paragon of the virtues that Democratic liberalism preached. O'Neill's belief in using tax dollars to do good deeds was unabashed: he boasted that he had promoted federal spending to help midgets grow.

Tip O'Neill was in many respects well suited to lead the House in the democratic period. His personality was amenable to the greater openness and communication that the culture of the House demanded.

If he was less of a policy maker than some members wanted, he was open to broad member participation in developing policy. O'Neill was a shrewd politician, and his orientation to the office was often political rather than institutional or substantive. It was his fate, however, to bring his sharp political instincts and strong liberal views to office during a conservative period in American politics. The O'Neill speakership was defined by a complex interplay of politics and policy, as the speaker sought to control the extent of the damage to liberal programs wrought by Jimmy Carter and Ronald Reagan.

Tip O'Neill came to Congress in 1952, elected to the seat vacated when John F. Kennedy was elected to the Senate. He had served as the first Democratic speaker of the Massachusetts legislature, and was a creature of urban Democratic politics. His father had been a sewer commissioner in Cambridge, and had used patronage power to gain influence in local politics.[2] Thomas P. O'Neill, Jr., was a product of the Cambridge streets, and had politics in his blood from an early age. He graduated from Boston College, where he had been an average student, but his real lessons were learned in his neighborhood and community. Politics for Tip O'Neill was always "local," as he liked to put it, and in understanding the people of his community he found his political strength. As speaker in Massachusetts, O'Neill was a powerful figure but not a legislative disciplinarian. The one element of traditional machine politics that he seemed to lack was a willingness to use the patronage powers at his disposal punitively. As the first Democrat to control the House in the history of the state, O'Neill engaged in no housecleaning, and no one was fired.[3] Tip O'Neill was not a vindictive man.

O'Neill was not among Washington's most visible figures during the first fifteen years of his service. His career was built on the foundation of a safe congressional seat, a congenial personality, and the development of important political relations with John McCormack and the Kennedys. He became McCormack's protégé, and was rewarded with an appointment to the House Rules Committee in just his second term. There, he could deal regularly with party leaders and members across the entire legislative spectrum, without becoming too involved in legislative detail. O'Neill was a leadership supporter on the Rules Committee, but he got along well with Judge Smith, and in the great Rules fight of 1961, he "played a minor role."[4] O'Neill consistently associated himself with liberal and reform goals without taking the leadership of the movement. When in 1957 "McCarthy's Mavericks" challenged the status quo, O'Neill refused to sign their "liberal manifesto." He understood that his climb to the top of the ladder would be better served by loyalty to McCormack than by joining a move to challenge the leadership. From the beginning of the reform movement to its end,

O'Neill was able to take advantage of an association with the reformers without alienating the elder statesmen of the old regime.

Until he entered the leadership, Tip O'Neill was a member of the "Tuesday-Thursday Club," typically spending only three days a week in Washington. His family remained in Cambridge, and for years he shared a Washington apartment with Massachusetts colleague and close personal friend Edward Boland. Dining out regularly during the week, O'Neill became well known to members even though he had little public visibility. From his first election in 1952 to his appointment as majority whip in 1971, Tip O'Neill was never a major power-broker in the House. He was, however, popular, and because of his close ties to McCormack, he was a link to the party leadership for many northeastern liberals. His political base in the Democratic caucus was narrow but firm.

A transformative event in O'Neill's career came with his open break with Lyndon Johnson on the Vietnam War in 1967. His was among the first of a series of Democratic defections that eventually led to Johnson's decision in March of 1968 to retire from the presidency. O'Neill turned against the war for moral reasons, revealing for the first time a dovish inclination in foreign policy; but the break with Johnson helped in his subsequent rise to the party leadership. In allying himself with the antiwar forces in the House, he positioned himself as a leader among liberal members of the caucus before the McGovern wing took control of the national party in 1972. He enhanced his status among liberal Democrats without getting caught up in the divisive attempts to dump McCormack or change the rules of the caucus. The members that O'Neill might have alienated on the war issue would probably not have supported him in a contested leadership election anyway. O'Neill's position on the war was not a political strategy, but a reflection of a deeply seated world-view. As speaker, he would become more involved in foreign policy than any of his predecessors, and his view of the world was profoundly shaped by his reaction to the Vietnam War.

O'Neill had an opportunity to compete for the elected position of majority leader in 1970, and chose not to enter the contest. Instead, he used his influence on behalf of Hale Boggs and was rewarded by appointment as whip. When Boggs was killed in an airplane crash two years later, O'Neill was elected majority leader without opposition. During his entire period of service in the House, Tip O'Neill never ran in a contested caucus election and after his first election in 1952, he had no serious challenge in his district. O'Neill's political outlook ripened with experience, but was never tempered by the serious threat of losing an election. As Carl Albert's majority leader, O'Neill served as a link to younger and more liberal members, just as Albert had for Rayburn and McCormack. Still, the two were at odds on some important policy issues. Albert supported administration policy on Vietnam until the war was virtually over, while O'Neill was one of the administration's strongest critics. In the Watergate affair, O'Neill aggressively pursued first Agnew and then Nixon, while Albert was more cautious. In each case Albert's positions were closer to the more senior, southern Democrats whose influence still predominated, while O'Neill sided with the liberal wing in the caucus, which was growing larger with each election. Tip O'Neill, the product of the ward-heeling politics of the past, appeared as a man of the future.

It is important to understand O'Neill's strategic location in the Democratic caucus. Speaker Albert's border state roots placed him near the center of the congressional party; Speaker O'Neill was firmly lodged on the party's left wing. During the mid 1970s the liberal wing of the party was growing in strength. The large number of new members elected in 1974 and 1976 combined with the cohort of liberals elected in the 1960s to dominate the Democratic caucus; the size of the Democratic majority promised to make it possible for the liberals to govern. The disenchantment that some of them felt with Speaker Albert was in large part a result of frustration that liberal goals were not being achieved. O'Neill was at home among the liberals, could serve as a beacon for liberal policy making, and was expected to be an aggressive speaker.

O'Neill's election as speaker coincided with an extensive revamping of the House Democratic leadership. Hale Boggs's death in 1972 and Carl Albert's retirement in 1976 had cost the House two strong links to the Rayburn/McCormack era. Then, in the Ninety-fourth Congress Wilbur Mills, the chairman of the Ways and Means Committee, and Wayne Hays, the chairman of the House Administration and Democratic Campaign Committees, fell prey to scandal. As majority leader, O'Neill played a major role in driving Hays from his leadership positions; a major thorn in Carl Albert's side would not be around to bother him.[5] A third controversial figure, Congressman Phillip Burton from California remained, and sought to become the party's majority leader. Burton had served as the chairman of the Democratic caucus during the heated debates over the Vietnam War and school busing, and was a leader of the most liberal faction within the caucus. With liberal strength increased, Burton became a leading candidate for majority leader. Facing off against Burton were Richard Bolling of Missouri, another titan of the old order, Democratic Whip John McFall of California, and dark-horse candidate Jim Wright of Texas. In the closest leadership election in the history of the House, Wright won by a single vote over Burton on the last ballot. His election indicated that the conservatives in the Democratic caucus would be a force with which to reckon.

Tip O'Neill and Jim Wright selected John Brademas of Indiana as whip and Dan Rostenkowski as chief deputy whip. Together, these four Democrats were a balanced leadership group, O'Neill and Brademas to the left, Wright and Rostenkowski to the right.[6] The new House leadership was joined by new leadership in the Senate, as West Virginia's Robert C. Byrd replaced retired Majority Leader Mike Mansfield of Montana. The task lying before the new Democratic leaders was simple to define: the Democrats needed to prove that they could govern. Tip O'Neill was determined to avoid the image problems from which his two immediate predecessors had suffered. To do so it was necessary that he lead the Congress in enacting the Carter program. O'Neill's reputation was tied to Carter's performance. Only if the administration were successful in passing its program in the House could O'Neill lay claim to a strong speakership. The speaker's ability to forge majorities was dependent upon the support that he would receive from the president, as events proved; yet O'Neill acted as though he could control his own fate. "I intend to be a strong Speaker," O'Neill pronounced. "I hope to make some innovative changes around here." He had learned a lesson from Albert's experience: no matter how successful a speaker may be in managing the business of the House, or even in winning votes, he must nurture his image. On cue, *Newsweek* commented: "O'Neill now stands to become the most potent man about the House since Rayburn."[7] And why not? A new and assertive speaker, clothed in increased institutional power, enjoying sizable majorities, working with a president of his own party, and leading an energetic flock of new troops had everything going his way. Speaker Albert's "veto-proof" Ninety-fourth Congress hadn't been, but Tip O'Neill's Ninety-fifth Congress would accomplish all that the Democrats had sought in the veto wars with President Ford.

Instead of a harmonious tenure, however, Speaker O'Neill was confronted with two very different situations, each in its own way presenting difficult challenges. The circumstances that O'Neill encountered in dealing with Democratic President Jimmy Carter were different in many crucial respects from those he faced in dealing with Republican President Ronald Reagan. So different was the O'Neill speakership during the Carter and Reagan administrations that it is necessary to analyze each separately. While the institutional context of the speakership with respect to House rules and norms did not change, O'Neill's strategic position and political role were fundamentally transformed. During the Carter administration he sought to survive as a loyal supporter of a president of his own party. During the Reagan administration he became the leading opponent of a president of the other party.

The Speaker as Loyal Supporter

A speaker's constitutional obligation is to facilitate the legislative process, but that his duty is to support the policies of a president of his own party has more often been accepted by Democratic than Republican speakers. Speakers generally loyal to presidents with whom they served have included Democrats such as Macon with Jefferson, Stevenson with Jackson, Carlisle with Cleveland, and Clark with Wilson. Speakers who viewed their role largely as independent of the presidency have included Whig Henry Clay and Republicans Blaine, Reed, Cannon, and Longworth. In the twentieth century, Democrat Sam Rayburn most clearly identified the role of the speaker as loyal supporter of a president of his own party. This concept of a speaker's duty was more compelling in a political system in which the power of the presidency was the main motive force; significantly, it developed during the three decades after 1932 when the presidency and the Congress were for the most part in Democratic hands. With the White House occupied by presidents with sweeping legislative programs to enact, such as Franklin Roosevelt, Truman, Kennedy, and Lyndon Johnson, it was natural for speakers Rainey, Burns, Bankhead, Rayburn, and McCormack to define their role in relationship to the president's legislative agenda.

Tip O'Neill accepted this concept of his role as speaker, and intended to put the force of his office behind the legislative program of the Carter administration. That program promised to be as sweeping as any since the Great Society. President Carter inundated the Congress with legislative proposals that included a comprehensive energy program, tax and welfare reform, the creation of three new cabinet-level departments (energy, education, and consumer affairs), comprehensive civil service reform, and an extensive effort to deregulate the economy. O'Neill shared Rayburn's understanding that the House of Representatives cannot function well when its circuits are overloaded. He advised Carter to limit his legislative priorities while setting one of them, the enactment of a comprehensive energy program, as the first goal for the House.

The speaker recognized that the new administration would enjoy a relatively brief honeymoon period within which it would be likely to have strong support on the Hill. It was important that it use this window of opportunity to try and pass its highest priority legislation, while establishing a positive tone for the balance of the term. O'Neill understood that it was as important for him to establish his reputation in the House as a speaker who could deliver the votes on major bills. In making the Carter energy program the major initial goal, O'Neill hoped to establish his position while laying the foundation for a successful presidential administration. O'Neill's approach to the Carter energy bill offers insights into the speakership and about the speaker. He had little to do with the formation of the Carter energy package. Carter relied upon James R. Schlesinger, his choice to head the new cabinet-level energy department proposed in the program, and there was little communication with the senators and congressmen upon whom the passage of the program would ultimately depend. This was the kind of mistake that the Carter administration would repeatedly make in dealing with the Congress, and ran contrary to the advice pressed upon the president by Speaker O'Neill and Senate Majority Leader Robert C. Byrd of West Virginia.[8] There was little that Speaker O'Neill could do to influence the legislative package unless the administration sought congressional input. Tip O'Neill's "reputation-maker" was a complex legislative program imposed upon the Congress by the administration.

Intent upon pushing the program through the House, O'Neill demonstrated for the first time as speaker two qualities that would serve him well: assertiveness on procedure and distance from policy. The "new-age" Democrats wanted a speaker who would be aggressive in the development and pursuit of a policy program. O'Neill was capable of being assertive, but was well known for his indifference to the details of policy. He understood that a speaker who becomes too closely associated with policy runs more risks than one who does not. Distance from policy permits distance from legislative defeats and policy failures. A speaker's powers are inherently procedural and political, and it was in these terms that O'Neill chose to define his role. If passing the president's energy program was in his interest, he would find a way to do it that depended upon procedural control rather than substantive input.

His device was borrowed from an innovation of Speaker Albert— an ad hoc committee. By tradition, the House uses ad hoc committees to study and to investigate, but not to legislate. The legislative labyrinth that had evolved during the years after World War II was loaded down with overlapping jurisdictions and it had become difficult to deal with complex policy issues. This is why Albert sought to reform the committee system in 1974. Failing in that attempt, Albert decided to experiment with an ad hoc committee to deal with policy on the use of the outer continental shelf. This was the first ad hoc House committee to be given legislative jurisdiction. In 1977 Speaker O'Neill decided that the best way to ram the Carter energy program through the House was to set up a special ad hoc committee to deal with it. The creation of an ad hoc energy committee had been suggested in 1976, but Speaker Albert decided against it when several key committee chairmen opposed the move. O'Neill faced the same opposition, and had to settle for a committee that would serve as a "clearing house" for legislative proposals made by authorizing committees of original jurisdiction. The Carter program would be farmed out to the standing committees according to their jurisdictions, and the committees were given deadlines to report bills to the special committee. The special committee could then propose amendments, but each section of the bill would be managed on the floor by the chairman of the committee having jurisdiction over it.

Speaker O'Neill appointed Congressman Thomas (Lud) Ashley of Ohio to chair the special committee, and was aggressive in pressing the committees to meet their deadlines. His appeal was based on the need for the Democratic party to demonstrate its capacity to govern. In the 1976 election the Democrats had castigated the Ford administration for its failure to come up with a comprehensive energy program, and O'Neill understood that it was politically imperative for the Democrats to pass a program of their own. It was also politically imperative for the speaker to appear as a leader who could make the House work. O'Neill knew instinctively that the Carter honeymoon period was his own best opportunity to win votes in the House.

President Carter's energy program was consumer-oriented.[9] The president proposed to discourage consumption by increasing price through taxation. The tax harvest would be rebated to low-income consumers. At the heart of the program was a crude-oil equalization tax that would raise the domestic price to world levels. The alternative was simple price deregulation. But deregulation was regressive and would offer its profits to the domestic oil industry at the expense of consumers. Carter saw no reason to permit the domestic industry to profit from a cartel price. Speaker O'Neill and his ad hoc committee pushed the Carter program to the floor of the House in four months, a remarkable accomplishment; but there the program ran into a serious challenge. A recommittal motion instructing the ad hoc committee to knock out the equalization tax was offered by Congressman William A. Steiger of Wisconsin. The motion was defeated by a narrow 203–219 majority.[10] O'Neill's appeal to party loyalty was barely sufficient to win a majority in the House. Still, the passage of the Carter program virtually intact had a salutary effect on O'Neill's reputation. By the summer of 1977 sympathetic reporters were heralding his power.[11]

But O'Neill's power was procedural and not substantive. From April 1977 until the final passage of the energy program in 1978, the speaker insisted that the only way to pass an energy program in the House was to take it to the floor en masse. In the Senate, the Carter program was farmed out to the standing committees, where it was dramatically altered.[12] Senator Russell Long of Louisiana, chairman of the Senate Finance Committee led a revolt against the taxing provisions, while the administration was forced into a compromise on natural gas pricing after a struggle between Senator Lloyd Bentsen of Texas and Senator

Henry M. (Scoop) Jackson of Washington. By the time the Senate package reached conference, its key provision had become the natural gas compromise. The crude-oil equalization tax had been knocked out in favor of partial deregulation of domestic oil prices.

When the conference report hit the House floor, the conservative coalition moved to defeat it by forcing a separate vote on the natural gas provision. In a cliff-hanger, the strategy was defeated on a 206–207 vote, with Speaker O'Neill banging a quick gavel as soon as he saw a majority in his favor. The action was reminiscent of Speaker Rayburn's assertive role in the chair in 1941 when the military draft was preserved by a single vote, but the appearance of force obscured an underlying weakness. O'Neill was just as assertive in defending the conference report in 1978 as he had been in pushing through the original Carter program in the spring of 1977; but the program that O'Neill defended at the end was barely a shadow of the program that he had promoted at the beginning. O'Neill's strategy of holding the package together worked for both packages, and from the point of view of his own reputation, it made little difference that the two differed so widely. O'Neill revealed the limits of his power even as he exercised it. He could not dictate the terms of the bill, as Joe Cannon might have done, but his interest lay in seeing it passed.

The early passage of the Carter energy program in the House did more to enhance O'Neill's reputation than Carter's. The president absorbed the gutting of the energy bill into his own reputation, while the speaker gained credit for having driven the initial administration bill through the House. The establishment of his reputation was a key first step in his speakership. As Jimmy Breslin had put it: "Tip O'Neill at all times has one great political weapon at his disposal. He understands so well that all political power is primarily an illusion. If people think you have power, then you have power. If people think that you have no power, then you have no power. This is a great truth in politics that I was able to recognize in O'Neill's ways."[13] Breslin's perception is astute and typically modern. To Breslin, the politician's capacity is fundamentally defined by the drive for power. Yet the remark also reveals just how shallow are the streams in which power flows. O'Neill understood that the quest for power is less important than the appearance of it. Usually, the illusionist is limited by forces beyond his power to control. Tip O'Neill was a master at creating the illusion of power, but he recognized that his own image was linked to Carter's fate.

Two factors served to define Tip O'Neill's speakership during the Carter years. They occurred within the context of the postreform House, but both were more important than any institutional arrangements that the speaker confronted. The first was that the Carter administration was unable to deal effectively with the Congress; the second was that Tip O'Neill was more liberal than Jimmy Carter. The problems that Jimmy Carter encountered in pressing his legislative agenda on the Congress were traceable to his character, on the one hand, and to his staff on the other. Jimmy Carter was a very intelligent man and a man of strong personal convictions. He viewed the presidency as a trust, and his own responsibilities as that of a trustee.[14] This attitude left little room for the spirit of compromise and conciliation that is demanded by the Congress. It was typical for the Carter administration to develop major legislative proposals without sufficient consultation with the Congress, in the belief that its policies would argue their own case on the Hill. This attitude characterized the development of major administration initiatives in tax and welfare reform, executive branch reorganization, and the energy bill. An important early indicator of the administration's sanctimonious attitude toward legislative politics came when the president proposed to eliminate nineteen water projects that had been approved by the Congress. Members in the affected states and districts were not consulted, on the theory that they would have the most reason to oppose rational policy making. Their resentment, and the inherent legislative resistance to presidential intrusion into pork-barreling, ensured that the administration would largely fail in its mission; but the bitterness engendered by the effort cast a shadow over the administration's relations with the Congress thereafter.[15]

President Carter's attitude toward the Congress was reflected in that of some members of his staff. This led to the development, especially early in the term, of inattention to congressional perquisites and sensibilities in a variety of smaller matters. This pattern touched upon Speaker O'Neill himself. At the time of the president's inaugural the new speaker requested extra tickets for the ball and got back row seats. When he complained to Carter's closest adviser, Hamilton Jordan, he was told that he could have his money back. O'Neill cursed Jordan, and started calling him "Hannibal Jerkin."[16] Injuries were added to insult. The speaker's recommendation for director of the CIA was ignored. A potential political opponent of the speaker's son in Massachusetts, former Nixon jack-of-all-trades Elliot Richardson, was named American ambassador to the United Nations' Law of the Sea Conference, and O'Neill was not consulted. The president planned a speaking engagement in Massachusetts and failed to notify O'Neill. Then he appointed a Massachusetts Republican as White House chief of protocol without notifying the speaker. All of this occurred within the first three months of the Carter administration.[17]

These slights to Speaker O'Neill were characteristic of the administration's approach to the Congress, which quickly landed Carter in trouble. By the end of January 1977, Speaker O'Neill and Senate Majority Leader Robert Byrd had gone public with a demand for better consultation by the administration.[18] The *Congressional Quarterly* described the president's relationship with Congress as "fragile," and Carter threatened to go over the Congress's head to the people. Meanwhile, Carter's assistant for congressional liaison, Frank Moore, acquired a reputation for failing to return phone calls. In his first presidential press conference on February 8, Carter acknowledged his difficulties in dealing with the Congress; in his second press conference two weeks later, he said that he was very pleased with his congressional relations.[19] Yet nothing much had changed in the meantime. Ironically, the difficulties that the administration faced in dealing with the Congress played into O'Neill's hands. He became portrayed as the elder statesman upon whom the new president would lean.[20] Because of Carter's problems in dealing with the Congress, O'Neill's reputation for power grew just as Rayburn's reputation had profited from Truman's difficulties with the Congress in the late 1940s.

But if O'Neill's reputation was enhanced by the perception that the president needed him, his task of marshaling majorities was made no less difficult. In spite of appearances, O'Neill needed Carter a lot more than Carter needed O'Neill. The speaker proved to be a willing innovator in congressional management, as his handling of the energy bill attested; but experience proved that techniques of legislative management are of little avail to a speaker in support of an administration that has lost its base of support on the Hill, and when the tide of public policy moves against the speaker's preferred positions. And that is precisely what happened to Tip O'Neill. At the end of March 1977, the *National Journal*, in a perceptive article, noted that the president's shaky relationship with the Congress was tied less to the incompetencies of his staff than to the direction of his policy priorities.[21]

The rightward shift in American public policy became more visible in 1978. Two good examples of this were the Humphrey-Hawkins Full Employment bill and the FY 1979 budget resolution. In both cases the legislation offered opportunities for a liberal Democratic congressional majority to work with a progressive Democratic administration to move public policy to the left. In both cases Speaker O'Neill had recourse to extraordinary steps in legislative management. And in both cases public policy was dragged toward the right in spite of the speaker's best efforts. The Humphrey-Hawkins bill was the last testament of Hubert Humphrey, the man who symbolized all that was best in New Deal liberalism. Co-authored with Congressman Augustus Hawkins of California, the bill required the government to set full-employment as its primary economic goal, and required that this be given central consideration in the congressional budget process.

In March of 1978 Humphrey-Hawkins passed the House as a result of a major effort by the Democratic leadership.[22] Humphrey-Hawkins was a declaration of the economic principles of the Democratic party. It was a counterpoise to the Republican Kemp-Roth tax proposal that symbolized traditional Republican economic philosophy. The Democrats had passed the Full Employment Act in 1946. The Republicans swept into office in 1947 and proposed a major tax cut, and the voters expelled the Republicans in 1948. In 1978 the Democrats hoped that the passage of Humphrey-Hawkins would ensure the health of the economy and their party's continued control of the government. The Congress enacted Humphrey-Hawkins, but the version passed into law was only a shadow of the vision shared by its authors. Instead of being incorporated into the budget process as a set of binding goals, the bill merely provided for the president to submit annually, along with his budget recommendations, a report setting five-year economic goals for maintaining a full-employment economy. Congress was afforded a review of economic policy during the consideration of each year's budget resolution. The debate over the Humphrey-Hawkins bill revealed the three basic economic philosophies dividing the congressional community. The liberal Democratic majority stood for economic stimulus through direct government spending. Conservative Democrats and Republicans were concerned about a balanced budget. The Republican new right pressed its program of tax cuts guided by the supply-side economic theory.[23]

The Democrats were able to fend off amendments that would have transformed the bill entirely, but the narrowness of many of the votes was indicative of the mood of the Congress. Republican Jack Kemp's three-year tax cut proposal was framed as an amendment to Humphrey-Hawkins and lost by only 22 votes, 194–216. A balanced budget alternative offered by Republican John Ashbrook lost by only 10 votes, 205–215. An amendment by Democrat Otis Pike that would have had the effect of raising the unemployment target substantially was defeated by only 5 votes, 199–204. Finally, the Democrats had to come forward with an amendment that required that economic goals include curbing the rate of inflation. Congressional Democrats could not use the bill as an excuse to propose liberal spending programs without attention to the inflationary impact of federal deficits; nor could Republicans stand for huge tax cuts without considering their tendency to promote inflation. As amended, the bill passed by a 257–152 margin, but 41 Democrats voted against it, 41 Democrats who would hold the balance of power in a more closely divided House.[24]

The leadership made Humphrey-Hawkins a priority and appointed a task force headed by North Carolina Congressman Charles Rose to work the bill. In a pattern that was characteristic of the Democratic leadership operation under O'Neill, the task force worked with the whips and liberal organizations such as the AFL-CIO. The Rules Committee structured debate so as to enable both sides to bring forward key amendments, position papers were prepared for each key amendment, and Democratic substitutes were developed for politically dangerous Republican amendments, giving to Democratic members acceptable positions on inflation and budget balancing. Given the closeness of several key votes, this effort was not wasted, but the majority party in the country, controlling both houses of the Congress and the presidency, had great difficulty in passing a highly symbolic bill incorporating its philosophy of government. It was able to pass the bill only by taking extraordinary steps in legislative management. The final bill was a much watered-down version of the original proposal on which it was based.

The second indication of the rightward shift in policy came with House consideration of the first budget resolution for FY 1979. In 1977 the House had rejected the first FY 1978 budget resolution, and Speaker O'Neill was determined to avoid a similar embarrassment in 1978. As a result, the leadership became more involved in shaping the FY 1979 budget resolution in committee, and geared up a full task force effort headed by Congressman Butler Derrick of South Carolina in order to pass the bill.[25] That Derrick was chosen was not coincidental since the leadership's defections were likely to be among southern Democrats. However, in order to bring a bill from committee and pass it on the House floor, the leadership had to move its position to the right as well. The result was an FY 1979 budget resolution that was the most conservative produced by the budget process to date, one that ushered in "the end of the era when most great social reform is passed."[26] The contrast between Congress's approach to the economy in 1977 and 1978 was striking. In the pattern of debate that had prevailed when President Ford was in office, Ford had stood for tax cuts to stimulate the economy while holding spending down with the veto. Ford's FY 1977 budget reflected that philosophy, but the revised budget that the Congress produced under Carter's leadership reversed the priority, proposing a lower tax cut and increased spending for public service jobs and public works. By contrast, the FY 1978 budget proposed an inflation-adjusted increase in spending of less than 1 percent, while President Carter called for a flat budget for FY 1980.[27] The final FY 1979 budget called for limits on public works programs, linking tax cuts to inflation (thus acknowledging the primacy of inflation over stimulus as the nation's major economic concern), and cut less from Carter's defense request than had been done in previous years. No major social program initiatives were proposed.[28]

Speaker O'Neill's use of legislative task forces to help in majority formation was designed to increase member involvement. Recognizing that the new, therapeutic Democrats wanted a sense of participation, O'Neill sought to foster loyalty through the use of ad hoc groups of members, who were asked to assist the leadership at the floor stage of legislation. While this task would naturally fall to the majority leader and party whips, O'Neill found it useful to broaden the base of participation and shape it to the demands of particular bills. He wanted members to feel as though they were a part of the leadership operation.

The task forces were an innovation in political management well suited to the culture of the therapeutic generation of younger Democrats, but were politically efficacious only in some circumstances. Under Speaker Albert task forces had been formed by the Steering and Policy Committee to develop Democratic positions on policy. Speaker O'Neill's task forces were designed to marshal support for legislation on the floor. O'Neill wanted to involve numerous members on behalf of the leadership, providing the sense of involvement that members wanted. He used the task forces, though, only when he had a sufficient majority with which to work. In the Ninety-fifth Congress, with the Democrats holding a decisive 302–133 margin, task forces were involved in nineteen roll-call votes, on all of which the leadership prevailed. An average of 60 Democrats defected on these votes, fewer than the number of southerners who might have sided with the Republicans (there having been 81 southern Democrats in that Congress). In the Ninety-sixth Congress the Democrats had a smaller margin (275–159) and a larger number of southerners (86). Across eleven task force votes, 66 Democrats defected on average, and the leadership won eight and lost three.[29] In both congresses, the leadership's primary defections were among southern Democrats, but the leadership's margin was sufficiently large to ensure victories in spite of them.

In the Ninety-seventh Congress, facing 179 Republicans and 79 southern Democrats and a White House and Senate controlled by the Republicans, the speaker decided that the task forces were no longer wise. He did not have the votes to win. This suggests that the task forces were useful for stirring activity and encouraging attendance by a majority party in solid control, but were less likely to swing votes when the partisan alignment was closer. The benefits were not worth the cost of embarrassing defeats. Since task force participation occurred mostly among party loyalists, it appears that they were not as valuable in winning the support of the less loyal members. In the Ninety-fifth and Ninety-sixth Congresses respectively, 63 and 80 percent of southern Democrats failed to serve on a single task force.[30]

The two external forces shaping O'Neill's speakership during the Carter years were the attitude of the Carter administration toward the Congress and the shift to the right in public policy. The Carter administration did have some legislative accomplishments to its credit. Among these were the reorganization of the executive branch, which included the creation of two new cabinet departments (education and energy); civil service reform; the Panama Canal Treaty; the Humphrey-Hawkins full employment bill; and the annual budget resolutions and the passage of most of the annual appropriations bills. President Carter won support for 78 percent of his legislative requests in 1977 and 75.4 percent in 1978.[31] But the administration's success rate was low by historical standards and its victories were often obtained by a policy shift to the right. This led to considerable criticism of Speaker O'Neill within the Democratic caucus. The early stories about the sage speaker as the legislative pillar of the new administration gave way to complaints that Democratic unity had been shattered.

Nowhere was this better illustrated than in the aftermath of the passage of the Conable-Jones tax bill in 1978. This was the first tax reform bill in over a decade that was not designed to increase the progressivity of the tax code. In the House Ways and Means Committee a coalition of centrists led by Oklahoma Democrat James R. Jones and ranking Republican Barber B. Conable, Jr., of New York, joined to send to the House floor a tax bill that was kinder to middle-income taxpayers and business than it was to the working poor. The bill was designed to stimulate business investment and provide incentives for savings. It presaged the direction of federal tax policy in the 1980s, and it passed the House in exactly the form in which it emerged from the committee. The bill was a major defeat for the Carter administration.[32]

Speaker O'Neill's handling of the tax bill demonstrated his dilemma and his art. The Ways and Means Committee had revolted against the liberal Democratic majority in the House. Chairman Ullman was forced to join forces with Jones and Conable in order to get a bill out of committee. Faced by a loss of control in committee, O'Neill wanted to avoid a direct vote on the Republican Kemp-Roth proposal for steep across-the-board cuts in marginal tax rates.[33] He insisted that the obliging Rules Committee deny a floor vote to Kemp-Roth. Then he stood back and allowed the conservative coalition to control the issue (even to the extent of disallowing a liberal social security amendment in the Rules Committee). Criticism from House liberals was predictable. The

Democrats were in "disarray," held Colorado Congressman Tim Wirth.[34] O'Neill's response was to blame the defeat on Carter. "The administration has been tardy in bringing tax legislation to this body," he declared.[35] O'Neill had about him many qualities that served him well in the speakership, but none more than this: among his contemporaries he had only one equal at plausibly blaming his defeats on other people: Ronald Reagan.

Tip O'Neill's dilemma was clearly defined by the end of the Ninety-fifth Congress, and was played to its conclusion in the Ninety-sixth. The 1978 elections increased Republican strength in the House considerably, and the hope that the Carter administration would find its legislative bearings gave way to a fear that its problems would lead to a general debacle in 1980. The first half of 1979 saw a further shift to the right as the Carter administration sought to restrain inflation by producing a balanced budget. The idea of a balanced budget became a fad on the Hill with a variety of proposals floated by conservative Democrats and Republicans alike, including one by Majority Leader Jim Wright.[36] The liberal reaction to this conservative shift was swift and strong. Said George Meany of the AFL-CIO, "Austerity. I see it as a major attack on the living and working standards of average Americans, further widening the gap between the 'haves' and the 'have-nots.'" Carter's prospective opponent for the 1980 Democratic presidential nomination, Ted Kennedy, held that "the fact is that the Administration's budget asks the poor, the black, the sick, the young, the cities and the unemployed to bear a disproportionate share of the billions of dollars of reductions." Speaker O'Neill drew a verbal line in the dust: "I didn't become Speaker to dismantle programs I've fought for all my life."[37]

Unsurprisingly, the House budget, which was passed on schedule in May, was to the left of the Carter proposal. In nine tense days of floor debate, a narrow Democratic majority fended off attacks on the bill. The leadership used one of its task forces to hold a fragile coalition of liberals and moderates together. The Senate budget was closer to the Carter proposal, and the final conference report adopted was more conservative than the House bill, but Speaker O'Neill supported it.[38] The limits of O'Neill's power were clear: he was loyal to the president and committed to the budget process, and therefore had to support policies that were too conservative for him. The passage of the budget should have portended good things for the Carter administration, but unfortunately other factors were at work that would in the end undermine the Carter presidency and demonstrate how greatly dependent Speaker O'Neill was upon the president. The Iranian revolution led to a crisis in world oil supply and shortages in the United States. In response the administration sought authority for standby gas rationing and proposed to decontrol the price of oil. In a reflection of the general decline in President Carter's support in the country, he was resoundingly rebuffed on both counts in the House in May 1979.

Even the president's success in negotiating the Camp David accords between Israel and Egypt did not retrieve his public standing. The Carter administration was rarely permitted the luxury of basking in its successes, because they were often covered in the shadow of embarrassing public defeats.

> Carter's popularity surged after his Middle East successes. Immediately after the Camp David meeting, Carter's rating went from 39 percent approval to 59 percent. The popularity created by the Mideast summit did not maintain itself, however. As the peace failed to materialize, some of the glow wore off. By the last week of March, 1979, Carter had once again declined to 39 percent approval, 50 percent disapproval. By May, with inflation rising, no energy solution in sight, and Carter's government in disarray, only 26 percent would give a "good" or "excellent" rating for the overall job done by Carter; 52 percent would rate him only "fair." A CBS–New York Times poll of June 5 showed Carter's popularity had dropped to a low of 30 percent support. It looked as if Carter was indeed heading for the end of his presidency.[39]

As May wore on into June, the oil crisis worsened. States were forced to adopt odd-even plans for selling gasoline, lines at the pump became common, and the public's mood soured further. While attending the Tokyo economic summit, the president resolved to make a renewed effort to move the Congress on the energy issue by addressing the nation. President Carter realized that the energy crisis was only a part of the problem that the country faced. The public had become skeptical of government and of government's ability to cope with the problems that faced it. He knew that he, more than any other person, was responsible and obligated to find the cure. His administration had reached a period of crisis from which he would either spring to reelection in 1980 or fall into jeopardy of losing the Democratic nomination. And so Jimmy Carter withdrew to the mountaintop retreat at Camp David to hold council before addressing the American people. To him came leaders from government, business, civil rights, religion, academia, and other walks of public life. Speaker O'Neill was among a number of congressmen who were called to his side. The president also arranged to meet with groups of private citizens, seeking as he always did to find his roots in the people. Over a seven-day period, July 7–13, 1979, Carter received over 100 pilgrims.[40] On July 15 he descended from the mountain to address the nation.

In one of the most remarkable presidential addresses in American history, the American people confronted the spectacle of a president who came to them to confess a failure of leadership. What had he learned on the mountaintop? "Mr. President," he was told, "you're not leading this nation. You're just managing the government." And even as a manager, Jimmy Carter had his shortcomings: "You don't see the people enough any more," ran one comment. "Some of your Cabinet members don't seem loyal. There is not enough discipline among your disciples," ran another.[41] Yet underneath the veneer of self-deprecation lay a deeper expression of doubt about America, one that by implication exonerated Carter from responsibility. In proclaiming a "crisis of confidence," Carter sought to shift the focus from his own failings as a leader to the failure of Americans as a people. Instead of blaming himself for lacking the inspirational qualities in a leader that a polity requires, he implied that the American people were at fault for failing to follow him. America did not face a crisis of leadership; it faced a crisis of followership. And if the president's "disciples" were disloyal, what was required was discipline, rather than inspiration, from above.

Thus, Carter's first act was one of retribution. In the most extensive cabinet shake-up in recent times, Carter sacked Treasury Secretary Michael Blumenthal, Secretary of Energy James R. Schlesinger, Health, Education and Welfare Secretary Joseph A. Califano, Jr., and Secretary of Transportation Brock Adams. These, presumably, were the disloyalists of whom the president had spoken, but they were also, in the eyes of many on Capitol Hill, among the most capable members of the cabinet. With the 1980 election only sixteen months away, it would be difficult for a new cabinet team to bring continuity to the administration in time to have an effect on policy and legislation. The supporters of those who had been deposed would have ample opportunity to exact retribution if they chose. And the widespread perception that more power was to be concentrated in the hands of a White House staff dominated by Georgians and now headed formally by Hamilton Jordan further added to an atmosphere of distrust and discontinuity among the Washington community.[42]

Tip O'Neill, who thought "ousted Health, Education, and Welfare Secretary Joseph Califano is great and considers some of the top White House staff not great, but is loyal to President Carter," appeared nonchalant. Saying that what's done is done, O'Neill expressed the view that the entire matter would blow over in "forty-eight hours . . . at most . . . well, give it a week." But had the speaker's opinion of White House congressional liaison chief Frank Moore improved? "Next question," growled O'Neill.[43] O'Neill's interest, as well as that of the president, lay in putting the episode behind them. Yet President Carter's problems put Speaker O'Neill in a very difficult situation, one to which he could not have been as indifferent as he pretended to be. O'Neill cared about two things: his power and the policies for which he had fought during his congressional career. Both were threatened by the Carter administration. O'Neill was caught in a Catch-22. If Carter was successful, it would mean retrenching programs to which O'Neill was committed; if Carter failed, O'Neill's reputation might suffer.

The catharsis of July 1979 gave way to the lengthy August recess, and a resumption of battle in September. As if to confirm the problems that the Carter presidency was causing the O'Neill speakership, a legislative debacle ensued. The crisis hit on September 19 and ran for a week. On that day the House voted down the second budget resolution for FY 1980.[44] On the twentieth the House voted down the Panama Canal Treaty implementing legislation.[45] On September 22 the speaker was forced to extend the deadline that he had set for the House Commerce Committee to report a hospital cost containment bill due to a parliamentary filibuster by committee opponents.[46] In the same week, the Congress defeated a continuing appropriations bill and a bill extending the public debt limit.[47]

This was probably the worst legislative week that any speaker has suffered in the twentieth century. One would have to go back to the days of obstructionism to find the House so paralyzed on legislative matters. Speaker Albert had been criticized for the failure to produce two-thirds majorities to override three presidential vetoes of controversial bills, but that week Speaker O'Neill could not muster simple majorities to pass basic legislation needed to run the government. These major defeats, coming one on top of the other, had an adverse effect on the administration and on the Democratic leadership in the House, even though every defeat was eventually reversed. The debt ceiling and Panama Canal bills were passed in September, the continuing resolution passed in October, and the second budget resolution was adopted in November. But in spite of these victories (along with a major victory on September 27 when the Congress cleared the conference report on the Department of Education bill), the damaging perception of chaos remained. Enter the speaker of the House, the master of damage control:

> "Everything fell apart," said House Speaker Thomas P. O'Neill, Jr. . . . "We came back after our August vacation and it was clear Kennedy was going to run [for president]. The members were telling us Carter was weak. What were they going to do? They were thinking, 'How am I going to protect myself?' "[48]

This statement says a lot about Speaker O'Neill and offers a lesson on the speakership. Who was at fault for the legislative debacle of mid

September, 1979? Well, nobody; everything just "fell apart." Yet wasn't
the speaker in charge? Well, it was "clear that Kennedy was going to
run." Of what relevance was this? A Kennedy candidacy would not hurt
O'Neill, but it does hurt Carter, since "members were telling us that
Carter was weak." Of course, O'Neill might have responded by saying:
"No, Carter isn't weak; he is strong, and I want you to support him."
He didn't because he knew that Carter was weak, and he knew that
the members knew it. Just as the members tried to distance themselves
from the president by voting against him, Speaker O'Neill had to distance himself from Carter rhetorically. The speaker's obligation to support the president ended where the threat to his own reputation began.
By putting some space between himself and Carter, O'Neill sought to
avoid identification with the president's difficulties.

In reaction to the legislative defeats of September both the administration and the House leadership talked tough but carried a little stick.
Assuming an LBJ-like demeanor, President Carter threatened retaliation.
Grants to cities, invitations to the White House, requests for campaign
help, and patronage requests would be based on the record of presidential support. "Some of you in Congress haven't supported me at
all," Carter threatened. "I'll be damned if I'll send my wife into your
district for a fundraiser."[49] The effect that such a threat could be expected
to have on members who were, according to their speaker, "trying to
protect themselves" by voting against the president, can only be estimated. Tough talk also emanated from the House Democratic leadership. In one of their episodic bursts of enthusiasm for party responsibility, the speaker and majority leader spoke of using the committee
assignment club to discipline those who failed to toe the party line on
key votes. O'Neill called a few members in for "confession."[50] But it
made no sense for the speaker to go to the mat in support of Jimmy
Carter. O'Neill's major interest lay in preserving his own reputation
without damaging the basis of his power. To the extent that the defeats
were perceived to lie at his feet, then his own reputation would suffer.
But with a convenient scapegoat such as Jimmy Carter available, there
was no need for the Democratic leadership to try and punish the members on whose votes their own power rested.

The demise of the Carter presidency in the 1980 election was foretold
by the events of 1979. When Ted Kennedy announced his intention to
challenge the president for the Democratic nomination, Speaker O'Neill
was caught in a conflict between his loyalty to an incumbent Democratic
administration, his close association with the Kennedys, and his liberal
policy preferences. He chose to sit out the conflict by serving as the
chairman of the Democratic convention at Carter's request. This permitted him to remain publicly neutral between Carter and Kennedy.

Throughout 1980, O'Neill steered around political and policy conflicts that were increasingly affected by electoral politics. He avoided the negotiations over the budget, sat on the sidelines in the presidential contest, and waited to see what would materialize.

A weakened presidency led to a government that was often in disarray, and there was little that O'Neill could do about it, as was illustrated in May 1980. On May 21 the House approved a defense authorization bill $6.2 billion above the budget resolution. On May 22 the Ways and Means Committee voted against the president's imposition of an oil-import fee. On May 29 the House rejected the conference report on the FY 1981 budget. Both the president and the speaker felt that the conferees had been too sympathetic to the Senate's position on defense numbers and opposed the conference report. However, in a speedy turnaround, the House voted to instruct its conferees to insist on the same defense number that had brought about the downfall of the first conference report. The historically unreliable liberal contingent in the House had called it a night—ninety-seven of them had gone home—thus enabling a coalition of Republicans and conservative Democrats to defeat a routine motion for adjournment. Seizing their opportunity, the conservatives moved to instruct the conferees. Lamented O'Neill: "I can't even get some of my friends in there to give me a motion to adjourn."[51]

Tip O'Neill suffered several significant defeats at the president's side, yet his public reputation never really suffered much. He was able to seem powerful just at the moment when he was losing. He fostered the impression that if the administration would simply follow his advice, everything would be alright. The defeats became Carter's, and not O'Neill's. Yet his natural talent for turning media criticism aside was less effective in assuaging his own members. While it protected him against the kind of press criticism that Speaker Albert had suffered, it could not shield him from the disenchantment of Democratic members who tended to blame him for their problems. After all, the Democrats had won big at the polls while Carl Albert was speaker. Now they worried that Carter's misfortunes would mean their own demise. If the speaker was as powerful as his reputation suggested, members had reason to wonder why the House Democratic party could not govern. Some members claimed that, despite his reputation for openness, O'Neill was too distant from the daily task of policy making and insufficiently assertive in presenting the congressional case to the administration.

The criticisms of O'Neill bore some validity. For all of his posturing about reaching out to members, working through members, and serving as a confessor for members, he was in plain fact older, more liberal, and culturally different from the majority of House Democrats. Many

Democrats felt excluded from the deliberations of their party because they *were* excluded; the Democratic caucus was relatively inactive during the Carter years. The therapeutic techniques by which the Irish speaker sought to mollify his members were of little avail when the tide of external forces turned against him. The factors that served most to shape O'Neill's conduct and fortunes during the Carter administration were the president, the state of the economy, and the mood of the country, all of which were beyond his control. Thus, the speakership of the House, in a united government, with a large partisan majority and led by a fairly assertive speaker, was seen to be what it usually is, a reactive institution. In playing the role of loyal supporter in the context of the postreform House, Tip O'Neill demonstrated that while the tactics of leadership were driven by institutional factors, the strategic role of the speakership depended more on two forces that were extrinsic to the House: the presidency and the policy agenda.

The Speaker as Loyal Opponent

On November 4, 1980, Tip O'Neill was transformed from a prospective lame duck speaker to the leading elected Democrat in America. The policy agenda shifted further to the right during the Reagan administration, and O'Neill's strategic position was altered as well. The loss of the presidency to the Republicans freed O'Neill from the millstone of the Carter administration. He was no longer forced to support a president for whose policies he had little enthusiasm and on whose performance he could not rely. Now, however, the speaker faced a new and more formidable challenge, for President Reagan threatened the policies for which O'Neill and the Democratic party had long stood.

The loss of the Senate to the Republicans for the first time since 1954 denied to O'Neill the support of a Democratic Senate in facing the Reagan onslaught, but he assumed a greater voice in defining his party's positions. Senator Robert Byrd of West Virginia became the minority leader and left to O'Neill the glare of national publicity and the obligations that came along with it. Whereas during the Albert speakership the lines of regular communication were between the speaker and Democratic Senate Majority Leader Mike Mansfield, during the second O'Neill speakership the speaker found it more often necessary to deal with Republican Senate Majority Leaders Howard Baker of Tennessee and Robert Dole of Kansas. The House Democrats were now much more likely to lose, but the speaker's position was enhanced as their leader.

Marshaling Democratic majorities in the House presented a difficult challenge. The loss of the White House shifted the leverage to the

Republicans. The loss of the Senate meant that House-passed bills would have to be compromised in conference. O'Neill's best strategy was to start out on the left in order to bargain back to the center, but with the narrowed House majority, a move to the left brought with it the danger of defeat on the House floor. A swing of just twenty-seven Democratic votes to a unified Republican minority would shift the balance of power in the House to the Republicans. The old opposition game, in which a Democratic Senate and House played off of each other to mutual advantage, cooperated in conference strategy, and shared responsibility, was not available. Instead, the House Democrats and their speaker stood alone in a hostile environment. Although played out in the context of the postreform House and shaped by the therapeutic culture of the new generation of members, O'Neill's speakership was fundamentally different during the Reagan administration than it had been during that of Jimmy Carter. His role during the Carter administration had been to support the president's program, but during the Reagan administration, his obligation was to oppose it. Speaker O'Neill assumed the major responsibility for defining the position of his party with respect to the challenge to Democratic liberalism posed by Ronald Reagan. He entered into a symbolic struggle with the president that lent a new dimension to the speakership.

A speaker's first task is to secure his political base. In his district and within the Democratic caucus, still dominated by liberals, O'Neill was secure; but on the House floor, he was threatened by the conservative coalition. The swing votes lay among southern, conservative Democrats who organized as the Conservative Democratic Forum (CDF). The CDF brought forward statistical analyses demonstrating their systematic underrepresentation on key House committees. This was in marked contrast to the heyday of the conservative coalition in the 1950s and 1960s. Then, the southern Democrats used their hegemony over the committee system to frustrate liberal aims. A faction can remain comfortably within the majority party so long as it is protected by the party's rules and holds positions of power commensurate with its needs. When it is excluded from positions of power it has an incentive to bolt the party and work with the minority party. Thus, when southern Democrats were threatened by the party's caucus during the Clark-Underwood regime, they demanded a two-thirds rule to ensure a veto over the caucus. When under Uncle Joe Cannon's iron fist the progressive Republicans were shorn of their committee assignments, they joined the Democrats in the revolt against Cannon.[52] History instructed Speaker O'Neill to be careful.

The Republicans tried to lure the southern Democrats away, but O'Neill assuaged them with the increased committee slots they sought.

Then, in order to maintain his own programmatic control, he increased the ratios of the major committees. Although the Democratic majority in the House was about 5–4, O'Neill set the ratios of the Rules Committee and the Ways and Means Committee at 2–1, and of the Appropriations and Budget Committees at 3–2, adding enough liberal Democrats to offset the influence of newly appointed conservatives.[53] The 1980 election had brought about the defeat of two key members, Whip John Brademas of Indiana and Ways and Means Chairman Al Ullman of Oregon. Congressman Dan Rostenkowski of Illinois, who had been the chief deputy whip, decided at O'Neill's request to become the chairman of Ways and Means. O'Neill selected caucus chairman Tom Foley of Washington as the new whip. The other major leadership vacancy was at the Budget Committee. In a contested caucus election in which O'Neill played no overt role, the Democrats selected Congressman Jim Jones of Oklahoma. Jones defeated two liberal members, David Obey of Wisconsin and Paul Simon of Illinois. His election indicated that the conservative tide had pushed the Democratic center of gravity to the right. Jones had been instrumental in shaping a more conservative Democratic program since 1978.[54]

Ronald Reagan's "revolution" was consummated during the first seven months of his presidency. The conditions under which the Reagan administration functioned subsequently were determined by the adoption of the president's economic program in the spring and summer of 1981. The passage of the budget and tax bills in 1981 demonstrated the manner in which a shift in the nation's policy agenda affected the structure of politics in Washington. It also revealed the dilemma that would shape the balance of Tip O'Neill's speakership, and his characteristic method of responding to it. In confronting the Reagan onslaught, Tip O'Neill had three related goals: he wanted to resist the attack on Democratic social programs, he wanted to build his House majority in the 1982 election, and he wanted to preserve his own power. O'Neill realized that the Reagan honeymoon would be unusually romantic, but he doubted that the Reagan program would have staying power. Expecting the president to win on his first major legislative initiative, the FY 1982 first budget resolution, O'Neill decided to distance himself from the defeat. While Budget Chairman Jim Jones struggled to put together a Democratic proposal that might win on the House floor, O'Neill took a trip to Australia. Knowing he was going to get clobbered, the speaker did not want anyone to think that he had really fought. He aimed to give Reagan his victory and then let the president suffer the political fallout.

O'Neill assumed that the damage on the first budget resolution would not be too bad, and it was in this that he miscalculated. In 1980

O'Neill had pushed President Carter's "balanced budget" to passage in the House by imposing reconciliation on the first budget resolution instead of the second, as specified in the budget act. Borrowing a page from the Carter-O'Neill strategy, the Republicans sought to do the same thing in 1981. This meant that the stakes would be high, since a House victory for the administration on the first budget resolution would position them to impose a major reordering of federal priorities in just two votes, the vote on the resolution and a vote on an omnibus reconciliation bill that would actually impose budget cuts. With a collateral victory on the Reagan tax package, the game would be over soon after it began. This is exactly what occurred. The Republican substitute, Gramm-Latta I, was authored by Delbert Latta of Ohio, the ranking Republican on the Budget Committee, and Texas Democrat Phil Gramm, a renegade on the Democratic side. On May 7 the House passed Gramm-Latta I by a 253–176 margin, with sixty-three Democrats joining a unanimous Republican minority. In June the reconciliation package proposed by the Democratic Budget Committee was brought to the floor. By then Speaker O'Neill had learned his lesson, and the Democrats sought to make the Republicans vote for cuts individually. On June 25 the Republicans blocked the strategy by defeating the rule on the bill by a vote of 210–217, and the following day the House adopted the Republican Gramm-Latta II substitute by a similar vote of 217–211.[55]

O'Neill's last chance to stall the Reagan program came on the tax bill. The Reagan proposal was based on the Kemp-Roth scheme to cut marginal rates by 30 percent over three years. This was the most serious threat to the welfare state posed by Reaganomics, since if the Republicans were wrong in their prediction that lowered marginal rates would spur savings, investments, and revenues, the revenue base would be taken out from underneath the government. This would lead to huge budget cuts or massive borrowing. The Reagan program represented the newest incarnation of old-style Republican trickle-down economics, handing out most of its direct benefits to the wealthy. The debate over the tax bill would be a rehash of the fight between John Nance Garner and Andrew Mellon in the 1920s, and the Democrats could win it. O'Neill could appeal to liberals, who wanted to preserve the tax base underlying the welfare state, and to conservatives, who believed in balanced budgets.

The Democratic Ways and Means Committee, under Dan Rostenkowski's leadership, produced a tax-cut proposal that was friendlier to lower-income taxpayers and gentler on the government's revenue base. The Democratic proposal had some appeal to Senate Republicans who doubted the premises of supply-side economics, and feared a budget debacle if the administration proposal were to pass. On June 1 a meeting was held at the White House to explore grounds for compromise. Speaker O'Neill, Majority Leader Jim Wright, and Rostenkowski met with Senate Finance Committee Chairman Robert Dole of Kansas, White House Chief of Staff James Baker, Treasury Secretary Donald Regan, and the president. This was one of the most important meetings of the Reagan-O'Neill era, for it fundamentally defined the speaker's attitude toward the president and those around him. For years thereafter pundits and politicians would speak of a grand, yet evanescent, budget compromise. It did not occur during the Reagan-O'Neill watch because the president and the speaker would not make the necessary concessions. On June 1, 1981, Tip O'Neill decided that Ronald Reagan did not want to compromise with the House Democrats. From then forward his operating assumption was that Republican overtures were designed to set a political trap for the Democrats. Emerging from the meeting, O'Neill called the Reagan tax plan a "windfall for the rich," and accused the White House of trying to set him up as an unreasonable obstructionist.[56] From then forward Tip O'Neill was suspicious of Republican "deals."

Having decided that compromise was beyond reach, O'Neill and Rostenkowski decided to fight. Rostenkowski joined in a bidding war with the administration, trying to win floor votes by offering tax concessions. The administration was willing to offer more and had the force of a very popular president on its side. In the end, the bidding war drove up the cost of the tax bill without changing the outcome. Rostenkowski's tax plan would have cut taxes in the aggregate by about $40 billion in FY 1982 in contrast to the Reagan administration's request for a cut of $54 billion.[57] In early June both sides began to adjust, the administration floating a "bipartisan" plan (this time co-sponsored in the House by ranking Ways and Means Republican Barber Conable and another Texas Democrat, Kent Hance) calling for $37.4 billion in cuts in FY 1982 and the Democrats edging up to $40 billion by offering some additional sweeteners.[58] By the end of June, the Senate Finance Committee's reported bill was estimated to cost $37 billion in 1982, although the out-year revenue losses would have been significantly higher than those projected by the Democrats' two-year marginal rate cuts. The Conable-Hance bill in the House was less expensive than either the Senate bill or the Rostenkowski bill in FY 1982, but more expensive than either of the other two bills over the five-year budget cycle.[59] On July 29 the Conable-Hance bill passed by a vote of 238–195 and once again, Ronald Reagan triumphed in the Democratic House.[60]

The passage of the Reagan economic program was a blow to Speaker O'Neill's reputation. This time he could not shift the blame to a Democratic administration. In the spring of 1981, commentary stressed the speaker's tenuous hold over his troops. The *Congressional Quarterly* held that the "budget fight show[ed] O'Neill's fragile grasp," and *Time* proclaimed that "Tip O'Neill [is] on the ropes."[61] Both publications cited the criticisms being made of the speaker by his own members. By the end of July, as the last of the battles loomed on the horizon, the commentaries reflected a different aspect of the problem. With the Republicans running national advertising portraying O'Neill as the epitome of the Democratic philosophy of tax and spend, the speaker himself had become a symbolic issue.[62] O'Neill had built his political career by adroitly turning criticism of his conduct to the side. But how could he disguise who he was? "Today," said one commentator, "he is familiar to anybody who watches television as the white-haired ghost of Congress past, struggling to adjust to the Reagan era like a dinosaur confronting evolution."[63] O'Neill's challenge was to find a way to turn the tide of the symbolic battle against his adversary in the White House.

In seeking to meet this challenge, Tip O'Neill developed a new conception of the speaker's role. He decided to fight the president on his own turf. If the Republicans wished to portray O'Neill as the symbol of all that was worst in Democratic liberalism, O'Neill would respond by standing for all that was best. He gambled that the notoriety that the Republican attacks had visited upon him could be turned to his advantage if he stood visibly for the average American who struggled to pay the bills. Tip O'Neill would be the advocate for the old, the poor, and the middle-class American who was threatened by economic recession and the loss of government services. O'Neill stood as the symbol of opposition to Reagan and awaited the opportunity to go on the attack. When, in September of 1981, the Reagan administration proposed further cuts in social security benefits, he found the opportunity for which he had been waiting. The problems facing the social security system were serious. The 1977 bail-out had raised taxes, but the high rates of inflation in the years following had driven up the indexed benefit base so far that the system was once again actuarially unsound. In the House of Representatives, a Ways and Means subcommittee headed by Congressman Jake Pickle of Texas had been studying the issue. In the summer of 1981, O'Neill called Pickle in and announced that no Democratic social security plan would be brought forward. The speaker had decided that any proposal would deny the social security issue to the party in the 1982 elections. Politically, the Democrats' wisest course of action was to wait the Republicans out on social security.

The administration's September proposal elicited a storm of criticism. The House Democratic caucus unanimously repudiated the proposed cuts and the Senate passed a resolution condemning them by a vote of 96–0.[64] Faced with the unhappy prospect of being once again pilloried on social security, the president, in a television address on September 25, abandoned the proposals and called for a bipartisan commission to study the social security system. In a letter to Speaker O'Neill, Reagan said: "Last spring, I proposed what I believe to be a fair, balanced and workable solution to the social security problem. However, it is now evident that there are so many proposals and so many different views of the problem that a comprehensive long-term solution is not possible in the immediate future."[65]

In lieu of his earlier proposals, Reagan called for interfund borrowing to float the system while a "bipartisan Blue Ribbon Task Force" studied the problem. The proposed task force caught O'Neill off guard. Responding on the floor of the House the next day, the speaker said: "This is a new idea, which the president has never discussed with me. The first notice I had of this was last night."[66] O'Neill knew that he was trapped—he could not oppose a commission—but he also sensed danger. If the commission's report were favorable to the Republican view of the social security problem, the Democrats would be placed on the defensive. The mere existence of the commission might take the matter out of the 1982 election, denying to the Democrats the only issue that seemed to be cutting in their favor. O'Neill's response was guarded:

> I want to emphasize my personal determination that the Social Security System remain solvent. If we are to form a new commission, it is vital that this new panel be fully committed to the future of Social Security. It should be established in consultation with the Ways and Means Committee, and any reform of Social Security should be consistent with congressional processes. I await further discussions with the President on this matter. I remain fully committed to assuring that the budget will not be balanced on the backs of Social Security recipients.[67]

This caution was well placed. Reagan proposed a task force of fifteen members, five to be named by him, five by Senate Majority Leader Howard Baker, and five to be named by O'Neill. The president called for the commission to report in "one or two years," that is, after the 1982 election. O'Neill insisted on a more even division of the commission and a reporting date in April 1982. Reagan conceded on the makeup of the commission, allowing for three appointments by both O'Neill and Baker and two each by Senate Minority Leader Robert Byrd and House Minority Leader Bob Michel, but held firm for a December 1982 reporting date.[68]

The social security debate demonstrated O'Neill's political position. He had become the principal adversary of the president of the United

States. It was a battle of David and Goliath, in which most of the power and resources lay on Reagan's side. Yet O'Neill had found the president's weakness, and knew that in proposing a commission, Reagan was searching for a way out of the dilemma in which he had allowed himself to be placed. O'Neill's political incentive was to leave Reagan dangling on social security, but he had to weigh several other considerations. One was the political risk of appearing to obstruct the president. Another was the danger of permitting Reagan to get off of the hook before the 1984 election. But O'Neill's overriding obligation was to the social security system itself. The commission's purpose was to ensure the solvency of social security, and O'Neill could hardly opt out of it. The speaker was caught between his obligation and his interest, and he put his obligation first.

Reagan's retreat on social security was the first indication that the his honeymoon was over. It seemed that the policy tide might be turning in O'Neill's favor. In the House, shell-shocked Democrats searched for a new direction. At a September 16 meeting of House Democrats billed as a "unity caucus," the members were able to vent their frustrations. In his remarks to the caucus, Speaker O'Neill evoked the themes by which both he and the party would be guided in the period that lay ahead. Drawing on his long career in public service, he reminded his troops that, in politics, the pendulum swings continuously, and would sooner or later swing back toward the Democratic side. He pointed with pride to the accomplishments of the Democratic party: "I remember the 1930s when 51 percent of America was impoverished. Today only 8 percent of America is impoverished. It isn't by chance that America has changed . . . It was the programs of our party along the line . . . We have built middle America and make no mistake about it." But if the Democrats were responsible for the progress of the past fifty years, the Republican party was to be responsible for what would happen next: "As of August 4, when you passed the tax bill, the program was the President's: the President's interest rates, the President's unemployment rates, the President's inflation rates . . . The President and his supporters went home with glee. They had everything they wanted."[69] Noting that the economic outlook appeared bleak, the speaker announced that the House Democrats would take the Congress on the road, holding field hearings around the country to highlight the suffering of those who were unemployed and the plight of those whose federal benefits would be cut in the Reagan budget. O'Neill realized that the war with Reagan was a battle to win public opinion, yet the congressional Democrats had many fewer resources to fight this war than did the Republican administration.

Inevitably the Democrats faced the question of what to do about their two renegades, Gramm and Hance. The episode offers a good lesson about the role of the Steering and Policy Committee under O'Neill's leadership. The furor over the support that Phil Gramm and Kent Hance had given to the Republicans had led to calls for caucus sanctions against the two. Speaker O'Neill still walked a narrow line between his liberal caucus majority and the rebellious southerners. In an attempt to stay out of the direct line of fire, he referred the question of discipline to the Steering and Policy Committee, which decided against sanctions. After the meeting, Majority Leader Jim Wright announced a four-point statement of principles on party loyalty. Wright's announcement was his own initiative, and not a Steering Committee recommendation to the caucus. O'Neill did not support a formal disciplinary policy, because it would tie his hands. He sought to use the Steering and Policy Committee as a foil to his own position. This was a typical O'Neill stratagem. He wanted to nurture his party and mediate its conflicts, and not to enforce discipline in a political situation in which consensus was unattainable. Normally, when Tip O'Neill referred a matter to Steering and Policy, he wanted it to disappear or he wanted someone else to appear responsible for the decision.[70]

The avoidance of responsibility was endemic to the political culture of the 1980s. One of the distinguishing characteristics of the democratic period was the government's routine recurrence to abnormal methods of policy making. The social security commission was only one example among many. During the Reagan administration, commissions were asked to address Central America, the MX missile, federal pay, and government efficiency. The commissions were designed to provide cover for politicians who did not have the courage to vote their convictions. They were paralleled inside the Congress by the use of special rules and voting procedures intended to obfuscate responsibility, by the use of omnibus legislation that obscured decision making, and by the constant reliance on the rump groups, retreats, and meetings that were the cocaine of the congressional culture. This was government by adhocracy, by decision-making groups without authority, without responsibility, and too often without success. The division in control of the government between the two parties and the symbolic character of the issues with which they dealt led to the use of such devices, which were only slightly better when they worked than when they didn't.

A good example of this came during the so-called "Gang of Seventeen" negotiations over the budget in the spring of 1982. These negotiations arose naturally out of the policy situation that the enactment of the Reagan program had created. The recession had undermined the economic assumptions on which the Reagan policies had been predicated, and huge budget deficits were now projected. "Deficit reduction" became, and would remain, the catchword of federal policy making. In March 1982 White House Chief of Staff James A. Baker sought to move the budget impasse off of dead center by proposing private negotiations between the administration and congressional leaders.[71] During the first three weeks of April, seventeen negotiators conducted thirteen meetings in an effort to reach agreement on a deficit reduction plan. The negotiations culminated in a dramatic meeting between the president and the speaker on April 28, 1982 that failed to resolve the impasse. The president was unwilling to have his tax reduction program undermined in the first year of its operation, and the speaker was unwilling to acquiesce in reductions in social security cost-of-living increases. With the "principals," as they were called, immovable on these issues, no agreement was possible.

The deep ideological differences between Reagan and O'Neill precluded compromise, but did not preclude political posturing. Throughout April, O'Neill maintained a steady drumbeat of criticism of the president. At his April 6 press conference he alleged that there was "no equity, fairness or balance to what the Republicans have been offering us."[72] Charging the administration with false numbering, the speaker reiterated his opposition to cuts in social security. By April 21 the negotiators had reached an agreement on the numbers, including the projected deficits and the target range for deficit reduction. President Reagan addressed the nation on April 20, claiming to have gone the extra mile for a compromise; but at his April 21 press conference O'Neill placed the blame for the economic situation on the president, saying, "He has to go first." In a prepared statement O'Neill said, "Mr. President, we are waiting."[73] The "we" in this case referred to the House Democrats; but it was intended to connote the American people, whom the House Democrats and their speaker presumed to represent. On April 26 O'Neill raised the level of rhetoric again. Likening Reagan to a drowning man fighting his rescuer (in this case the Democrats), O'Neill promised that the Congress (by implication, congressional Democrats) would "help as long as we can. If it goes under one time, we will pull him up. If it goes under the second time, we will pull him up. And we will keep trying to help him reach the shore. If he just makes it impossible, it will be very difficult, but we will keep trying with patience." While transforming himself from the conciliator to the savior, O'Neill continued to berate Reagan for the inequity of a tax program that delivered such large tax cuts to the wealthy. Noting Reagan's stubborn resistance to compromise, the speaker held out hope: "We always have to believe in redemption [laughter]."[74]

After the climactic April 28 meeting, O'Neill took the offensive again. Dropping the role of compromiser and rescuer, the speaker put on his gloves and came out swinging. The president, he said, "offered a raw deal to the Democrats and the American people [linking the two]. He advocated that we continue his economic program, which has brought hardship to millions . . . When it came down to it . . . the president offered more of the same: an economic program that is not working; soft treatment for the well-to-do; and another brutal cut at those who have already been hurt the most by the Reagan program."[75] As O'Neill's rhetorical posture shifted, his tactics changed. The Congress would now return to the task of writing a budget that would rescue the drowning president—but the Republican Senate would be the first in the water. "The Republican Party in the Senate has that responsibility and he is the president of the United States. We will follow very closely what they are doing in the Senate. Their schedule will be ahead of ours on the budget."[76] Within a week Tip O'Neill, presidential savior, had become an apprentice lifeguard. Most striking about this entire exercise was not so much O'Neill's political and theatrical skill, which in its own way rivaled Reagan's, as much as the difficulty he faced in competing with the president for the public mind. A speaker's press conference, however well handled, is a very limited vehicle for reaching the American people. Reagan had far more direct access to the public. O'Neill's attempts to define the issue were mediated by the interpretation of a press corps of varying ability, ideology, and perseverance. He could not easily reach the American people himself, but could hope to influence the perceptions of opinion leaders in Congress and in the media.

O'Neill's main political goal was to pick up seats in the 1982 congressional elections. In the Ninety-seventh Congress his capacity to force compromise with the administration was very limited. His main assets were the declining economy and rising deficit, which caused the Republican Senate to be more receptive to revenue increases than the administration. In the fall of 1982 O'Neill actually found himself cooperating with the Senate and administration to pass a tax "reform" bill that produced substantial new revenues. The following month Ronald Reagan suffered his first major legislative defeat when the Congress overrode his veto of a supplemental appropriations bill that shifted money from military to domestic spending.[77] The importance of this veto override to Speaker O'Neill should be emphasized. After ten months during which Reagan had regularly beat him around the head, the speaker had finally marshaled a two-thirds majority against the president and had done so on a traditionally Democratic issue. The veto override vote confirmed in his own mind the soundness of the political strategy that he had pursued the entire year. Emboldened, the Democrats rushed a supplemental appropriations bill containing a new federal jobs program to the House floor the following week, which passed.[78] In the

Senate, a jobs bill sponsored by Indiana Republican Dan Quayle and Massachusetts Democrat Edward Kennedy found majority support, and in October of 1982 Ronald Reagan put his signature to a public jobs bill.

Even as he sought such targets of opportunity to shape policy around the margins, O'Neill recognized that in the long run his ability to force compromise with the administration depended upon an enlarged House majority. To do this he was willing to lose legislatively in order to win politically. While taking the heat from members every time he lost a major vote, O'Neill hoped to convince voters that the Republican policies were responsible for their plight. This strategy was quite dependent on the Democrats' ability to win the support of middle-class swing voters. Their support would be determined less by the speaker's rhetorical appeals than by their own actual economic circumstances. Thus, while Tip O'Neill sought to wait out the Reagan onslaught, the battle was being waged on his behalf by the Federal Reserve Board and its chairman, Paul Volcker, whose policy of wringing inflation out of the economy by tightening the money supply had been in place since the end of the Carter administration. The tight money policy bit down before the massive Republican tax cuts enacted in 1981 could help reheat the economy. The recession that ensued in 1981 and 1982 was the most severe since the Depression, and led naturally to a Democratic resurgence at the polls. It was the underlying condition of the economy, more than the speaker's rhetorical attacks, that led to a gain of twenty-six Democratic seats in the 1982 elections.

With an enlarged House majority, Speaker O'Neill's strategic situation shifted in the Ninety-eighth Congress. The combination of southern Democrats and a unified Republican minority was not as easily able to defeat the Democratic majority on the House floor. O'Neill had a chance to pass leadership bills on the House floor and to bargain with the Republican Senate in conference. The rearguard strategy of the Ninety-seventh Congress gave way to a more aggressive posture in the Ninety-eighth. The speaker's first step was to strengthen his procedural control over the House.[79] O'Neill supported rules changes that he had resisted in 1981, when he did not want to alienate conservative Democrats. In two steps aimed directly at the Republican minority, the Democratic caucus voted in December of 1982 to amend the House Rules to limit riders on appropriations bills and to make it more difficult to discharge committees of proposed constitutional amendments.[80] The speaker was also empowered to put off routine votes that sometimes were used by the minority to delay House business (such as a vote to approve the previous day's journal), and the Democratic caucus decided to strip the seniority of any member who switched party during a session of the Congress. The outraged Republicans accused the Democrats of legislative tyranny.[81]

The caucus voted to remove Texas's Phil Gramm from the Budget Committee in retribution for his cooperation with the Republicans in the Ninety-seventh Congress, but this was the only act of retribution that the Democrats took.[82] Instead of further punishment, Speaker O'Neill sought to bind the party together while tightening his grip on the committee system. Committee ratios were enlarged in order to reflect the Democrats' larger House majority, and the leadership used the extra vacancies to assure control and assuage feelings.[83] When the rules changes approved by the Democratic caucus were brought to the floor, the leadership backed off of the proposed change affecting constitutional amendments because of southern Democratic opposition. O'Neill leavened the Budget Committee's membership with seven new liberal Democrats. The Democrats had their first chance to pass a budget in 1983, and Tip O'Neill wanted to make sure that it was a budget drafted on liberal terms.[84] Yet when disputes arose over assignments to popular committee seats, the speaker chose to stay out of the fights.[85] Having improved his strategic position, he wanted to avoid involvement in intraparty squabbles. His position, while improved, was not commanding.

In 1983 O'Neill's main goal was to lay a foundation for Democratic victories in the 1984 senatorial and presidential elections. His enhanced majority enabled him to pursue an affirmative legislative strategy in addition to the rhetorical battle with the president. O'Neill wanted to pass Democratic legislation that would clarify the differences between the two parties on major domestic and foreign policy issues. He succeeded in doing so in several instances in 1983. The House passed a measure to rescind the third-year rate cut that had been enacted in the 1981 tax bill, two public-service jobs bills, and for the first time since 1980, a Democratic budget resolution. The social security commission's report laid the basis for a bail-out of the system that incorporated the speaker's proposal to tax the benefits of higher income recipients. On budget, taxation, jobs, and social security, O'Neill had found a new offensive capability. Of course, passing bills on the House floor was not tantamount to enacting public policy. In each case the speaker and his Democratic House majority had to bargain in conference with the Senate and the administration. But that the two sides were more nearly equal was apparent in some of the outcomes. One of the public service jobs bills was enacted into law and the social security bill passed by substantial majorities on terms that O'Neill could accept.

In pushing his legislative program in 1983, O'Neill demonstrated his capacity to operate in the new environment of policy making within the Democratic caucus. He found it necessary to cater to the thirst for participation among the new-breed Democrats through more frequent caucus discussions of issues, the appointment of task forces to study policy, and wider-ranging personal contacts. He also had to deal with a set of ambitious committee chairmen who were not always supportive of his program. A phenomenon well known to House insiders but scarcely recognized by the public is the manner in which individual career paths affect the legislative process. Congress always has two agendas: the public legislative agenda and the secondary, private agendas of the politicians who are asked to address it. The politics of secondary agendas permeates the legislative process. In the early 1980s there were at least four Democrats (Jim Wright, Tom Foley, Jim Jones, and Dan Rostenkowski) who coveted the speakership. Among them, Jones and Rostenkowski also fought to protect their prerogatives as committee chairmen. Sometimes, this placed them in conflict with O'Neill. For example, in pressing the House to pass legislation rescinding the third-year cut in tax rates, O'Neill found himself in direct opposition to Ways and Means Chairman Dan Rostenkowski, who floated a proposal for a tax "freeze" in order to put a floor under federal revenues.[86] At a heated private leadership meeting O'Neill, Rostenkowski, and Majority Leader Jim Wright argued about party strategy.[87] At his daily press conference, the speaker reiterated his support for the elimination of the third-year cut. "So do you want the cap?" he was asked by a reporter. "Does your brother eat onions?" O'Neill gruffly replied.[88] Rostenkowski backed off of the tax freeze idea, and the House passed O'Neill's proposal.

At the Budget Committee, Chairman Jim Jones looked for his first chance to pass a committee budget on the House floor. Jones preferred a bipartisan approach to budget making, and his policy views were more conservative than O'Neill's; but now the speaker had stacked his committee against him, and he had no choice but to join with O'Neill in seeking to pass a Democratic budget that would be too liberal to gain bipartisan support. In an effort to control the shape of the budget, O'Neill announced that the entire Democratic caucus would hold several meetings to discuss economic and budget policy.[89] In the search for a "consensus budget," the Democrats underwent all of the hand-holding, surveying, and communicating that had become the hallmark of the therapeutic culture.[90] The term *consensus* was, in fact, misleading. The Democrats had little hope of reaching a substantive policy consensus within their own ranks. The party was too badly divided on fundamental issues. They could, however, reach a temporary accord on a budget plan with which a sufficient majority could live. The search for consensus was in reality an effort to build a psychological consensus where a genuine political consensus was lacking. The therapeutic techniques to which the party resorted reflected a culture in which the feeling of solidarity was often more important than substantive agreement. O'Neill functioned like a marriage counselor who preaches that a shared understanding can substitute for shared goals. With Speaker O'Neill and Jim Jones pressing for consensus, the Democratic members of the Budget Committee produced a unanimous vote in favor of a Democratic plan, which was later sustained on the House floor.[91] The Democrats proved for the first time that they were a force to be reckoned with on budget policy. After a prolonged struggle in the Senate, the Congress finally passed a budget resolution, but the tax and reconciliation bills that it presupposed proved harder to come by.

The enhanced position of the speaker and his Democrats led to a predictable result: stalemate. A more unified House Democratic party was able to produce governmental deadlock. By the end of the first session of the Ninety-eighth Congress neither the tax bill nor the reconciliation bill required by the budget had been enacted into law. The Ways and Means Committee produced a minor revenue bill, but in a curious reversal of form, the House of Representatives refused to pass a tax bill supported by the speaker and the Senate refused to pass a reconciliation bill supported by the majority leader. The tax-and-spend Democrats refused to tax, and the budget-cutting Republicans refused to cut the budget.[92] "We're Unable to Act," proclaimed a *Time* headline, quoting Senator John Danforth.[93] "We have confessed to an already doubting nation that we are ruled by political fear rather than economic courage," pontificated Chairman Dan Rostenkowski.[94] Said Speaker O'Neill, "Why put your own members and party through that ordeal for symbolism?"[95]

Why did it appear that Speaker O'Neill had "lost his grip on the House?"[96] O'Neill had his finger on the problem: symbolism. The budget process is inherently symbolic. All of the decisions made there must be made again in the actual process of taxing and spending, and the out-year projections defy rational calculation. Because budgets are symbolic, they more easily lend themselves to ideological posturing. When the time comes to translate budgets into appropriations and tax bills, the pragmatic instincts of the legislator normally take over. But when the budget dilemma offered such politically unpalatable alternatives, with such high political and economic stakes, the space normally allowed to those pragmatic legislative instincts had shrunk considerably. The result was that the only bills around which a consensus could be formed were grossly inadequate to address the problem at hand. Instead, each side fought to saddle the other with the blame for what might occur. Faced with a choice between dubious action and cautious inaction, the Congress chose to be cautious.[97]

President Reagan and Speaker O'Neill contributed greatly to this paralysis. Each chose to raise the symbolic stakes by portraying the other as representing a political evil. Reagan castigated O'Neill as the representative of a bankrupt philosophy of government that had brought about the problems of the modern welfare state. O'Neill castigated Reagan as a tool of the upper class, a heartless man who was out to undo all the good that the New Deal and Great Society had accomplished.[98] Both of these views contained an element of truth, but the caricatures distorted as much as they revealed. Reagan and O'Neill realized that the struggle in which they were engaged was for the heart and soul of the American polity, and that the battle would be fought over the symbols by which the polity's self-interpretation would be shaped. The symbolic battle impeded compromise and prevented governance.

The direct cause of the deadlock was the fact that the Democrats could now control their own destiny in the House. This enabled O'Neill to bargain when before he could only posture. But the goal of bargaining is compromise, and compromise proved difficult to attain. The reasons were essentially political. The government was split three ways, between the administration, the Senate Republicans, and the House Democrats.[99] Senate Republicans broke the cord that tied them to the Reagan administration, but could not reach a compromise with House Democrats so long as the president was unwilling to support it. The administration was unwilling to compromise the program that it had so recently enacted, and the Democrats would not do the dirty business of raising taxes for a president who would surely use the issue against them. The new-found power at O'Neill's disposal was not sufficient to enable him to make policy, although it did strengthen his hand politically.

In the Ninety-eighth Congress, Tip O'Neill's opposition to Ronald Reagan extended its reach to foreign policy. Traditionally, speakers of the House have not been centrally involved in foreign policy, and have sometimes been burned when they have. Both Henry Clay and Thomas Brackett Reed were strong speakers, yet both suffered defeats in foreign policy matters. Speaker Rayburn supported President Roosevelt's war policy and Truman's reconstruction program, and contributed importantly to the development of a bipartisan foreign policy during the Eisenhower administration. Speakers McCormack and Albert were internationalists who supported Presidents Johnson and Nixon on the Vietnam War. After his break with Johnson on the war in 1967, O'Neill's policy views were those of the liberal wing of the Democratic party; as a result, he became the first speaker in the twentieth century to consistently oppose the foreign policy of the administration with which he served.

O'Neill developed a dual posture toward foreign policy designed to enable him to oppose the administration without committing Democratic members to his positions. On the one hand, the speaker defined substantive foreign policy issues as matters of private conscience rather than party position; on the other hand, he attacked the administration for usurping congressional prerogatives.[100] O'Neill strongly opposed the MX missile and the administration's interventionist policy in Central America, and supported the nuclear freeze movement. Two incidents in 1983 revealed the depth of his opposition to the Reagan policy, and the constraints that he lay under as speaker in voicing that opposition.

In the summer of 1983 O'Neill was convinced by National Security Advisor Robert C. McFarlane that an American presence in a United Nation's peace-keeping force in Lebanon would contribute to stability in the Middle East.[101] Both the administration and the Democratic leadership were cautious about the possible effect on the 1984 presidential election of a protracted debate over American involvement in Lebanon, and the continuing controversy over the constitutional status of the War Powers Resolution further complicated matters. An agreement was reached within the framework of the resolution to commit American troops to the U.N. force for eighteen months (until after November 1984), in order to depoliticize the issue.[102] When in October of 1983 a terrorist bomb killed 250 Marines barracked at the Beirut airport, the political ramifications could not be avoided.

At first, O'Neill supported a continuing American presence.

> In my opinion, [withdrawing] would be the worst possible thing we could do. We are committed to the Middle East. I think it would be a victory for our adversaries, particularly Russia, and, I think, Syria, who is acting as a satellite of Russia . . . It is easy to say, "Bring our boys home." But what is the depth behind the whole thing. Do we want to split Lebanon and have it taken over by the Syrians? . . . What would happen to free Europe in the event they would lose the oil fields to Russia? . . . We are committed to the Middle East regardless [of the circumstances].[103]

Within a few months, however, the speaker turned against the administration. He appointed a fifteen-member congressional advisory committee, which reported to him in January. On its advice, he announced that unless diplomatic progress were quickly forthcoming, he would call for a withdrawal of American troops.[104] At a meeting with President Reagan on January 25, the speaker called administration policy simplistic and misleading.[105] In the first week in February he moved from hedging to attack. Pushing for a nonbinding resolution calling for the withdrawal of American troops, O'Neill proclaimed: "It's his policy. I had no voice in setting the policy." Reagan was quick to respond: O'Neill "may be ready to surrender, but I'm not."[106]

President Reagan eventually did surrender, ordering the "redeployment" of American troops to ships at sea in February. The end of American troop presence only served to escalate the rhetorical battle in Washington. Reagan accused the Democrats of "losing" Lebanon.[107] At his daily press conference O'Neill responded with one of his sharpest attacks on the president:

> Q.: A lot of Republicans are saying that the president's attack on you will be politically profitable to him.
> THE SPEAKER: It is hard for me to conceive, because there is no question in my mind that the president's foreign policy will be an issue in this campaign. His Lebanon policy was a disaster . . . The one person in America who is responsible for the loss of the marines and the failure in Lebanon is the president of the U.S. . . . . There is no question that his policy has been a failure. We [Congress] had no decision in putting together that policy.[108]

O'Neill's shift is easy to explain. When 250 American soldiers are blown up in their sleep, wise politicians put as much distance between themselves and the policy that has led to the disaster as possible.

The other major foreign policy event in 1983 was the American invasion of Grenada, which occurred the day after the Lebanon bombing. In this case the speaker's initial reaction was strongly critical.

> The issue was that several Caribbean nations asked us to help. It seemed to be secondary that the lives of our citizens [were at stake] . . . He [the president] broke international law. I don't like that. I think he is wrong. To be perfectly truthful, he frightens me. I think he was looking for a reason to go there, and he found the opportunity last week . . . We can't go with gunboat diplomacy. The marines did a tremendous job down there, but we can't continue that route—going into Nicaragua and places like that. His policy is wrong and frightening.[109]

Yet this time a fact-finding expedition sent by O'Neill to Grenada supported the decision to invade, forcing the speaker to back away from his criticism. "Fortunately for the president, the right thing was done. But I believe that he was looking for two years to go in there, and the

Grenadians gave him the opportunity for action . . . If I have any criticism it's that we should have been trying to straighten out the Grenada situation long ago."[110] Here, O'Neill's instinctive ideological response was tempered by a political reality: the American public strongly supported the invasion, and it little availed the speaker to be too assertive on the wrong side of public opinion. Wise politicians do not oppose popular invasions.

These two examples illustrated the nature of the foreign policy debate and the role that O'Neill played in it. The American people were, in the 1980s, ambivalent about foreign policy. They liked assertiveness and the jingoism that went along with it; yet they opposed putting American troops at risk in strange, faraway places. President Reagan's policies played to the militant instinct, while Speaker O'Neill's opposition drew on the pacifist concern. O'Neill's position was always reactive. The first move in the foreign policy game was always the president's to make. O'Neill's political strategy was to find targets of opportunity in the armature of the Reagan foreign policy.

In fact, in head-to-head legislative competition, O'Neill had considerable success in fending off Reagan foreign policy initiatives. The administration came into office in 1981 intent on the deployment of a hundred MX missiles; yet by the time Reagan left office in 1989 only fifty missiles had been authorized, and the abandonment of the MX remained a viable policy option. In Central America, the administration's support of the Nicaraguan Contras became the main point of controversy. Between 1983 and 1986 Speaker O'Neill fought relentlessly against American military aid to the Contras. During these years the House voted eight times on military aid, and the House sided with O'Neill seven times. Across this set of votes, an average of 211 Democrats voted with O'Neill against Reagan, while 160 Republicans sided on average with Reagan. The swing votes lay among a group of moderate Democrats and Republicans led by Oklahoma congressman Dave McCurdy.[111] In 1984 and 1985 the Congress placed restrictions on American military aid to the Contras, and it was not until 1986 that President Reagan was finally able to win congressional approval for a renewal of aid. In the interim the administration pursued a policy of providing secret support, which culminated in the Iran-Contra scandal. The scandal undermined public support for the administration's policy, and when O'Neill retired in 1986, he could claim that the implementation of the Reagan doctrine in Central America had been forestalled.

Tip O'Neill's best year in his war with Ronald Reagan was 1983. In both domestic and foreign policy, O'Neill was successful in winning support for his policies in the House, and was able to bargain with the Senate and the administration. Social spending was on the increase, social security had been made solvent, and the administration seemed vulnerable entering the 1984 election year. One measure of the climate of early 1984 can be gleaned from the fact that in January 1980 the polls showed Ronald Reagan trailing the incumbent Jimmy Carter by thirty points, but in January 1984, the polls showed Walter Mondale within ten points of Reagan.[112] Tip O'Neill remained the nation's leading elected Democrat until Mondale was nominated. His goal was to articulate the issues on which the 1984 campaign would be fought. The Democrats would stand for equality, fairness, and peace, the Republicans for elitism, unfairness, and war.

In 1984 O'Neill turned from the issues to the ticket. He endorsed Walter Mondale in February, and a month later announced his own intention to retire from the House after the Ninety-ninth Congress ended in 1986. O'Neill wanted to make sure that he was not an issue in the 1984 campaign. O'Neill pushed Mondale's cause in the House Democratic caucus, many members of which were uncommitted convention delegates. When Colorado Senator Gary Hart won the New Hampshire primary the speaker extended a hand, or rather a foot, to the dark horse: "I have a foot in the bucket of the future. While I am old hat, I am only with my right leg. My left leg is in the future." "Are you comfortable with Hart?" he was asked. "The answer is absolutely 'yes.' "[113] When in June it had become evident that neither Hart nor black leader Jesse Jackson could defeat Mondale, O'Neill sought to sooth the losing candidates' feelings in order to promote harmony at the convention. Meeting with Hart in early June, the speaker received the senator's assurances that he would not carry his campaign over to a divisive floor fight at the convention.[114] A special party committee appointed by the speaker and headed by Arizona Congressman Morris Udall sought to assuage the Jackson forces by considering their demands for convention representation in proportion to Jackson's percentage of the primary vote. The Udall effort failed to produce an agreement, but it assuaged the Jackson camp to some extent.[115]

O'Neill was also influential in the choice of Geraldine Ferraro as Mondale's running mate. O'Neill had pushed Ferraro's career in the House, where she had become Democratic caucus secretary with the speaker's support. Ferraro had been the head of a caucus task force that drafted planks for the 1982 midterm convention, and as the permanent chairman of the convention, O'Neill named her to head the platform committee in 1984. When Mondale decided that his best electoral strategy lay in placing a woman on the ticket, O'Neill pushed hard for Ferraro. When Ferraro's selection was announced, O'Neill hailed the decision.[116] The speaker had every reason to be satisfied; uniquely among the leaders of the Democratic party, Tip O'Neill had stood behind the choice of this ticket. As one pundit put it, Speaker O'Neill was the "man behind the woman," the man to whom Walter Mondale owed much of his own support, the choice of his running mate, and even the articulation of his campaign theme—the unfairness of the Reagan program.[117] More than in any other recent presidential election, the national ticket was influenced by the speaker of the House. With this identification, however, came responsibility; when the Mondale-Ferraro ticket was defeated in November, Speaker O'Neill felt the pain.

A sidelight to the 1984 campaign suggested the toll that partisan politics was taking in the House of Representatives. The role that O'Neill had assumed as a Democratic party spokesman led to Republican charges that he was guilty of excessively politicizing the speakership. If O'Neill accused Reagan of being unfair to America's poor and downtrodden, then House Republicans wanted Americans to know that the speaker was himself unfair to the poor and downtrodden of the House of Representatives, the Republican minority. A group of Republican ideologues led by Georgia's Newt Gingrich, styling themselves as the Conservative Opportunity Society (COS), took to the House floor during special order time to castigate Democrats. On one occasion the object of their attack was the recorded opposition of some Democrats to the Vietnam War. In a special order speech, Gingrich recited Democratic members' statements from the *Congressional Record*, implying that their opposition to the war showed a lack of patriotism. While the special order time was carried live over the Cable-Satellite Public Affairs Network (C-SPAN) to a sizable audience, the viewers had no way of knowing that the House chamber was virtually empty, and the members of whom Gingrich spoke were not present. Gingrich's theatrics suggested that the members in question were present in the chamber and unwilling to respond to his allegations. A livid Speaker O'Neill decided to turn the tables on the COS by ordering the television cameras to pan the chamber during their next onslaught. A few days later Pennsylvania Republican Robert Walker was in the midst of a diatribe against the Democrats when the cameras swung around to reveal that he was in fact speaking to empty chairs. Embarrassed and enraged, the Republicans accused the Democrats of dirty tricks. In a floor confrontation Speaker O'Neill called Gingrich's charges "the lowest thing I have ever seen," a violation of House etiquette that enabled the Republicans to have the speaker's words "taken down" (i.e., stricken from the *Congressional Record*). O'Neill, having made his point, did not seem to care. The COS attacks on the Democrats were to be expected, but the fact that Republican leaders Robert Michel of Illinois and Richard Cheney of Wyoming sprang to the defense of Gingrich and Walker indicated the extent to which partisanship was seeping into the political culture of the House of Representatives.[118]

President Reagan's landslide victory and Speaker O'Neill's impending retirement again transformed the strategic circumstances of O'Neill's speakership. In spite of the scope of the Reagan victory, the Republicans picked up only fifteen seats in the House, leaving the speaker with a diminished but safe margin. More significant than the reduced size of his majority, however, was the manner in which his stature in the Democratic caucus was undermined. Friendly commentators could try to puff him up, but the reality was that Tip O'Neill's strength was seriously reduced in the Ninety-ninth Congress.[119] Once again the speaker was under attack by the CDF. Its leader, Congressman Charles Stenholm of Texas threatened to run against O'Neill if he would not step down.[120] Younger members, led by Tony Coehlo of California and Richard Gephardt of Missouri, demanded a greater role in shaping party policy.[121] O'Neill's position as speaker was not seriously threatened. He had done too many favors and was too widely liked for the malcontents to unseat him; yet their concern was bottomed on a reality that O'Neill understood. Many Democrats paid a high price in their districts by retaining O'Neill as their leader. The impression of the party nationally would continue to be presented primarily through their control of the House, and many members felt that it was important to free the party of an image steeped in the liberal politics of old that O'Neill symbolized. The complaints of the younger members were especially telling, since they represented the party's future. O'Neill acceded to their request that a party executive committee be established, that younger members be afforded a greater role in party decision making, and a more visible role as party spokesmen.

To those with an institutional memory, this set of demands must have fostered a sense of déjà vu. It was precisely the same kind of demand that this same crowd had placed upon Speaker Albert in 1975, when many of them were in their first term. The circumstances then were quite different; the Democrats were in the ascendancy. They had won a landslide congressional election and were poised to retake the White House in 1976. They had no reason to complain that Speaker Albert was a liability in their districts, yet they demanded from their leadership better communication and a more clearly articulated and forcefully expressed vision of the party and its future. A decade later, they complained of a lack of party vision and inadequate intraparty communications. Their leader was "a relic of the party's past, out of touch with the voting mainstream."[122] The demand for participation proved to be a consistent theme of the therapeutic generation. They got older, wiser, and more beholden to the system, but they never lost their affection for communication. Their culture was different from Tip O'Neill's culture, and although the speaker's Irish personality was well suited to a collegial and participatory environment, O'Neill remained a white-haired, liberal ward heeler in a Democratic caucus comprised increasingly of blow-dried policy entrepreneurs. Both the southern conservatives and the younger moderates thought that Tip O'Neill was too far to the left to lead the party effectively. The conservatives wanted to dump him, the moderates did not. In the end, neither group tried.

Why did the House Democrats cling to a speaker who had clearly been to the left of the electoral mainstream during his entire term of office, the second longest in the history of the House? Here, the most useful comparison is to Uncle Joe Cannon. During his eight year speakership, Cannon became an increasingly controversial national figure. In 1908 the Democrats made his control over the House and his conservative politics a national political issue. Within his own party he was constantly attacked by the progressives, who eventually joined with the Democrats to undercut his power. Yet even then, Cannon was not unseated as speaker, although he offered the House that choice by vacating the chair.

From 1908 until the 1980s, no speaker of the House became a national campaign issue; in the 1980s Tip O'Neill did. But even though he was widely regarded as a political liability to the Democrats, no one ever challenged him in the Democratic caucus. Several factors serve to explain this seeming paradox. Like Cannon, O'Neill had the support of an ideological majority in his own caucus. It would have been difficult for any challenger to have defeated him, and the costs of a failed challenge would have been high. O'Neill, like Cannon, was personally very popular. It should not be forgotten that George Norris, the man who earned his profile-in-courage badge by removing Speaker Cannon from the Rules Committee in 1910, respected Uncle Joe and opposed the motion to vacate the chair.[123] Speaker O'Neill was also widely liked, even by those who opposed him. One does not easily attempt to end the political career of a person whom one likes. In the larger historical view, House Democrats have always recoiled at the prospect of a divisive leadership fight. In the twentieth century the Democratic caucus has witnessed only three challenges to an incumbent leader: Morris Udall mounted a symbolic candidacy against John McCormack in 1969, and John Conyers of Michigan won about twenty votes in two quixotic runs against Carl Albert in the 1970s. By contrast, two Republican leaders have been unseated since World War II: Martin by Halleck in 1958 and Halleck by Ford in 1966. The Republicans are a party of leader factions; the Democrats are a party of regional and ideological factions. The leaders of these factions have not been willing to challenge one another. Finally, Tip O'Neill played his retirement shrewdly throughout his tenure. Every time the criticism seemed likely to boil over, he suggested that he was considering retirement. In the fall of 1984 he had firmly committed to retire at the end of the next congress. To challenge him was not worth the fight; it was easier to wait him out. Tip O'Neill had become a lame duck.

The organization of the Ninety-ninth Congress demonstrated how restive the younger Democrats were. In an important change in procedure, the caucus voted to elect the party whip beginning in the 100th Congress. Then, in a revolt led by Oklahoma Congressman Dave McCurdy, the caucus voted to unseat aged Arms Services Committee Chairman Melvin Price in favor of Congressman Les Aspin of Wisconsin. In a noticeable indication of his circumstances, O'Neill turned over to Majority Leader Jim Wright the task of negotiating committee ratios with the Republicans. While the Democrats retained ratios slightly more favorable than the partisan balance in most cases (decisively so on the Rules and Ways and Means Committees), they turned over thirty committee slots to the Republicans.[124]

As a lame duck, O'Neill's strategy changed. It was no longer necessary for the speaker to lambast the president at every opportunity. O'Neill held fewer press conferences, and they were less strident.[125] In the election year of 1984, O'Neill issued forty-three prepared statements during 101 daily press conferences. Almost all were harsh attacks on Reagan. In 1985, he issued only twenty-one statements at 75 press conferences; many of these dealt with pending legislation and were addressed to the Senate Republicans, twenty-two of whom would stand for reelection in 1986.[126] The positive legislative and political strategy of the Ninety-eighth Congress gave way to a new kind of defensive approach. The speaker sat back and awaited the Reagan administration's second-term policy initiatives, which he sought to reshape. The two major policy achievements of the Ninety-ninth Congress, the adoption of the Gramm-Rudman-Hollings balanced budget proposal and the enactment of the 1986 tax reform bill, both illustrated O'Neill's approach. The former (authored by Republican senators Phil Gramm of Texas and Warren Rudman of New Hampshire, and Democrat Ernest Hollings of South Carolina) involved recourse to a leadership task force, while the latter was routed through the normal committee process; but in both cases the Democrats ended up refashioning Republican proposals in order to make them more acceptable.[127]

The Gramm-Rudman bill sought to address the central piece of unfinished business between Ronald Reagan and Tip O'Neill, the budget deficit. Neither man was willing to take the initiative to address the problem, and so Gramm-Rudman brought the issue to them. The proposal mandated a five-year declining deficit path, and required mandatory budget cuts if the annual deficit targets were not met. The budget-balancing initiative came from the Republican-controlled Senate rather than from the Democratic House. The Republican senators had never been enamored of deficit spending, and with a substantial number of them up for reelection, Republican control of the Senate was at stake.

Senate passage of Gramm-Rudman threw the House Democrats on the defensive. Tip O'Neill's insistence that the president and the Senate go first in any attempt to raise taxes made sense in light of habitual Republican attacks on the Democrats as taxers and spenders, but it left the Democratic party with no plan to address the deficit problem. The politically difficult proposals—raising taxes and cutting entitlement spending—had come from the Senate and not from the House. While the Gramm-Rudman plan smacked of gimmickery, it was a dramatic step toward addressing the deficit. Many Democrats were critical of O'Neill for having allowed Senate Republicans, especially Phil Gramm, to have stolen the march from the Democrats on the deficit issue.[128] Scurrying to respond, the speaker appointed Majority Whip Tom Foley to head a task force to develop a Democratic response to the Republican plan. O'Neill knew that the House would not resist passage of a balanced-budget plan of some sort once it came to a vote. The problem for the Democrats was to pass their own plan in the House in order to bargain with the Senate in conference. Over the next few weeks Foley, caucus Chairman Dick Gephardt, and other Democratic leaders met frequently to plan the Democrats' response. The Democrats were forced to accept the basic terms of the Republican bill, but hoped to be able to bend it toward traditional Democratic positions. The Democrats wanted more social spending put off limits and more defense spending left subject to the automatic cuts. Whereas the Senate had generously put the first round of cuts off until after the 1986 election, the House Democrats wanted the bill to take hold immediately. If there was pain to be felt, the Democrats wanted Republican Senators up for reelection in 1986 to feel it.

The Democrats passed their plan on November 1, and the two chambers went to conference. On December 12 a conference report was signed into law by President Reagan. The Republicans were able to set certain categories of defense spending off limits, while the Democrats protected entitlement programs. The passage of the Gramm-Rudman Act placed great pressure on Congress to do something about the federal deficit. If the Congress did not act, the automatic cuts would ravage many federal spending programs. If the act worked, it would lead to reduction in the federal deficit. Speaker O'Neill left the House with a law on the books that aimed to solve the great unsolved issue of his tenure, the federal deficit. Like other deals struck between O'Neill and Reagan, this one promised to protect basic Democratic interests. If Gramm-Rudman were to work, it was as likely to eventuate in tax increases or cuts in defense spending as in cuts in welfare programs. But the reliance on this shotgun device did not reflect well on the government that chose it.

A Congress free to pass a balanced-budget act was also free to ignore it. In 1987 the Supreme Court invalidated the enforcement mechanism in a suit brought by Oklahoma Congressman Mike Synar, forcing the Congress to rely on a secondary enforcement plan that included passage of a joint resolution by the Congress to put sequestration into effect. Facing that reality in September 1987, the Congress passed a revision of the Gramm-Rudman law that enacted a new automatic procedure and stretched out the timetable to a balanced budget by two years, reducing the amount of deficit reduction required in FY 1988 accordingly. In the era of political symbolism the Congress labeled this capitulation a "reaffirmation" act, but the financial markets were not fooled, and the stock market crashed the following month. Only in the face of the worst financial debacle since the great crash of 1929 was the government able to reach accord on a two-year plan to reach the Gramm-Rudman targets.[129]

The other major domestic accomplishment of the Ninety-ninth Congress was the enactment of the most sweeping reform of the tax code in a generation. President Reagan had made the reform of the tax code the principal domestic priority of his second administration. On the Democratic side, the concept of a modified flat tax had been pushed by New Jersey Senator Bill Bradley and Missouri Congressman Dick Gephardt. Speaker O'Neill recognized that tax reform was potentially a good issue for Democrats, but only if the party could get out in front with an innovative proposal that would appeal to the political mainstream. The basic element of reform, embraced by Reagan as well as the Democrats, was simple: lower rates and fewer loopholes. The trade-off was to offer to the rich and to corporations a sharp decrease in the marginal rate of taxation, and to the poor a higher bottom bracket that would effectively remove millions from the tax rolls. The rich would be asked to pay for their rate reductions by the elimination of frequently used deductions. In the past the Congress had purchased reform by allowing inflation to push taxpayers into higher brackets; now, with bracket creep terminated by tax-rate indexing, reform would be purchased by eliminating preferences for individuals and corporations.[130]

The tax reform issue presented a classical example of a factor that has often proven essential to effective legislating in the Congress, a committee chairman who had a strong incentive to get a bill. President Reagan was joined in his drive for tax reform by Dan Rostenkowski, the chairman of the House Ways and Means Committee.[131] Rostenkowski wanted tax reform to pass the House, and he wanted the House tax bill to be his product, not Tip O'Neill's, Dick Gephardt's, or anyone else's. Since 1981 the chairman had for the most part been kicked around by the Republican Senate on tax matters. Rostenkowski wanted to leave behind a major revision of the tax code as a legacy of his chairmanship.[132]

Speaker O'Neill had less of a personal stake in the matter than Chairman Rostenkowski. For O'Neill, the primary concerns were to protect his Democratic members and to protect the interests of the national party. The failure of tax reform would not hurt Democratic members unless the public really wanted a new tax bill and the Democrats were perceived to have blocked the way to its enactment. The speaker had to support Rostenkowski's efforts to put together a bill that could pass the House, but he did not crusade for the bill, as he had for the 1977 energy bill. While at the outset O'Neill stated the need for the bill clearly—"I have to have a bill, the Democratic Party has to have a bill, and Danny's got to put one together that will sell . . . [or else] we'll be clobbered over the head by the President of the United States"—he later hedged his bets when it appeared that the House would fail to pass it: "I have found very little sentiment for the tax reform bill, very little sentiment . . . The people in the street never mentioned it . . . There is no desire to change a law which has been in effect for 75 years. The Democrats and Republicans have the same feeling."[133] O'Neill's public statements reflected the mood at the time each was made. At the outset, when a major tax reform bill seemed inevitable, the speaker wanted a Democratic bill; when, later, the momentum seemed to have gone out of the reform effort, O'Neill did not want anyone to think it was an important Democratic priority. Tip O'Neill always protected his party and his own reputation.

In his effort to pass a tax reform bill in the House, Dan Rostenkowski demonstrated his adaptability to the culture of the House in the democratic period. Rostenkowski was a Chicago ward heeler by nature, and like O'Neill, he was entirely comfortable in the back rooms where deals are cut. In order to rally his committee, the ward heeler held bipartisan retreats to foster a sense of commitment to the prestige of the Ways and Means Committee and a sense of solidarity among its members; he joined the therapeutic generation and became a leader in it. Realizing that tax reform cut across too many vested interests to be enacted incrementally, the chairman sought to forge a committee majority behind the bill by appealing to its group instincts. He sought to convince his members that their own interests would be served by joining in a reform effort that was perceived to be progressive and fair, even if their own constituencies had to lose some tax benefits in the process. In order to preserve the climate of reform, he asked his members to refrain from staking out fixed positions on particular provisions. Committee members understood that the chairman would try to accommodate those provisions of most importance to them, but he did not want the committee to become the captive of the vast array of special interests by which it was besieged.[134]

When Speaker O'Neill publicly supported the retention of the state and local tax deduction, Rostenkowski heatedly told O'Neill to back off. Rostenkowski had seen the budget deadlock of the preceding four years. He knew that one key element of the deadlock was O'Neill's intransigence on social security COLAs. If the speaker's proper strategic role was normally to stake out a polar position on the Democratic left, the better to be drawn back into the center, now Rostenkowski did not want him to polarize the House by setting himself in concrete on any particular feature of the tax code. Dan Rostenkowski was a man who liked to win, and would not let ideology stand in his way. He wanted to win very badly, and winning meant passing a tax bill in the House. He wanted O'Neill's support, but he did not want the speaker to define the terms of the debate.[135]

On December 3 Rostenkowski succeeded in producing a committee bill that had a Democratic stamp.[136] The bill lowered tax rates, eliminated many deductions, knocked poor people off of the tax rolls, and yet preserved features that were most popular with key Democratic constituencies. It went to the House floor with bipartisan committee support, but there it ran into a surprise: the Republicans turned against it and the House defeated the rule.[137] The defeat of the rule sent a signal to the White House that House Republicans were tired of being left out of the deal when it came to tax reform.[138] In part, Republican resentment derived from Rostenkowski's way of handling the reform effort. He wanted a bipartisan consensus, but did not seek one by attempting to reach accord with the Republican party leadership; instead, he chose to broker deals with committee Republicans, five of whom supported the bill in committee. On the floor, however, only fourteen Republicans voted to approve the rule. It was apparent that the five Republican committee votes did not reflect a House Republican consensus. Therapy only works on those who participate in it.

Speaker O'Neill took the opportunity to take a swipe at President Reagan. Noting that the rule had failed because of Republican opposition, the lame-duck speaker proclaimed Reagan to be a lame-duck president. O'Neill exercised dormant parliamentary muscle and announced that no attempt would be made to revive the tax bill until the president could promise the delivery of at least fifty Republican votes.[139] Put to the challenge, President Reagan responded with yet another virtuoso performance. Meeting with the Republican conference in the Rayburn House Office Building, the president appealed for support for his major domestic initiative, pointing out rightly that the death of tax reform in the House meant the death of tax reform during the Reagan administration. Promising to veto any tax bill that did not meet criteria important to the House Republicans, the president pleaded with the members of his party to give the Republican-controlled Senate a chance to work its will on the bill. The plea was heard, and a week later the House approved the rule and brought the tax bill to the floor. Speaker O'Neill, by now a supporter of the bill, spoke strongly on its behalf. On the key vote on the rule, 56 Republicans and 10 Democrats switched their votes from no to yes, and the rule carried easily, 258–168. In an anticlimax indicative of the uncertainty that members felt on the tax reform issue, the House finally passed the measure by voice vote.[140]

In 1986 the Senate Finance Committee produced an even more radical bill by a unanimous vote. The committee proposal was later approved almost unanimously by the full Senate. In conference Dan Rostenkowski was successful in returning to the bill some of the provisions of the House bill, but the basic bill that was enacted into law came from the Republican-controlled Senate. In the end, neither party could claim sole credit for the achievement. Indeed, the 1986 elections returned control of the Senate to the Democrats. Speaker O'Neill's political strategy and Dan Rostenkowski's legislative strategy had succeeded in neutralizing a potent political issue. Unlike the Gramm-Rudman deliberations, which had been undertaken by a leadership task force appointed by O'Neill, the tax negotiations followed the normal committee process. But the results of the two negotiations were very similar. In each case, fundamental change in law and policy had been enacted through a process of bipartisan negotiation, with minimal political impact on the fortunes of either party. For all of the partisan rhetoric, the outcomes were acceptable to both sides.[141]

An important sidelight to the tax reform debate was the position taken by the speaker-apparent, Jim Wright. The tax reform bill was acceptable to Reagan and O'Neill, but Wright consistently criticized it. As a congressman from Texas, Wright feared the effect of tax reform on the oil and gas industry; as a party leader, he believed the federal deficit to be the more compelling public policy issue. He did not want to use the revenues gained by preference elimination to purchase tax reform when they might be used to lower the deficit. Wright's opposition to the position of the speaker and the chairman of the Ways and Means

Committee harbingered changes to come in the next congress. The disagreement between the speaker and his majority leader over the position of the party on taxation revealed their very different personalities and political outlooks. The question of the Democrats' posture toward new revenues arose again and again. During the speaker's daily press conferences, O'Neill was asked about it no fewer than twelve times.[142] The speaker refused to budge from the position that he had held since 1984: all proposals for new revenues must emanate from the White House or Senate and must have the express support of the president, Senate Majority Leader Bob Dole, and House Minority Leader Bob Michel. O'Neill would not permit the Democrats to face another campaign in which the Republicans could accuse them of being the party of taxation and spending. O'Neill favored increased revenues to bring the budget toward balance; but he placed the protection of his party's political interest (as he understood it) above his concern for a balanced federal budget.

By contrast, Jim Wright was willing to say publicly that the Democratic party should advance budgets responsive to the deficit problem and that included such new revenues as the party was willing to stand behind as a policy matter. In order to allay the badgering from the press about a rift in the leadership's ranks, O'Neill issued a statement in support of the tax reform bill that acknowledged the difference in their views and reiterated his own often-stated position.

> The House will very soon be voting on the tax reform conference report. It is a good bill and deserves to pass . . .
>
> Ever since 1984, I have made the calculation that it is impossible to make a substantial change in this country's fiscal policy without the support of the President . . . I have insisted that no such change be undertaken in a partisan fashion. Any shift in revenue policy must be bi-partisan and have the support of the President.
>
> Jim Wright has been adamant since 1981 that the Congress needs to take the lead in restoring the revenues lost through the misconceived fiscal policies of 1981. He has recognized the political risks in this position, but he has stuck to his guns. I respect his position, but I also believe that tax reform is a value in itself. I think that Chairman Rostenkowski deserves credit for fighting to keep the bill revenue neutral against those forces in the other body who were willing to see a further loss of revenue.[143]

This public acknowledgment of the differences in the two leaders' positions on the crucial issue of taxation revealed just how different in philosophy, temperament, and geopolitical base O'Neill and Wright were, and harbingered significant changes for the House of Representatives during a Wright speakership.

In the final months of the Ninety-ninth Congress Jim Wright was asked by Speaker O'Neill to take primary leadership responsibility for the budget negotiations, the trade bill, the drug bill, the immigration bill, and the antiterrorism bill. Each of these bills passed the House with bipartisan support by substantial majorities. These bills addressed major national policy issues and the congressional response was in each case centrist. The attainment of bipartisan agreement was all the more remarkable in light of the heightened sense of partisanship that had marked the House in the Ninety-ninth Congress. Partisan voting in the House was higher in 1985 and 1986 than at any time since 1970; yet at the end of the Ninety-ninth Congress, major bills were passed with the support of both Democrats and Republicans.[144] Obviously, House Democrats and Republicans found it in their mutual interest to reach agreement in the period immediately preceding the 1986 election. The conditions under which bipartisan agreement was attained in an otherwise highly partisan chamber were shaped by the force of electoral politics, but the House's center of gravity was shifting toward the middle as well. Jim Wright had an opportunity to steer the House in a more centrist direction, reflecting his own political coalition in the House. Wright's active involvement in these issues also suggested that, as speaker, he would be far more engaged in the details of policy than Speaker O'Neill had chosen to be.

In the autumn of 1986 Tip O'Neill's political career came to a close and awaited its apotheosis. Already, his friends had it under way. "His ten years as speaker have defined that office certainly for the rest of this century," said his old roommate Eddie Boland.[145] The encomiums were by themselves proof of one fact that they alleged: Tip O'Neill was the best-known speaker of the House in the history of the Republic. "Sam Rayburn could have walked down the streets . . . without anybody noticing him," said Tom Foley. "Tip O'Neill couldn't do that."[146] Television carried the image of Tip O'Neill to the public at large, with the help of Ronald Reagan.

When a man who has been in public life for over thirty years, ten of them at the pinnacle of his political profession, retires with a good reputation, it is itself an indication that his tenure has been a success. But Tip O'Neill did not "define the speakership for the balance of the century." O'Neill filled the speakership well, but the enlarged public role that he played was due to the political circumstances in which he was placed by the 1980 election. The fact that he was so colorful lent to his role an air of drama that it might otherwise have lacked. A speaker who was not in the same strategic position or who was less of a personality than O'Neill would have enjoyed less of a symbolic role.

In fact, O'Neill's ability to take advantage of the unusual circumstances in which he found himself during the Reagan administration reflected a fact that he would perhaps be reluctant to acknowledge: Tip O'Neill and Ronald Reagan were very much alike. The essence of Ronald Reagan's presidency and Tip O'Neill's speakership both lay in symbolic leadership. Neither man was well versed in the details of the policies over which they fought; both men relied on others to do the nuts-and-bolts work of political leadership. Each was guided by strong ideological commitments. O'Neill was often called powerful, but such power as he had was severely circumscribed. His influence on policy was more often owing to positioning than to power, and his position was more often defensive than offensive. Even when the House Democrats sought to pass party position bills during the Reagan years, they knew that their policies would rarely prevail over those of the administration. The best that they could hope for was a reasonable compromise. On public policy matters, Tip O'Neill's speakership was usually reactive.

Without doubt, Tip O'Neill will be best remembered as a partisan Democrat. Since he chose to define his own goals in partisan terms, he is entitled to be judged for his effectiveness, and the judgments will be mixed. O'Neill's political instincts were as finely honed as those of any political leader in American history. While many wondered if O'Neill's liberal image was good for the Democratic party, few doubted the speaker's sagacity in playing that image to the hilt. Yet by placing such high priority on partisan goals, the speaker perpetuated a political deadlock that had grave repercussions for the country. There were occasions on which Speaker O'Neill placed the electoral interests of the party above a search for bipartisan consensus on legislation, on the theory that only by winning power could the Democrats implement their policies. For Speaker O'Neill, the battle for power was part of a fight over the future of the country.

And it is precisely in considering its impact on the direction of the country that Speaker O'Neill would wish to have his legacy judged. The conservative shift in public policy that occurred during the 1980s was something to which Tip O'Neill was opposed body and soul. That it occurred is a sufficient indication of the limits of his power. Historians of this era will write that, in the latter part of the twentieth century, the American public demanded a pause in the evolution of the welfare state. As the nation's leading welfare-state liberal, Tip O'Neill tried to preserve as much of the Democratic policy structure as he could by fighting a political war with Ronald Reagan. To a great extent he succeeded. If Ronald Reagan is remembered as the man who put the lid on the welfare state, Tip O'Neill will be remembered as the man who led the fight against the Reagan revolution. Neither man did it alone. Reagan's revolution was undergirded by grass-roots personal support and a prevailing conservative breeze that enabled him to govern; but Tip O'Neill's counterrevolution was undergirded by a deeper, if more silent, acceptance of the fundamental presuppositions of the welfare state that he defended. Both men were symbolic leaders whose positions had deep public support. Together, the two Irish antipodes created a policy impasse that was not in the national interest. At the end of their struggle, it remained to be seen whether or how the impasse that they had created would be resolved. By 1987 many Democrats were convinced that the country could no longer afford the luxury of the ideological war that had raged since 1981. A lack of policy direction was the single most consistent criticism of Speaker O'Neill among members and commentators. The newer and younger generation of Democrats wanted a speaker who would take a more forceful hand in shaping a Democratic policy agenda. With Jim Wright's election as speaker, it appeared that these Democrats would get the policy maker they had long sought.

The Speaker as Policy Maker

On December 8, 1986, the House Democratic caucus selected Jim Wright of Texas to be its candidate for speaker in the 100th Congress. The Democrats selected Congressman Tom Foley of Washington as their majority leader, and for the first time elected a whip, Congressman Tony Coehlo of California. Once again, the leadership ladder produced an uncontested speakership nomination, and since the Democrats controlled 258 of the House's 435 seats, Wright's election as speaker was assured. In Jim Wright the Democrats selected a leader who was a blend of the old and the new. His career had been built on the pork-barrel politics of the Public Works Committee, yet he had been the most issue-oriented majority leader of the modern era. While his critics caricatured him as a southern snake-oil salesman, in fact Wright was a man of strong convictions and an equally strong desire to see them implemented in public policy.

The history of the speakership yields no example of a speaker whose fundamental character traits changed upon assuming the office. In no previous case has a speaker's early career provided a clearer indication of his propensities than did Jim Wright's. Wright inherited from his father a hard-nosed populism and pugnaciousness that was reflected throughout his career. A boxer and Golden Glove coach, Wright knew how to fight and liked to win. Elected to the Texas House of Representatives in 1946, Wright was defeated in seeking reelection in 1948. He spent the next six years in Weatherford, Texas, serving as mayor and involving himself in a variety of community activities. In 1954 he took on an incumbent congressman who was supported by the largest newspaper in Fort Worth, and won the election by running against the editor of the paper.[147]

Jim Wright often said that his role-model was Speaker Sam Rayburn, who in 1955 returned to the speakership at the pinnacle of his power in the House. Actually, Wright was not among Rayburn's closest protégés and Wright did not get the seat that he sought on the Foreign Affairs Committee. Instead, he was placed on Public Works, where he was launched on a career path that would be very different from the speakers who preceded him. O'Neill, Albert, and McCormack had been products of the leadership system. None had played a major role on a substantive committee. Rayburn had been a powerful chairman of the Commerce Committee, and had made his role by passing major legislation in the House. By contrast, Jim Wright established his position in the House by effective pork-barreling:

> He became a legend for funneling federal dollars to his home town. A 1979 study found that his district got the highest "return" per tax dollar of any in the country . . . for most of his House career, Wright was best known as a tireless advocate of federal water projects . . . he was elected [majority leader] by a single vote . . . subsequent analysis revealed that he had won because he was a friendly guy, a Southerner, and had courted his colleagues over the years by helping them with their pet projects on Public Works.[148]

This account captures the foundations of Wright's House career. In his years in the party leadership, he would continue to do favors for members. It misses entirely, however, the geopolitical factors that enabled Wright to jump on the leadership ladder.

Among the four men who ran for majority leader in 1976, Jim Wright was the most conservative. He received the southern vote, while Richard Bolling, John McFall, and Phillip Burton split the northern vote. After McFall dropped out, the caucus gave Burton 107 votes to 95 for Wright and 93 for Bolling. Then, in a head-to-head confrontation Wright edged Burton by a single vote. Many claimed to have had a hand in Wright's election. Speaker Albert urged him to run and worked on his behalf privately.[149] Tip O'Neill guarded his vote, but certainly supported Wright against Burton.[150] Dan Rostenkowski of Illinois managed Wright's campaign and later claimed to have swung the key vote.[151] The explanation of Wright's victory lay in his more centrist position in the caucus, on the one hand, and his own willingness to take a risk, on the other. This was the first time since Henry Rainey upset the establishment in running for majority leader in 1930 that an outsider had won his way into the House leadership in a contested election. Jim Wright demonstrated in 1976 that he had the guts to take a major risk; this proved to be a harbinger of his speakership.

During his decade of service as majority leader, Wright traveled to hundreds of congressional districts, did many favors for members, and managed business on the House floor. He certainly had more daily contact with members than did O'Neill. Still, Wright was an essentially private man who held his own counsel. His was a combination of fiery temperament and cool aloofness, and his impetuous character was in marked contrast to the avuncular O'Neill. Wright was not of the therapeutic generation that he was called upon to lead and lacked some of the qualities that its members desired in their speaker. While he was comfortable with the mechanics of Democratic party governance, he was not one to reach out to members in a personal way. His strong sense of privacy and a stubborn independent streak risked running afoul of the desire of his Democratic members for an open and participatory speakership. Yet the mechanisms of Democratic party government had, by 1987, become well refined, and Wright had helped refine them. There was little doubt of his willingness to use the caucus, the whips, and the Steering and Policy Committee in marshaling Democratic majorities. But the formal process of invoking the mechanisms of party government for constructive dialogue was merely that. The crucial test came in eliciting from the process party positions that would have widespread support, would serve the interests of the party and the nation, and would bear the stamp of the speaker's leadership.

Jim Wright sought to rise to this challenge of office, embarking upon a thirty-month speakership that was among the most provocative in American history. In June 1989 he became the first speaker to resign the office as the result of an ethics investigation into alleged violations of House rules governing the personal finances of members. The high drama associated with Wright's resignation brought the speakership to the attention of the public in a way that his management of the House had not. It is important to understand the end of Wright's speakership in relationship to his conduct of office and its character. What happened to Jim Wright was, in the end, caused not simply by the manner in which he conducted his personal affairs or by his having violated House rules. Instead, Wright's fate was sealed by the chemistry of his personality, his approach to the speakership, the institutional circumstances in which he functioned, and the partisan environment that he helped create. Jim Wright set one aspect of the democratic speakership, its policy-making role, against its therapeutic and symbolic functions, and came up the loser. The analysis of the Wright speakership must begin with his conduct of office.

Speaker Wright followed three strategies in the 100th Congress. First, he sought to develop consensus positions within the Democratic party on a specific, yet confined, agenda of major policy issues. Second, he used his control over the Rules Committee to structure floor consideration so as to ensure that the Democratic bills would not be threatened by disabling Republican amendments, especially those emanating from the far right.[152] This effectively precluded the conservative coalition from forming against him, and left moderate Republicans with little choice but to support the Democratic bills. Finally, when major bills reached the stage of conference deliberation, Wright was often willing to make concessions to the right, especially since those concessions were as often made to more conservative Senate bills, rather than to proposals made by the conservative wing of the House Republican party. Wright bargained very little with the Republican leadership. This was not a return to the Rayburn-Martin era. To the contrary, Wright was intent upon laying the basis for unity within his own party, and he would not risk jeopardizing it by trucking with the Republicans.[153]

Wright's aggressive use of his powers for partisan advantage was in contrast to his more cooperative attitude in 1986, when as majority leader he worked toward bipartisan cooperation on several bills. Several factors serve to explain this. The political dynamics of the 1986 election year took the edge off of many issues. This was especially true in the Senate, where Republicans strived to retain their majority. In the House, Wright dealt with issues that had reasonable prospect of bipartisan support, and as majority leader, he was without the powers of the speakership. Wanting to ensure his nomination by the Democratic caucus, he had little incentive or opportunity to pursue partisan advantage. As speaker in 1987, Wright had both opportunity and incentive. His incentive was to establish his reputation; the opportunity was provided by the Iran-Contra investigation, which weakened President Reagan and rendered him impotent in many Democratic congressional districts. The swing votes within the Democratic caucus had more to fear from Jim Wright than from Ronald Reagan.

In his quest to establish a strong speakership, Wright was willing to press his powers under the rules to their limits in a way that no speaker had done since Joe Cannon. The reform movement had left as its legacy both a fragmented House and a much strengthened speakership. Speaker Albert had been constrained by circumstance and disposition from taking full advantage of the recovered powers of the office, and Speaker O'Neill had done so only sporadically. Speaker Wright was the first speaker in the democratic period to use the powers of office systematically to pass his own legislative agenda. Eventually he pushed too hard. On October 29, 1987, the speaker set a modern precedent in the assertive use of the powers of the chair. From the outset of the 100th Congress, Wright had insisted that responsible action on the federal deficit required new tax revenues.[154] For this example of political candor, he was rebuked by many Democrats, who shared O'Neill's position; but as the end of the first session drew near, and in the wake of the stock market crash on October 24, the Budget Committee brought to the floor a reconciliation bill that included $12.8 billion in new revenues and a controversial welfare reform package. Some Democrats opposed the tax increases and others the welfare reform provision, while the Republicans were strongly against both. While the speaker, with other congressional leaders, was at a White House budget summit to discuss the stock market crash, a coalition of Democrats and Republicans defeated the rule and blocked floor consideration of the bill by a 217–203 vote.

Returning to the Hill, Speaker Wright immediately reconvened the Rules Committee and brought the reconciliation bill back to the floor without the welfare provisions. However, the standing rules of the House posed an obstacle. Rules passed by the Rules Committee must lay over for one legislative day before they can be considered on the floor. Undaunted, Wright adjourned the House and reconvened it for the legislative day of October 30 on October 29. This enabled him to win passage of the rule on a 238–182 vote. But on final passage the fifteen-minute voting period expired with a 205–206 majority against the bill. In order to reverse the result, the speaker held the vote open for ten minutes until a Texas Democrat was prevailed upon to switch his vote. As soon as he did, Wright gaveled the vote closed.[155]

Wright had several reasons for being insistent. The stock markets were understandably jittery in the wake of the crash, and the speaker thought that a demonstration of seriousness of purpose in reducing the budget deficit would reassure them. Just the previous month the Congress had stretched out the Gramm-Rudman plan for an additional two years. In the wake of the stock market crash, Wright knew that budget negotiations with the administration were imminent and he wanted to strengthen his bargaining position with the White House and Senate by having a House-passed tax increase in hand. Wright also wanted to show that he could produce a voting majority on the House floor even in the most difficult of circumstances.[156] However compelling these motives may have been, Wright's insistence had adverse consequences. This was the first major floor fight of his tenure in which he suffered serious defections from Democratic ranks. His success to that time had been based upon a relatively unified Democratic caucus. Wright was able to win in this case only by rolling over some Democrats as well as some Republicans, and he opened the door to what any speaker wants least, intraparty factionalism.[157]

Some of the Democrats were mad, and all of the Republicans were furious.[158] The Republicans were as angry at Jim Wright as Democrats had been at Uncle Joe Cannon. An indication of the damage to interparty relations that Wright's strategy had done came in May of 1988 when the Republican leadership took to the floor of the House en masse under a special order addressed to the abusive practices of the Democratic leadership.[159] The Republicans provided statistics that argued the extent of Democratic efforts to control the floor of the House. The data demonstrated that in the 100th Congress, the House had passed fewer bills, held fewer hearings, had increased the number of appropriations enacted without prior authorization, had granted more waivers of the budget act, had increased the use of restrictive rules on the floor, had more frequently denied to the Republicans the right to seek to recommit with instructions, and had used the rules themselves to pass substantive legislation. The Republican catalogue suggested a Democratic leadership intent upon closing the door on deliberation on the floor of the House. As significantly, it revealed a Republican party embittered by its treatment at the hands of the majority Democrats.

The Republican data demonstrate a clear trend, but a full analysis of it must take into account factors in addition to the imperiousness of the Democrats and their leader. The reform movement shattered the power structure of the House and made it very difficult for normal business to proceed. Many of the modified rules were designed to protect the committee product on the floor and not the leadership's program. Often they were supported by both Democrats and Republicans. The reforms opened the legislative process and made it more vulnerable to legislative mischief; the Republicans were the worst abusers of the floor stage in their efforts to craft politically inspired amendments. Prior to 1970, members were routinely protected by the unrecorded teller vote. It was the imposition of the recorded teller vote and then electronic voting that permitted members to be put on the spot. Doing so became a pastime of the most conservative Republicans. The leadership used self-executing rules (rules that upon passage amended standing law) in order to avoid public pressure, and often the beneficiaries were from both parties. The budget crisis of the 1980s that made the use of waivers necessary was due in large part to policies that the Republicans enacted in 1981. The legislative strategies employed by the Democrats were designed to protect members in their districts. This is a natural goal of a legislative party, and there can be little doubt that a Republican-controlled House would lay similar pressure on a Republican speaker.

A balanced view of the trend toward controlled management of the House floor suggests causes that lay deeper than the partisan motives of an overbearing majority; yet it does not preclude the possibility that this is sometimes what in fact occurred. The litmus test that should be applied to the use of the rules is this: are they being used so as to facilitate timely, rational, orderly, and fair consideration of legislation? The rules of the House should be used to foster the conditions of deliberation and not to enable the majority to impose its will on the minority arbitrarily. When the rules are used for partisan political purpose, they derogate from the House's capacity to deliberate. Control supersedes comity, and the legislative body is damaged at its core. This is what happened during the partisan period. The discussion in chapter 2 traces the last period of centralized power in the House. Then, it was the Republican party that served as the main vehicle of centralized control. Republican leader Bob Michel could have borrowed the speeches of John Sharp Williams and Champ Clark, and Speaker Wright could have taken his script from Tom Reed and Joe Cannon.

Some people thought that Jim Wright simply wanted to maximize his power in order to control public policy. Evidence for this interpretation is found in the speaker's approach to American policy toward Nicaragua. The trend toward greater involvement by the speaker in foreign affairs began during Speaker Albert's tenure and was given more emphasis by Speaker O'Neill's opposition to President Reagan. But neither Albert nor O'Neill would have gone as far as Jim Wright did in the 100th Congress. Fluent in Spanish, Wright had a long-standing personal interest in Latin American affairs. His Fort Worth, Texas, district was conservative on foreign policy and national defense matters, and some of the largest private contributors to the Contra cause had been from Texas. Yet Wright could not forget that the liberal wing of the Democratic caucus shared Tip O'Neill's views on Central America, and would not welcome an attempt by Wright to endorse the Reagan program. The Contra question divided the Democratic caucus and threatened to crush the speaker between his district and his caucus majority. He needed to find a way to put the Contra question to sleep.

The speaker's solution was a clever gambit with the Reagan administration. Soon after the Iran-Contra hearings were brought to a close, the administration approached Wright to suggest that he join with President Reagan in sponsoring a peace plan.[160] Wright gambled that his association with the proposal would force action among Central American governments on a peace initiative of their own that was then being discussed. When a few days later, President Oscar Arias of Costa Rica announced the Central American plan, Wright jumped on board, leaving the administration with no choice but to voice support for the proposal as well.[161] Pressing his advantage, Wright pushed through a small amount of stop-gap humanitarian aid for the Contras and became actively involved in the discussions leading to the opening of formal talks between the Nicaraguan government and the rebels.[162] The speaker's actions brought forth a predictable condemnation by the administration, leading some Republicans to call him the "Speaker of State." In the end, former Democratic National Chairman Robert Strauss of Texas was called upon to negotiate articles of peace between the speaker and Secretary of State George Schulz.[163]

Speaker Wright's approach to the Contra question reflected his position and district, and also his desire to play a major role in foreign policy. It was a risky venture, since if the peace process failed and the Sandinista regime became more entrenched, the Democrats would be accused of "losing" Nicaragua to the communists. But the other alternative was an acceptable negotiated settlement, an alternative that the American public seemed clearly to prefer by 1987. In either event, the speaker would be able to claim to have "given peace a chance" in Central America.[164] Aside from Wright's immediate personal and political motives, however, his role in the Nicaraguan debate raised important questions about the proper role of the speaker in foreign affairs. In the democratic period the House of Representatives has been more heavily involved in foreign affairs than ever before. The speaker now has a statutory role and a political incentive for more active engagement in foreign policy. To a great extent the role that speakers play depends upon the foreign policy agenda. That a speaker should play a role is natural and inevitable; that the speaker should seek to preempt the executive's constitutional prerogatives in foreign affairs would be very unwise. Jim Wright's fate will be a caution to future speakers who might be tempted to play on the world stage.

In pushing his power and policies to the hilt, Jim Wright had the advantage of riding a favorable policy tide. After six years of budget paralysis and reductions in many public programs, the public was ready to see Congress take action to address major national problems. The 100th Congress was able to act in a variety of substantive areas where its immediate predecessors had failed to act because of the deadlock between Reagan and O'Neill. The Democrats' legislative agenda hardly smacked of Great Society liberalism; instead, it was largely aimed at the political center. For example, the trade bill that Wright had made the centerpiece of the Democratic program was in the end shorn of both the protectionist Gephardt amendment and a controversial plant closing provision.[165] At the end of the first session, under the pressure of the stock market crash, the Democratic leadership joined in a budget summit with the Senate and the White House. This was precisely the sort of summit that Wright had called for since 1985. Yet now the speaker resisted summitry as an infringement upon House (i.e., his) prerogatives. In the end, Wright agreed to a deficit reduction package that swung to the right.[166]

In 1988 the Congress passed three major bills that reflected a centrist policy consensus. Catastrophic health care had become a major national concern and the administration had proposed a plan to provide it through the Medicare system. Liberal Democrats tried to leaven the bill with a major program for long-term health care authored by venerable Congressman Claude Pepper of Florida. Wright agreed to give the proposal a vote, but the Pepper amendment was defeated when key committee chairmen such as Dan Rostenkowski and John Dingell opposed it. The bill that was in the end passed with substantial bipartisan support was largely the administration's bill.[167] The Democrats managed to add on a provision for prescription drugs, with Speaker Wright leading the way, but it was a measure of how far Democratic liberalism and Republican conservatism had come that the Republicans wanted to pay the bills, leaving the Democrats to buy the pills. A second revealing piece of legislation was the welfare reform bill. Welfare, even more than health, was a traditional Democratic issue. In the heyday of Democratic liberalism, liberals had opposed work requirements, while conservatives had supported them. This welfare reform bill, like the catastrophic health bill, was drafted on moderate terms. Democrats and Republicans supported work requirements, and only differed on how stringent they should be.[168] Finally, in one of its last actions the 100th Congress passed a major bill to deal with the drug problem. Traditional Democratic liberalism would treat drug users as the victims of society and provide for their rehabilitation. This bill provided for harsher penalties for dealers, cut off some federal benefits for users, and toughened enforcement and interdiction. A moderate bill drafted by the House Select Narcotics Committee was significantly toughened on the floor and the resultant bill passed with only thirty opposing votes.[169]

All three of these bills passed with substantial bipartisan support, and each was moderate. Republicans willingly supported health and welfare legislation that thirty years before they would have opposed, but the Democratic congressional majority was more moderate than at any time since the Great Society. When bargains were made, they were to the right rather than the left. Jim Wright was able to pass these bills because the Democrats were more unified and the legislative program was near enough to the center to hold a governing coalition together. The greater unity among Democrats was due to generational turnover. Both the old-style southern conservatives and the old-style northern liberals were passing from the scene. The most liberal group did not extend much further than the Black caucus, and the new southern Democrats were much more moderate than their conservative forbears. Thus, Wright's success was due more to positioning than to power. His leadership was forceful, however, and the personal element cannot be left out of account. He pushed the House hard and demanded action from the legislative committees. Meeting frequently with Democratic committee caucuses on major legislation, he was firm in insisting on reporting deadlines. He was far more involved in the details of legislation than had been his predecessor, and was unwilling to delegate as much legislative responsibility to his staff. Speaker O'Neill had permitted key staff members to act on his behalf in dealing with members and with the press; Speaker Wright liked to handle these matters himself.[170]

A lesson about the speakership may be gleaned from Jim Wright's first Congress. The contextualist thesis relies heavily on the assumption that institutional factors shape leadership style. In terms of the way that business is conducted in the House, this notion proved reasonably accurate. While Speaker Wright was far more assertive in controlling the legislative agenda than Speaker O'Neill had been, the democratic practices that had evolved within the Democratic caucus were continued.[171] The caucusing, task-forcing, and retreating, what Tip O'Neill had called the "dialoguery," were unabated. However, the contextualist view tends to be insensitive to the major differences that the personal element of the power equation makes. Whether one looks at Wright's position on the major issues of taxation and Contra aid, or to his approach to policy formation in the House, the differences between him and O'Neill are striking. Wright's strategic situation was different from O'Neill's, as was his persona. The lesson to be drawn from this in the search for understanding of the speakership is simple: institutional context affects the methods by which a speaker may seek to lead the House, but it does not determine them, or the goals in pursuit of which they are employed. An approach to interpreting the speakership that leans wholly on institutional factors will fail to grasp the complex interplay of institutional arrangements, political alignments, policy positions, and personal factors involved in the process of governance. For a decade scholars had claimed that the problem with the postreform House was that power was too diffuse; in the 100th Congress, Jim Wright showed that power could be centralized in the speakership.

Three aspects of Jim Wright's conduct during the 100th Congress warrant close examination from the perspective that these pages have developed. The democratic speakership is policy-oriented, therapeutic, and symbolic. Wright was clearly policy-oriented, but hardly a counselor in the O'Neill mold. To the contrary, his sometimes aloof manner and his lack of strong friendships with members were among the most often remarked-upon aspects of his character. That Jim Wright was not a therapeutic personality does not mean that the House was not a therapeutic institution. In fact, many House Democrats were extremely uneasy about Wright's close-to-the-vest style and tolerated it only because they were winning votes. But a speakership that lasts at all long will not be one in which the speaker consistently wins. Successful speakers are those who manage to survive and be effective even when they are losing. Wright's reception among a sufficient number of Democrats left him very little margin for error. He was not able to fall back on the personal affection of members as O'Neill had done in adverse times.

The therapeutic culture of the House did not go away; instead, it became routinized in the whip organization. Tony Coehlo was a leader in the therapeutic generation, and his expansion of the whip organization, the routinization of task forces, and the constant efforts to extend communication among members, represents the institutionalization of the therapeutic function. This is not to say, however, that a nontherapeutic speaker can thrive by institutionalizing the therapeutic function and ignoring it himself. Today members want a speaker they trust, in whom they can confide, and with whom they can communicate. They will not be happy with a father figure or a power-broker, and they will not elect either in a contested election. The future of the speakership lies within the therapeutic culture.

Jim Wright did not possess Tip O'Neill's natural capacity for reaching out to members, and it seemed unlikely that he would come to play the same symbolic role. When the Democrats recaptured the Senate, the speaker lost his distinct role as national party spokesman. With the Reagan presidency in its twilight, the edge was taken from the contest in which Reagan and O'Neill had been engaged. While O'Neill symbolized the better instincts of New Deal liberalism, Wright's image suggested to many people its worst features. The caricature of the Texan as a snake-oil salesman was hard to discourage. In the end Wright did become a symbol for the Democrats, albeit in a way that he would have done much better to have avoided. By his aggressive approach to the speakership, he shaped a public image as a man determined to use the powers at his disposal assertively, if not ruthlessly; when his political opponents were able to call his personal conduct into question, his role as a symbol of the Democratic party and the House of Representatives became untenable, and he was forced to resign. The story of Jim Wright's resignation is among the bitterest tales in the history of the House, but in it is revealed very clearly the character of the speakership of the House of Representatives in the democratic era.

It was not unprecedented for a speaker to become subject to allegations of personal misconduct. Clay was accused of trading his support to John Quincy Adams for the presidency in return for appointment as Adams's secretary of state. Colfax and Blaine were implicated in the Crédit Mobilier scandal, and Randall was accused of using his position to steer government contracts to a paper mill in which he owned an interest. Keifer practiced nepotism in office. Garner was accused of excessive drinking and cozy relations with the railroads. McCormack was tainted by charges that lobbyist Nathan Valoshen operated from the speaker's office and used his letterhead, while Albert and O'Neill faced accusations related to the Korean bribery scandal. Among these speakers, only Colfax was found to have been guilty of violating the law or House rules, and by then he was serving as Grant's vice president. In the 100th Congress Jim Wright came under attack on a variety of grounds for violations of House rules and the House ethics code. It was alleged that he had used his power improperly on behalf of the Texas savings and loan industry; that he had circumvented House rules by taking an extraordinary royalty on a vanity book, in lieu of honoraria and in excess of outside earning limits; that he had accepted unreported gifts from a Texas friend, George Mallick, in connection with the employment of Wright's wife, Betty, by an investment firm jointly owned by the two families; and that he had publicly divulged classified information obtained in his official capacity.

On May 26, 1988, Speaker O'Neill's nemesis, Republican Congressman Newt Gingrich of Georgia, lodged a formal complaint against Wright with the House Committee on Standards of Official Conduct, commonly known as the House Ethics Committee.[172] Gingrich's Conservative Opportunity Society, whose self-proclaimed mission was to win Republican control of the House by pressing a conservative policy agenda, now saw an opportunity to make headway by a direct assault on Speaker Wright. Gingrich was a well-known opponent of Wright's, and harassment from him was to be expected. His case gained respectability when the self-styled citizens' lobby Common Cause joined in calling for an investigation into the speaker's affairs.[173] Common Cause had long been identified with liberal politics, and its call for an investigation ensured that the Democrats would not be able to dismiss the Gingrich charges as politically motivated. Gingrich's motives were, no doubt, political, but it was one measure of the depth of Republican feelings about Wright that seventy-one other Republicans joined in the Georgian's complaint.[174]

The Ethics Committee's investigation hung over Jim Wright's head like a thundercloud during the balance of 1988. With the election of the Bush administration, the speaker's approach to the legislative agenda for the 101st Congress was positively timid in comparison with his prime ministership during the preceeding congress.[175] Then, at the outset of the new congress the speaker fell into the middle of a quagmire over a proposed congressional pay raise that did much to undermine his support in the House. Congressional pay raises have frightened members ever since the voters turned out a large number of congressmen after the pay grab of 1816. The average voter makes less than the average congressman, and many voters find it hard to believe that members of Congress cannot get by on the money they are making, no matter what the salary level is. Because of this, Congress finds it politically dangerous to vote itself a pay raise. Since congressional pay is tied to that of the executive and judicial branches, the federal salary schedule is often held hostage to congressional timidity.

Seeking a way out, Congress created a commission on federal pay mandated to recommend increases in federal pay every four years. The "Quadrennial Commission" as it became known, proposed in 1988 to significantly raise federal pay scales. The Congress was to be the beneficiary of a 50 percent increase in salary. The members wanted the money, but did not want to have to vote on it. Therefore, they had provided by law that the pay increase would go into effect unless vetoed by both houses of the Congress and the president. In this manner the Senate, the House, or the president could ensure that the pay raise would take effect. When public gadfly Ralph Nader launched an attack on the pay increase, the public reaction was strongly adverse. The Senate caved in to the pressure immediately, solaced by the fact that senators are able to earn more in honoraria than are members of the House.

All of the pressure came to focus on the House and on Speaker Wright. From the beginning the strategy had been for Wright to avoid a House vote until the legislatively mandated deadline for congressional action had passed. By inaction the House would earn a 50 percent pay increase. Under tremendous pressure from members who wanted the raise, and in the face of opposition from those who wished to make a political issue out of the pay grab, Wright caved in and scheduled a House vote. The inevitable result was that the raise was defeated. Even as he braced for the results of the ethics investigation, Wright alienated many of his strongest supporters by denying them a pay increase that they very much wanted. There can be no doubt that the pay grab fiasco contributed to the weakening of Wright's support in the Democratic caucus at a time when he most needed it. Republican sentiment against the speaker reached a new pitch when, as a result of the bitter Senate fight over the nomination of John Tower to be secretary of defense, the House Republicans elected Wright's accuser, Newt Gingrich, to replace Richard Cheney, the secretary of defense designate, as their new whip.[176]

After ten months of investigation by a special counsel, the Ethics

Committee announced on April 17, 1989, that it had "reason to believe" that the speaker had committed sixty-nine violations of House rules in two areas: the business relationship between Wright, his wife, and George Mallick; and the sales of Wright's book *Reflections of a Public Man* in bulk to organizations in lieu of honoraria for speeches.[177] The committee dismissed all of the original charges brought by Gingrich, as well as other charges having to do with Wright's business dealings and his interventions in the regulatory process with respect to the Texas savings and loan industry. While the committee deliberated, other allegations against Wright surfaced. National and Texas newspapers had launched extensive investigations of Wright's affairs. By the spring of 1989 new revelations had become almost a daily occurrence. Wright was alleged to have accepted free rides from businesses having an interest in legislation, was claimed to have made excessive profits through a blind trust on transactions that suggested possible insider information, was accused of promoting a business in which his wife was employed in the *Congressional Record*, faced further accusations that his wife had accepted employment for which she did no work, and was alleged to have promised to intervene on behalf of savings and loans in return for campaign contributions. None of these charges were substantiated, or even brought within the purview of the ethics investigation then in process. Some of them might have been included in the committee's investigation had it proceeded; but in the end Wright had no choice but to resign both the speakership and his seat in the House in order to spare himself, his family, his party, and the House the burden of further investigations.[178]

Jim Wright's downfall came in May of 1989. On May 11 his key staff assistant, John Mack, resigned after it was revealed that he had been convicted as a young man for a felonious assault on a woman.[179] On May 17 a group of House Democrats met and openly discussed the need for the speaker to resign. On May 23, in a televised hearing, the speaker's lawyers argued before the Ethics Committee that the charges against Wright be dismissed on the grounds that his actions were not in violation of the rules as alleged in the committee's bill of particulars. When it became apparent that the committee had no intention of dismissing the charges on technical grounds, thus necessitating a full hearing on the substance of the charges themselves, Wright decided to resign. On May 31, 1989, he gave a passionate defense on the floor of the House against the main charges against him, and announced his resignation effective upon the election of a new speaker on June 6. He also indicated his intention to resign his seat in Congress by the end of June, thus bringing to a close the congressional inquiry into his affairs.[180]

In his resignation speech Wright appealed to the House to put behind

it the partisan "blood-letting" that had come to poison the legislative
environment. "Let me give you back this job you gave me," he said,
"as a propitiation for all of this season of bad will that has grown up
among us."[181] Wright was in part correct in portraying himself as the
victim of a political vendetta. There can be no doubt that the partisan
acrimony in the House was greater in 1988 and 1989 than at any time
since the reign of Uncle Joe Cannon. Even in the fierce partisan conflict
during the Cannon speakership, however, members did not commonly
employ attacks upon the personal ethics of other members as a political
strategy. The personal acrimony that came to characterize American
politics in the late 1980s was the product of a new style of political
campaigning in which symbolic and personal attacks through mass
media of communication proved effective in influencing voters in both
presidential and congressional elections. Speaker Wright did fall prey
in this environment, but his apologia ignored his own role in contributing
to the creation of it. It is precisely here that the lesson of Jim Wright's
speakership is to be found.

The American speakership is a hybrid of parliamentary and partisan
functions that sometimes do not mix together well. During the parliamentary period the speaker's role as presiding officer was predominant.
While the speakers of this period were no doubt partisan, their role was
shaped largely by the demands of the chair; they were not the leaders
of entrenched political parties. Especially during the two decades prior
to the Civil War, speakers understood that their most important duty
was to maintain the conditions under which deliberative government
could be conducted in the House. It was after the Civil War, during the
partisan period, that speakers came to accept primary responsibility for
party leadership. With the defeat of obstructionism and the practices
that supported it, the way was paved for an overbearing majority to
impose its will on the House. In the first decade of the twentieth century,
the House reacted against the practices associated with Cannonism, and
adopted a more decentralized system of governance. This led to the
evolution of the feudal system, in which the standing committees governed the House under the benign guidance of speakers who were forced
to broker where their predecessors had ruled. It was in the feudal period
that the norms of deference to seniority and comity among members
became embedded in the folkways of the House. Likewise, the feudal
period was marked by a greater degree of bipartisanship in policy making
than had been possible during the partisan era, especially after the
emergence of the conservative coalition in 1937.

During the evolution of the office, speakers retained two essential
obligations: the first was to embody the authority and dignity of the
House, and the second was to preside impartially over its proceedings,

dealing fairly with all members. To be sure, there have been many occasions when a speaker has sacrificed these obligations on the altar of his party's program, and the partisan period in particular was often characterized by a sacrifice of the speaker's parliamentary obligations to the pursuit of legislative victories. But the House rose up against Uncle Joe Cannon precisely because his conception of the speakership was at odds with its fundamental character. Members of the House will always prefer a fair speaker to a powerful one, and the speaker who forgets this places himself in harm's way.

Jim Wright was by nature an aggressive man, oriented to the use of power. He had chafed for years under the often relaxed approach of the popular Tip O'Neill. Upon assuming the speakership, he ached to govern. He intended, as he put it, to explore the limits of his power, and eventually he found them. Wright's most basic mistake lay in fostering in his political opponents the desire to get rid of him. It is apparent that any speaker who is worth his salt will at times alienate members, within his own party and across the aisle. A speaker who is too assiduous in courting members will come to be regarded as lacking in backbone. There is a difference, however, between a speaker who occasionally crosses individual members and a speaker who fosters widespread and continuing antipathy among many members of the opposite party, while sustaining only lukewarm support within his own. Jim Wright gave the Democrats the kind of forceful leadership that many had sought, and he succeeded in leading a very productive 100th Congress. But along the way he failed to nurture an environment in which his speakership could thrive. Instead, he dissipated his personal and political capital in the single-minded pursuit of his policy goals.

Still, he might have survived as speaker had he not been vulnerable to charges of ethical violations. In the larger scheme of things, the charges against Wright were small potatoes. He may well have been correct in claiming that much of what was alleged against him was not in technical violation of House rules, the amounts of money were small in any case, and there was little demonstrated connection to his role in shaping public policy. Among the most striking aspects of the Wright affair is that one so high could have been brought low by so little. Wright's congressional career was in many respects distinguished. No one doubted his devotion to his country or to the House of Representatives. His accusers were no doubt politically motivated, and it was not apparent that Wright was less honorable or less devoted to the House than the typical Republican. Yet in the end Wright had to resign, and his resignation was, under the circumstances, inevitable. Speaker Wright made his own confession in saying that he had used bad judgment. His speakership was forfeit not just in propitiation of the partisan animosity that led to the charges against him, but in atonement for his having come to symbolize a kind of petty profiteering inconsistent with the dignity of the office of speaker.

Speaker Wright was forced to resign because of the confluence of two factors. His manner of leading the House ran afoul of the spirit of comity that is and will remain essential to its deliberative capacity, and his personal conduct was, although in a rather trivial way, impugnable. Both elements were required. If Wright had not been vulnerable to the ethics charges brought against him, it is unlikely that his Republican opponents could have undermined his support in the Democratic caucus. However, if Wright had led the House differently, neither Republicans nor Democrats would have had a sufficient motive to seek to unseat him.

Wright's fate conflicted with the character of the office in the democratic era. The democratic speakership is policy-oriented, therapeutic, and symbolic. Wright was the most policy-oriented speaker in modern times, but he collided with the therapeutic and symbolic dimensions of the office. This need not have happened. The circumstances in which Wright was forced to resign included the institutional context of the House, the partisan environment, the long period of Democratic hegemony, the Republican frustration to which it gave rise, and Wright's character. Wright's assertive leadership and involvement in policy making were a good thing for his party and for the House; but he could have led the House in a less alienating way. Here we see that policy-making leadership and deliberative leadership are not the same thing. One can provide policy leadership within a party caucus and by using the powers of the chair to drive through a legislative program; but a deliberative leader's job is to foster the conditions under which rational debate over policy can be sustained over time among the assembled representatives. The drive that led Wright to the speakership shaped his conduct in office, and it seems likely that this same drive was related to the way in which he conducted his personal affairs. What is most interesting about the saga of Wright is how very personal the factors that shaped his speakership and led to its tragic end were. Let his case, then, put to rest any lingering belief that the speakership of the House is wholly defined by contextual factors. Who the speaker is makes an enormous difference, as Speaker Wright surely proved.[182]

Wright's resignation was a shattering blow to the House Democratic caucus, but not the only one that it received in May 1989, a black month in the party's history. On May 28, in a related and equally shocking development, House Democratic Whip Tony Coehlo of California announced his intention to resign from the House effective June 15. Coehlo was the subject of allegations about a junk-bond transaction facilitated by the Wall Street firm of Drexel Burnham and Lambert, which had just the previous year been levied over half a billion dollars in fines for insider trading violations. Coehlo had borrowed the money for the investment from a California savings and loan association and had neglected to report it. He had shared Wright's concern about the effects of federal regulation on savings and loans, and as chairman of the Democratic Congressional Campaign Committee in the early 1980s solicited substantial campaign contributions from Drexel Burnham. Facing a protracted investigation similar to that which Speaker Wright had suffered, Coehlo decided to quit.[183]

The resignations of its first and third ranking leaders shook the House Democratic caucus. The normal pattern of leadership succession was thrown into turmoil, the politics of secondary agendas was compacted and distorted. The Democrats understood that it was essential that the party proceed to an orderly election of new leaders, and that the new leaders be untouched by personal scandal. Influential members aspiring to the speakership had to consider whether they wished to have their personal lives made subject to the kind of scrutiny that Wright and Coehlo had suffered. The various ideological and regional factions within the Democratic caucus searched for leadership candidates who would be above reproach. The task was made more complicated by the political climate of the day. Caucus Chairman Bill Gray of Pennsylvania pondered a race for majority leader or whip, but his candidacy was called into question when unsubstantiated leaks suggested a Justice Department investigation into the management of his congressional office. Gray's example illustrated the extreme sensitivity of the ethics issue and its susceptibility to manipulation by political opponents.

From this catharsis a new House leadership team emerged. Majority Leader Thomas S. Foley of Washington was elected speaker on June 6, 1989.[184] A moderate Democrat from a Republican-leaning district in eastern Washington state, Foley had come to the House in 1965 to join the generation of reformers who razed the power structure in the House. In 1975 Foley became the direct beneficiary of the reform movement when the Democratic caucus unseated Agriculture Committee Chairman W. R. Poage of Texas and elected Foley to the post. In 1977 Foley was elected chairman of the Democratic Caucus, and in 1980 he was tapped by Speaker O'Neill to succeed John Brademas as the party's whip. His election as majority leader in 1986 was uncontested.

Tom Foley offered the Democrats much that they needed in their speaker. Mild-mannered and judicious, Foley had on many occasions demonstrated his ability to work with the participatory mechanisms by which the Democrats ran the House in the democratic era. In 1985 he had taken the lead in negotiating the Gramm-Rudman-Hollings Act for

the House Democrats, and in 1987 he was the leader of the House
Democratic team that negotiated a two-year budget agreement with the
Reagan administration and the Senate. While his voting record had
shifted to the left during his years in the Democratic leadership, he
remained moderate in disposition and had established excellent relations
on the Republican side of the aisle. If there was any rap against Tom
Foley, it was that he was sometimes too cautious. It was said of him
that he was a man who saw all three sides to every question. In the
bitter atmosphere in which he was called to the chair, Foley's level-
headed character would be of advantage in restoring comity in the
House. It remained an open question, however, as to whether comity
was in the cards. The thirst for revenge among hard-nosed politicians
is not easily quenched, and there remained many thirsty congressmen
on both sides of the aisle. Tom Foley had the ability to extend the reach
of the democratic speakership; it remained to be seen if the House of
Representatives would give him the opportunity.

As their new majority leader the Democrats elected Richard Gephardt of Missouri.[185] This was an historic twist of fate for him and for
the House of Representatives. First elected to the House in 1976, Gephardt had come to symbolize the new generation of House Democrats.
From his seat on the Ways and Means Committee, and through service
on leadership-appointed task forces and ad hoc committees, Gephardt
had become involved across a wide range of policy areas and had
repeatedly demonstrated his ability to forge consensus within his own
party and, on occasion, across the aisle. His political outlook was that
of a pragmatic progressive, reflecting the orientation of many new members toward the careful construction of public policy. So successful was
his congressional career that in 1984, when he was beginning just his
fifth term in the House, he was elected chairman of the Democratic
caucus. In 1987 he launched a two-year campaign for the presidency,
winning the important Iowa caucuses by a plurality, but withdrawing
after a poor showing in the "Super Tuesday" southern primaries. One
indication of Gephardt's popularity among House Democrats is the fact
that scores of his colleagues endorsed his presidential candidacy in 1988
and worked in their districts on his behalf.[186]

Gephardt was joined in the Democratic leadership by Bill Gray, who
became the first black member of the House to win the position of
party whip.[187] Paralleling the significance of the introduction of a black
man into the leadership was the fact that—for the first time since
Champ Clark, the Democratic leader who opposed Uncle Joe Cannon
in the twentieth century's first decade—the Democratic leadership was
without a southern representative. The leadership elections of Gephardt
and Gingrich accelerated the transfer of power to the new generation of

House members who have come to define the institution during its democratic era.[188] As Gephardt personified the policy-oriented and therapeutic membership on the Democratic side of the aisle, so did Gingrich among the Republican leaders. Together, they indicated a possible new step in the evolution of the speakership.

Conclusion

The conditions surrounding the democratic speakership are increasingly clear. The period of transition from the feudal to the democratic order marked the end of the expansion of the American welfare state. Lyndon Johnson's Great Society was the last gasp of the positive state. The burst of federal regulatory activity in the late 1960s and early 1970s brought an expansion of federal power; but more significantly, it moved the government away from positive spending programs and toward regulatory policy. By 1977 the political tide had already turned against major federal spending initiatives and the expansion of federal regulations. Tax reduction became a cause, and the resources of the federal government would no longer be commensurate with its commitments. In these crucial respects, Ronald Reagan simply furthered a policy agenda that had taken root during the Carter administration. The move "from the positive to the regulatory state" altered the character of legislative politics.[190] The federal budget became the focal point of political debate, and the politics of the budgetary process suppressed much in the way of new spending initiatives. During the Carter and Reagan administrations the Congress was often unable to pass its appropriations bills by the end of the fiscal year, and recourse to omnibus spending bills was common. The budget reconciliation bills were often used to package together changes in basic law. The Congress, an institution by tradition wedded to a piecemeal incrementalism, developed a fondness for legislation in bulk.

Increasingly, the House floor became a center of its action. The more open, democratic, and therapeutic culture opened the door for increased partisanship. In the feudal period, floor consideration usually served to ratify committee bargains; in the democratic period, the floor of the House was often the stage for guerrilla theater. The increasingly common overlap of committee jurisdictions, the vast scope of many major bills, and the culture of a new generation of politically independent and policy-oriented members, combined to make floor management a difficult and politically charged business. The response of the House as an institution, and of the majority Democratic party, was to develop new techniques of floor management through the use of complex rules that often limited the scope of amending activity.

The task of coalition building became much more challenging. It became more difficult for bipartisan coalitions to develop, and increasingly the majority Democrats had to search for majority consensus within their own ranks. This led them to develop new techniques for seeking consensus, techniques that reflected the democratic, symbolic, and therapeutic culture of the Democratic caucus. It is conceivable that House Democrats held more formal and ad hoc meetings from 1977 to 1990 than they did prior to 1977. The constant caucusing, retreating, task-forcing, whipping, prayer-meeting, work-outing, study-grouping, floor-gabbing, ad-hoc-this-ing and rump-group-that-ing that characterized the Democratic caucus reached a level never before seen. When Carl Albert was criticized by the class of 1974 for inadequate communication, he pointed out that he had met more often with the whips and committee chairmen than any speaker before him, but it was not enough. By the end of Tip O'Neill's tenure, Democrats were meeting daily and on any pretext, and still many members complained about inadequate communication. Under Jim Wright, the leadership made more extensive efforts to institutionalize the therapy than had been done under O'Neill, and yet the most common criticism of Wright among Democrats was a lack of consultation.

It was evident that talking was not alone sufficient to govern. The members possessed a desire to communicate, but they were driven by a single common fear: defeat at the polls. Knowing that their every vote had the potential for district discomfort, members became diffident. In the "condition of mere nature," man is driven by fear, especially the fear of violent death (Hobbes, *Leviathan* 1.13). The social-contract thinkers argued that fear would drive men into civil society in order to protect their lives, liberty, and property. The most important property that a member of Congress has is his seat. Hobbes recommended a Leviathan as the solution to the social problem. In the 100th Congress, some members thought that Jim Wright had sought to become a Hobbesian Behemoth. Wright held the support of his members until he threatened their most fundamental political interest, reelection. When the ethics investigation made him a political liability, he was forced to resign.

In order to protect members and win votes, Tip O'Neill and Jim Wright engaged in legislative positioning. On major bills and on politically dangerous amendments to them, the Democratic leadership sought to limit the political damage that the pesky Republicans could cause. The Democrats used their control over the Rules Committee to limit debate and to make politically viable amendments so that Democratic members could show well in their districts. "Give 'em a vote they can go home with" became the motto of the Democratic leadership. When that was not possible, on those occasions when reality visited itself squarely upon the solons, the House would become paralyzed. "We're unable to act." "The House is in disarray." "The election is determining everything that we do." "Everything fell apart." These are the characteristic comments of the democratic period. They are counterpoised by "This speaker is an S.O.B.," which in translation meant that the Democrats had managed to win by using their power in a way that the Republicans did not like. The House was often torn between anarchy and tyranny.

The difficulties that O'Neill and Wright faced were not due only to the culture of the House, the diffidence of its members, and the nature of the policy agenda. The speakership in the democratic period was strongly influenced by its relationship to the presidency. Jimmy Carter and Ronald Reagan did not have anything to do with the intrinsic factors shaping the speakership, but the presidency was the extrinsic force that set the table at which these speakers had to eat. Both the Congress's agenda and the political environment in which it was considered were influenced by the presidency more than any other single factor. From a constitutional point of view, the relationship between the speaker and the president is defined by the speaker's obligation to facilitate congressional consideration of the policy agenda. Tip O'Neill felt compelled to support Jimmy Carter even when he disagreed with his policies, and he acknowledged his obligation to give Ronald Reagan's program its day on the House floor. In the 101st Congress, Speaker Wright made it clear that the House Democrats would provide a fair hearing for the policy initiatives of the Bush administration even while advancing a legislative agenda of their own.

From a political point of view, however, the relationship between the speakership and the presidency is more complex. Speakers are torn three ways, between their own policy preferences (usually reflecting those of their congressional districts), the center of gravity within the party caucus (that other constituency to which speakers must attend), and the pull of the president's program. When the president is of the same party as the speaker, this relationship is smooth only if the president and the speaker are generally in accord on policy and the administration is effective in the art of legislative relations. When this is not the case, as in the relationship between Speaker O'Neill and President Carter, the speaker's job will be difficult. When the president is of the opposite party, the speaker is free to resist. This situation faced Speaker Albert from 1971–76 and Speaker O'Neill from 1981–86. The nature of his opposition will depend upon several factors. One is the president's popularity. It is apparent that Tip O'Neill had a much more difficult time in dealing with Ronald Reagan from 1981 to 1986 than Jim Wright did in 1987 and 1988, simply because Reagan was weakened politically during the 100th Congress. A second factor is the degree of consensus on policy within the speaker's own party. Speaker Albert's task had been made difficult because of the deep rift among House Democrats. O'Neill's options were constrained by the threat of the CDF to bolt to the Republican side. The divisions within the Democratic caucus had been its historical hallmark, but with each succeeding election they diminished as older liberals and conservatives were replaced by a new generation of pragmatic centrists. The Democratic caucuses in the Ninety-ninth and 100th Congresses showed more unity in voting than their predecessors in large part because the members were more unified on policy. A third and vital factor is the speaker's approach to policy making. It makes a difference if the speaker has an agenda of his own and the force of will to pursue it. The main difference between Tip O'Neill and Jim Wright lay in the latter's sometimes obdurate insistence on passing a legislative agenda that was distinctly his own. Tip O'Neill preferred to let consensus gestate; Jim Wright sought to impose it from above. That he had considerable success in doing so in the 100th Congress depended on these things: Reagan was weak, the Democrats were relatively united, and Wright was insistent. Of these factors, only the third was within Wright's power to control.

The differences between Tip O'Neill and Jim Wright, and especially the fate of the latter, remind us forcefully of the personal element to the speakership. Of the two, O'Neill's persona responded better to the therapeutic and symbolic character of the democratic speakership, Wright's to the policy orientation of its members. Yet both were very much the product of the House as it had been shaped by the Democratic party during its long period in the majority. They were Democratic speakers during the democratic era. Speaker Tom Foley differed from both O'Neill and Wright in personality and disposition, but like them he was a product of the culture of the Democratic party. It fell to his lot to perpetuate the Democratic regime while seeking to restore a sense of order and comity to the House. Foley's judicious temperament seemed at the time to be well suited to that challenge. Unfortunately for Speaker Foley, the seeds of discord that had been planted during the 1980s came to full bloom on his watch. Speaker Wright had sown the wind, and Speaker Foley would reap the whirlwind. The former became the first speaker to resign office; the latter became the first since the Civil War to be defeated at the polls. And in 1995 America welcomed, for the first time in the lives of most Americans, a Republican-controlled House of Representatives, led by Speaker Newt Gingrich.

6 ☆ The Republican Speakership

The Demise of the Democratic Regime

Tom Foley took the oath of office as speaker of the House on June 6, 1989. On November 5, 1994, he was defeated for reelection, the first sitting speaker to suffer defeat at the polls since William Pennington in 1860. In a brief, five-year span the House Democrats had suffered the first forced resignation of a speaker and the first electoral defeat of a speaker in 134 years. The resignation of Jim Wright, the defeat of Foley, and the Republican takeover of the House in the 104th Congress reflected an underlying change in American politics and in the House of Representatives. In the 1980s the realignment of the South to the Republican party created more cohesive legislative parties.[1] The Republican party became more conservative and the Democratic party became increasingly dominated by its liberal wing. For the first time in three generations, Congressional Democrats and Republicans on occasion behaved like legislative parties.

Speaker Foley's pacific leadership style was in sharp contrast to that of Jim Wright and was initially warmly welcomed by Democrats and Republicans alike.[2] It appeared for a moment that a semblance of harmony might be restored to the House. The Republicans (and many Democrats) had complained bitterly about Wright's heavy-handed control of the House, and Foley promised to be a more fair-minded and conciliatory leader. If a renewed sense of collegiality and comity had been a high priority for members, then Foley would have been the ideal speaker. However, it soon appeared that comity and collegiality were not high on anyone's agenda. The Republican insurgents, led by Newt Gingrich, had taken a major step toward their goal of capturing control

of the House, but they had not attained that ultimate objective. Foley
was a less vulnerable target but also a less formidable opponent. On the
Democratic side of the aisle, ideological division and factional conflict
soon split the party asunder. It became apparent that unity within the
Democratic caucus had depended precisely on the strong hand Wright
had played. The Democrats were now more vulnerable than ever.

Foley's honeymoon was brief indeed. In September 1989 sixty-four
Democrats defected to vote with the Republicans in support of a capital-
gains tax cut proposed by President Bush.[3] Foley's consensus-building
approach, widely hailed just two months before, was faulted. The
party's defeat on capital gains reflected the underlying political dynamics. The political center of gravity of the American polity had been
steadily shifting to the right. The Republicans attacked moderate and
conservative Democrats in their districts. To survive, these Democrats
had to move toward the center. Jim Wright had held the Democratic
caucus together by controlling the House floor to protect members
against politically threatening votes. In this case Foley was unable to
hold his conservative flank in line and lost on a key vote.

Tom Foley was committed to building consensus within the Democratic caucus, to working with the committee leaders in fashioning
legislation, and to bipartisan cooperation with the House Republicans
and the Bush White House. He wanted to solve problems, to govern by
compromise and consensus.[4] This approach led to several notable
achievements. Foley was able to resolve the lingering issue of member
pay by winning a salary increase in exchange for the elimination of
honoraria. He led the Democrats in the 1990 fiscal summit that
produced the Omnibus Budget Reconciliation Act of 1990, in which
President Bush accepted tax increases as part of a deficit-reduction
package. This agreement was criticized from the left in the Democratic
party and from the right in the Republican party. It was a compromise
package that made substantial inroads in the deficit while protecting
entitlements. It was vintage Foley. Yet in spite of these significant
accomplishments there remained an undertone of doubt about Speaker
Foley's leadership. In 1991 he came under increasing criticism by
Democrats. Ironically, although many Democrats had chafed under
Wright, many now wanted more assertive leadership. Foley was
perceived to be too deferential to committee chairs, insufficiently willing
to make fundamental institutional changes, and too cautious to take
reasonable risks. His conciliating style was useful when protracted
negotiations were needed but a liability when partisan confrontation
occurred or legislative arm-twisting was required. Within the Democratic caucus, Foley's leadership was criticized by liberals who wanted a
more aggressive partisanship and by moderates who wanted more in the

way of institutional reform. The former sought to challenge the Republicans ideologically, the latter to preempt a GOP reform agenda. Foley was insufficiently assertive to satisfy either group.[5]

In these circumstances one of Speaker Foley's real strengths—his willingness to defend the House against its critics—became a liability. The speaker, as Foley later wrote, must "speak for the House."[6] His obligation is to defend its prerogatives and its reputation. In 1991 and 1992 scandal again erupted when it was revealed that scores of members, Democrats and Republicans, had overdrawn their accounts at the House Bank. This institution was on the order of an internal credit union in which members' overdrafts were covered by other members' deposits. Loose administration had enabled some members to extend their credit by tens of thousands of dollars, in effect interest-free loans. Public reaction was predictably negative and the congressional response characteristically defensive. The public saw the bank scandal as simply another example of the members of Congress behaving like a privileged class; the Democratic leadership saw it as providing another opportunity for insurgent Republicans to tar the Democratic majority for simply perpetuating traditional practices. Speaker Foley's initial instinct was to protect the members by withholding full disclosure of their names and the amounts of their overdrafts.[7] Newt Gingrich was in full attack. It made little difference to him that many Republicans were affected; to Gingrich, this was simply a further indication of the manner in which House Republicans had assimilated the culture imposed upon them by the Democrats.

Eventually, Speaker Foley implemented several modest administrative reforms, but the Democratic regime was incapable of fundamentally reshaping the House as it had in the early 1970s.[8] There were now too many entrenched power centers. Ironically, Tom Foley, staunch defender of the House, became a focal point for criticism of it. Nowhere was Speaker Foley's dilemma more clearly defined than on the issue of term limits for members of Congress. The term-limits movement had strong Republican support. In his home state of Washington, voters in 1992 enacted a state law imposing term limits on the state's congressional delegation. Foley opposed term limits in principle and believed that it was unconstitutional for a state to impose limits on the terms of members of Congress. He therefore joined in a legal challenge to the constitutionality of the Washington law. This handed Republicans an issue upon which to challenge him. Tom Foley became the speaker who had sued his own constituents. He was also the leading defender of the status quo.[9]

In spite of these difficulties, Speaker Foley and the Democrats were able to retain control of the House in the 1992 elections despite losing

10 seats to the Republicans. A frustrated electorate denied President Bush a second term in office, giving 19 percent of the vote to independent Ross Perot and electing Arkansas Governor Bill Clinton as president with only 43 percent of the vote. In an election that witnessed the largest turnover in House seats since the New Deal, the Democrats were returned to power with a 258-seat majority that included 63 freshmen members, many of whom had campaigned on behalf of political reform. Seeking to avoid the errors of the Carter administration, Speaker Foley held regional meetings with the freshmen Democrats in which he argued that the message of the election was that the voters wanted an end to governmental gridlock.[10] By uniting behind a policy agenda, the Democrats hoped to earn the confidence of the electorate. Speaker Foley's message was not "To get along, go along" but "Work together, don't rock the boat." The congressional Democrats chose policy over reform. To assuage the reform sentiment, the speaker joined with Senate Majority Leader George Mitchell of Maine to appoint a special joint committee on congressional reform. The committee held hearings in 1993 and 1994, but Congress did not consider its recommendations.[11]

The emphasis on policy instead of reform could succeed only if President Clinton and the congressional Democrats produced substantial legislative accomplishments. The first great legislative battle of the Clinton administration was the president's 1993 budget plan, which sought more than $500 billion in deficit reduction in part by raising marginal tax rates on the wealthy and imposing new taxes on energy and on gasoline at the pump. Faced with unanimous Republican opposition, Clinton was forced to seek the lowest common denominator among Democrats. After a monumental struggle the bill passed the House by just two votes. In the Senate, Vice President Al Gore cast the tie-breaking vote. Although congressional moderates were able to remove some controversial components of the bill, such as a broad-based energy tax, the final bill raised taxes substantially, cut defense by more than the president had proposed in the campaign, and provided red meat for Republican challengers in the 1994 elections. In this, his first major legislative battle, President Clinton governed from the left, alienating support among Democratic centrists in the Congress. Ironically, it was precisely these members who were most vulnerable to Republican attacks.[12]

The second great battle of the Clinton administration was over the president's health-care-reform plan, produced by a task force headed by First Lady Hillary Rodham Clinton. This attempt at comprehensive reform of the health-care system would have affected one-seventh of the American economy and touched the lives of every American. By seeking comprehensive reform Clinton united reform opponents and provided to them a common object of attack. The hospitals, doctors, insurance companies, and pharmaceutical companies opposed the plan for different reasons but to the same purpose—its defeat. Republicans attacked the plan as a form of socialized medicine, a characteristic product of a liberal Democratic administration. At the end of Clinton's first biennium, health-care reform came crashing down as moderate Democrats fled from the Clinton administration.[13]

The battles over the Clinton budget and health-care reform indicated the nature and limits of Speaker Foley's leadership. Working with other Democratic leaders in the House and Senate, the speaker was effective in rallying a congressional majority for the budget bill. It would not have passed but for effective work by the congressional party leadership. Foley had for many years been in the middle of complicated budget negotiations as Democratic whip and majority leader. His style was well-suited to the patient negotiation and horse-trading required by budget politics. Health-care reform was much more complicated. It touched upon the jurisdictions of many House committees and subcommittees. It engendered opposition from entrenched and well-organized interests. Its matrix of policies made logrolling very difficult. In the end, Republican opposition hardened and moderate Democrats had to protect themselves. The failure of the health-care-reform plan was the dénouement of the 103d Congress.

The Democrats had made no progress on campaign-finance reform or institutional reform. Speaker Foley resisted the former reforms because he recognized that the large cohort of freshmen Democrats would need the fundraising advantages afforded to incumbents to get past their first and most critical reelection campaign. Committee chairmen such as Dan Rostenkowski at Ways and Means and John Dingell at Energy and Commerce resisted the latter reforms because they might undermine their power and autonomy. By November 1994 the Democrats had little in the way of achieved reforms to present to the voters, and the policy accomplishments of the 103d Congress lay buried in the rubble of the health-care fiasco. In Washington's Fifth District, Speaker Foley faced a capable and well-financed opponent. As the leader of the House Democrats, he was forced to defend the party position on taxes and health care. As speaker, he had sought to defend the constitutional prerogatives of the House by suing the citizens of Washington over their congressional term-limits law. In the 1994 election Speaker Foley was swept from office along with the Democratic congressional majority, the ultimate casualty of Newt Gingrich's long struggle for power in the House.

Gingrich had always had a single goal: Republican control of the

House of Representatives. In the 1978 election campaign that brought him to the House, he attacked the entrenched Republican leadership as well as that of the Democrats. Instead of following the traditional career path, that is, investing himself in legislative committee work and constituent service, he chose to build a career dedicated to political opposition grounded in organization and ideas. The founding of the Conservative Opportunity Society in 1983 was the first step. It became the vehicle for the Republican C-SPAN strategy and eventual confrontation with Speaker O'Neill (see p. 252). In 1986 Gingrich was invited by Delaware Governor Pete DuPont to chair GOPAC, a political action committee dedicated to the recruitment of Republican candidates for state local offices. Gingrich developed GOPAC into a fundraising machine and a farm team for GOP candidates. During each election cycle from 1988 to 1994, Republican candidates at every level were instructed at GOPAC seminars and inspired by GOPAC audio tapes featuring homilies by Gingrich. GOPAC was the foundation upon which Gingrich rose to the party leadership in 1989. During the 1990 and 1992 election cycles the Democrats clung to their House majority; but on the Republican side, Gingrich gained more and more support. While devoting most of his attention to party building rather than to the traditional legislative role of a party whip, in 1990 he demonstrated his influence by leading a block of Republicans in opposition to the budget agreement President Bush had reached with the Democratic leadership. In 1993 he emerged as the leading Republican strategist in opposing the program of the Clinton administration. In the fall of 1993 Republican Leader Bob Michel announced his intention to retire at the end of the 103d Congress, and Gingrich was his heir apparent. By the summer of 1994 the only question was, would he be speaker or minority leader?

Several factors combined to prepare the ground for the Republican electoral sweep in 1994. The wave of Democratic retirements that had begun in 1992 continued in 1994; there were thus a large number of vulnerable first-term Democrats and Democratic open seats. Voters were fed up with the federal government, especially the Congress. The Republican attacks on the Democrats had been buttressed by independent presidential candidate Ross Perot's antipolitics campaign in 1992; Perot called for the election of Republicans in 1994. The Republicans had recruited candidates to challenge Democratic incumbents in a large number of districts, especially first-term and southern Democratic members. Disaffection with the Clinton administration led to increased campaign contributions by business groups. Thus, the conditions were ripe for the Republicans to elect a House majority for the first time since the election of 1952.[14]

It is to Newt Gingrich's credit, however, that the Republicans were able to capitalize on the opportunity. First, he had articulated the ideological ground on which the 1994 election was fought. The election became a referendum on the Democratic party and its control of the government. It became a philosophical contest between the Republicans, as the party of smaller government and less taxation, and the Democrats, as the party of more government and higher taxation. Second, Gingrich had orchestrated the Republican campaign in every aspect, including candidate recruitment and training, issue articulation, and fundraising. Third, Gingrich had forged a unity of purpose among incumbent Republicans and Republican challengers. He insisted that the incumbents raise money in support of challengers, making their support a precondition of their role in a Republican House administration. Finally, Gingrich led the GOP leadership in developing the Contract With America legislative agenda for the 104th Congress, providing both an electoral platform and a governing program. When the 1994 election results were in, the Republicans had swept to a 230-seat House majority, had recaptured the Senate, and had captured many state legislative seats. Strikingly, not a single Republican incumbent was defeated in any national or state legislative race in 1994.

The GOP Regime

How would the first Republican majority in forty years govern the House?[15] The party's historical tendency has been toward more centralized party leadership than the Democrats can typically sustain. During the 80th and 83d Congresses Speaker Martin evoked something of Sam Rayburn's demeanor, but the Republicans ran the House according to customary practices dating back to Speaker Longworth (see pp. 120–25). Republican speakers from Blaine to Longworth had led more centralized party regimes than had any Democratic speaker. So it was unsurprising that Speaker Gingrich sought to impose more centralized leadership, but the extent of the Republican transformation of the House was nonetheless remarkable. Under Gingrich's leadership the Republicans sought to dismantle entirely the power structure the Democrats had put in place during their forty years of uninterrupted control and to replace it with new mechanisms that reflected the culture and values of the Republican party. Gingrich's goal in organizing the House during the 104th Congress was to refashion its culture thoroughly. From the committee system to the House's administrative apparatus to the seniority rule to the informal caucuses to the culture of the Republican conference, Gingrich sought to root out every vestige of the Democratic regime and to replace it with a new Republican regime that would be as lasting as the Democrats' had been.[16]

The new leadership team was centered in the Speaker's Advisory Committee (SAG), which included the elected party leadership (Majority Leader Dick Armey of Texas, Whip Tom DeLay of Texas, Conference Chair John Boehner of Ohio, and Campaign Committee Chair Bill Paxon of New York) and was chaired by Gingrich ally Robert Walker of Pennsylvania. The concept of a leadership steering committee had deep roots in the Republican conference, dating back to the Longworth regime in the 1920s. Every Republican majority since has utilized some variation of this committee. The Republican leadership also implemented a coordinated staff structure within the leadership and between the leadership and the committee staffs, reducing the potential for factionalism within the party. Paralleling the coordinated staff system was a coordinated public-relations effort led by the speaker's press secretary and communications director and extending to communications directors in all Republican congressional offices. The Republican communications operation paralleled that of the White House and far transcended those of previous speakers.[17]

The Republicans eliminated three committees (Merchant Marine and Fisheries, District of Columbia, and Post Office and Civil Service) and renamed several others (e.g., Education and Labor became Education and Educational Opportunities, Armed Services became National Security, and Public Works and Transportation became Transportation and Infrastructure). Committee staffs were reduced by one-third, and the leadership asserted a voice in the selection of key committee staff members. The Republicans revamped their committee-assignment process. James R. Mann's burdensome and decentralized committee on committees (see pp. 99–101) was replaced with a new committee on which the speaker directly or indirectly controlled one-fourth of the votes.[18] The Democratic regime had become root-bound in the committees. Committee chairs regularly frustrated party leaders. Powerful Democratic speakers such as Sam Rayburn and Tip O'Neill had survived by working with, rather than running over, the barons. The decentralization wrought by the reforms of the 1970s had weakened the committee chairs only to strengthen the hand of subcommittee chairs. Still, some powerful committee chairs had stood in the path of Speaker Foley's limited reform agenda.

Speaker Gingrich was determined to ensure that no committee or sub-committee chair could impede the party agenda. In nominating committee chairs, the committee on committees had skipped seniority in three cases (naming Henry Hyde of Illinois at Judiciary, Robert Livingston of Louisiana at Appropriations, and Thomas Bliley of Virginia at Commerce). By skipping seniority in these three instances he sent a message to all members that the seniority rule was no longer inviolate.[19] The Democrats had on occasion unseated senior members from chairmanships, but only by a vote of the caucus. The party leadership had always supported the seniority rule and had defended senior members against insurgent challenges. In the 104th Congress such decisions were made by the speaker. Gingrich also insisted on three-term limits for committee chairs (accepting a four-term limit for the speaker). Proxy voting in committees, a major source of power for the chair, was eliminated. The reduction in committee staffs struck at the heart of committee power because the scope of committee activity is delimited by its resources. Smaller and more cohesive committee staffs working in cooperation with an enlarged leadership staff afford more control to the party leadership. Furthermore, the elimination of three committees served to consolidate committee jurisdictions. The committees that were eliminated had strong ties to traditionally Democratic interest groups (federal workers, maritime unions, civil rights groups). Congressional committee power is grounded in interest-group links; narrow committee jurisdictions lead to stronger linkages. By transferring the jurisdictions of these three committees to other committees of more general jurisdiction the Republicans diluted the influence of some Democratic interest groups in the committee system.

The organizational changes facilitated the imposition of a leadership program that undermined the roles of the committees even further. The initial agenda for the 104th Congress was, of course, the Contract With America. Determined to enact the Contract's provisions by the self-imposed 100-day deadline, Speaker Gingrich and SAG turned to a series of party task forces to develop legislation on Contract items and other major issues, such as the budget, Medicare reform, and congressional reform. These task forces drew their membership from among the relevant congressional committees but included other members as well. External advisers and interest-group representatives participated in task-force deliberations. The task forces effectively supplanted the committees as drafters of Contract legislation. Although precedent existed for ad hoc committees to develop legislation (see pp. 202 and 217), and although the two parties had each used intraparty task forces to help pass or defeat legislation on the floor (see p. 224), the use of party task forces to draft legislation at the expense of the authorizing committees was without precedent. The committee reforms, the staff reductions, and the undermining of seniority all aimed at transforming an entrenched committee structure; the use of the task forces aimed at circumventing the committee process altogether.

The committees are the repositories of congressional expertise. In defending the use of task forces, Speaker Gingrich offered an alternative theory of expertise grounded in contemporary management theories that favor flexible and adaptable organizational arrangements.[20] He argued that the task forces combined the expertise of members from several committees along with that of staff and lobbyists. Of course, only Republican committee members, Republican staff, and sympathetic lobbyists were included in task-force deliberations. Here lay the real reason for bypassing the committees: they included Democrats, and Speaker Gingrich was determined to impose his agenda by means of a unified party majority rather than a bipartisan coalition. He did not want the Democrats to have an opportunity to dilute the legislation or disrupt the party program. In fact, Gingrich's goal was to destroy the organizational foundation of Democratic power in the House. The reduction of committee staff combined with turnover in committee ratios to throw thousands of experienced Democratic staffers out of work. The elimination of special-interest caucuses (legislative service organizations, or LSOs) further eroded the foundations of the Democratic power structure and attacked its premise directly. By defunding LSOs such as the congressional black and Hispanic caucuses and the venerable Democratic Study Group, the Republicans sought to impede communications and the flow of information between their adversaries. They also called into question the essence of the Democratic regime, its reliance on decentralized power rooted in constituency support. Of course, the Republicans were no less beholden to special interests than the Democrats, but Gingrich sought to ensure that Republican interest-group links would be to the party leadership.

In abolishing the Democratic power structure the Republicans sought also to erode its cultural foundations. Gingrich understood that political parties are cultures and that the majority party will impose its culture on the institution. The longer the party is in power, the more deeply ingrained its culture will become in the institution, and the Democrats had been in the majority for a very long time. Essential to Gingrich's understanding of the cultural foundations of power was the perception that the minority party absorbs the dominant culture and comes to embrace it. In Gingrich's view, the congressional "norms" described in textbooks about Congress, such as comity, reciprocity, deference, specialization, and logrolling, were not the natural tendencies of a legislative body but products of the culture of the Democratic party. Deeply divided between its southern and northern wings, between liberals and conservatives, between hawks and doves, and between rural and urban areas, the Democrats had found it necessary to develop norms that permitted intraparty accommodation. The Republicans, shut out of power, had adopted those norms in order to function within the Democratic power structure. But by assimilating the culture of the Democratic party, the Republicans had made it difficult to effectively challenge the Democrats at the polls. Gingrich's attacks on the Democratic power structure constituted a cultural onslaught that inevitably addressed both individual and institutional practices. In reshaping the culture of the House on Republican values, Gingrich sought to refashion behavior as well as to reshape institutions.[21]

This effort embodied the therapeutic tendencies of modern culture, which permeated the management theories to which Gingrich subscribed. From the beginning he had been the most therapeutic of the new generation of Republicans. His leadership motto—Listen, learn, help, lead—is taken directly from contemporary management theory. His leadership theory—vision, strategies, projects, tactics—is taken from military command doctrine. The two bodies of theory are in fact closely related because they stress group cohesion as the critical component of collective action. Since the electoral incentives of members of Congress often divide them (just as soldiers in the field have a naturally occurring incentive to cut and run), group cohesion depends upon the culture of the organization, which shapes attitudes and perceptions. The role of the leader is not simply to command but to nurture a climate of reciprocal feelings in which collective action becomes possible. Leadership on this model is less transactional and more integrative. Thus, Speaker Gingrich rarely chairs a meeting, preferring to sit among the members and listen to what they have to say. He is the therapist who listens; they are the patients who talk. When he finally talks they are prepared to listen.

The Republican reforms extended to the administrative apparatus of the House, long a bastion of Democratic patronage and a deep reflection of Democratic culture. The scandals that rocked the House in the early 1990s revealed the rot. When the Republicans took control of House administration they moved quickly to transform it. Realizing immediately that most of the apparatus was beyond repair, they treated it in the manner of the Iraqi army during the Persian Gulf War: they cut it off and killed it. Instead of preserving, they eliminated; instead of reforming, they privatized. The post office, the Folding Room, the barber and beauty shops, and the shoeshine booths were privatized. Ice delivery to members' offices was eliminated. The House Printer office was abolished. Fire sales of surplus furniture and equipment brought in hundreds of thousands of dollars. A warehouse was then sold. The Office of Doorkeeper was eliminated. The Office of Clerk was reduced by 90 percent and restricted to the management of legislative process. The Office of Sergeant at Arms was professionalized. The House Administration Committee, long a bastion of patronage and political favoritism, was renamed as the Oversight Committee and stripped of its power. Twelve layers of House administration were reduced to two. The new

Office of Chief Administrator was created, reporting directly to the speaker. A professional audit of House operations conducted by Price Waterhouse found the House management system to be the most inefficient organization Price had ever examined, with management practices and ledger-keeping dating to the Continental Congress. Price recommended more than two hundred management reforms. An automated financial system was put in place, and the first inventory of the House was conducted. The operation of the House was reconceptualized on a business model, with each office treated as a small business and given a "representational allowance" and flexibility in regard to its expenditure. Allocation of House resources was no longer to be based on political preference.[22]

These changes met with some resistance from more senior members on both sides of the aisle, but the momentum of reform and the commitment of the speaker carried the day. Opposition to administrative reform was deeply rooted in the culture of the Democratic party and of the House that the Democrats had shaped. It was also a reflection of the electoral needs of all members. Among the first substantive laws enacted by the Republican-controlled 104th Congress was a provision to apply all laws passed by the Congress to itself. Congress had exempted itself from such basic laws as those affecting equal employment opportunity, racial and sexual harassment, and occupational health and safety. The justification lay putatively in the constitutional separation of powers: these laws were enforced by the executive branch and adjudicated by the judiciary. In reality, the congressional exemptions from them were grounded in political expediency: the members did not want to become vulnerable to embarrassing investigations and allegations. Similarly, the resistance of some members to administrative reform indicated lingering concern that there should be some allowance for political considerations and the belief that in a representative assembly the members were sovereign, their needs paramount.

The administrative apparatus adopted by the Republicans transferred the locus of power away from the individual members and their committees to the party leadership. It would be the speaker who would ultimately resolve the tensions between political and managerial needs. While the number of House officers reporting directly to the speaker declined (for all of his concern for management, Gingrich did not like to manage), the power of the speakership was greatly enhanced. Under the Democrats, chairs such as Wayne Hays of Ohio and Charlie Rose of North Carolina could establish independent power bases at House Administration and frustrate the party leadership. Gingrich sought to avoid this.

The Republican regime demonstrated a remarkable unity of purpose. Not all Republicans supported all aspects of it. Many believed that the intrusions on the committee system had gone too far (especially through the task forces). Others disliked the new administrative apparatus. Some were offended by the degree of power asserted by SAG. A few distrusted Gingrich. Still, the Republicans clung together as the Democrats never could, uniting to reform the House and to pass the Contract With America. In the 104th Congress the average GOP party unity score on floor votes was 91 percent in 1995 and 87 percent in 1996; the average Democratic party unity score was 80 percent in both years.[23] The trend toward greater party unity that had begun in the mid-1980s was accelerated. This was just as Speaker Gingrich would have had it. His goals were to control the House and impose a responsible party regime on it. The best measure of his success was not the behavior of Republicans but the behavior of Democrats. Republicans had sometimes tended to act like a political party; the Democrats rarely had. Minority leader Dick Gephardt inherited a relatively united Democratic caucus. He owed this to the Democrats' nemesis, Newt Gingrich.

Speaker Gingrich

Newt Gingrich is a man of many parts. He is a historian who fits contemporary events into broad historical cycles. He is a teacher who purveys his particular conception of history to students. He is a futurist, a devotee of Alvin Toffler, who envisions the House of Representatives as a model for twenty-first-century legislatures. He is a military strategist who sees politics as a genre of war. His strategies are influenced by the United States Army's Training and Doctrine (TRADOC) approach (he utilized Pentagon congressional fellows to conduct "after-action reviews" of key House votes). He is a devotee of contemporary management theories such as those of W. Edwards Deming and Peter Drucker and seeks to impose business theories on political organizations. He is an ideologue who motivates supporters by stirring their passions. He is a novelist who grounds narratives in a sweeping view of history. He is a cultural figure who condenses meaning: he symbolizes the best of American politics to his supporters and the worst to his detractors. He is the most complex person to have served as speaker of the House, and his speakership reflects the complexity of his persona.[24]

Newt Gingrich has devoted his life and his career to a single-minded pursuit of power in the House. His goal has been to transform American politics. He has always been a politician. Among his many role models is Benjamin Disraeli, who recast English conservatism, rebuilt the Tory party, and reshaped British politics in the nineteenth century. Disraeli had a grand vision for England, and he understood that to realize that vision it was necessary for his party to seize and hold power. In the

1840s he organized a philosophical movement, Young England, which preached a new conservative populism aimed at winning support from the rising bourgeoisie. In the 1850s he fought from the back bench for control of the party. In the 1860s he emerged as its leader and put in place a new party organization. He supported electoral reform in order to place his party on the winning side of an inevitable historical movement. In the 1870s his party won control of Parliament, and he became prime minister. He ushered in a new era of Tory domination of British politics that came to full fruition only after his death.[25]

Gingrich's career has been inspired by just such a grand vision. Among American speakers only Henry Clay had similarly sweeping goals. Clay was a great national leader who transcended the speakership that he shaped. Newt Gingrich has sought to have an enduring impact on the American political system. He has conceived of himself as an institution builder whose measure of success will lie less in winning the political battle of the day than in refashioning the way the war is fought. He has sought to recreate American politics along lines of party responsibility, in the process establishing the Republican party as the natural majority party during the next era in American history. It is unusual for a speaker to be guided by such a grand historical vision, but to suggest that Speaker Gingrich is abnormal is to presuppose an institutional normality that he rejects. In his view, institutions are what leaders make them to be. Gingrich has aimed to reshape the House in his image rather than to be shaped by it.

The speakership Newt Gingrich created in the 104th Congress was a mirror image of his persona. It was expansive and complicated and extended its reach far beyond the House of Representatives. Previous speakers were, in Tip O'Neill's phrase, men of the House; Newt Gingrich was not. For him, winning the speakership was neither the culmination of his life's ambition nor the principal goal of his political career. Gingrich built his career in the House, and this led him to the speakership. But unlike his Democratic predecessors, Gingrich did not seek simply to fill the speakership for as long as possible; he sought to use the speakership to further his larger ambition. He expanded the office inside and outside of the House.

The Gingrich organization was rooted in Georgia's Sixth Congressional District. His local organization was linked to the district office in Washington, which in turn was connected to the solar system of the speakership. At the center of that solar system was the staff of the speaker's office, coordinating with those of the majority leader, the majority whip, the Republican conference, and the Republican National Campaign Committee. The leadership's unified staff coordinated the activities of committee staffs.[26] SAG advised the speaker on policy and political decisions. The speaker's communications office coordinated the Republican message with member communications staffs. Party legislative task forces were appointed by the speaker and coordinated by leadership staff. The chief administrator, clerk, sergeant at arms, and counsel reported to the speaker. There were some tensions between the speaker's staff and those of other party leaders, committee chairs, and members. The leadership occasionally acted by fiat. Coordination sometimes broke down. In terms of simple span of control, there was too much for the speaker to superintend. Still, by any historical comparison, the Republican regime was more unified and coordinated than any previous administration in the history of the House, and the speaker had more organizational control than any speaker since Cannon.

This extensive House infrastructure was simply one aspect of an acronymic political universe extending well beyond Capitol Hill. Much of it was put in place before Gingrich became speaker. He had his own political action committee, the Monday Morning Club, through which he raised money for member campaigns. He resigned the chairmanship of GOPAC but retained influence over it. He worked closely with conservative activist Paul Weyrich in establishing the Free Congress Project (FCP) and its progeny, National Empowerment Television (NET), a network devoted to the conservative movement. He founded the Progress and Freedom Foundation (PFF), his own think tank, which sponsored distribution of videos of his college lectures through the Mind Extension University (MEU). He started Earning By Learning (EBL), a private organization to promote literacy by paying children to read books. He controlled the Abraham Lincoln Opportunity Foundation (ALOF), whose original charter was charitable but through which he sponsored two television series, American Citizens Television (ACT) and American Opportunities Workshop (AOW), which aimed at promoting conservative activism. ALOF was funded largely through GOPAC, a subject of later ethics allegations. He launched the American Campaign Academy (ACC), which was designed to promote political participation. He was closely (although not officially) connected to the Citizens for Tax Justice, the Christian Coalition, and the world of conservative talk radio and its leader, Rush Limbaugh.

Newt Gingrich's political universe is as multifaceted as his character; one finds an organization for each of his indulgences. He produced a continuous flow of ideas, and then he created organizations to implement them. He is at the center of a universe that he created. Its core is his core. But what is to be found there? An interpretation of previous speakerships traces its path to their districts and local constituencies, and from there to a seat in the House and finally a place on the leadership ladder. Thus, Sam Rayburn, John McCormack, Carl Albert, Tip

O'Neill, Jim Wright, and Tom Foley grew up in or near the congressional districts they came eventually to represent, rooted their political careers in native soil, transplanted them to the House of Representatives, and nurtured them there over a prolonged period of time by adapting to the congressional milieu. Newt Gingrich's career was entirely different. He transplanted himself into a self-selected district, overcame its local culture in his third run for office, refused to assimilate the culture of the House once he got there, and in fact built his career by seeking to destroy it. He was a weed in the congressional garden.

Gingrich has always sought to impose himself upon institutions rather than to allow institutions to impose themselves upon him. In his second year at West Georgia State College he proposed himself as president of the college: the place needed to be transformed. When he arrived in the House of Representatives he sought to shake up the Republican conference: it needed revitalization. The instinct to create or reshape institutions is central to his nature. The institutional arrangements he has sought have reflected his persona and have served his interests. The various presentations of self—the warrior, the ideologue, the scholar, the futurist—have been but manifestations of the underlying drive to impose upon the political system the kind of politics at which Newt Gingrich excels: adversarial, party politics. This brand of politics demands ideologically coherent and organizationally unified political parties led by politicians who see politics as a kind of war. It demands allies and adversaries. Politics is a Manichean struggle between good and evil, between us and them. As Gingrich likes to put it, politics is a team sport, and the question should be, whose side are you on?

This conception of politics involves a different perspective on the role of the legislative party and its leadership, and a different role for the speakership, than that upon which the Democratic House was built. Internally divided, the Democrats sought to soften partisan edges. Gingrich's conception embraces partisanship and accepts bipartisanship only on terms that are favorable to his party. It requires a mind-set that places the interest of the party above the autonomy of the member. It rejects norms of reciprocity, deference, and comity when adherence to them sacrifices the party interest. It echoes the Republican doctrine of Reed, Cannon, and Longworth, but those earlier Republican speakers rested their theories of party governance on a political doctrine of majority rule, and not on organizational theories that stress group cohesion and integrative management. Speaker Gingrich proposed to go farther than any of his Republican predecessors. He sought not only to impose a system of party governance, but also to establish a new culture among House Republicans and eventually among all members. This gestalt (or in military parlance, "command doctrine") would guide the party and reshape the culture of the House. It would ingrain a new understanding of the character of the House and a new way of resolving conflict within it. Under the Democratic gestalt, conflict was resolved by seniority, reciprocity, logrolling, and committee and subcommittee autonomy. Getting along and going along usually meant supporting the committee or subcommittee chair. Under the GOP gestalt, a member might still be expected to get along by going along, but as a member of the party team. Thus, Gingrich's goal was to fundamentally change the character of the House as a legislative institution. Newt Gingrich's contribution to American political science was to provide an experiment in party government of the House of Representatives in an era when political parties are in many respects weaker than at any time in American history. That experiment took place in the 104th Congress, the Congress of the Republican revolution.

The Republican Revolution

The centerpiece of the Republican revolution in the 104th Congress was, of course, the Contract With America.[27] Crafted initially as an election-year campaign platform, the Contract provided a blueprint for the new GOP majority during the first four months of 1995, which the Republicans called the "Contract period." The specific provisions of the Contract were selected because polling and focus group data had indicated their broad public support. They included requiring Congress to abide by all laws that it imposes on everyone else, a limit on unfunded federal mandates to the states, a statutorily imposed and limited line-item veto for the president, enactment of a balanced-budget amendment to the Constitution, a crime bill, welfare reform, child-support legislation, a child tax credit, restricting U.N. authority over U.S. troops, increasing earnings limits for social security recipients, a reduction in the capital-gains tax, tort reform, and congressional term limits. The Republicans were committed to floor votes on these issues. To translate the Contract into law, Gingrich appointed a series of Republican task forces that eventually produced thirty-one separate pieces of legislation. Task-force bills were pushed through the committees and to the House floor before the 100-day deadline. Eventually, all Contract bills except congressional term limits passed in the House, with the Republicans nearly unanimous in support of them. On April 7, 1995, Speaker Gingrich punctuated House completion of the Contract with an unprecedented national television address outlining the Republican legislative agenda and vision for the future. The speaker had become premier, but only of the House. In the Senate, resistance by Democrats and some moderate Republicans slowed the pace of the GOP revolution, defeating the balanced-budget amendment and proceeding slowly on other Contract bills. By the summer of 1995 only five Contract provisions had cleared the Congress and only three had been enacted into law.[28]

While the Senate dawdled on the Contract, the House moved on to other major issues, including a seven-year balanced-budget plan, Medicare reform, telecommunications reform, and agricultural-crop-subsidy reform. In approaching several of these issues, Gingrich once again chose to appoint task forces instead of relying on committees. He was determined to ensure that the party program would not be held up in the committee rooms. Gingrich himself headed Republican efforts to shape a balanced-budget plan and to reform Medicare. In the spring and summer of 1995 the speaker was at the apex of power and influence. He was able to bypass legislative committees at will, major bills were drafted in his office, the Rules Committee was used to refashion bills produced by committees and to add substantive riders to appropriations bills, and members were disciplined for opposing leadership initiatives. Gingrich demonstrated a mastery of complicated policy issues, a remarkable ability to negotiate compromises within the party and between the Republicans and external interest groups, and a sure-footed grasp of the political ramifications of the Republican program.[29]

The Democrats were distraught. The Republican juggernaut denied them any meaningful role in shaping legislation. Although the Republicans issued fewer restrictive rules for floor legislation than had been customary for the Democrats, they imposed time limits on debate that effectively constrained the Democrats' ability to offer amendments. And when votes were taken the Republican majority voted in unison. Having watched helplessly as the GOP dismantled the power structure that had sustained them in office, the Democrats now suffered as the Republicans sought to reduce or dismantle federal programs the Democrats had put in place. Democratic frustration led to angry outbursts in the committee rooms, on the floor, and in the hallways. From the Democrats' point of view, the Republican program went far beyond policy correction; it aimed at eroding the social safety net and destroying the legislative process. If, as Woodrow Wilson held as far back as 1885, congressional government is committee government, then congressional government was at an end. In its place was government by majority party fiat.

Helpless in policy and procedural struggles, the Democrats attacked at the only vulnerable point, bringing ethics charges against Gingrich himself. Gingrich had been Jim Wright's principal accuser, and the Democrats were not reluctant to deal with him in kind. Led by Party Whip David Bonior of Michigan, the Democrats attacked Gingrich relentlessly, eventually bringing seventy-four charges to the bipartisan House Committee on Standards of Official Conduct (Ethics Committee) and raising a steady drumbeat of criticism on the House floor. The charges covered a spectrum of alleged abuses of House rules and campaign-law violations. In essence, Gingrich was accused of commingling political and nonpolitical organizational structures and functions in order to raise money for his various projects by circumventing House rules, federal campaign-finance laws, and federal tax law. Organizations such as GOPAC, PPF, NET, ALOF, and ACC formed a set of interlocking directorates under Gingrich's influence or control. The question confronting the Ethics Committee was, did these complex arrangements violate House rules or public law? The committee quickly became divided along partisan lines. Finally, in late 1995 it appointed an independent counsel to investigate several of the charges. The appointment of a special counsel put the charges against the speaker on a procedural back burner, but on the House floor the Democrats continued to keep the heat on.[30]

In the fall of 1995 congressional and public attention focused on the struggle between the Republican Congress and the Clinton White House over the budget. The House and Senate had adopted (at Gingrich's insistence) a seven-year plan to balance the federal budget. The GOP budget included $270 billion in Medicare savings to extend the program's solvency and an additional $170 billion in Medicaid cost savings. The Republicans also proposed $245 billion in tax cuts, that included a $500 child tax credit, repealing the increased tax rates in the Democrats' 1993 budget bill, and a reduction in the capital-gains tax. This policy mix enabled the Democrats to claim that the Republicans aimed to impose benefit reductions for elderly and poor people while offering tax savings to the rich. President Clinton, by contrast, proposed to balance the budget over nine years while imposing fewer than half the spending reductions and offering fewer than half the tax reductions sought by the Republicans.[31]

From October 1995 through April 1996 Speaker Gingrich and GOP Senate Majority Leader Robert Dole of Kansas, the front-runner for the party's presidential nomination, led Republican negotiators in talks with the White House over the terms of a budget agreement. The legislative vehicles for the budget debates were the budget reconciliation bill that embodied the Republican's seven-year balanced-budget plan, a series of continuing resolutions to keep the government running after the end of the fiscal year on September 30, and bills extending the government's ability to borrow money by raising the debt ceiling. The congressional politics was convoluted. In the House, Republican deficit hawks and tax cutters were at odds on policy. Conservative ideologues sought to use the mandatory bills to enact pet legislation. In the Senate, Republican moderates sought to maintain a higher level of social spending than the House proposed. Democrats in both chambers opposed the Republican program, leading to near party-line voting. At the other end of Pennsylvania Avenue, President Clinton wielded the veto pen. By January 1996 Clinton had vetoed six budget bills, and substantial parts of the federal government had been shut down for more than three weeks.[32]

The budget impasse, and not the Contract With America, was the defining event of the 104th Congress. At its outset the Republicans took advantage of their electoral momentum to reform the House, to pass almost all of the Contract on the floor, and to move forward on other significant legislation, such as telecommunications reform. At its end Republicans and Democrats compromised in enacting welfare reform, an increase in the minimum wage, and other legislation. But for the seven-month period from October 1995 to April 1996 the deadlock on the budget dominated congressional and public attention. And it is here that we find the critical decision of Newt Gingrich's speakership.

Republican speakerships typically assert the principle of party responsibility, and Republican speakers have to figure out how far they can push it. Gingrich had taken advantage of the very unusual circumstances surrounding his election as speaker to establish a more secure foundation of institutional power than had been enjoyed by any speaker since Cannon. His goal was to use his power base and new-found public reputation to revolutionize American politics and public policy. He recognized that it would take many years for the Republicans to consolidate their power and implement their programs, but he believed that the momentum of the 1994 election offered an opportunity to build a long-term GOP majority on the footings of an initial victory on the budget. Ronald Reagan had expressed his great insight by a simple metaphor. The federal government, he had often said, is like a child; if you want to teach it responsibility, you must reduce its allowance. Reagan had succeeded in cutting the federal government's allowance, but in the House of Representatives Tip O'Neill and the Democrats had been able to sustain federal spending programs they believed in. In order to finally lock in place a policy revolution it was necessary to enforce a balanced budget. Gingrich set as the most important Republican goal in the 104th Congress the enactment of a seven-year balanced budget scored by the Congressional Budget Office.

The initiative for a balanced budget would come from the House, and then it would require Senate concurrence and finally President Clinton's signature. The Democrats had sufficient votes to sustain presidential vetoes. Gingrich had to plan a strategy that would begin with a House bill and end with a presidential signature. In developing this strategy, he made two assumptions: first, that the House would have to compromise its position with both the Senate and the president, and second, that it was in the president's interest to sign a balanced-budget agreement into law. His strategy was to develop a House bill with large tax reductions (initially $345 billion) and substantial cuts in Medicare ($270 billion) and Medicaid ($170 billion), with the intention of compromising along the path to a balanced budget that President Clinton would sign.[33]

Gingrich's assumption that Clinton would eventually compromise with the Republican Congress was grounded in a political and personal assessment of President Clinton. The political assessment suggested that Clinton's most secure path to reelection was to move to the center and present himself as a leader who could work with an opposition Congress to enact a fiscally responsible budget. The attainment of a budget agreement would leave the Republican presidential nominee with no issue upon which to challenge him. The personal assessment was that Clinton was a politician who was adaptable to circumstances. He had run as a centrist to avoid being labeled a liberal (as Democratic nominees Mondale and Dukakis had been). Once elected, he had been dragged to the left by the Democratic congressional leadership, leading to the debacle of 1994. With a conservative Republican majority in Congress, he would be pulled back to the center and would agree to some modified version of the GOP budget. These political incentives would eventually be catalyzed by the various triggering mechanisms in the budget process. The government had to be funded, and until the budget was balanced the debt ceiling had to be raised. On several occasions in the 1980s the government had been shut down for brief periods when a Republican White House had played an end game with a Democratic Congress. In the 104th Congress the two parties' institutional positions were reversed but the game was the same, and it would likely yield the same result: first conflict, then compromise. This, at least, was Gingrich's calculation.

It was not, however, how the game played out. In December and January the budget impasse led to two partial government shutdowns lasting more than three weeks total. At each step the House Republicans sought to impose their policy preferences on the administration, and President Clinton stood firm against them. The congressional Republicans moved substantially toward the center, halving their proposed tax cut and reducing Medicare savings. Even these concessions were resisted in the Republican conference. By defining the House GOP position on terms initially acceptable to the conference's most zealous members, including the seventy-three freshmen, Gingrich created a severe constraint on his ability to bargain. In setting his goal of a seven-year balanced budget in stone, he had established a benchmark against which

GOP conservatives would measure any compromise. The two sides engaged in more than fifty hours of negotiations prior to and during the shutdowns, to no avail. President Clinton, it turned out, did not want a deal.

After the 1994 election President Clinton had two paths to reelection. He could work with the Republican Congress in order to present himself to the voters as a centrist president working effectively with a Republican Congress; this was the path Gingrich assumed Clinton would take. Or he could run against the Republican Congress, defining it as too extreme and presenting himself as Horatius at the bridge. This path would ally Clinton with the congressional Democrats with whom he had fallen in 1994. Newt Gingrich had proven himself to be an extraordinary party builder and a shrewd tactician. His political instincts were normally well honed. In this instance, however, he misread the political situation. Newt Gingrich thought that Bill Clinton's best strategy was to act like George Bush, conciliating the Congress and cutting a deal. Bill Clinton concluded that his best strategy was to act like Harry Truman, castigating the Congress and running against it. Bush had lost and Truman had won. Indeed, when Bush had proposed to cut a deal with congressional Democrats in 1990 Gingrich had opposed him and led the opposition among Republicans. Gingrich's position in 1990 had been that Bush needed to define the differences between Republicans and Democrats; now he expected Clinton to blur those differences by compromising. Later Clinton did move to the center, coopting potentially Republican political space; but first he chose to define the House Republicans as extremists. To do so he needed visible evidence of extreme Republican behavior. The government shutdown handed him just the evidence he needed. Clinton was able to capture the passion of the Republican revolution and turn it against the Republicans. In the middle of the shutdown, as public opinion turned against the GOP and the Senate caved in, Gingrich realized his mistake. The shutdown had to end.

However, many Republicans, especially the freshmen, remained intransigent. In order to turn them around Gingrich engaged in a brilliant feat of legislative leadership, conducting a full day of meetings with various elements of the conference and concluding near midnight after a three-hour meeting of the full conference. The next day, he called the conference together and announced that the government was going to be reopened and that the only condition would be that President Clinton submit a seven-year balanced-budget plan. This, the speaker knew, the president was prepared to do. Any House Republican that disagreed was free to challenge him as speaker. Any House Republican that did not vote with the party leadership should look for no future favors. With only fifteen dissenting Republican votes, the House voted to end the shutdown on January 26, 1996.[34]

In this episode the contours of Newt Gingrich's speakership are revealed. We observe the position of institutional strength from which he proceeded; it was the House Republicans who set the terms of the debate. We see the unity in the Republican conference that enabled it to make a balanced budget the centerpiece of federal policy. We also witness the ideological divisions within the Republican party that eventually constrained it. We find Speaker Gingrich following a legislative strategy in pursuit of his larger political goals, employing all of the skills that enabled him to lead the GOP to power in the House. We also encounter the two main constraints that the constitutional system imposes upon the speakership: bicameralism and the separation of powers. For Newt Gingrich could not, in the end, govern the country from the speakership because the Senate and President Clinton would not allow it.

The potential of the speakership has always been defined in relationship to the Senate and the presidency. Because the speaker is empowered by the rules of the House, the office has more institutional power than does the office of the Senate majority leader. Gingrich collected more institutional power than any recent speaker. When a speaker has the support of a united and substantial party majority, it is very difficult to move public policy in a direction he opposes. However, that the speaker can sometimes control the House does not mean that he can control the government. A determined minority of U.S. senators can often block legislation, and a president supported by a one-third minority in either house of Congress can sustain a veto. Much of Newt Gingrich's Republican revolution ran aground in the Republican-controlled Senate, and most of the rest was defeated by Bill Clinton's veto pen. Even a united Republican Congress was unable to impose its will on the administration in the great budget war of the 104th Congress.

A speaker can sometimes win a legislative stand-off with a president, but he can rarely win a public-relations battle; otherwise, Uncle Joe Cannon would be enshrined on Mt. Rushmore instead of Teddy Roosevelt. When Newt Gingrich underestimated Bill Clinton he also underestimated the presidency itself. The platform the White House affords is substantially higher than that of the speakership. The president is clothed in the authority of the American people who elect him; the speaker's authority is grounded in a congressional district and a congressional party caucus. The president has the power to act as well as to speak; he has executive authority. The speaker can act within the rules of the House and of his legislative party, but he cannot act under the authority of public law. The president commands the attention of the media and can convey his message to the public through it. Speaker Gingrich attracted more media attention than any previous speaker, but he could not control his own message through it. It was unsurprising, then, when President Clinton won the spin war over the government shutdown: the public blamed it on the congressional Republicans by a 2–1 majority, according to public-opinion surveys.

The budget battle became the fulcrum for a full-scale attack on Speaker Gingrich by labor unions, the Democratic National Committee, and, later, the Clinton reelection campaign. The Republicans had on occasion sought to attack Democratic speakers Tip O'Neill and Jim Wright, but the scale of the Democratic attack on Gingrich was without precedent. His political adversaries sought to make him the symbol of a reactionary, Republican-controlled House of Representatives. By his own estimation, by midsummer 1996 the speaker was the object of more than fifteen thousand attack ads nationwide. By the time of the November 5, 1996, election he estimated them to as numbering more than seventy-five thousand. Every Democratic congressional candidate sought to link the Republican opponent to Gingrich and the GOP budget. President Clinton attacked the Republicans for proposing allegedly draconian "cuts" in Medicare even though the Republican budget called for increases in Medicare spending. Advertisements attacking Republican presidential nominee Robert Dole of Kansas linked him to Gingrich and the GOP budget. The attacks had their intended effect: Gingrich's approval ratings sank below 30 percent, the lowest ratings for any speaker since pollsters began asking about them in the 1970s.[35]

It was thus a wounded Newt Gingrich who sought to guide the House Republicans to a second historical milestone, the reelection of a GOP majority for the 105th Congress. The GOP had not retained control of two consecutive congresses since the years 1927–30. The speaker's strategy was to burrow into the underground of the Republican base, traveling from one safe haven to another, in order to shore up party spirits and build its campaign war chest. During the spring of 1996 Gingrich disappeared from political radar. The leader who emerged for the summer's primary-campaign season was verbally combative but kept a much lower profile than the insurgent leader of the 1994 election had done. In Washington, House Republicans moved quickly to the political center, passing an increase in the federal minimum wage, health-insurance portability, and a compromise welfare-reform bill. As the 104th Congress moved toward adjournment the budget logjam broke and appropriations bills began to move. One clear indication of the change in the political tide was the fact that congressional Republicans raised federal spending for a variety of discretionary programs by about $15 billion above 1995 levels. The Republicans were out to save themselves.[36]

The 1996 congressional elections were an Armageddon. Democrats were determined to regain control of the House and knew that their best chance was in 1996, when seventy-three freshmen Republicans would be in their first and most vulnerable reelection campaigns. Allied with liberal interest groups and organized labor, the Democrats launched a full assault on the House Republicans and their leader, Newt Gingrich. They almost pulled it off. As the campaign headed into the last two weeks, national and state polls indicated one of the closest elections in American history, with a slight advantage to the Democrats. It was clear that the slightest shift in public sentiment might swing the election to either party. The Democratic strategy of softening the Republicans with the early advertising blitz had given the party the lead, but at the campaign's end it was the Republicans, not the Democrats, who had cash left to spend. The advantages of money and incumbency combined with late-breaking reports of illegal foreign campaign contributions to the Democratic party to tip the electorate to the Republicans in many swing districts. In the end, the GOP lost 8 seats and entered the 105th Congress with a majority of 227–208.

The Republican Regime in Transition

The Republicans had preserved their opportunity to entrench control of the House, but Gingrich was markedly weakened. When the Republicans met in November 1996 to organize for the 105th Congress the changed political environment was evident. A few Republicans called for the speaker to step aside until the ethics investigation was completed. Most, however, rallied around Gingrich, and he was unanimously chosen by the GOP conference as its nominee for speaker. In accepting the nomination, Gingrich evoked a conciliatory tone and message.[37] Noting that President Clinton had campaigned on Republican policy positions, such as a balanced budget that included tax cuts, the speaker promised to work with the administration and the congressional Democrats. Labeling the 105th Congress the "implementation congress," Gingrich abandoned the revolutionary rhetoric of the 104th. The speaker's more moderate tone reflected the changing political context of his leadership.

Gingrich made concessions to the committee chairs and to moderate Republicans. SAG was disbanded in favor of a larger leadership group that included the chairs of five major committees: Ways and Means, Rules, Budget, Appropriations, and Commerce. Policy recommendations of the leadership group would be taken to the party's policy

committee, which comprised members from all regions and factions in
the conference. Members were assured that in the 105th Congress
legislation would be written in committee and not in the speaker's office.
When committee chairs were named, there were no skips in seniority.

A move to confirm subcommittee chairs by the conference was
defeated, thus protecting moderates from the conservative conference
majority. The subcommittee chairs would continue to be named by the
chairs of the full committees. The leadership contemplated no further
changes in the committee system. In a significant step, the speaker
accepted the resignation of House Administrator Scot Faulkner and
transferred supervisory responsibility for that office to the House Oversight Committee. Just as Faulkner had replaced longtime Democratic
staffers with reform-minded Republicans, Faulkner loyalists were led to
the door. While the speaker would continue to name all House officers
subject to floor confirmation, he would no longer oversee the day-to-day
operations of any administrative office. This was a victory for the
committee chairs who had come into conflict with Faulkner over the
scope and direction of administrative reform. It was a clear setback to
Speaker Gingrich's effort to control House administration.[38]

Although the numerical balance of the 105th Congress did not differ
greatly from that of the 104th, with Clinton in the White House, a
narrow House majority, and a more conservative, Republican Senate
majority enlarged by two seats to 55, the political landscape was in fact
quite different. The ideological center of the House was narrow space
occupied by about seventy "Blue Dog" Democrats and "Lunch Bunch"
Republicans, as the moderate factions in each party were known.
Laboring under an ethics cloud, Speaker Gingrich received critical support from GOP moderates, who preferred him to others in the leadership hierarchy that a conservative conference majority might select. The
moderates hoped to pull the conference to the center with Gingrich's
support.[39] Once again a House speaker was forced to modify his
approach as the changing political landscape altered the conditions of
his speakership. Gingrich was confronted by limitations on his power so
familiar to his Democratic predecessors. The force of the presidency, the
expectations of members, and the institutional character of the speakership itself forced him to retrench. Yet in modifying his approach, Newt
Gingrich still served as a *Republican* speaker. The moderates would
have a greater voice in the 105th Congress, and the committee chairs
would be drawn more closely into the leadership circle, but the Republicans would continue to adhere to the principle of party government
with an expectation of party loyalty. Gingrich would continue to be the
leader of the House Republicans, and the Republican speakership would
continue to be stronger than any Democratic variation of the office.

It was against this backdrop that Gingrich decided in December 1996 to acquiesce to the Ethics subcommittee's finding that he had violated House rules by using tax-exempt organizations for political purposes and by making false statements to the Ethics Committee.[40] These admissions ensured that he would face discipline from the House by reprimand or censure. A censure would require him to relinquish the speakership. The speaker's public admission and apology caused stress fractures in the GOP conference as several members called for him to step aside until the ethics process was completed. Various proposals were advanced for the Republicans to appoint an interim speaker pending final resolution of the case. Democrats, led by Bonior, called for the Republicans to find a new leader. The Republican leadership group rallied around Gingrich, launching a public-relations campaign, organizing conference calls among members to provide information, and encouraging wavering members to vote for him for speaker when the House convened on January 7, 1997. With a margin of only nineteen votes, a handful of Republican defectors could deny Gingrich reelection and throw the House into chaos. On the eve of the vote Gingrich met with the GOP conference in a three-hour session; the following morning the Republicans met for two more hours. In these meetings Gingrich sought to assure members that his transgressions had been unintentional and that there were no further skeletons in his closet. Gingrich supporters put the case on partisan grounds: the Democrats were using the ethics process to deny the Republicans the right to elect the leader of their choosing. To the majority of Gingrich loyalists, supporting Gingrich was a matter of party principle. Potential defectors put the case on ethics grounds: the Republicans should not choose to be led by a tarnished leader.[41]

The drama was played out on Tuesday, January 7, 1997, as the House convened at noon. Unlike the United States Senate (a continuing body presided over by the vice president of the United States, who also serves as president of the Senate), the House must renew itself every two years. By statute the clerk of the House presides over its opening session, in which the first order of business is the election of the speaker. After GOP Conference Chair John Boehner of Ohio placed Newt Gingrich's name in nomination, Democratic Caucus Chair Vic Fazio of California moved that the House defer the election of speaker and move to elect an interim speaker. Boehner moved to table the motion, and the motion to table was approved along a largely party-line vote of 222–210, with four Republicans supporting the Democrats' motion. The Democrats then placed in nomination their leader, Dick Gephardt, and the House moved to a roll-call vote for speaker. In a moment of high drama, nine Republicans refused to vote for Gingrich. Five members voted present, two voted for Jim Leach of Iowa, a senior moderate who had come out against Gingrich's election, and one vote each was cast for former members Robert Michel of Illinois and Robert Walker of Pennsylvania. Under the precedents of the House, a candidate must command the votes of a majority of members casting their votes for candidates by name. In this case, 425 votes were so cast, of which Newt Gingrich claimed 216 and Dick Gephardt 205. Six members (including Gephardt) voted present, and four (including Gingrich) did not vote. Gingrich thus was elected speaker, the first speaker since Gillett to claim office by plurality vote.[42]

The members of the Ethics Committee in the 104th Congress were extended in their service until January 21, 1997, by which date they were required to complete their investigation of the speaker. After considerable squabbling over the schedule and a dispute about an intercepted cellular telephone conversation in which the speaker was alleged to have violated his agreement with the committee, committee counsel James Cole filed his report on January 16, 1997, and televised hearings were held the following day. On January 17 the committee voted 7–1 to accept the negotiated penalty recommended by the counsel: that the speaker be reprimanded and assessed $300,000 for having violated House rules. On January 21, 1997, the House voted 395–28 to impose this penalty. Gingrich entered the 105th Congress at least temporarily free from internal House investigative procedures but facing the possibility of further inquiry by the Justice Department and/ or the Internal Revenue Service into his possible use of tax-exempt foundations for political purposes. The final committee report did not find that Gingrich had violated any laws or intentionally misled the committee, but Cole's report implied that he had.[43]

Newt Gingrich thus became the first speaker to be formally reprimanded by the House. Although subsequent investigations by the Justice Department or the Internal Revenue Service might still threaten his leadership, he had weathered the storm for the time being. The willingness of the Republican majority to stand behind Gingrich was a testament to the unity of the party and to the obligation many of its members felt to him. There could be little doubt, however, that Gingrich's hand was greatly weakened. How could he resurrect his speakership? It appeared that Gingrich would have to change course in the 105th Congress. In his acceptance speech he indicated that he intended to work with all members and through the committee system to address the nation's needs. He called for a focus on implementation as opposed to confrontation. He apologized to the House for having brought discredit upon it. These remarks were in stark contrast to the ebullience of 1995 and were an indication of an altered strategy to meet altered circumstances.[44]

Gingrich had sought to develop among House Republicans a strong and unified culture. His payoff came when the Republican conference stood by him through the ethics controversy. In his weakened circumstance it became more important than before to nurture the bonds of GOP unity, yet the task would now be more difficult. Gingrich would have to listen, learn, help, and lead the House; he would also have to refashion his public image. Politicians often recreate their images. America welcomed several renditions of the "new" Richard Nixon, for example, and President Clinton repositioned himself after the 1994 election debacle. Gingrich faced a harder task. A speaker's ability to reach the public is limited. The enormous media coverage that Gingrich received during the 104th Congress was unusual and, as it turned out, not really within his power to control. His image was defined in part by his enemies but also in part by the House of Representatives, to which he was institutionally hostage; when the public got mad at the House, it got mad at him. A president has more opportunity to shape his image than does a speaker because he is better able to control his own destiny. President Clinton built his career as an adaptable politician, melding into the background even as it changed hue; he was most effective when standing aloof from party allegiance. Newt Gingrich built his career as a party politician whose very strength derived from the sharp edges of his political identity. To soften those edges would be to sacrifice an element of his strength. Gingrich was an icon among conservative Republicans; he galvanized the base. His challenge, then, would be to restore public confidence in his leadership while maintaining the loyalty of his staunchest partisan supporters.

During 1996 Gingrich had sought to step back from active management of the House in order to assume the role of conceptualizer and strategist for the Republicans; as the 105th Congress convened, he announced that he intended to continue this posture.[45] This choice of strategies offered insight into Gingrich's character. Gingrich sees himself as a national political leader of world-historical proportions, as a party leader, and as an organizational leader who builds and runs institutions. In the first role he is the visionary who inspires by the force of ideas—a cultural figure. In the second role he is a grass-roots organizer and motivator who sees politics as war by other means. In the third role he is an institutional leader in the Drucker-Deming mold. Disraeli had merged the roles of visionary, party builder, and institutional leader effectively within the framework of a parliamentary regime. The American constitutional regime, however, resists responsible party government. In focusing on his role as a political strategist for the Republicans, Gingrich returns to his roots. At his core Newt Gingrich is a partisan politician; but a speaker of the House must be more than that.

Conclusion: A New Era?

Did the election of a Republican majority in the 1994 elections mark the beginning of a new historical era in the evolution of the House of Representatives and the speakership? It seems quite possible. Historical transitions in the office have been marked by a period of disequilibrium leading to a catalytic event. In the 1980s the House became increasingly divided along partisan lines. Between the summer of 1989 and the winter of 1996 a powerful Democratic House speaker was forced to resign, his Democratic successor was evicted by his own constituents, and the new Republican speaker became the most unpopular political figure in America, winning reelection to the speakership by a plurality and becoming the first speaker to be reprimanded by the House. This instability in the speakership is without parallel in American history. During the parliamentary era the office experienced frequent turnover, but this was at the option of speakers, by the choice of their party's caucus, or due to a change in party control of the House. In the revolt against Speaker Cannon the House defeated a motion to vacate the chair, thus continuing him in office. What explanation can be given for the upheaval the House and its speakership have experienced, and what do these events suggest about the office itself?

Contextual explanations of Congress suggest that party leaders' behavior is shaped by institutional arrangements. I accept this general proposition and have sought to describe in this book how the changing institutional context of the House of Representatives has influenced the evolution of the speakership. I have also suggested that institutional context is affected by broader forces affecting the political system, on the one hand, and by the influence of individual political actors, on the other hand. Institutional context mediates systemic change and the actions of leaders; it reflects the former and is affected by the latter. The historical and analytical framework I have deployed to explain the speakership presents the office's evolution through definable periods. These periods relate to, but are not coextensive with, patterns in the evolution of the party system and electoral realignments. I have chosen to demark them by specific events in the history of the House. The transition from the parliamentary period to the partisan period began during the upheavals of the 1850s and was marked by Pennington's election as speaker, coterminous with Lincoln's election and the onset of the Civil War. The transition from the parliamentary to the feudal period began with the struggle between progressive and standpat Republicans in the first decade of the twentieth century and was marked by the revolt against Cannon and the election of a Democratic House in 1912. The transition from the feudal to the democratic era began with the fight to pack the Rules Committee, followed by Sam Rayburn's death, and culminated in the reforms of the early 1970s. The forced resignation of Jim Wright, the defeat of Tom Foley, and the election and reelection of Newt Gingrich may well indicate a turning point in the history of the House, with the 1994 election the key event.

If the speakership is entering a new period in its development, its beginning offers a poor vantage point for assessment. Analytic histories are, as I have said, constructs and not facts. History may prove unfriendly to predictions based on current trends, and analysis always proceeds more securely from a retrospective point of view. As long as Gingrich serves as speaker, he can continue his experiment in party government; however, his diminished stature also diminishes his prospects. Another Republican speaker might not be able to continue the transformation Gingrich has begun. No matter who their leader is, the Republicans face the challenge of imposing a regime of their own. The defining characteristic of the House of Representatives in its democratic era has been the autonomy of its members. The Democratic party's long period in the majority spanned the speakership's feudal and democratic periods and offered two variations of decentralized administration, one in which power resided with the committee chairs and the other in which power was spread among the party leadership, the committees and their subcommittees, and the Democratic caucus. Although the Democrats clung to their House majority, underlying political conditions changed. The realignment of the South, the growth of middle-class suburbs and the development of shared political interests in them, and the settling of the Baby Boom generation into a middle-aged conservatism all contributed to a reshaping of the electorate. The increasing power and unity of the Republican party reflected these changes. In the 1980s the Democrats began to demonstrate more cohesive voting patterns, and their speakers were given more power to control floor debate. But the culture of the Democratic party resisted any serious attempt at party governance. Jim Wright's leadership of the 100th Congress was a brief exception that proved that rule; Wright's resignation and Tom Foley's speakership confirmed it.

In the 104th Congress the Republicans demonstrated their historical tendency toward party government. The rare circumstances in which Speaker Gingrich came to office afforded him an opportunity to establish a more powerful speakership than any since Uncle Joe Cannon's. From the speaker's chair Gingrich set the legislative agenda for the House and the policy agenda for the nation. He brought the committee system to heal, he cleaned out the patronage bins of House administration, and he brought to the speakership a new approach to party leadership. In the process, he made himself the symbol of all that the Democrats and their interest-group allies opposed. Democratic speakers had been able to hide behind the committee system; Gingrich sat astride it and absorbed into his reputation all of the opposition to the Republican agenda. The behavior of speakers has never been wholly determined by institutional context, but only two other speakers have been able to reshape the environment of office as Newt Gingrich did: Clay and Reed. Opportunities for speakers to fundamentally alter the conditions of House governance are rare and depend upon Machiavellian fortune as well as Machiavellian art.[46] Gingrich had both. There exists no clearer example in the history of the House of Representatives of a political leader who created the conditions of his own leadership. He transformed the culture of the Republican conference, he defined the terms upon which the Republicans would challenge the Democrats, he organized the Republican machine, he recruited the candidates and raised the money for their campaigns, he led the party to victory, he shaped the new regime they put in place, and in spite of his missteps he led them to retain control of the House in the 1996 elections. No theory that makes leadership style wholly contingent upon institutional context can explain all of that. The independent force of Newt Gingrich's leadership must be acknowledged.

Some aspects of the new Republican regime are endemic to the party's culture, some are due to the unusual circumstances in which they came to power in 1995, and some are due to Speaker Gingrich's proclivities. The more centralized leadership model, the use of a party steering committee to set a party policy agenda, and the greater degree of coordination between the party leadership and the committees are characteristically Republican. The dominant role of the party leadership and the speaker in the 104th Congress, the use of task forces to draft major legislation, the bypassing of committees, and even the cult of personality surrounding Gingrich himself were by-products of the 1994 election. The use of private-sector and military management models, the rhetorical tone, and the complex organizational matrix of Gingrich's political universe all reflected Gingrich's idiosyncrasies. Yet each of these three facets of the Republican project reflected the character of the party. The election of a Republican majority at long last enables political science to assess the role of the two parties as a variable in analyzing the House. It is now demonstrable that there are significant differences in the cultures of the two major parties and that these differences affect their manner of governing in the House. Some of the Republicans' changes simply served to bring modern management practices to the House and are likely to become institutionally embedded. Other changes wrought by the Republicans, such as the abolition of special-interest caucuses, the abolition of proxy voting, and the reduction in committee staffs, affect the culture of the House and are of more uncertain duration. But a lesson learned in the 104th Congress is that the institutional context of the House of Representatives is fundamentally affected by the culture of its governing party. Republicans and Democrats are different.

If the House of Representatives has entered a new era, its defining feature is likely to be found in new approaches to party organization. During the late nineteenth century the party system rested on control of nominations and strong partisan identification on the part of the electorate. Neither is the case today. Nominations are determined by competition in open primaries, and members of Congress will remain independent of party control. Voters are increasingly independent, and party allegiance is weak. The realignment of the South has had the effect of making the Democratic and Republican parties more demographically and ideologically homogeneous, creating an opportunity for party leaders to nurture cohesive majorities. Ideological cadres within the major parties can be organized at the grass roots to recruit candidates, raise money, and control nominations. National leaders can seek to harness grass-roots activism to support national party agendas. As leader of the legislative party, the speaker may assume a new role as strategist, as Gingrich has done. In order to maintain cohesion, speakers can pursue recruitment, electoral, and public-relations strategies. The speaker's role will transcend the House.

Speaker Gingrich has provided an indication of how the speakership might develop along these lines. In many respects, his speakership is *sui generis:* the combination of the circumstances in which he came to power, his personal qualities, his organizational predilections, and his leadership philosophies will not all be replicated by other speakers. But future speakers will have strong incentives to pursue leadership strategies similar to those Gingrich has pioneered in the House. In the 104th Congress, House Democrats sought to emulate Gingrich's leadership approach even as they castigated his style. Democratic leader Richard Gephardt adopted some of Gingrich's tactics, including a defined legislative agenda. Gephardt's principal constraint was the character of the Democratic caucus, which remained inhospitable to central party leadership. Still, under Gephardt the Democrats reached new levels of cohesion in part because the realignment of the South had made the party more homogeneous but in larger part because the Democrats wanted to win. When Gingrich is replaced by another Republican leader, we should expect a continuation of more centralized party control, and the Republicans' new leader will be likely to follow many of the precedents set by Gingrich. Both Republican and Democratic speakers will play a significant role outside the House to build the party base.

And it is in creating the conditions of party cohesion that the essence of the speakership is presently to be found. The American regime rejects responsible party government as the human body would a transplanted organ; but stronger and more cohesive parties are possible. The task is one of leadership. As I have noted, legislative leadership has tradition-ally been regarded as inherently transactional. Surely legislative leaders will always cut deals, but increasingly they will engage in integrative strategies. The Democratic variation has been to stress participation in the caucus and when legislation is ready to come to the floor. In between, the committee barons have shaped policy. I have labeled this kind of leadership activity therapeutic: everyone felt better, but the chairs still had the power. In the Republican model integrative leader-ship is carried to a new level. The leader sets the tone and direction and then enlists the rank and file as members of the team. Gingrich prefers to couch this approach in military terms; another speaker might not. The military doctrine is simply a variation of contemporary private manage-ment theories that stress team-building. The approach is essentially integrative and inherently therapeutic. It derives less from that branch of organization theory influenced by economics than from that influenced by the discipline of group psychology.

The documents released by the Ethics Committee indicate the scope and method of Gingrich's leadership.[47] In 1992 we find him articulating a vision for the party, defining a political strategy, and putting in place an enormously complex set of organizational arrangements to pursue both. Yet Gingrich's approach will be familiar to students of contempo-rary management theory and practice. We have before us a potentially new model for the speakership. The speaker has been a presiding officer, a party boss, a legislative broker, and a symbolic leader. But no speaker has ever really been a transformational leader in the sense in which the term is used in management theory. Newt Gingrich is the first to try. He has sought to join together a theory of organizational leadership and a theory of political leadership. He has sought to be at one and the same time a new kind of speaker of the House and a national political leader whose aim is a fundamental restructuring of American politics. Yet, while his real skill and greatest passion is as a partisan, his most enduring legacy may be in shaping a new role for speakers as organi-zational leaders. Ironically, it is possible that Gingrich is not the leader to institutionalize the changes his revolution has wrought. His temperament may prove unsuited to the demands of the theories he espouses. It is perhaps for this reason that his preferred emphasis is on party strategy. Sooner or later the Republicans will find it necessary to select a new leader, who will have the task of institutionalizing the leadership regime developed by Gingrich. The Republicans will have to find a path to stable leadership succession that will ensure that their chosen leader is suited to the conditions the party's culture imposes. The Democrats have preferred the seniority rule and the leadership ladder. It is not evident that these devices are suited to the needs of the Republican party. Contested speakership nominations in the Republican conference could be the norm.

Gingrich's Republican successor will confront a reality that he refused to recognize. Gingrich's transformational project is in crucial respects at cross-purposes with the institutional character of the House of Representatives and indeed of the American political system itself. Newt Gingrich sought, like Disraeli, to forge a new party machine and a new partisan majority. He attacked the Democratic regime, which he believed perpetuated itself by corrupting the House. He launched a political war to "storm the gates," and he succeeded. In implementing a new regime, however, he swept too broadly. Believing that institutions bend entirely to political will, he sought to impose a form of centralized leadership on the House that was at odds with its character. Eliminating special-interest caucuses is one thing; bypassing the committee system is quite another. The House of Representatives is made up of elected representatives of the American people. Every member of the House has a right and obligation to participate in the legislative process on behalf of his or her constituency. The rules of the House ensure the rights of members to effective participation even as the rules ensure the right of voting majorities to make final decisions. It is the duty of the speaker to enforce the rules of the House and to protect the rights of its members. Legislative voting majorities are not coextensive with legislative party majorities. In seeking to impose a responsible party regime on the House, Gingrich regarded institutional qualities as mere products of party culture. Institutional norms such as deference, reciprocity, specialization, and especially comity are not simply instruments of party control or expressions of the legislative needs of the Democratic party. They are endemic to the nature and culture of the House of Representatives.

Gingrich sought power, as many before him had, but in the final analysis the Hobbesian view of politics with which the present study began provides an inadequate foundation for understanding the House of Representatives and the speakership. The essence of the American speakership lies in the balance between political power and institutional obligation. Speakers of the House must be attuned to the uses of power, but power itself should not be the sole object nor the primary standard by which they are evaluated. Power is a means and not an end. A speaker cannot be effective without it, but he should not be consumed by the desire for it. Whether power is found to lie in the rules of the House, in a strong governing majority, or even in a public image, it must be understood and evaluated in relationship to the ends to which it is put. Some of the most important ends a speaker of the House is obligated to seek may be made more difficult to attain by the heavy-handed imposition of his will. A legislative body requires a sense of comity, a respect for procedure, and a spirit of mutual forbearance. A legislature is, after all, a venue of representative government. It is a place where deliberation about the public weal must be possible. The exercise of power without judgment is worse than the possession of judgment without power; a good speaker must have and use both.

In no area is the exercise of judgment more important to a speaker than in the conduct of his personal and public affairs. Several speakers have had controversial personal lives. Others have had their public conduct questioned. A speaker has an obligation to set the highest ethical standards in the conduct of both private and public life. A speaker who is found to have made serious violations of House rules or public law should not be surprised when his fitness for office is questioned. Speaker Wright was forced to resign the office amid ethics charges because he lacked sufficient support in the Democratic caucus; Speaker Gingrich, despite a reprimand and assessment, managed to win reelection to the office because his support among House Republicans was strong. Unless his public approval ratings recover, his support in the Republican conference will no doubt wane. Their experiences demonstrate that the penumbra surrounding formal rules is constantly shifting. The speakership of the House embodies its authority and dignity, as Speaker Muhlenberg first understood. A speaker who brings discredit upon the House fails an obligation of the office.

The House and the speakership will be affected, as it was in the past, by the broad currents of American politics. In the gradual process of political and social evolution, individual speakers will be able to shape the character of the office if they choose to try. Over the course of American history, the House of Representatives has sometimes preferred average to exceptional leaders. But today the speakership is more important in the scheme of government than at any time since the revolt against Cannon, and more is demanded of government now than was the case then. Representative government depends on the capacity of citizens and representatives to choose leaders. It is important that they choose well.

Appendix: The Speakers of the House of Representatives

Speaker	Period of Service in House	Period of Service as Speaker
(Date of Birth) Party Affiliation State	*Dates Congresses*	*Dates Congresses*
Frederick A. C. Muhlenberg (Jan. 1, 1750) Federalist/1st Congress Democratic-Republican/ 3d Congress Pennsylvania	Mar. 4, 1789–Mar. 3, 1797 1st–4th Congresses	Apr. 1, 1789–Mar. 3, 1791 Dec. 2, 1793–Mar. 3, 1795 1st and 3d Congresses
Jonathan Trumbull (Mar. 26, 1740) Federalist Connecticut	Mar. 4, 1789–Mar. 3, 1795 1st–3d Congresses	Oct. 24, 1791–Mar. 3, 1793 2d Congress
Jonathan Dayton (Oct. 16, 1660) Federalist New Jersey	Mar. 4, 1791–Mar. 3, 1799 2d–5th Congresses	Dec. 7, 1795–Mar. 3, 1799 4th and 5th Congresses
Theodore Sedgwick (May 9, 1746) Federalist Massachusetts	Mar. 4, 1789–June, 1796 Mar. 4, 1799–Mar. 3, 1801 1st–4th, and 6th Congresses	Dec. 2, 1799–Mar. 3, 1801 6th Congress

Speaker	Period of Service in House	Period of Service as Speaker
(Date of Birth) Party Affiliation State	*Dates Congresses*	*Dates Congresses*
Nathaniel Macon (Dec. 17, 1757) Democratic-Republican North Carolina	Mar. 4, 1791–Dec. 13, 1815 2d–14th Congresses	Dec. 7, 1801–Mar. 3, 1807 7th–9th Congresses
Joseph B. Varnum (Jan. 29, 1750) Democratic-Republican Massachusetts	Mar. 4, 1795–June 29, 1811 4th–12th Congresses	Oct. 26, 1807–Mar. 3, 1811 10th and 11th Congresses
Henry Clay (April 12, 1777) Democratic-Republican Kentucky	Mar. 4, 1811–Jan. 19, 1814 Mar. 4, 1815–Mar. 3, 1821 Mar. 3, 1823–Mar. 6, 1825 12th–16th, 18th and 19th Congresses	Nov. 4, 1811–Jan. 19, 1814 Dec. 4, 1815–Oct. 28, 1820 Dec. 1, 1823–Mar. 3, 1825 12th–16th, 18th Congresses
Langdon Cheves (Sept. 17, 1776) Democratic-Republican South Carolina	Dec. 31, 1810–Mar. 3, 1815 11th–13th Congresses	Jan. 19, 1814–Mar. 3, 1815 13th Congress
John W. Taylor (Mar. 26, 1784) Democratic-Republican/ 16th Congress National-Republican/ 19th Congress New York	Mar. 4, 1813–Mar. 3, 1833 13th–22d Congresses	Nov. 15, 1820–Mar. 3, 1821 Dec. 5, 1825–Mar. 3, 1827 16th and 19th Congresses
Philip P. Barbour (May 25, 1783) Democratic-Republican Virginia	Sept. 19, 1814–Mar. 3, 1825 Mar. 4, 1827–Oct. 15, 1830 13th–18th, 20th, 21st Congresses	Dec. 4, 1821–Mar. 3, 1823 17th Congress

Andrew Stevenson   Mar. 4,1821–June 2,   Dec. 3, 1827–June 2,
(Jan. 21, 1784)   1834   1834
Democrat   17th–23d Congresses   20th–23d Congresses
Virginia

John Bell   Mar. 4, 1827–Mar. 3,   June 2, 1834–Mar. 3,
(Feb. 15, 1797   1841   1835
Whig   20th–26th Congresses   23d Congress
Tennessee

James K. Polk   Mar. 4, 1825–Mar. 3,   Dec. 7, 1835–Mar. 3,
(Nov. 2, 1795)   1839   1839
Democrat   19th–25th Congresses   24th–25th Congresses
Tennessee

Robert M. T. Hunter   Mar. 4, 1837–Mar. 3,   Dec. 16, 1839–Mar. 3,
(April 21, 1809)   1843   1841
Democrat   Mar. 4, 1845–Mar. 3,   26th Congress
Virginia   1847
                          25th–27th, and 29th
                          Congresses

John White   Mar. 4, 1835–Mar. 3,   May 31, 1841–Mar. 3,
(Feb. 14, 1802)   1845   1843
Whig   24th–28th Congresses   27th Congress
Kentucky

John W. Jones   Mar. 4, 1835–Mar. 3,   Dec. 4, 1843–Mar. 3,
(Nov. 22, 1791)   1845   1845
Democrat   24th–28th Congresses   28th Congress
Virginia

John W. Davis   Mar. 4, 1835–Mar. 3,   Dec. 1, 1845–Mar. 3,
(April 16, 1799)   1837   1847
Democrat   Mar. 4, 1839–Mar. 3,   29th Congress
Indiana   1841
                          Mar. 4, 1843–Mar. 3,
                              1847
                          24th, 26th, 28th, and
                          29th Congresses

Speaker	Period of Service in House	Period of Service as Speaker
(Date of Birth) Party Affiliation State	Dates Congresses	Dates Congresses
Robert C. Winthrop (May 12, 1809) Whig Massachusetts	Nov. 9, 1840–May. 25, 1842 Nov. 29, 1842–July 30, 1850 26th, 27th, 28th–31st Congresses	Dec. 6, 1847–Mar. 3, 1849 30th Congress
Howell Cobb (Sept. 7, 1815) Democrat Georgia	Mar. 4, 1843–Mar. 3, 1851 Mar. 4, 1855–Mar. 3, 1857 28th–31st Congresses and 34th Congress	Dec. 22, 1849–Mar. 3, 1851 31st Congress
Linn Boyd (Nov. 22, 1800) Democrat Kentucky	Mar. 4, 1835–Mar. 3, 1837 Mar. 4, 1839–Mar. 3, 1855 24th, 26th–33d Congresses	Dec. 1, 1851–Mar. 3, 1855 32d–33d Congresses
Nathaniel P. Banks (Jan. 30, 1816) American Party (Coalition with Democrats) Massachusetts	Mar. 4, 1853–Dec. 24, 1857 Dec. 4, 1865–Mar. 3, 1873 Mar. 4, 1875–Mar. 3, 1879 Mar. 4, 1889–Mar. 3, 1891 33d–35th, 39th–42d, 44th–45th, and 51st Congresses	Feb. 2, 1856–Mar. 3, 1857 34th Congress
James Orr (May 12, 1822) Democrat South Carolina	Mar. 4, 1849–Mar. 3, 1859 31st–35th Congresses	Dec. 7, 1857–Mar. 3, 1859 35th Congress

William Pennington (May 4, 1796) Whig New Jersey	Mar. 4, 1859–Mar. 3, 1861 36th Congress	Feb. 1, 1860–Mar. 3, 1861 36th Congress
Galusha A. Grow (Aug. 31, 1823) Republican Pennsylvania	Mar. 4, 1851–Mar. 3, 1863 Feb. 26, 1894–Mar. 3, 1903 32d–37th, 54th–57th Congresses	July 4, 1861–Mar. 3, 1863 37th Congress
Schuyler Colfax (Mar. 23, 1823) Republican Indiana	Mar. 4, 1855–Mar. 3, 1869 34th–40th Congresses	Dec. 7, 1863–Mar. 3, 1869 38th–40th Congresses
Theodore M. Pomeroy (Dec. 31, 1824) Republican New York	Mar. 4, 1861–Mar. 3 1869 37th–40th Congresses	Mar. 4, 1869 40th Congress
James G. Blaine (Jan. 31, 1830) Republican Maine	Mar. 4, 1863–July 10, 1876 38th–44th Congresses	Mar. 4, 1869–Mar. 3, 1875 41st–43d Congresses
Michael C. Kerr (Mar. 15, 1827) Democrat Indiana	Mar. 4, 1865–Mar. 3, 1873 Mar. 4, 1875–Aug. 19, 1876 39th–42d, 44th Congresses	Dec. 6, 1875–Aug. 15, 1876 44th Congress
Samuel J. Randall (Oct. 10, 1828) Democrat Pennsylvania	Mar. 4, 1863–Apr. 13, 1890 38th–51st Congresses	Dec. 4, 1876–Mar. 3, 1881 44th–46th Congresses
J. Warren Keifer (Jan. 30, 1836) Republican Ohio	Mar. 4, 1877–Mar. 3, 1885 Mar. 4, 1905–Mar. 3, 1911 45th–48th, 59th–61st Congresses	Dec. 5, 1881–Mar. 3, 1883 47th Congress

Speaker	Period of Service in House	Period of Service as Speaker
(Date of Birth) Party Affiliation State	*Dates* *Congresses*	*Dates* *Congresses*
John G. Carlisle (Sept. 5, 1835) Democrat Kentucky	Mar. 4, 1877–May 26, 1890 45th–51st Congresses	Dec. 3, 1883–Mar. 3, 1889 48th–50th Congresses
Thomas B. Reed (Oct. 18, 1839) Republican Maine	Mar. 4, 1877–Sept. 4, 1889 45th–56th Congresses	Dec. 2, 1889–Mar. 3, 1891 Dec. 2, 1895–Mar. 3, 1899 51st, 54th–55th Congresses
Charles T. Crisp (Jan. 29, 1845) Democrat Georgia	Mar. 4, 1883–Oct. 23, 1896 48th–54th Congresses	Dec. 8, 1891–Mar. 3, 1895 52d–53d Congresses
David Henderson (Mar. 14, 1840) Republican Iowa	Mar. 4, 1883–Mar. 3, 1903 48th–57th Congresses	Dec. 4, 1899–Mar. 3, 1903 56th–57th Congresses
Joseph G. Cannon (May 7, 1836) Republican Illinois	Mar. 4, 1873–Mar. 3, 1891 Mar. 4, 1893–Mar. 3, 1913 Mar. 4, 1915–Mar. 3, 1923 43d–51st, 53d–62d, 64th–67th Congresses	Nov. 9, 1903–Mar. 3, 1911 58th–61st Congresses
James B. (Champ) Clark (Mar. 7, 1850) Democrat Missouri	Mar. 4, 1893–Mar. 3, 1895 Mar. 4, 1897–Mar. 2, 1921 53d, 55th–66th Congresses	Apr. 5, 1911–Mar. 3, 1919 62d–65th Congresses

Frederick H. Gillett (Oct. 16, 1851) Republican Massachusetts	Mar. 4, 1893–Mar. 3, 1923 53d–68th Congresses	May 19, 1919–Mar. 3, 1925 66th–68th Congresses
Nicholas Longworth (Nov. 5, 1869) Republican Ohio	Mar. 4, 1903–Mar. 3, 1913 Mar. 4, 1915–Apr. 9, 1931 58th–62d, 64th–72d Congresses	Dec. 7, 1925–Mar. 3, 1931 69th–71st Congresses
John N. Garner (Nov. 22, 1868) Democrat Texas	Mar. 4, 1903–Mar. 3, 1933 58th–73d Congresses	Dec. 7, 1931–Mar. 3, 1933 72d Congress
Henry T. Rainey (Aug. 20, 1860) Democrat Illinois	Mar. 4, 1903–Mar. 3, 1921 Mar. 4, 1923–Aug. 19, 1934 58th–66th, 68th–73d Congresses	Mar. 9, 1933–Aug. 19, 1934 73d Congress
Joseph W. Byrns (July 20, 1869) Democrat Tennessee	Mar. 4, 1909–June 4, 1936 61st–74th Congresses	Jan. 3, 1935–June 4, 1936 74th Congress
William B. Bankhead (April 12, 1874) Democrat Alabama	Mar. 4, 1917–Sept. 15, 1940 65th–76th Congresses	June 4, 1936–Sept. 15, 1940 74th–76th Congresses
Sam Rayburn (Jan. 6, 1882) Democrat Texas	Mar. 4, 1913–Nov. 16, 1961 63d–87th Congresses	Sept. 16, 1940–Jan. 3, 1947 Jan. 3, 1949–Jan. 3, 1953 Jan. 5, 1955–Nov. 16, 1961 76th–79th, 81st–82d, 84th–87th Congresses

Speaker	Period of Service in House	Period of Service as Speaker
(Date of Birth) Party Affiliation State	*Dates Congresses*	*Dates Congresses*
Joseph W. Martin, Jr. (Nov. 3, 1884) Republican Massachusetts	Mar. 4, 1925–Jan. 3, 1967 69th–89th Congresses	Jan. 3, 1947–Jan. 3, 1949 Jan. 3, 1953–Jan. 3, 1955 80th, 83d Congresses
John W. McCormack (Dec. 21, 1891) Democrat Massachusetts	Nov. 6, 1928–Jan. 3, 1971 70th–91st Congresses	Jan. 10, 1962–Jan. 3, 1971 87th–91st Congresses
Carl B. Albert (May 10, 1908) Democrat Oklahoma	Jan. 3, 1947–Jan. 3, 1977 80th–94th Congresses	Jan. 21, 1971–Jan. 3, 1977 92d–94th Congresses
Thomas P. O'Neill, Jr. (Dec. 9, 1912) Democrat Massachusetts	Jan. 3, 1953–Jan. 3, 1987 83d–99th Congresses	Jan. 4, 1977–Jan. 3, 1987 95th–99th Congresses
James C. Wright, Jr. (Dec. 22, 1922) Democrat Texas	Jan. 3, 1955–June 30, 1989 84th–101st Congresses	Jan. 6, 1987–June 6, 1989 100th–101st Congresses
Thomas S. Foley (March 6, 1929) Democrat Washington	Jan. 3, 1965–Dec. 20, 1994 89th–103d Congresses	June. 6, 1989–Dec. 20, 1994 101st–103d Congresses
Newton L. Gingrich (June 17, 1943) Republican Georgia	Jan. 3, 1979– 96th Congress	Jan. 3, 1995– 104th Congress

Sources: Adapted from Jill Spier, Frederick H. Pauls, and Paul S. Rundquist, "Information concerning Speakers of the House of Representatives," *Congressional Research Service* Report no. 77–147 G, June 15, 1977, mimeographed. Information on Speakers O'Neill, Wright, and Foley provided by the author.

Notes

Prologue: The Speakership in History

1. Joseph Alsop and Robert Kintner, "Never Leave Them Angry," *Saturday Evening Post*, January 18, 1941, 22.
2. Ibid.
3. Richard Bolling, *Power in the House: A History of Leadership of the House of Representatives* (New York: Dutton, 1968).
4. Mary Parker Follett, *The Speaker of the House of Representatives* (1902; reprint, New York: Burt Franklin, 1974).
5. Robert L. Peabody, *Leadership in Congress: Stability, Succession and Change* (Boston: Little, Brown, 1975).
6. Barbara D. Sinclair, *Majority Leadership in the U.S. House* (Baltimore: Johns Hopkins University Press, 1983).
7. Joseph Cooper and David W. Brady, "Institutional Context and Leadership Style: The House from Cannon to Rayburn," *American Political Science Review* 75 (1981): 411–25. See also David W. Rhode and Kenneth A. Schepsle, "The Ambiguous Role of Leadership in Woodrow Wilson's Congress" (paper delivered at the American Political Science Association Meeting, New Orleans, 1985); Steven S. Smith, "O'Neill's Legacy for the House," *Brookings Review* 5 (Winter 1987): 28–36.
8. Sinclair's *Majority Leadership* is premised on the institutional context of the postreform House, which is its strength and its limitation.
9. "Yet what we need from history, and why the social scientist must also, among other things, be a historian, is not merely comparable information about the past, but some idea of how we have gotten from the past to the present, in short, a narrative. Narrative is a primary tool and powerful way by which to know about a whole. In an important way, what a society is . . . is its history" (Robert N. Bellah et al., *Habits of the Heart: Individualism and Commitment in American Life* [Berkeley and Los Angeles: University of California Press, 1985], 302).
10. Richard L. McCormick, "The Party Period and Public Policy: An Exploratory

Hypothesis," *Journal of American History* 66 (September 1979): 279–98; id., *The Party Period and Public Policy: American Policy from the Age of Jackson to the Progressive Era* (New York: Oxford University Press, 1986).

11. Everett Carll Ladd, Jr., *American Political Parties* (New York: Norton, 1970); Walter Dean Burnham, *Critical Elections and the Mainsprings of American Politics* (New York: Norton, 1970).

12. McCormick, *Party Period and Public Policy*; Stephen Skowronek, *Building a New American State: The Expansion of National Administrative Capacities, 1877–1920* (Cambridge: Cambridge University Press, 1982).

13. Shakespeare *Macbeth* 5.5.21–23.

14. The literature is far too vast to list comprehensively. A selection would include David W. Brady, *Congressional Voting in a Partisan Era: A Study of the McKinley Houses and a Comparison to the Modern House of Representatives* (Lawrence: University of Kansas Press, 1973); id., *Critical Elections and Congressional Policy Making* (Palo Alto, Calif.: Stanford University Press, 1988); Joel H. Silbey, *The Shrine of Party: Congressional Voting Behavior, 1841–1852* (Pittsburgh: University of Pittsburgh Press, 1967); Ladd, *American Political Parties*; McCormick, *Party Period and Public Policy*.

15. David Brady, for example, stresses the significance of the electoral transformation of the 1890s, but clearly identifies the revolt against Cannon in 1910 as having ended an era in the speakership. Compare *Critical Elections and Congressional Policy Making*, ch. 3, with *Congressional Voting in a Partisan Era*, p. 186.

16. Ladd, *American Political Parties*, 67.

17. Thomas Alexander, *Sectional Stress and Party Strength: A Computer Analysis of Roll-Call Voting Patterns in the United States House of Representatives, 1836–1860* (Nashville: Vanderbilt University Press, 1967).

18. Morton Keller, *Affairs of State: Public Life in Late Nineteenth Century America* (Cambridge: Harvard University Press, 1977); Skowronek, *Building a New American State*.

19. Alonzo L. Hamby, ed., *The New Deal: Analysis & Interpretation* (New York: Longman, 1981).

20. Harold Seidman and Robert Gilmour, *Politics, Position, and Power: From the Positive to the Regulatory State* (New York: Oxford University Press, 1986), ch. 6.

21. Ladd, *American Political Parties*.

22. Nelson Polsby, "The Institutionalization of the House of Representatives," *American Political Science Review* 62 (1968): 144–68.

23. Bellah et al., *Habits of the Heart*, 122.

24. "In actual life every historical event, every human action, is quite clearly and definitely understood, without a sense of the slightest contradiction in it, although every event is conceived of partly as free, and partly as necessary" (Tolstoy, *War and Peace* [1865–72], trans. Constance Garnett [New York: Modern Library, 1931], 1125). See also Robert Nisbet, *Social Change and History* (New York: Oxford University Press, 1969), 280.

25. Milan Kundera, *The Art of the Novel* (New York: Grove Press, 1986), pt. 4.

26. Cooper and Brady, "Institutional Context and Leadership Style."

27. Ladd, *American Political Parties*; McCormick *Party Period and Public Policy*.

Chapter 1. The Parliamentary Speakership

1. General histories of the British speakership are Arthur Irwin Dasent, *The Speakers of the House of Commons* (1911; reprint, New York: Burt Franklin, 1966); Philip Laundy, *The Office of Speaker* (London: Cassell, 1964); J. S. Roskell, *The Commons and Their Speakers in English Parliaments, 1376–1523* (New York: Barnes & Noble, 1965).

2. This was the only time in English history when a monarch entered the House of Commons while in session. Speaker Lenthall's famous response to Charles I was as follows: "May it please Your Majesty, I have neither eyes to see, nor tongue to speak in this place, but as the House is pleased to direct me, whose servant I am here; and I humbly beg Your Majesty's pardon that I cannot give any other answer than this to what your Majesty is pleased to demand of me" (Laundy, *Office of Speaker,* 211).

3. Many political issues marked American colonial development. Underlying all of them was the question, who should make the decision? With the development of institutions of self-government, the American colonies faced the issue of the authority of their legislative assemblies in relationship to that of the royal governors. In the end, this conflict was only resolved by revolution. See Ronald M. Peters, Jr., *The Massachusetts Constitution of 1780: A Social Compact* (Amherst: University of Massachusetts Press, 1978), for an analysis of the theoretical problem.

4. Sources on the colonial speakership are scant. Published sources forming the basis for this account are Philip A. Bruce, *The Institutional History of Virginia in the Seventeenth Century* (New York: G. P. Putnam's Sons, 1910), 469; Mary Patterson Clarke, *Parliamentary Privilege in the American Colonies* (New Haven: Yale University Press, 1943), 133; Mary Parker Follett, *The Speaker of the House of Representatives* (1902; reprint, New York: Burt Franklin, 1974), 13–14; E. B. Greene, *The Provincial Governor in the English Colonies of North America* (Cambridge: Harvard University Press, 1898), 149–50; Ralph Volney Harlow, *The History of Legislative Methods in the Period before 1825* (New Haven: Yale University Press, 1917); Herbert Levi Osgood, *The American Colonies in the Seventeenth Century,* (New York: Macmillan, 1904), 1: 248–51; John Gorham Palfrey, *A Compendious History of New England from the Discovery by Europeans to the First General Congress of Anglo-American Colonies* (Boston: Houghton Mifflin, 1873), 1: 273–74, 317–18.

5. Publius [pseud. for Alexander Hamilton, James Madison, and John Jay], *The Federalist Papers* (1787–88; reprint, New York: Modern Library, 1975), no. 70:454.

6. Ibid., no. 1:6.

7. In the sixth *Federalist,* Hamilton says that by nature men are vindictive and rapacious. Why would the executive for life that he proposed at the Constitutional Convention not be so as well?

8. Publius, *Federalist Papers,* no. 58:381–82.

9. This is a synthesis of the theoretical points made by Madison in *Federalist Papers,* nos. 52–58. He does not, of course, address the speakership per se.

10. Publius, *Federalist Papers,* no. 10:59.

11. Ibid., no. 53:352.

12. *Annals of Congress,* 1st Cong., 1st sess. (Washington, D.C.: Gales & Seaten, 1834), 103–4. On the speaker's ceremonial obligations, see William Maclay, *The Journal of William Maclay* (New York: Frederick Ungar, 1965). Maclay roomed in the same boarding house with Muhlenberg. Elias Boudinot expresses reservations to his wife about becoming speaker precisely because of the extent of the anticipated social and ceremonial obligations. See Elias Boudinot to Mrs. Boudinot, April 2, 1789, First Congress Project Collections, George Washington University, Washington, D.C.

13. Phillip Muhlenberg to John Hubley, April 4, 1789, First Congress Project Collections, George Washington University, Washington, D.C.

14. Frederick A. C. Muhlenberg to Benjamin Rush, March 6, 1789, First Congress Project Collections, George Washington University, Washington, D.C.

15. William Maclay to Benjamin Rush, March 6, 1789, First Congress Project Collections, George Washington University, Washington, D.C.

16. Frederick A. C. Muhlenberg to Benjamin Rush, March 21, 1789, First Congress Project Collections, George Washington University, Washington, D.C. See Joseph B. Varnum, Jr., *The Seat of Government of the United States* (Washington, D.C.: R. Farnham, 1854).

17. Oswald Seidensticker, "Frederick Augustus Conrad Muhlenberg, Speaker of the House of Representatives in the First Congress, 1789," *Pennsylvania Magazine of History and Biography* 19 (1889): 184–206.

18. *Annals of Congress,* 1st Cong., 1st Sess., 99–100.

19. Kenneth R. Bowling, "Politics in the First Congress, 1789–1791" (Phd. diss., University of Wisconsin, 1968), 50.

20. Frederick A.C. Muhlenberg to Benjamin Rush, May 30, 1790, First Congress Project Collections, George Washington University, Washington, D.C.

21. "Journal of the House of Representatives," in *Documentary History of the First Federal Congress, 1789–1791* (Baltimore: Johns Hopkins University Press, 1977), vol. 3.

22. James Sterling Young, *The Washington Community, 1800–1828* (New York: Harcourt, Brace, & World, 1966), 14–20; Varnum, *Seat of Government.* Later the Pennsylvania cause was lost to a compromise on the assumption bill. According to Jefferson's diary this was worked out over a dinner at his house with Hamilton, Madison, and other members of the Virginia delegation. Alvin M. Josephy, Jr., *On the Hill: A History of the American Congress from 1789 to the Present* (New York: Simon & Schuster, 1979), 72–73, questions this account.

23. Harlow, *History of Legislative Methods in the Period before 1825,* 123; Lauros G. McConachie, *Congressional Committees* (New York: Crowell, 1898), 155–56.

24. "The Speaker has promised to go among the members and rouse them with all his power," Maclay, *Journal,* 46, reports with reference to the tariff question. For other references to Muhlenberg's activities see ibid., 133, 146, 151, 180, 187, 227, 261, 282.

25. William Nesbit Chambers, *Political Parties in a New Nation: The American Experience, 1776–1809* (New York: Oxford University Press, 1963), 182. The Federalists controlled the House in 1790, 1792, 1796, and 1798. The Republicans controlled the House in 1794 and 1800. The Federalists controlled the Senate until 1800.

26. John C. Miller, *The Federalist Era, 1789–1801* (New York: Harper & Row, 1960), 81, provides a good account of the Federalist and Republican outlooks.

27. Chambers, *Political Parties in a New Nation*, 42. Out of this barrage of criticism emerged the Sedition Act, which contributed to the decline of the Federalist party.

28. Miller, *Federalist Era*, 81.

29. Harlow, *History of Legislative Methods in the Period before 1825*, 156–57.

30. Chambers, *Political Parties in a New Nation*, 87; Joseph Cooper, *The Origins of the Standing Committees and the Development of the Modern House*, Rice University Studies, vol. 56, no. 3 (Houston: William Marsh Rice University, 1971), 4; Harlow, *History of Legislative Methods in the Period before 1825*, 157; Miller, *Federalist Era*, 163.

31. Joseph M. Bessette, "Is Congress a Deliberative Body?" in *The United States Congress: Proceedings of the Thomas P. O'Neill, Jr., Symposium* (Chestnut Hill, Mass.: Boston College, 1982); Woodrow Wilson, *Congressional Government: A Study in American Politics* (Boston: Houghton Mifflin, 1885), 85.

32. Beckley's activities are described by Chambers, *Political Parties in a New Nation*, 70, 85, 117–19, 132. See also Edmund Berkeley and Dorothy Smith Berkeley, *John Beckley: Zealous Partisan in a Divided Nation* (Philadelphia: American Philosophical Society, 1973).

33. Chambers, *Political Parties in a New Nation*, 171; Cooper, *Origins of the Standing Committees*, 47; Josephy, *On the Hill*, 122; Marshall Smelser, *The Democratic Republic, 1801–1815* (New York: Harper & Row, 1968), 51; Young, *Washington Community*, 128–30.

34. Chambers, *Political Parties in a New Nation*, 185; William E. Dodd, *The Life of Nathanial Macon* (Raleigh: Edwards & Broughton, 1903), ch. 13; Follett, *Speaker of the House*, 68–69; Smelser, *Democratic Republic*, 106. Thomas Perking Abernethy, *The South in the New Nation, 1789–1819* (Baton Rouge: Louisiana State University Press, 1961), 313–14.

35. Dodd, *Life of Nathanial Macon*, 144. On Randolph's split with Jefferson over Florida, see Henry Adams, *History of the United States of America during the Administration of Thomas Jefferson* (New York: A. & C. Boni, 1930); Joseph G. Baldwin, *Party Leaders: Sketches of Thomas Jefferson, Alexander Hamilton, Andrew Jackson, Henry Clay and John Randolph of Roanoke* (New York: Appleton, 1855); Jonathan Daniels, *Ordeal of Ambition: Jefferson, Hamilton and Burr* (Garden City, N.Y.: Doubleday, 1970); and Dumas Malone, *Jefferson the President: Second Term, 1806–1809* (Boston: Little, Brown, 1974), vol. 5 of *Jefferson and His Times*.

36. The Tertium Quids were Republicans who opposed Jefferson and who wished to distinguish themselves from "the two great parties." See J. Franklin Jameson, *Dictionary of United States History, 1492–1984* (Boston: Puritan Publishing, 1894), 577; Norman K. Risjord, *The Old Republicans: Southern Conservatives in Congress, 1800–1824* (New York: Columbia University Press, 1965), 40–71.

37. Harlow, *History of Legislative Methods in the Period before 1825*, ch. 10, provides a good account of the difficulties Jefferson encountered and his method of dealing with them.

38. Chambers, *Political Parties in a New Nation*, 185.

39. Josephy, *On the Hill*, 131.

40. Nathan Schachner, *Thomas Jefferson: A Biography* (New York: Thomas Yoseloff, 1951), 876–87.
41. Wilfred E. Binkley, *American Political Parties: Their Natural History* (New York: Knopf, 1958), 91.
42. Schachner, *Thomas Jefferson,* 887.
43. Chambers, *Political Parties in a New Nation,* 193–95; Clement Eaton, *Henry Clay and the Art of American Politics* (Boston: Little, Brown, 1957), 24; Harlow, *History of Legislative Methods in the Period before 1825,* 199; Josephy, *On the Hill,* 143; Smelser, *Democratic Republic,* 208.
44. Gerald R. Leintz, "House Speaker Elections and Congressional Parties, 1789–1860," *Capitol Studies* 6 (1978): 68; Bernard Mayo, *Henry Clay,* (New York: Archon Books, 1966), 403.
45. Robert G. Brookshire and Dean F. Duncan III, "Congressional Career Patterns and Party Systems," *Legislative Studies Quarterly* 8 (February 1983): 65–78; Nelson W. Polsby, "The Institutionalization of the House of Representatives," *Ameircan Political Science Review* 62 (March 1968): 146; Young, *Washington Community,* 89–90.
46. Cooper, *Origins of the Standing Committees,* 57–65; Harlow, *History of Legislative Methods in the Period before 1825,* 219.
47. The definitional issue is broached by Chambers, *Political Parties in a New Nation,* 46–50, and Young, *Washington Community,* 113–31. Their approaches and conclusions are different. Chambers focuses upon six major functions of political parties: "nominating; electioneering; shaping opinion; mediating among groups, brokerage, or finding formulas of agreement; managing government; and supplying connections between the branches of government" (p. 46). He finds that the Federalist and Republican groups in the early congresses came to perform these functions and concludes that a party system was present. Young focuses upon presidential nominating caucuses, speakership elections, policy outcomes, and associational activity, and concludes that by these tests a party system did not develop until after 1828. For a voting study bearing upon party formation during the Federalist era, see Rudolph M. Bell, *Party and Faction in American Politics: The House of Representatives, 1789–1801* (Westport, Conn.: Greenwood Press, 1973).
48. Follett, *Speaker of the House,* 73–74; Eaton, *Henry Clay,* 23.
49. In one case Clay constrained Randolph by denying him the floor absent a motion under consideration. When Randolph made the required motion, Clay ruled that it could not be considered unless the House accepted it; following Clay's lead, the House declined to do so. In another case Clay ruled that Randolph's motion to reconsider the Missouri Compromise was out of order until the morning business was completed. Then Randolph moved to have the bill held until a motion to reconsider would be in order, which Clay also ruled out of order. In effect, Clay stalled Randolph until the House-passed bill was reported to the Senate. By the time Randolph obtained the floor, it was too late to reconsider the bill. See Follett, *Speaker of the House,* 73–74. During Clay's service as secretary of state to Adams, his relationship with Randolph, then a U.S. senator from Virginia, took a turn for the worse, and a duel was fought. Shots from either side failed to hit the mark and, honor served, the two made amends. Benton's eyewitness account offers an interesting insight into the code of honor. See Thomas Hart Benton, *Thirty Years' View; or, A*

History of the Working American Government for Thirty Years from 1820–1850 (1854–56; reprint, New York: Appleton, 1893), 1:70–76.

50. Follett, *Speaker of the House*, 82.

51. De Alva Stanwood Alexander, *History and Procedure of the House of Representatives* (1916; reprint, New York: Burt Franklin, 1970), 84.

52. Young, *Washington Community*, 131–35; Follett, *Speaker of the House*, 131–35.

53. Mayo, *Henry Clay*, 425.

54. Young, *Washington Community*, 131–32; David W. Rhode and Kenneth A. Schepsle, "The Ambiguous Role of Leadership in Woodrow Wilson's Congress" (Paper delivered at the American Political Science Association Meeting, New Orleans, 1985), argue that Clay used his power over committee appointments to preserve his base of power. Both Follett and Schurz contend that Clay was careful to use his power of appointment to further his policy aims (Follett, *Speaker of the House*, 80; Carl Schurz, *Life of Henry Clay* [New York: Houghton Mifflin, 1892] 1:78). Young's finding that Clay spread his appointments across boardinghouse groups (members living in the same boardinghouse who were presumed to share political interests) is not incompatible with the partisan use of the appointment power unless one assumes, as Young does, that boardinghouse groups were the basic factional units into which the House was divided.

55. Young, *Washington Community*, identifies the seven issues with Clay, and argues that Clay lost in five cases. Interestingly, the "War Hawk" lost on four issues related to foreign policy, where he was out of step with the Monroe administration. That Clay, as speaker, should have been involved in foreign policy issues at all is striking, and confirms my impression that he always regarded himself as a national leader who happened to be speaker.

56. Joseph Cooper and David W. Brady, "Institutional Context and Leadership Style: The House from Cannon to Rayburn," *American Political Science Review* 75 (1981): 411–25; Rhode and Schepsle, "Ambiguous Role."

57. Rhode and Schepsle argue in "Ambiguous Role" that Clay fostered the committee system in order to solidify his position. Harlow argues, however, that Clay was primarily concerned to increase the efficiency of the House, noting in evidence, that several of the new committees were housekeeping devices; that four of six new committees were proposed while Clay was not speaker in 1815, and were established in 1822, when he was also not speaker; and that the establishment of a separate committee on manufactures failed twice while he was speaker (*History of Legislative Methods in the Period before 1825*, 218–19).

58. *The Diary of John Quincy Adams, 1794–1845*, ed. Allan Nevins (New York: Charles Scribner's Sons, 1951), 207, 237, 253, 262.

59. James K. Polk was the other, but he served as governor of Tennessee after leaving the speakership and before his election as president.

60. *Diary of John Quincy Adams*, ed. Nevins, 263.

61. George Dangerfield, *The Awakening of American Nationalism, 1815–1828* (New York: Harper & Row, 1965), ch. 8; Richard P. McCormick, *The Second American Party System: Party Formation in the Jacksonian Era* (Chapel Hill: University of North Carolina Press, 1966), 330.

62. Alexis de Tocqueville, *Democracy in America* (1835), trans. George Lawrence (Garden City, N.Y.: Doubleday, Anchor Books, 1969), 278.

63. Michael F. Holt, *The Political Crisis of the 1850s* (New York: John Wiley & Sons, 1978), 22.

64. Everett Carll Ladd, Jr., *American Political Parties* (New York: Norton, 1970), 88–93.

65. Francis Fry Wayland, *Andrew Stevenson: Democrat and Diplomat, 1785–1857* (Philadelphia: University of Pennsylvania Press, 1949), 35.

66. Ibid., 74.

67. Ibid., 75.

68. Ibid., 76.

69. Ibid., 81–84.

70. Follett, *Speaker of the House*, 85; Wayland, *Andrew Stevenson*, 97.

71. Follett, *The Speaker of the House*, 84.

72. Ibid.

73. Ladd, *American Political Parties*, 57–91.

74. Ibid., 97.

75. William Brock, *Parties and Political Conscience: American Dilemma, 1840–1850* (Millwood, N.Y.: KTO Press, 1979), ch. 3; McCormick, *Second American Party System*, 338–41; Glyndon G. Van Deusen, *The Jacksonian Era, 1828–1848* (New York: Harper & Row, 1959), 112.

76. Brock, *Parties and Political Conscience*, 25; McCormick, *Second American Party System*, 342; David Potter, *The Impending Crisis, 1848–1861* (New York: Harper & Row, 1976), 225–46.

77. McCormick, *Second American Party System*, 345–49.

78. For further information about these speakers, see Joshua Caldwell, "John Bell of Tennessee: A Chapter of Political History," *American Historical Review* 4 (1899): 652–64; Powell Moore, "The Revolt against Jackson in Tennessee, 1835–1836," *Journal of Southern History* 2 (1936): 335–59; Powell Moore, "James K. Polk: Tennessee Politician," *Journal of Southern History* 17 (1951): 493–516; Charles Grier Sellers, Jr., *James K. Polk, Jacksonian* (Princeton: Princeton University Press, 1957), especially chs. 8–10; Fred Harvey Harrington, *Fighting Politician: Major General Nathaniel P. Banks* (Philadelphia: University of Pennsylvania Press, 1948); Johns Eddins Simpson, *Howell Cobb: The Politics of Ambition* (Chicago: Adams Press, 1973); Zachary Taylor Johnson, *The Political Policies of Howell Cobb* (Nashville: George Peabody College, 1929).

79. Prior to the Civil War, the principal concern relating to the speaker's right of floor recognition pertained to the desire of most members to keep the slavery issue off of the floor; after the Civil War, speakers faced a proliferation of potential business, and the power of floor recognition came to be used as an instrument for determining the business of the House more generally. In the latter context it became a potent political device.

80. There has been so much debate among scholars about the role of slavery in the antebellum state and its relationship to the causes of the Civil War that there is nothing to be added here. It only remains to state the perspective that guides the present analysis. Obviously slavery was neither the sole factor contributing to the causes of the Civil War nor steadily a salient matter on the national issue agenda. If one measures the agenda by party platforms, legislation, or other objective indicators, then there are periods when slavery did not dominate the antebellum agenda. Even where it does emerge, it is not easy

to differentiate from associated economic and social phenomena. Acknowledging these evident truths, one may still reasonably claim that slavery, for so long as it existed, was the fundamental fact of American national life, was central to the circumstances that impeded national economic and political development prior to the war, and was the direct cause of it. Lincoln's second inaugural address states the truth of the matter. One account that argues this view is William J. Cooper, Jr., *The South and the Politics of Slavery, 1828–1856* (Baton Rouge: Louisiana State University Press, 1978).

81. Potter, *Impending Crisis,* 249.

82. Accounts of the breakdown of the second party system are to be found in Potter, *Impending Crisis,* and Holt, *Political Crisis of the 1850s.*

83. An overview of these contests for the speakership is Follett, *Speaker of the House,* 51–63. The most detailed account of these speakership elections is Richard F. Bensel's "The Antebellum Political Economy and the Speaker's Contest of 1859" (paper delivered at the American Political Science Association Meeting, New Orleans, 1985). Bensel's exhaustive research is a model for others who seek a historical understanding of the Congress. He presents the political maneuverings during the speakership election of 1859 in detail and traces their roots to the conflicts over the great issues of the day (slavery and tariffs), the career ambitions of members (committee assignments), and the control of House patronage. His conclusion, that "no solution to sectional conflict could have emerged from the antebellum state itself" (p. 83) is shared here.

84. Bensel, "Antebellum Political Economy," discusses the impact of committee appointments on the deadlocked election of 1860. Alexander, *History and Procedure,* ch. 5, stresses the importance of the appointment power to the speakership, noting that speakers of the parliamentary period were often accused of partiality in making committee appointments; but Alexander does not describe them as having used the power to enforce party positions.

85. Consider, for example, a confidential letter from Thomas Henry, a member of Congress, to Speaker Hunter: "My position on the Committees is to me a little mortifying. I do not profess to be worthy of much consideration; but you have undoubtedly placed me in a situation, the last but one on the last and least important Committee. Which will give occasion to political enemies to reproach me and to reproach my friends in the highly respectable district I have the honor to represent. I shall feel more sensibly the taunts of enemies, because I was among the first, who broke away from the marshalled forces of the Whigs, and sustained you to the end, for the highly honorable station you occupy . . . It may hereafter be in your power to remedy, I will not say the wrong, but the injury you have unconsciously inflicted on me" *Correspondence of Robert H. T. Hunter, 1826–1876,* ed. Charles H. Ambler [New York: Da Capo Press, 1971], 31).

86. Follett, *Speaker of the House,* 96.

Chapter 2. The Partisan Speakership

1. Everett Carll Ladd, Jr., *American Political Parties* (New York: Norton, 1970), ch. 4.

2. In the Thirty-sixth Congress (1859–60) the partisan alignment in the House

of Representatives was 114 Republicans and 92 Democrats; in the Thirty-seventh Congress (1861–62) it was 105 Republicans and 43 Democrats. The Republicans remained the dominant party until 1874, holding margins of 102 to 75 in the Thirty-eighth Congress (1863–64), 145–46 in the Thirty-ninth Congress (1865–66), 143–49 in the Fortieth Congress (1867–68), 170–73 in the Forty-first Congress (1868–69), 139–104 in the Forty-second Congress (1870–71), and 203–88 in the Forty-third Congress (1872–73).

3. Michael Les Benedict, *A Compromise of Principle: Congressional Republicans and Reconstruction, 1863–1869* (New York: Norton, 1974), 22–24; Morton Keller, *Affairs of State: Public Life in Late Nineteenth Century America* (Cambridge: Harvard University Press, 1977), 17–30; George H. Mayer, *The Republican Party, 1854–1964* (New York: Oxford University Press, 1977), 93–98.

4. Congressional Research Service, *Major Acts of Congress and Treaties Approved by the Senate,* Report no. 82–15b GOV (Washington, D.C.: GPO, 1982) 43–44.

5. Richard B. Cheney and Lynne V. Cheney, *Kings of the Hill: Power and Personality in the House of Representatives* (New York: Continuum, 1983), 65; Alvin M. Josephy, Jr., *On the Hill: A History of the American Congress from 1789 to the Present* (New York: Simon & Schuster, 1975), 214.

6. George Rothwell Brown, *The Leadership of Congress* (Indianapolis: Bobbs-Merrill, 1922), 59; Hubert Bruce Fuller, *The Speakers of the House* (Boston: Little, Brown, 1909), 159. O. V. Hollister, *Life of Schuyler Colfax* (New York: Funk & Wagnals, 1986), provides a sympathetic biography. James A. Barnes, *John G. Carlisle: Financial Statesman* (New York: Dodd, Mead, 1936), 156, lists Colfax among the great speakers.

7. Josephy, *On the Hill,* 219.

8. Mary Parker Follett, *The Speaker of the House of Representatives* (1902; reprint, New York: Burt Franklin, 1974), 101–02.

9. Fuller, *Speakers of the House,* 158.

10. The best study of one-party politics in America is V. O. Key, Jr., *Southern Politics in State and Nation* (New York: Knopf, 1949).

11. Keller, *Affairs of State,* 167; Matthew Josephson, *The Politicos: 1865–1896* (New York: Harcourt, Brace, 1938), 104–5.

12. Josephson, *Politicos,* 68–77, 94–99, 319–23; Keller, *Affairs of State,* 256–57, 310–12; Mayer, *Republican Party,* 16–18, 204–7.

13. David Saville Muzzey, *James G. Blaine: A Political Idol of Other Days* (New York: Dodd, Mead, 1935), 87–99; Russell H. Conwell, *The Life and Public Service of James G. Blaine* (New York: E. C. Allen, 1884), 307–21; Gail Hamilton, *Biography of James G. Blaine* (Norwich, Conn.: Harry Hill, 1895), 347–63. An interesting account of the Crédit Mobilier scandal and the involvement of Schuyler Colfax and James G. Blaine is to be found in Charles Edward Russell, *Blaine of Maine: His Life and Times* (New York: Cosmopolitan Book Corporation, 1931), 211–56. A recent convention paper by Don Wolfensberger, Minority Counsel to the Subcommittee on the Legislative Process, House Committee on Rules, traces allegations of misconduct against speakers Blaine, Clay, Randall, and Kerr, indicating that in none of these cases was misconduct proven (Don Wolfensberger, "The Roles, Styles, and Conduct of House Speakers: 1789–1987" [paper delivered at the American Political

Science Association Meeting, Washington, D.C., 1988], 23–25).
14. Follett, *Speaker of the House,* 104.
15. Ibid., 188–89; Thomas B. Reed, "A Reply to X.M.C.," *North American Review* 151 (1890): 229.
16. Edward Stanwood, *James Gillespie Blaine* (Boston: Houghton Mifflin, 1905), 117–20.
17. Lauros G. McConachie, *Congressional Committees* (New York: Crowell, 1898), 161.
18. Albert V. House, Jr., "The Contributions of Samuel J. Randall to the Rules of the United States House of Representatives," *American Political Science Review* 29 (1935): 838; Fuller, *Speakers of the House,* 203.
19. Follett, *Speaker of the House,* 110–11; Ralph M. Goldman, *Search for Consensus: The Story of the Democratic Party* (Philadelphia: Temple University Press, 1979), 87; De Alva Stanwood Alexander, *History and Procedure of the House of Representatives* (1916; reprint, New York: Burt Franklin, 1970), 44.
20. House, "Contributions of Samuel J. Randall," 839; Alexander, *History and Procedure,* 194–98; U.S. Congress, House, *A History of the Rules Committee* (Washington, D.C.: GPO, 1983), 49–51. Follett, *Speaker of the House,* holds that "the history of the House of Representatives shows that the consolidation of power has been an inevitable development," and again that, "entirely irrespective of party tenets, there is at present an inevitable tendency towards the centralization of power." Follett was correct in identifying the tendency to centralization in the partisan period, but that it was not inevitable was quickly demonstrated when, within ten years of her study, the House revolted against Cannon. It is more precise to say that the tendency to centralization in the latter part of the nineteenth century was endemic to the conditions of that era, affected both parties, and was most strongly felt in the Republican party.
21. Alexander, *History and Procedure,* 239; House, "Contributions of Samuel B. Randall," 838.
22. Follett, *Speaker of the House,* 113–14; Congressional Research Service, *Major Acts of Congress,* 62.
23. Barnes, *John G. Carlisle,* 67–72.
24. Ibid., 81.
25. Ibid., 95–97.
26. Ibid., 99–101, 108–11.
27. Ibid., 97, 112.
28. Ibid., 116–17, 126, 131–40.
29. In the Sixty-fifth and Seventy-second Congresses the Democrats held six-vote majorities.
30. William A. Robinson, *Thomas B. Reed, Parliamentarian* (New York: Dodd, Mead, 1930), 182–86; Samuel W. McCall, *The Life of Thomas Brackett Reed,* (1914; reprint, New York: AMS Press, 1972), 167.
31. Follett, *Speaker of the House,* 179–214; Thomas B. Reed, "Obstruction in the National House," *North Ameircan Review* 149 (1889): 421–28.
32. Robinson, *Thomas B. Reed,* 208–9; Joseph G. Cannon, "Dramatic Scenes in My Career in Congress: When Reed Counted a Quorum," *Harper's* 140 (1920): 433–37; McCall, *Thomas B. Reed,* 162–72; Follett, *Speaker of the House,* 191–216; Alexander, *History and Procedure,* 155–79.
33. Robinson, *Thomas B. Reed,* 217–27.

34. Thomas B. Reed, "Rules of the House of Representatives," *Century* 37 (1889): 794–95; id., "Reply to X.M.C.," 228–36.

35. For typical statements of the Democratic view, see *Congressional Record,* February 10, 1890, 1178, statement of Mr. Mills of Texas; February 11, 1890, statement of Mr. Holman; February 12, 1890, statement of Mr. Lone of Illinois.

36. Publius [pseud. for Alexander Hamilton, James Madison, and John Jay], *The Federalist Papers* (1787–88; reprint, New York: Modern Library, 1975), no. 10: 57.

37. X.M.C. [pseud.], "Speaker Reed's Error," *North American Review* 151 (1890): 90–111; Reed, "Reply to X.M.C.," 228–36; id., "The Speaker and His Critics," *North American Review* 151 (1890): 237–50.

38. Thomas B. Reed, "A Deliberative Body," *North American Review* 152 (1891): 148–56.

39. Ibid., 148–56.

40. Bureau of the Census, *Historical Statistics of the United States: Colonial Times to 1970* (Washington, D.C.: GPO, 1975), pt. 2:1081.

41. Congressional Research Service, *Major Acts of Congress,* 67–68; Robinson, *Thomas B. Reed,* 235–54.

42. Robinson, *Thomas B. Reed,* 239.

43. Ibid., 243–44.

44. Ibid., 244.

45. Bureau of the Census, *Historical Statistics of the United States,* pt. 1: 224; pt. 2: 1104.

46. Keller, *Affairs of State,* 376–84; Mayer, *Republican Party,* 224–28.

47. Congressional Record, December 8, 1891, 8, 9.

48. Robinson, *Thomas B. Reed,* 300–304.

49. Bureau of the Census, *Historical Statistics,* pt. 1: 224; pt. 2: 1104.

50. Clay was a candidate in 1824. Joe Cannon had support in 1908, and Champ Clark led on several ballots in 1920. Cactus Jack Garner won the California primary and was Roosevelt's main opponent in 1932. Cannon was often spoken of as a presidential candidate, but never seriously competed. Polk and Blaine won party nominations, but at the time Polk was governor of Tennessee and Blaine a U.S. senator from Maine.

51. Robinson, *Thomas B. Reed,* 351–52.

52. Chang-Wei Chui, *The Speaker of the House of Representatives since 1896* (New York: Columbia University Press, 1928), 287–88.

53. Robinson, *Thomas B. Reed,* 353.

54. H. S. Boutell, "Speaker Cannon and the Presidency," *Independent* (1908): 896; Francis E. Leupp, "The New Speaker," *Outlook,* 21 (1903): 684–85; William Rea Gwinn, *Uncle Joe Cannon, Archfoe of Insurgency: A History of the Rise and Fall of Cannonism* (New York: Bookman Associates, 1957), 63–64; Cheney and Cheney, *Kings of the Hill,* 122–23.

55. It is alleged that Henderson was driven from the House due to an improper relationship with a senator's daughter (Neil MacNeil, *Forge of Democracy: The House of Representatives* [New York: David McKay, 1963], 119).

56. Blair Bolles, *Tyrant from Illinois: Uncle Joe Cannon's Experiment with Personal Power* (New York: Norton, 1951), 63.

57. Bolles, *Tyrant from Illinois,* 88–105; Gwinn, *Uncle Joe Cannon,* 72–98; Theo-

dore Roosevelt: An Autobiography (New York: Macmillan, 1913), 382–83. For a good analysis of the political currents of the era, see David W. Brady, *Congressional Voting in a Partisan Era: A Study of the McKinley Houses and a Comparison to the Modern House of Representatives* (Lawrence: University of Kansas Press, 1973).

58. Chiu, *Speaker of the House*, 297–98.
59. Gwinn, *Uncle Joe Cannon*, 94–95.
60. Congressional Research Service, *Major Acts of Congress*, 79–82.
61. Boutell, "Speaker Cannon," 817; Joseph G. Cannon, "The Power of the Speaker," *Century* 78 (1909): 309; id., *Speech of Hon. J. G. Cannon, Delivered at Kansas City, Missouri, Friday, November 26, 1909* (Washington, D.C.: GPO, 1909).
62. Claude E. Barfield, "Our Share of the Booty: The Democratic Party, Cannonism, and the Payne-Aldrich Tariff," *Journal of American History* 57 (1970): 308–23; Gwinn, *Uncle Joe Cannon*, 177–84; Bolles, *Tyrant from Illinois*, 183–95.
63. Gwinn, *Uncle Joe Cannon*, 158–76.
64. Ibid., 174; Kenneth W. Hechler, *Insurgency: Personalities and Politics of the Taft Era* (New York: Columbia University Press, 1940), 59–61.
65. Gwinn, *Uncle Joe Cannon*, 178–84.
66. Ibid., 184–85.
67. Cannon, "Power of the Speaker," 307.
68. Charles R. Atkinson, *The Committee on Rules and the Plot to Overthrow Speaker Cannon* (New York: Columbia University Press, 1911), 51–70.
69. Ibid., 71–94; John D. Baker, "The Character of the Congressional Revolution of 1910," *Journal of American History* 60 (1973): 686.
70. Brown, *Leadership of Congress*, 147–67; Bolles, *Tyrant from Illinois*, 214–22; Atkinson, *Committee on Rules*, 100–121; Gwinn, *Uncle Joe Cannon*, 206–16; L. White Busby, *Uncle Joe Cannon: The Story of a Pioneer American* (New York: Holt, 1927), 243–69; Chiu, *Speaker of the House*, 140–41.
71. Chui, *Speaker of the House*, 141.
72. Cannon's lieutenant, James E. Watson of Indiana, later claimed that Norris would not have opposed Cannon had the speaker given him the committee assignment he wanted. Even principled men can be practical. See James E. Watson, *As I Knew Them* (Indianapolis: Bobbs-Merrill, 1936), 115–16.
73. Nelson W. Polsby, Miriam Gallaher, and Barry Spencer Rundquist, "The Growth of the Seniority System in the United States House of Representatives," *American Political Science Review* 63 (September 1969): 804, demonstrates conclusively that Cannon's harshest tactics occurred toward the end of his reign as his political position weakened.
74. Bolles, *Tyrant from Illinois*, 98–103.
75. Ladd, *American Political Parties*, 152–57.
76. Atkinson, *Committee on Rules*, 74.
77. Ladd, *American Political Parties*, 115–23.
78. Richard L. McCormick, "The Party Period and Public Policy: An Exploratory Hypothesis" *Journal of American History* 66 (September 1979): 283–93; id., *The Party Period and Public Policy: American Politics from the Age of Jackson to the Progressive Era* (New York: Oxford University Press, 1986).

Chapter 3. The Feudal Speakership

1. Blair Bolles, *Tyrant from Illinois: Uncle Joe Cannon's Experiment with Personal Power* (New York: Norton, 1951), 230.
2. George Rothwell Brown, *The Leadership of Congress* (Indianapolis: Bobbs-Merrill, 1922), 171; Paul D. Hasbrouck, *Party Government in the House of Representatives* (New York: Macmillan, 1927), 9.
3. See Nelson Polsby, "The Institutionalization of the U.S. House of Representatives," *American Political Science Review* 62 (March 1968): 144–69; Nelson Polsby, Miriam Gallaher, and Barry Rundquist, "The Growth of the Seniority System in the U.S. House of Representatives," *American Political Science Review* 63 (August 1969): 787–807; David W. Brady, *Congressional Voting in a Partisan Era: A Study of the McKinley Houses and a Comparison to the Modern House of Representatives* (Lawrence: University of Kansas Press), 186.
4. Chang-Wei Chiu, *The Speaker of the House of Representatives since 1896* (New York: Columbia University Press, 1928), 302–3.
5. Ibid., 46–58, summarizes Clark's extensive participation in floor debate.
6. James S. Fleming, "Re-establishing Leadership in the House of Representatives: The Case of Oscar W. Underwood," *Mid-America* 54 (1927): 235; Evans C. Johnson, *Oscar W. Underwood: A Political Biography* (Baton Rouge: Louisiana State University Press, 1980), 137–42; Hasbrouck, *Party Government*, 11–13.
7. Hasbrouck, *Party Government*, 11–13. The Holman Rule is discussed on p. 58 above.
8. Fleming, "Re-establishing Leadership," 241.
9. Ibid., 240.
10. Wilder H. Haines, "The Congressional Caucus of Today," *American Political Science Review* 9 (November 1915): 696–706; James Holt, *Congressional Insurgents and the Party System, 1909–1916* (Cambridge: Harvard University Press, 1967), 84–85; Brown, *Leadership of Congress*, 178–81.
11. Fleming, "Re-establishing Leadership," 240; Congressional Research Service, *Major Acts of Congress and Treaties Approved by the Senate, 1789–1980*, Report no. 82–156 GOV (Washington, D.C.: GPO, 1982), 83–86.
12. Hasbrouck, *Party Government*, 5.
13. Chiu, *Speaker of the House*, 155.
14. House Rules Committee, *History of the Committee on Rules* (Washington, D.C.: GPO, 1982), 97–108. Speaker Albert won control of the Rules Committee for the speakership. Speaker O'Neill used this control to his advantage when the need arose. Speaker Wright did so systematically in the 100th Congress.
15. Chui, *Speaker of the House*, 154.
16. Polsby, Gallaher, and Rundquist, "Growth of the Seniority System," 804; Barbara Hinckley, *The Seniority System in Congress* (Bloomington: Indiana University Press, 1971).
17. T. Richard Witmar, "The Aging of the House," *Political Science Quarterly* 79 (1964): 526–37; Polsby, "Institutionalization of the U.S. House"; Samuel Kernell, "Toward Understanding 19th Century Congressional Careers: Ambition, Competition, and Rotation," *American Journal of Political Science* 21 (November 1977): 669–93; Robert G. Brookshire and Dean F. Duncan III, "Con-

gressional Career Patterns and Party Systems," *Legislative Studies Quarterly* 8 (February 1983): 65–78.

18. *Congressional Directory*, 1st ed., 63d Cong., 2d sess. (Washington, D.C.: GPO, 1913), 185–213.

19. Brown, *Leadership of Congress*, 179–81, emphasizes the degree of southern influence; and see George Rothwell Brown, *The Speaker of the House: The Romantic Story of John H. Garner* (New York: Brewer, Warren & Putnam, 1932), 126–36.

20. Seward W. Livermore, *Politics Is Adjourned: Woodrow Wilson and the War Congress, 1916–1918* (Middletown, Conn.: Wesleyan University Press, 1966), 137; Arthur M. Schlesinger, Jr., *The Crisis of the Old Order, 1919–1933* (Boston: Houghton Mifflin, 1957), 228; Hasbrouck, *Party Government*, 94.

21. Livermore, *Politics Is Adjourned*, 224.

22. Bascom N. Timmons, *Garner of Texas: A Personal History* (New York: Harper & Brothers, 1948), 111.

23. For an account of James R. Mann, see Brown, *Leadership of Congress*, 191–92. On Longworth's role in deposing Mann, see William Hard, "Nicholas Longworth," *Nation* 118 (1924): 88–89. On the role of Hays and Penrose, see Chiu, *Speaker of the House*, 25–27.

24. On the Mann coup, see Brown, *Leadership of Congress*, 191–93; Hasbrouck, *Party Government*, 43–45; Chiu, *Speaker of the House*, 75–76; Lynn Haines, "Your Government at Washington," *Searchlight* 4 (May 1919): 3–7.

25. Brown, *Leadership of Congress*, 194–96.

26. Ibid., 200–229.

27. Haines, "Your Government at Washington," 6–7.

28. Brown, *Leadership of Congress*, 211–21.

29. Hasbrouck, *Party Government*, 91–97.

30. On Longworth's action, see "You Can't Help Liking Nick," *Literary Digest*, November 21, 1925, 45–46; Duff Gilfond, "Mr. Speaker," *American Mercury*, August 1927, 457; Lynn Haines, "A Reversion to Cannonism," *Searchlight on Congress* 11 (December 1925): 9. For Uncle Joe Cannon's unreconstructed views of 1920s-style insurgency, see Joseph G. Cannon, "Party Discipline," *Saturday Evening Post*, September 27, 1924, 3–4, 71–72. Insurgency during the Wilson administration is examined by Holt, *Congressional Insurgents*.

31. "The Next Speaker," *Outlook* 139 (March 1925): 357.

32. William Hard, "Nicholas Longworth," *American Review of Reviews* 71 (1925): 371.

33. Gilfond, "Mr. Speaker," 453. See also Lucy Meriweather Calhoun, "Introducing the New Speaker," *World Review*, December 14, 1925, 177.

34. Neil MacNeil, *Forge of Democracy: The House of Representatives* (New York: David McKay, 1963), 81.

35. Gilfond, "Mr. Speaker," 453. See also William Tyler Page, "Mr. Speaker Longworth," *Scribner's* 83 (March 1928): 276–77.

36. Hard, "Nicholas Longworth," 88.

37. The famous Garner-Longworth drinking hideaway appears initially to have been called the "Bureau of Education" later revised to the "Board of Education" (see Joseph Alsop and Robert Kintner, "Never Leave Them Angry," *Saturday Evening Post*, January 18, 1941, 22). The Bureau or Board of Education

received its name from Congressman John McDuffie of Alabama (Alfred Steinberg, *Sam Rayburn: A Biography* [New York: Hawthorne Books, 1975], 85).
According to Steinberg, Longworth would occasionally perform on his Strad-
ivarius at the Board, an instrument that he could play "behind his back, over
his head, and between his legs" (Gilfond, "Mr. Speaker," 451). Garner continued the Board, but his predilection was for poker (Steinberg, *Sam Rayburn,*
85–86; Timmons, *Garner of Texas,* 121). The Board was discontinued by
Rainey, Byrns, and Bankhead, but reinstated by Rayburn. It was discontinued
by McCormack.

38. The following account relies upon Alonzo L. Hamby, ed., *The New Deal:
Analysis & Interpretation* (New York: Longman, 1981); Arthur M. Schlesinger,
Jr., *The Coming of the New Deal* (Boston: Houghton Mifflin, 1958); Raymond
Moley, *The First New Deal* (New York: Harcourt, Brace & World, 1966);
Rexford Tugwell, *The Democratic Roosevelt: A Biography of Franklin D.
Roosevelt* (Garden City, N.Y.: Doubleday, 1957); William E. Leuchtenberg,
Franklin D. Roosevelt and the New Deal, 1932–1940 (New York: Harper &
Row, 1963).

39. James T. Patterson, *Congressional Conservatism and the New Deal* (Lexington:
University of Kentucky Press, 1967), 170–76.

40. *Congressional Directory,* 63d Cong., 1st sess.; 71st Cong., 1st sess. (Washington, D.C.: GPO, 1913; 1929).

41. Polsby, "Institutionalization of the U.S. House," 146; "Loss of Democratic
Edge in House Hangs Heavy over Administration," *Newsweek,* February 28,
1944, 38.

42. These figures were culled from the *Congressional Directory,* 63d through 72d
Congresses. In his study of voting patterns in the 1890s, David Brady identifies
major committees empirically as those with the right to report bills at any time
(*Congressional Voting in a Partisan Era,* 156). This gives him a number of
substantive legislative committees and a few housekeeping committees such as
Accounts and Enrolled Bills. The figures in the text are based on the subjective
estimate of the value of the major legislative committees and those distributing
pork. They are: Agriculture; Appropriations; Banking and Currency; Coinage-
Weights-Measures; Foreign Affairs; Immigration; Interior and Insular Affairs;
Judiciary; Merchant Marine and Fisheries; Military Affairs; Naval Affairs; Post
Offices and Roads; Public Buildings; Public Lands; Rivers and Harbors; Rules;
and Ways and Means.

43. Timmons, *Garner of Texas,* 119. On Garner's four bills, see ibid, pp. 109–
10. On his opposition to Mellon, see pp. 107 and 115. Further description of
the Garner-Mellon battles is given by Schlesinger, *Crisis of the Old Order,* 62.
A biased account of the Mellon tax program is found in the progressive journal
Searchlight on Congress: "Mellon Tax Plan Meets a Just Fate," 9 (May 1924):
4–5; "The Mellon Tax Plan Again Up to Congress," 11 (October 1925): 8–
12; "Congress Asked to OK More of the Mellon Plan," 11 (November 1925):
3–9; "The New Mellon Bill Now Up to the Senate," 11 (December 1925): 4–
10; "Mellon Demonstrates Mastery over Congress," 11 (February 1926): 4–
8.

44. On Garner's fiscal conservatism, see Timmons, *Garner of Texas,* 138–51.

45. Ibid., 136.

46. Ibid.

47. Both Republicans and Democrats were fiscal conservatives in the sense of seeking a balanced budget. The Democrats favored public works and public relief financed by higher taxes on wealthy taxpayers; the Republicans favored fiscal retrenchment and lower taxes.

48. O. C. Fisher, *Cactus Jack* (Waco: Texian Press, 1978), 84–85; Schlesinger, *Crisis of the Old Order*, 229; Timmons, *Garner of Texas*, 141–51.

49. Fisher, *Cactus Jack*, 87; H. G. Dulaney, ed., *Speak Mr. Speaker* (Bonham, Tex.: Sam Rayburn Foundation, 1978), 43–44.

50. Robert A. Caro, *The Years of Lyndon Johnson*, vol. 1, *The Path to Power* (New York: Knopf, 1982), 560–71; Leuchtenberg, *Franklin Roosevelt and the New Deal*, 6–8; Schlesinger, *Crisis of the Old Order*, 295–314; Tugwell, *Democratic Roosevelt*, 224–27. Garner served as a loyal supporter of the New Deal until Roosevelt's second term. The relationship between the two had taken a bad turn as a result of Garner's opposition to the Court-packing plan and the attempt to purge southern Democrats in the 1938 election. Thus it is not surprising to find that the accounts of Garner afforded by those enamored of FDR differ greatly from those characterizing his earlier service in the House by those close to him there. Roosevelt himself called Garner "impossible" (James MacGregor Burns, *Roosevelt: The Lion and the Fox* [New York: Harcourt, Brace, 1956], 414). According to Rexford Tugwell, Garner was a "confused Texan who, as the most prominent congressional Democrat, had the responsibility for shaping alternatives to the Hoover policies . . . he was, however, a conservative and so lacking in imagination that nothing had occurred to him that Hoover had not thought of first" (*Democratic Roosevelt*, 226). To one Rooseveltian scholar, Garner was "an erratic leader of his party" who "had advocated both retrenchment and heavy spending" (Leuchtenberg, *Franklin D. Roosevelt and the New Deal*, 6). To another, he "was baffled by the Depression" and "vacillated between cooperation and obstruction in his attitude toward the [Hoover] administration" (Schlesinger, *Crisis of the Old Order*, 228). On Rainey's progressive tendencies and his conflicts with Garner, see Lynn Haines, "The New Mellon Bill Now Up to Senate," *Searchlight on Congress*, 11 (December 1925): 4–5. For a balanced view, see D. B. Hardeman and Donald C. Bacon, *Rayburn: A Biography* (Austin: Texas Monthly Press, 1987), 125, 133–43, 225, 229–30, 503n.

51. The quoted characterization is from Robert A. Waller, *Rainey of Illinois: A Political Biography, 1903–1934* (Urbana: University of Illinois Press, 1977), 181.

52. In the 1925 debate over the Mellon tax bill, Rainey was a leading critic of Mellon on the floor, although Garner was the effective leader of the Democrats. See Haines, "Mellon Tax Plan Meets a Just Fate" and "Mellon Bill Now Up to Senate."

53. Waller, *Rainey of Illinois*, 160–62.

54. Ibid., 163–167; Timmons *Garner of Texas*, 137.

55. Waller, *Rainey of Illinois*, 174–77. See also *New York Times*, November 10, 13, 17, 19, and 27, 1932; December 24 and 30, 1932; February 2, 16, 18, and 27, 1933; March 3, 1933.

56. *New York Times*, November 29, 1932.

57. *New York Times*, March 3, 1933.

58. Polsby, "Growth of the Seniority System," 794.

59. *Congressional Directory,* 72d Cong., 1st sess. (Washington, D.C.: GPO, 1932), 19131.

60. Moley, *First New Deal,* 203–4; Burns, *Roosevelt: The Lion and the Fox,* 175; *New York Times,* March 1, 1933.

61. Waller, *Rainey of Illinois,* 194–95.

62. Ray Tucker, "A Master for the House," *Colliers,* January 5, 1935, 22; *Time,* December 12, 1934, 9–10; Steinberg, *Sam Rayburn,* 124–25. See also *New York Times,* November 13, 22, and 25, 1934; December 13 and 16, 1934.

63. *Time,* December 24, 1934, 10.

64. *Time,* September 23, 1940, 17.

65. Caro, *Path to Power,* 318–21.

66. Ibid., 762–63, provides the most readable account. Caro's description of Rayburn is powerful. It is regrettable, in a way, that life is not as dramatic as Caro makes it seem. Caro mixes facts, anecdotes, and interpretation; a reader is well advised to differentiate among the three. For other accounts of Rayburn's effectiveness as chairman of the Interstate and Foreign Commerce Committee, see Hardeman and Bacon, *Rayburn,* chs. 9 and 10; Steinberg, *Sam Rayburn,* 90–91, 106–14; C. Dwight Dorough, *Mr. Sam* (New York: Random House, 1962), 224–26; Tucker, "Master for the House," 22, 149; "National Affairs," *Time,* September 23, 1940, 16–17.

67. "People of the Week," *U.S. News and World Report,* January 7, 1949, 40–41.

68. Alsop and Kintner, "Never Leave Them Angry," 23.

69. Joseph Cooper and David W. Brady, "Institutional Context and Leadership Style: The House from Cannon to Rayburn," *American Political Science Review* 75 (June 1981): 411–25.

70. Richard Bolling, interview with author, January 13, 1982; D. B. Hardemann, interview with author, July 19, 1979.

71. "National Affairs," *Time,* May 16, 1949, 24; "The Cloakroom Coup," *Newsweek,* February 12, 1945, 53, 55.

72. Steinberg, *Sam Rayburn,* 167–68. Hardemann and Bacon, *Rayburn,* 257–61.

73. Sam Rayburn, "The Speaker Speaks of Presidents," *New York Times Magazine,* June 4, 1961, 32.

74. Steinberg, *Sam Rayburn,* 168; Hardemann and Bacon, *Rayburn,* 277.

75. Steinberg, *Sam Rayburn,* 196, 211, 236–40, 256–57; Hardeman and Bacon, 311–12; Caro, *Path to Power,* 313, describes Rayburn's attitude toward friendship.

76. The federal budget jumped from 3.23 percent of GNP in 1918 to 16.59 percent in 1919. After peaking in 1920 at 22.01 percent, it fell to a low of 3.01 percent in 1927, and stood at 4.71 percent in 1931. In 1932 it jumped to 8.03 percent and ranged between 8.03 percent and 12.10 percent from 1932 to 1941. In 1942 it jumped again to 24.70 percent and peaked in 1944 at 45.20 percent. After the war, it declined to a low of 12.00 percent in 1948 and then steadily increased to a range of 19–22 percent through the 1970s. Figures for years prior to 1940 were reconstructed from Bureau of the Census, *Historical Statistics of the United States: Colonial Times to 1970* (Washington, D.C.: GPO, 1975), pt. 1: 224; pt. 2: 1105. Figures for years subsequent to 1939 were taken from *Historical Tables: Budget of the United States Government, Fiscal Year 1987* (Washington, D.C.: GPO, 1986) 1.2(1)–(2).

77. Steinberg, *Sam Rayburn*, 237; Susan M. Hartmann, *Truman and the 80th Congress* (Columbia: University of Missouri Press, 1971), 11, 75.
78. On "Meat Axe Taber," see Hartmann, *Truman and the 80th Congress*, 14.
79. Ibid., 76.
80. Ibid., 11.
81. William S. White, "Then Martin, Now Rayburn, and So On," *New York Times Magazine*, February 6, 1955, 36.
82. Hartmann, *Truman and the 80th Congress*, ch. 4.
83. Ibid., 19–20.
84. Ibid., 17, 128–30, 137, 211–12.
85. Truman's foreign policy achievements included the Marshall Plan (*Congressional Quarterly Almanac*, 1947: 607–30); the United Nations (ibid., 1945: 471–74); aid to Greece and Turkey (ibid., 1947: 35–37, 247–57); and several peace treaties (ibid., 1947: 263–68).
86. Steinberg, *Sam Rayburn*, 254.
87. "People of the Week," *U.S. News and World Report*, April 7, 1950, 39–40.
88. The 21-day rule was helpful in negotiating other legislation to the floor even when it was not invoked. In the Eighty-first Congress the rule was invoked for the anti-poll-tax bill and the rivers and harbors bill. The threat of its use forced action on the minimum wage, social security, and housing bills (*Congressional Quarterly Almanac*, 1949: 577). In the Eighty-second Congress the following bills were brought out of the Committee on Rules via the 21-day rule: the rivers and harbors bill, the flood-control bill, the joint resolution providing for U.S. participation in international organizations, bills granting statehood to Alaska and Hawaii, the National Science Foundation bill, the mining bill, the veterans' hospital bill, and the poll-tax bill (ibid., 1951: 336).
89. Fred I. Greenstein, *The Hidden-Hand Presidency: Eisenhower as Leader* (New York: Basic Books, 1982), 49.
90. "The Congress: Maneuvers on the Hill," *Time*, June 1, 1953, 14; and Steinberg, *Sam Rayburn*, 281.
91. "Congress: Maneuvers on the Hill," 14.
92. Greenstein, *Hidden-Hand Presidency*, 59. Eisenhower sought to use his friendship with the Texas oilman and Johnson bankroller Sid Richardson.
93. Hardeman and Bacon, *Rayburn*, 385, 395–96.
94. Alfred Steinberg, *Sam Johnson's Boy: A Close-up of the President from Texas* (New York: Macmillan, 1968), 379; "Last Roundup in Congress—Two Texans in the Saddle," *U.S. News and World Report*, August 22, 1958, 56–58; "Two Texans Who Call the Signals," ibid., January 17, 1958, 48–50; "41 Years of Experience to Help—or Hinder—Ike," ibid., November 19, 1954, 88, 90–91.
95. "People of the Week," *U.S. News and World Report*, December 17, 1954, 14; Steinberg, *Sam Rayburn*, 297.
96. Steinberg, *Sam Johnson's Boy*, 393; id., *Sam Rayburn*, 297; Hardeman and Bacon, *Rayburn*, 407.
97. "People of the Week," *U.S. News and World Report*, December 21, 1956, 18; Steinberg, *Sam Johnson's Boy*, 447–48; id., *Sam Rayburn*, 312.
98. Steinberg, *Sam Johnson's Boy*, 447.
99. *Congressional Record*, January 30, 1957, H1324–26.
100. Democratic Study Group, "A Short History of the Democratic Study Group, 1957–1979" (n.d., mimeographed). See also Kenneth Kofmehl, "The Insti-

tutionalization of a Voting Bloc," *Western Political Quarterly* 17 (June 1984): 256–62; Arthur G. Stevens, Jr., Arthur H. Miller, and Thomas E. Mann, "Mobilization of Liberal Strength in the House, 1955–70: The Democratic Study Group," in Robert L. Peabody and Nelson W. Polsby, eds., *New Perspectives on the House of Representatives* (Chicago: Rand McNally, 1977), 71–96. The precursor of McCarthy's Mavericks was a caucus of thirty-five progressive Democrats and Republicans in the 1930s led by Texas populist Maury Maverick, and called Maverick's Mavericks (see "House Mavericks Threaten a Fight," *New York Times,* April 14, 1935, 10).

101. This account is based on "People of the Week: Battle over Civil Rights," *U.S. News and World Report,* August 16, 1957, 16; Steinberg, *Sam Rayburn,* 314–15; "The Congress: Compromised Compromise," *Time,* September 2, 1957, 13–14; Richard Bolling, *House Out of Order,* (New York: Dutton, 1965), ch. 9; *Congressional Quarterly Almanac,* 1957: 562, 568–69.

102. *Congressional Quarterly Almanac,* 1957: 569. Thurmond's record of twenty-four hours, eighteen minutes surpassed the standard of twenty-two hours and twenty six minutes set by Democrat Wayne Morse of Oregon in 1953. As of 1990, the Thurmond record still stands.

103. Carl Albert, interview with author, May 11, 1979. A similar account was given by Speaker Albert to Anthony Champagne (*Congressman Sam Rayburn,* [New Brunswick, N.J.: Rutgers University Press, 1984], 149–51).

104. Bolling, *House Out of Order,* 181; Hardeman and Bacon, *Rayburn,* 421–22.

105. This account is based on "A Leader with Troubles: Division in the Ranks," *U.S. News and World Report,* September 7, 1959, 48–49; "As Speaker Rayburn Sees the Labor Issue," ibid., August 24, 1959, 90–91; Bolling, *House Out of Order,* ch. 8; and Hardeman and Bacon, *Rayburn,* 431–32.

106. Bolling, *House Out of Order,* 169.

107. Ibid., 172.

108. Steinberg, *Sam Rayburn,* 316.

109. Ibid., see also "National Affairs: Mister Sam's Skid," *Newsweek,* September 17, 1959, 36, 38; "The Congress," *Time,* February 10, 1961, 13.

110. Steinberg, *Sam Rayburn,* 324–35; "It Is Up to Mr. Sam," *New Republic,* February 8, 1960, 3–4.

111. Steinberg, *Sam Rayburn,* 324–35; "It Is Up to Mr. Sam," *New Republic,* February 8, 1960, 3–4. See also Bolling, *House Out of Order,* 216; Hardeman and Bacon, *Rayburn,* 447–65.

112. Robert L. Peabody, "The Enlarged Rules Committee," in Peabody and Polsby, eds., *New Perspectives on the House of Representatives,* 129–64; Steinberg, *Sam Rayburn,* 336–38; see also "People of the Week," *U.S. News and World Report,* February 13, 1961, 75; "Inside Story of a Fight for Control of the Congress," ibid., March 6, 1961, 75; "The Congress," *Time,* February 10, 1961, 11–14; "The Congress: At the Brink," *Time,* February 3, 1961, 17–18; "Congress a Lamb," *Newsweek,* January 30, 1961, 20, 22; "It Is Still . . . . The House That 'Mr Sam' the Speaker Runs," ibid., February 13, 1961, 26–28; "Help for Mr. Sam," ibid., February 6, 1961, 27–28.

113. Champagne, *Congressman Sam Rayburn,* provides an excellent account of Rayburn's district style; table 5, p. 177, details Rayburn's electoral opposition.

114. Richard Bolling, *Power in the House: A History of the Leadership of the House of Representatives* (New York: Dutton, 1968), 195, describes Rayburn's cau-

tion. On Rayburn's use of lieutenants see "Two Texans Who Call the Signals," 49.

115. Caro, *Path to Power,* ch. 18, is a good example.

116. D. B. Hardeman, interview with author, July 19, 1979; Steinberg, *Sam Rayburn,* 315, has Rayburn complaining about a majority of 282.

Chapter 4. Emergence of the Democratic Speakership

1. John Barriere, interview with author, July 18, 1979.

2. Randall Ripley, *Party Leaders in the House of Representatives* (Washington, D.C.: Brookings Institution, 1967). The term *collegial group* is his.

3. Ibid., 33–38.

4. Ibid., 67–72.

5. Ibid., 70, 150.

6. Richard Bolling, *House Out of Order* (New York: Dutton, 1965), 74–76.

7. Richard Bolling, *Power in the House: A History of the Leadership of the House of Representatives* (New York: Dutton, 1968), ch. 6.

8. Morris Udall, interview with author, June 5, 1979.

9. "McCormack Beats Back House Revolt," *Washington Post,* January 3, 1969; "Cleaning Up House," *New Republic,* January 4, 1969, 9–10; Robert L. Peabody, *Leadership in Congress: Stability, Succession, and Change* (Boston: Little, Brown, 1975), 164.

10. See Norman J. Ornstein, ed., *Congress in Change: Evolution and Reform* (New York: Praeger, 1975); Norman J. Ornstein and David W. Rohde, "Political Parties and Congressional Reform," in Jeff Fishel, ed., *Parties and Elections in an Anti-Party Age: American Politics and Crisis of Confidence* (Bloomington: Indiana University Press, 1978), 280–94; Thomas E. Mann and Norman J. Ornstein, *The New Congress* (Washington, D.C.: American Enterprise Institute, 1980); Burton D. Sheppard, *Rethinking Congressional Reform: The Reform Roots of the Special Interest Congress* (Cambridge, Mass.: Schenkman Books, 1985).

11. Sheppard, *Rethinking Congressional Reform,* 26–27.

12. The best summary account is in Ornstein and Rohde, "Political Parties and Congressional Reform." The Democratic Study Group produced a chronological list of the major reforms in a special report, "Reform in the House of Representatives" (November 6, 1978, mimeographed).

13. Ornstein and Rohde argue that the decentralizing reforms themselves created a power vacuum into which a willing and able speaker could step ("Political Parties and Congressional Reform," 292). Sheppard, whose view is representative of recent congressional scholarship, emphasizes the institutionalization of the dispersal of power (*Rethinking Congressional Reform,* ch. 7). There can be no doubt that the immediate effect of the congressional reforms of the early 1970s was to decentralize the House; however, the powers given to the speaker are those requisite to centralization of power in the speakership, as we shall see in ch. 5.

14. The importance of the regular monthly caucus is stressed both by Ornstein and Rohde ("Political Parties and Congressional Reform," 283) and by Sheppard, (*Rethinking Congressional Reform,* 42).

15. James T. Patterson, *Congressional Conservatism and the New Deal: The*

Growth of the Conservative Coalition in Congress (Lexington: University of Kentucky Press, 1967), 210.

16. Sheppard, *Rethinking Congressional Reform*, 42, 50.

17. Ornstein and Rohde, "Political Parties and Congressional Reform" 282. There are five methods of voting in the House of Representatives. They are by (1) ballot; (2) voice vote, in which the chair declares the outcome; (3) division, in which the chair counts the yeas and nays as they stand; (4) teller vote, in which members queue up in lines, yea and nay; and (5), since 1973, electronic device. The secret ballot is used only in party caucuses and is not a constitutionally valid method of voting in the Congress. The teller vote may be either recorded (the tellers take down the names of the members as they pass through the teller lines) or unrecorded (the tellers merely count heads by taking yea and nay cards). Prior to the Legislative Reform Act of 1970, teller votes were normally unrecorded in the Committee of the Whole. For a complete overview, see *Guide to Congress* (Washington, D.C.: Congressional Quarterly, 1976), 346.

18. Sheppard, *Rethinking Congressional Reform*, 49–53. The adoption of the recorded teller vote led directly to the implementation of electronic voting in the Ninety-third Congress in order to save time. An unintended consequence of the adoption of the electronic system for recording votes was the reduction in the amount of time members spent on the floor awaiting votes. This dramatically decreased their main opportunity for informal discussion and camaraderie. The therapeutic generation succumbed to technology.

19. Sheppard, *Rethinking Congressional Reform*, 53. Ornstein and Rohde, "Political Parties and Congressional Reform," 283.

20. Ornstein and Rohde, "Political Parties and Congressional Reform," 286; Sheppard, *Rethinking Congressional Reform*, 234–36.

21. *Business Week*, January 9, 1971, 66, 69; John Fischer, "The Upheaval in Congress," *Harpers'* 241 (October 1970): 36.

22. *Time*, February 1, 1971, 13.

23. *Business Week,* January 1, 1971, 69.

24. Charles S. Bullock III, "House Careerists: Changing Patterns of Longevity and Attrition," *American Political Science Review* 66 (October 1972): 1296.

25. Carl Albert, interview with author, May 9, 1979.

26. Nelson W. Polsby, "Two Strategies of Influence: Choosing a Majority Leader, 1962," in Robert L. Peabody, ed., *Leadership in Congress,* (Boston: Little, Brown, 1976), 66–99. See also "The House: Majority Winner?" *Newsweek,* December 4, 1961, 17–18.

27. Peabody, *Leadership in Congress,* 218; Thomas P. O'Neill, Jr., *Man of the House: The Life and Political Memoirs of Speaker Tip O'Neill* (New York: Random House, 1987), 217–18.

28. Carl Albert, interview with author, April 16, 1987; Steven C. Roberts, "A Most Important Man on Capitol Hill," *New York Times Magazine,* September 22, 1985, 44; O'Neill, *Man of the House,* 219.

29. Speaker Albert did not initiate Teague's challenge to Rostenkowski.

30. Democratic Study Group, "Reform in the House of Representatives," 11–18.

31. Richard M. Nixon, "State of the Union Address," January 22, 1971, *Congressional Quarterly Almanac,* 1971: 2A–5A.

32. *Congressional Quarterly Almanac,* 1972: 852–53; *Washington Post,* April 21,

1972; Fletcher Thompson to Carl Albert, January 26, 1972; Emanuel Celler to Carl Albert, May 12, 1972; John Barriere to Carl Albert, May 15, 16, and 30, 1972; Thomas P. O'Neill, Jr., to Carl Albert, May 24, 1972; Andrew J. Biemiller to Carl Albert, November 17, 1975. All primary sources cited in this chapter are to be found in the Carl Albert Collection, Carl Albert Center, University of Oklahoma.

33. John Barriere to Carl Albert, May 15and 16, 1972, May 16, 1972; Dan Cohen to Peter Rodino, October 22, 1975; Andrew J. Biemiller to Carl Albert, November 17, 1975; *Congressional Quarterly Weekly Report*, November 22, 1975, 2525.

34. Gary Orfield, *Congressional Power: Congress and Social Change* (New York: Harcourt Brace Jovanovich, 1975), 192–216.

35. John Barriere to Carl Albert, March 15, 1973.

36. John Barriere to Carl Albert, April 26, 1971; *Congressional Quarterly Almanac,* 1971: 192–93.

37. John Barriere to Carl Albert, April 26 and 28, 1971.

38. John Barriere to Carl Albert, May 6, 1971.

39. John Barriere to Carl Albert, May 7, 1971.

40. Orfield, *Congressional Power,* 223.

41. John Barriere to Carl Albert, May 24, 1971.

42. *Congressional Quarterly Almanac,* 1971: 181–83.

43. Ibid., 193–97. John Barriere to Carl Albert, February 10, 1971, March 19, 22, and 30, 1971, July 13, 1971; Carl Albert, press conferences, May 26, 1971, June 29, 1971.

44. *Congressional Quarterly Almanac,* 1971: 174.

45. John Barriere to Carl Albert, March 26, 1971.

46. Joint press conference on the minimum wage, March 4, 1971 (audio tape).

47. John Barriere to Carl Albert, April 26, 1971.

48. Wright Patman, "Dear Colleague," February 19, 1971; Wright Patman to Carl Albert, February 19, 1971; Wright Patman to Carl Albert, March 3, 1971; *Wall Street Journal,* March 3, 1971; Mike Reed to Carl Albert, March 4, 1971.

49. *Congressional Quarterly Weekly Report,* October 14, 1972, 2679–80.

50. Carl Albert to Holland Roberts, February 28, 1972.

51. Mike Reed to Carl Albert, July 29, 1971, August 8, 1971; Wilbur Mills to W. R. Poage, May 5, 1971; *Congressional Quarterly Almanac,* 1971: 481–93.

52. Mike Mansfield to Carl Albert, Wilbur D. Mills, Russell B. Long, John O. Pastore, and Herman E. Talmadge, June 30, 1971; Russell B. Long to Mike Mansfield, Carl Albert, Wilbur D. Mills, John O. Pastore, and Herman E. Talmadge, July 1, 1971; Mike Mansfield to Russell B. Long, July 6, 1971; Wilbur Mills to Mike Mansfield, July 12, 1971; Mike Mansfield to Carl Albert, August 9, 1971; Mike Mansfield to Carl Albert, Russell B. Long, John O. Pastore, and Herman E. Talmadge, November 3, 1971; Carl Albert to Mike Mansfield, November 4, 1971.

53. George Mahon to Carl Albert, August 3, 1972; *Wall Street Journal,* August 8, 1972.

54. John Barriere to Carl Albert, July 12, 1971; September 20, 1971.

55. *Congressional Quarterly Almanac,* 1972: 362.

56. Carl Albert to William M. Colmer, November 17, 1971; William M. Colmer to Carl Albert, November 18, 1971.

57. John Dent to Carl Albert, November 17, 1971.

58. Carl Albert to William Colmer, November 17, 1971.

59. William Colmer to Carl Albert, November 18, 1985. One measure of the ideological difference between Colmer and Albert is the fact that Colmer's administrative assistant, Trent Lott, was later elected to the House from Mississippi as a Republican and became the party's whip. In 1988 he was elected to the Senate.

60. *Washington Post,* March 3, and 15, 1972; *Congressional Quarterly Almanac,* 1972: 362–63; John Barriere to Carl Albert, April 10, 1972.

61. *Congressional Quarterly Almanac,* 1972: 363.

62. Ibid., 361.

63. House Rule X, clause 6(f), requires that "the Speaker shall appoint no less than a majority of members who generally supported the House position as determined by the Speaker." Usually conferees are drawn from the committees having primary jurisdiction over a bill or key provisions of it. When members oppose a key provision in a bill or a comprehensive substitute that is adopted by the House, they can create a prima facie case for being appointed to the conference by voting for the bill on final passage. When a substitute is adopted, it is possible that many, if not most, members of the committee reporting the bill will have opposed it. The claims of the committee members for seats in the conference may then come into conflict with the requirement that the majority of conferees have supported the bill, so long as each individual conferee voted for the bill on final passage. A speaker might well take advantage of this situation on occasion; but to commonly rig the conferences would violate the spirit of this rule and imply a speakership not in command of a House majority. See *Journal of the House of Representatives of the United States,* 98th Cong., 2d sess., 2163.

64. *Congressional Quarterly Almanac,* 1972: 370–71; John Barriere to Carl Albert, July 31, 1972.

65. *Congressional Quarterly Almanac,* 1973: 328–40.

66. *Congressional Quarterly Almanac,* 1974: 239–44.

67. Ibid., 324.

68. David J. Hadley and Ronald M. Peters, Jr., "The Speaker Votes" (paper delivered at the American Political Science Association Meeting, New York, 1981). The speaker does not normally vote except to make or break a tie. Albert's decision to vote in the Ninety-second Congress on recorded teller votes was intended to signal his position. He abandoned the practice of voting when the electronic voting system was initiated in the Ninety-third Congress.

69. William R. Anderson et al., "Dear Colleague," March 15 and 27, 1971; Thomas P. O'Neill, Jr., et al., "Dear Colleague," March 29, 1971; Carl Albert to Emanuel Celler, June 24, 1971; Bella Abzug, "Dear Colleague," June 28, 1971; Rowland Evans and Robert Novak, "The Doves Jump the Gun," *Washington Post,* April 26, 1972.

70. "The Custodian of the House," *Washington Post,* December 6, 1971; "Carl Albert Starting to Show Muscle," ibid., January 26. 1973; Richard Lyons, "Albert's Performance as Speaker Disappoints Some," ibid., December 8, 1971.

71. Richard E. Neustadt, *Presidential Power: The Politics of Leadership from FDR to Carter* (New York: John Wiley & Sons, 1980).

72. Hobart Rowen, *Washington Post,* January 30, 1973.

73. "$268.7 Billion Budget Seeks No Tax Rise," *Washington Post,* January 30, 1973.

74. David Broder, *Washington Post,* January 30, 1973.

75. Carl Albert, interview with author, May 13, 1979.

76. John Barriere, interview with author, July 18, 1979.

77. Carl Albert, "Impeachment and Resignation of Vice President Agnew," October 13, 1973 (audio tape).

78. Roger H. Davidson and Walter J. Oleszek, *Congress against Itself* (Bloomington: Indiana University Press, 1977), 62–68, 82–85.

79. Allen Schick, *Congress and Money: Budgeting, Spending and Taxing* (Washington, D.C.: Urban Institute, 1980), 46–48.

80. Gallup Poll, "Nixon's Popularity Rating, 1969–1973," as printed in *Watergate: Chronology of a Crisis* (Washington, D.C.: Congressional Quarterly Press, 1974), 2: 125.

81. Schick, *Congress and Money,* ch. 2; W. Thomas Wander, F. Ted Hebert, and Gary W. Copeland, eds., *Congressional Budgeting: Politics, Process, and Power* (Baltimore: Johns Hopkins University Press, 1984); Dennis S. Ippolito, *Congressional Spending* (Ithaca, N. Y.: Cornell University Press, 1981); Lance T. LeLoup, *The Fiscal Congress: Legislative Control of the Budget* (Westport, Conn.: Greenwood Press, 1980); Rudolph G. Penner, ed., *The Congressional Budget Process after Five Years* (Washington, D.C.: American Enterprise Institute, 1981); James P. Pfiffner, *The President, The Budget, and Congress: Impoundment and the 1974 Budget Act* (Boulder, Colo.: Westview Press, 1979). The most detailed account of the leadership's effort on the Impoundment Control Act is by Larry Dodd and Terry Sullivan, "Partisan Vote-gathering in the U.S. House of Representatives" (MS).

82. Schick, *Congress and Money,* 27, 47.

83. John Barriere to Carl Albert, January 15, 1973; Joel Jankowsky to Carl Albert, March 27, 1973.

84. John Barriere to Carl Albert, January 15, 16, and 18, 1973.

85. Arthur Maass to Senator Sam Ervin, attached to John Barriere to Carl Albert, February 2, 1973.

86. John Barriere to Carl Albert, February 20, 1973.

87. James R. Jones to Carl Albert, March 23, 1973; *New York Times,* July 26, 1973. Two members of Congress, John Culver of Iowa and John Brademas of Indiana, also submitted comprehensive critiques of the draft bill.

88. See *Congressional Quarterly Almanac,* 1974: 252–62.

89. John Barriere to Carl Albert, June 5, 1973, August 1, 1973.

90. Schick, *Congress and Money,* 384.

91. James L. Sundquist, *The Decline and Resurgence of Congress* (Washington, D.C.: Brookings Institution, 1981), gives an excellent account of the reform movement; the term *resurgence* is his.

92. Davidson and Oleszeck, *Congress against Itself,* 83–84; Sheppard, *Rethinking Congressional Reform,* chs. 4 and 5.

93. The Hansen substitute carried by 203–165. It was supported by 70 percent of the Democrats, whereas 65 percent of the Republicans voted for the Bolling proposal. Both Majority Leader O'Neill and Majority Whip McFall supported

the Hansen proposal against the expressed position of Speaker Albert, a sufficient indication that the matter was no longer regarded as a leadership issue (Davidson and Oleszeck, *Congress against Itself,* 250–54).

94. Carl Albert, interview with author, May 10–11, 1979; Richard Bolling, interview with author, June 12, 1980.
95. Carl Albert, "The First Session of the Ninety-third Congress" (press release, December 23, 1973, mimeographed), 1.
96. *Congressional Quarterly Almanac,* 1973: 7.
97. Carl Albert, "First Session," 12.
98. Carl Albert, interview with author, May 10, 1979; Spiro T. Agnew, *Go Quietly or Else* (New York: William Morrow, 1980), 165.
99. House Rule IX, Questions of Privilege, sec. 1, 664, *Manual and Rules of the House of Representatives, 93d Congress,* 92d Cong., 2d sess., 1973, H. Doc. 384, 329. A privileged resolution is entitled to supersede other pending business for immediate floor consideration.
100. "Albert Tells of Call in Agnew Case," *Washington Post,* October 10, 1973.
101. Jimmy Breslin, *How the Good Guys Finally Won: Notes from an Impeachment Summer* (New York: Ballantine Books, 1975), 60–61; O'Neill, *Man of the House,* 258.
102. Carl Albert, "The Most Dramatic Events of My Life," *Oklahoma State University Outreach* 5 (March 1974); Carl Albert, interview with author, May 11, 1979; John D. Ferrick, *The Twenty-fifth Amendment* (New York: Fordham University Press, 1976), 122–23; Richard M. Cohen and Jules Witcover, *A Heartbeat Away* (New York: Viking Press, 1974), 254–57; Roland Evans and Robert Novak, "Politics and Carl Albert's Decision," *Washington Post,* September 30, 1973.
103. Breslin, *How the Good Guys Finally Won,* 57–65; Ferrick, *Twenty-fifth Amendment,* 123.
104. Breslin, *How the Good Guys Finally Won,* 55.
105. Carl Albert and Richard Bolling, "Congressional Reform and Legislative Priorities," February 21, 1975 (audio tape). Bolling and Albert agree about Deschler's conservatism.
106. House Gingerly Pokes at Impeachment," *Washington Post,* September 21, 1973.
107. Breslin, *How the Good Guys Finally Won,* 65.
108. "The Reluctant Dragoon," *Time,* November 5, 1973, 31; Robert Sherrill, "Running from the Presidency," *New York Times Magazine,* December 9, 1973, 35, 130, 132, 134, 137–39, 141, 146–47, 150; "Every Other Inch a President," *Ramparts,* January 1974, 18–20.
109. "Speaker Albert Had Secret Blueprint for Transition to Presidency," *Sunday Oklahoman,* November 28, 1982.
110. Peter Rodino, interview with author, May 27, 1982.
111. Thomas P. O'Neill, Jr., statement (October 23, 1973, mimeographed).
112. Carl Albert, statement (October 23, 1973, mimeographed); Joseph Califano to Carl Albert, October 22, 1973, suggests a moderate tone for Albert's statement.
113. Carl Albert, interview with author, May 10, 1979; Breslin, *How the Good Guys Finally Won,* 76.
114. Albert had recommended Ford's nomination as vice president to Nixon.

115. David Broder, "Mr. Albert's Challenge," *Washington Post,* December 1, 1974.

116. Mary Russell, "A Most Frustrating Year for Speaker Albert," *Washington Post,* October 26, 1975.

117. "Task Force Press Conference," January 13, 1975 (audio tape).

118. Steve Bourke to Carl Albert, March 14, 1975.

119. Mike Reed and Joel Jankowsky, interview with author, November 2, 1981.

120. William Brodhead to Carl Albert, June 6, 1975.

121. Paul Tsongas and Tim Wirth, "Dear Colleague," June 18, 1975.

122. Robert N. Bellah, et al., *Habits of the Heart: Individualism and Commitment in American Life* (Berkeley and Los Angeles: University of California Press, 1985), 131.

123. Toby Moffett et al., memorandum to new members, June 10, 1975.

124. Bob Carr, press interview, June 17, 1975 (audio tape).

125. John Barriere to Carl Albert, June 19, 1975. Fourteen years later the leader of the Watergate Babies fessed up. The aim they really had in common was reelection. According to Toby Moffett: "I remember Sam Donaldson and Lesley Stahl were outside the gates of Airlie House, waiting to see what we were going to do next, because we had toppled those chairmen and changed the caucus rules. What they didn't know is that the conversation turned immediately to incumbency protection. That's what the weekend was spent on. . . . There were workshops on issues, but those were not nearly as popular. Everybody wanted to know how to get re-elected" (William Schneider, "JFK's Children: The Class of '74," *Atlantic,* March 1989, 38).

126. Memo for the record, confidential, June 12, 1975. This memo was probably prepared by the staff in the majority whip's office.

127. New Members Caucus Voting Profile, 94th Congress, 1st sess.; John Barriere to Carl Albert, June 17, 1975; Dodd and Sullivan, "Partisan Vote-gathering in the U.S. House."

128. Jamie O'Hara to Carl Albert, June 17, 1975, plus attachment.

129. Press Conference after meeting with freshman Democrats, June 17, 1975: remarks of Paul Tsongas, Carl Albert, and Bob Carr (audio tape).

130. Orfield, *Congressional Power,* 239–48; Democratic Study Group Special Report, "The 94th Congress" (September 27, 1976, mimeographed), 16–17.

131. John Barriere to Carl Albert, January 27, 1975; Gerald R. Ford, *A Time to Heal: The Autobiography of Gerald R. Ford* (New York: Berkeley Books, 1979), 235.

132. John Barriere to Mike Reed, June 3, 1975.

133. An important related exception to this general rule was the creation by Speaker Albert in 1975 of the Ad Hoc Select Committee on the Outer Continental Shelf. This energy-related committee was formed at the suggestion of Congressman John Murphy of New York. Its goal was to bring together members representing the various committee jurisdictions and seaboard interests affected by the development of the outercontinental shelf oil reserves. This was the first use of the power granted to the speaker to appoint select committees having the power to report legislation to the floor. While less publicized than the Select Energy Committee appointed by Speaker O'Neill in 1977 and chaired by Thomas L. Ashley of Ohio, the Murphy committee was the precedent upon which the Ashley committee was founded.

134. Ford, *Time to Heal,* 328.

135. Democratic Study Group, "94th Congress," 9.
136. "Whip News Special" (July 22, 1976, August 10, 1976, mimeographed).
137. "Whip News Special" (July 1, 1976, mimeographed); Democratic Study Group, 94th Congress," 3–5.
138. John Barriere to Carl Albert, February 2, 1976, June 23, 1976; Carl Albert to Honorable Committee Chairmen, June 19, 1976. Numerous responses by the committees are to be found in the Carl Albert Collection.
139. Carl Albert, retirement announcement (press release, June 5, 1976, mimeographed).

Chapter 5. The Democratic Speakership in the Postreform House

1. Edward Walsh, "The Man of the House Retires," *Washington Post,* October 19, 1986; Steven S. Smith, "O'Neill's Legacy for the House," *Brookings Review* 5 (Winter 1987): 28–36.
2. Thomas P. O'Neill, Jr., *Man of the House: The Life and Political Memoirs of Speaker Tip O'Neill* (New York: Random House, 1987), 12.
3. Paul Clancy and Shirley Elder, *Tip: A Biography of Thomas P. O'Neill, Speaker of the House* (New York: Macmillan, 1980), 64.
4. Ibid., 92–95.
5. Richard L. Lyons and Mary Russell, "Patman Loses House Chair; Hays to Stay," *Washington Post,* January 23, 1975; Bruce F. Freed, "Hays Resigns Post; Scandal Broadens," *Congressional Quarterly Weekly Report,* June 19, 1976, 1564–65.
6. Michael J. Malbin, "House Democrats Are Playing with Strong Leadership Lineup," *National Journal,* June 8, 1977, 940.
7. Tom Matthews, "The Man of the House," *Newsweek,* January 17, 1977, 20.
8. *Congressional Quarterly Weekly Report,* February 26, 1977, 361–63.
9. Congressional Quarterly, *Energy Policy* (Washington, D.C.: Congressional Quarterly Press, 1978), 1–44; James L. Cochrane, "Carter Energy Policy and the Ninety-fifth Congress," in Stephen H. Spurr, ed., *Energy Policy in Perspective* (Washington, D.C.: Brookings Institution, 1981), 547–608.
10. Richard Corrigan, "The Carter Energy Epic: Enter the Senate," *National Journal,* August 20, 1977, 1303–4.
11. Richard Lyons, "A Powerful Speaker," *Washington Post,* April 3, 1977.
12. Michael J. Malbin, "Rhetoric and Leadership: A Look Backward at the Carter National Energy Plan," in Anthony King, ed., *Both Ends of the Avenue* (Washington, D.C.: American Enterprise Institute, 1983), 212–45.
13. Jimmy Breslin, *How the Good Guys Finally Won: Notes from an Impeachment Summer* (New York: Ballantine Books, 1975), 31. Cf. Thomas Hobbes: "Reputation of power is power; because it draws with it the adherence of those who need protection . . . Also, what quality soever makes a man beloved or feared of many, or the reputation of such quality, is power, because it is a means to have the assistance and service of many" (*Leviathan* 1.10).
14. Charles O. Jones, *The Trusteeship Presidency: Jimmy Carter and the United States Congress* (Baton Rouge: Louisiana State University Press, 1988). Erwin C. Hargrove also captures Carter's resilient convictions in *Jimmy Carter as President: Leadership and Politics of the Public Good* (Baton Rouge: Louisiana State University Press, 1988).

15. Dom Bonafede, "Carter's Relationship with Congress: Making a Mountain Out of a 'Moorehill,' " *National Journal*, March 26, 1977, 416–63; "Meanwhile, Back on the Hill," *Newsweek*, March 28, 1977, 16–17; "Turning on the Water," ibid., April 4, 1977, 26.

16. Laurence Leamer, "Squaring Off in Washington: Tip O'Neill vs. Jimmy Carter," *New York*, May 16, 1977, 7–9.

17. Betty Glad, *Jimmy Carter: In Search of the Great White House* (New York: Norton, 1980), 417–19; Victor Lasky, *Jimmy Carter: The Man and the Myth* (New York: Richard Marek, 1979), 321–22; Martin Tolchin, "An Old Pol Takes on a New President," *New York Times Magazine*, July 24, 1977, 6.

18. "Hill Leaders Ask Carter to Improve Consultation," *Washington Post*, January 28, 1977.

19. Mercer Cross, "Carter and Congress: Fragile Friendship," *Congressional Quarterly Weekly Report*, February 26, 1977, 361–63.

20. "Tip O'Neill: The Great Accommodator," *Washington Post*, June 19, 1977; Tolchin, "An Old Pol," 6.

21. Bonafede, "Carter's Relationship with Congress," 456–63; "Behind the Growing Feud," *U.S. News and World Report*, May 23, 1977, 23.

22. See *Congressional Quarterly Almanac*, 1978: 275; Jim Wright, "Dear Colleague" (March 6, 1978, letter); "The Speaker's Humphrey-Hawkins Task Force" (March 6, 1978, mimeographed); Thomas P. O'Neill, "Dear Colleague" (March 7, 1978, letter); minutes of meeting on the Humphrey-Hawkins Full Employment bill (n.d.); summary of roll-call votes on Humphrey-Hawkins (n.d.); summary of H.R. 50, the Full Employment and Balanced Growth Act of 1978 (n.d.); staff memorandum for the files, Democratic Steering and Policy Committee (n.d.); memorandum, staff to Thomas P. O'Neill, March 14, 1978. Primary sources cited in this chapter are in the author's possession.

23. *Congressional Quarterly Almanac*, 1978: 272–73.

24. Ibid., 276.

25. Staff memorandum for the files, Democratic Steering and Policy Committee, May 25, 1978.

26. Gene Russell, press officer for the U.S. Conference of Mayors, as quoted by Robert J. Samuelson, "Writing a Federal Budget in the Age of the Squeeze," *National Journal*, September 23, 1978, 1496.

27. Ibid., 1496–97.

28. Joel Havemann, "A Good Year for the Congressional Budget Process," *National Journal*, September 23, 1978, 1501–8.

29. Barbara D. Sinclair, *Majority Leadership in the U.S. House* (Baltimore: Johns Hopkins University Press, 1983), 138–40.

30. Ibid., 141–46. See tables 5.1, 5.2, and 5.3. In a subsequent study of Speaker Wright's use of task forces during the 100th Congress, Sinclair indicates that they were "the standard way of handling legislation on which any significant leadership effort is deemed necessary." She fails to consider the implication of a fact she elsewhere in the same piece identifies: Wright's agenda was carefully crafted to win the support of most Democrats. It does not follow that the strategy of inclusion that the task forces are taken to exemplify will work when the political tide pulls the swing votes to the other side of the aisle. See Barbara D. Sinclair, "Majority Party Leadership in the House of Representatives: A Reassessment" (paper delivered at the American Political Science Association Meeting, Washington, D.C., 1988).

31. *Congressional Quarterly Almanac,* 1978: 22-C. The Carter figures were lower than those of any other president working with partisan congressional majorities since 1952, with the exception of Lyndon Johnson in 1968.

32. *Congressional Quarterly Weekly Report,* August 12, 1978, 2095–98.

33. Robert J. Samuelson, "Tax Cut Debate May Come Back to Haunt House Members," *National Journal,* August 5, 1978, 2095–98.

34. Richard E. Cohen, "Sophomore Democrats Are Restless on Taxes and House Procedures," *National Journal,* July 29, 1978, 1203.

35. *Congressional Quarterly Weekly Report,* August 12, 1978, 2095.

36. Richard E. Cohen, "Trying to Kick the Spending Habit," *National Journal,* April 21, 1979, 632. The Wright plan was similar to the Gramm-Rudman-Hollings Act of 1985.

37. Timothy Clark, "Now That Carter's 1980 Budget Is Out, Let the Battle Begin," *National Journal,* January 27, 1979, 133.

38. Sinclair, *Majority Leadership in the U.S. House,* 175–80.

39. Glad, *Jimmy Carter,* 443.

40. Carol Steinbach, "They Came to Camp David," *National Journal,* July 21, 1979, 1224–25.

41. "Text of President Carter's Address to the Nation," *Washington Post,* July 16, 1979; Jimmy Carter, *Keeping Faith: Memoirs of a President* (New York: Bantam Books, 1982), 115–20.

42. Dom Bonafede, "Carter Turns on the Drama—But Can He Lead?" *National Journal,* July 28, 1979, 1236–40.

43. Richard Lyons, "On Capitol Hill," *Washington Post,* July 24, 1979.

44. "In Surprise Move, House Votes Down '80 Budget Plan," *Washington Post,* September 20, 1979.

45. "House Votes Down Bill to Implement Canal Treaties," *Washington Post,* September 21, 1979.

46. "On Capitol Hill," *Washington Post,* September 22, 1979.

47. *Congressional Quarterly Alamanc,* 1979: 15.

48. Ibid.

49. "Carter Lashes Congressmen: Says to Expect Retaliation," *Washington Post,* September 21, 1979.

50. *Congressional Quarterly Almanac,* 1979: 15.

51. "House Votes to Bust Arms Budget," *Washington Post,* May 22, 1980; see also: "Ways and Means Votes against Carter's Oil Import Fee," *Washington Post,* May 23, 1980; "House Balks at Budget Plan," *Washington Post,* May 30, 1980; "The Budget: Who's in Charge Here?" *Newsweek,* June 23, 1980, 29.

52. See pp. 82–87; 93–95 above.

53. Richard Cohen, "Bipartisanship in the Wind," *National Journal,* December 13, 1980, 2131; *Congressional Quarterly Almanac,* 1981: 6–7.

54. Simon dropped out after running third on the first ballot; the second ballot saw Obey and Jones tied; on the third ballot Jones won by five votes (*Congressional Quarterly Almanac,* 1981: 9).

55. "House Democrats Challenge Reagan on Budget Voting," *Washington Post,* June 25, 1981; "Reagan Gains Major Budget Wins," ibid., June 26, 1981; "Reagan Triumphs in House Budget Vote," ibid., June 27, 1981; "House

Ratifies Savings Plan in Stunning Reagan Victory," *Congressional Quarterly Weekly Report*, June 27, 1981, 1127–29.

56. "Administration Toughens Stance on Tax Cut Plan," *Washington Post*, June 1, 1981; "Reagan, Democrats Unable to Agree on Terms for Tax Cut Plan," ibid., June 2, 1981.

57. "Tax Cut Compromise Barred as Committee Marks Ups Near," *Congressional Quarterly Weekly Report*, April 18, 1981, 670.

58. "Reagan and Rostenkowski Modify Tax Cut Proposals to Woo Conservative Votes," *Congressional Quarterly Weekly Report*, June 6, 1981, 979–80.

59. According to the Joint Committee on Taxation's estimates, the Democrats' bill would cost $37.8 billion in FY 1982 and $704.6 billion over five years; the Conable-Hance bill would cost $36.3 billion in FY 1982 and $752.7 billion over five years; the Senate Finance Committee bill would cost $37.0 billion in FY 1982 and $686.7 billion over five years (*National Journal*, August 1, 1981, 1391). By the time the bidding war was ended and the bill enacted into law, the Joint Tax Committee estimated the final cost to be $37.6 billion in FY 1982 and $747.3 billion over five years (*Congressional Quarterly Almanac*, 1981: 93). "Both Republicans and Democrats admitted their bills were more products of a political bidding war than blueprints for sound economic policy," according to the *Almanac* ("Reagan and Rostenkowski Modify Tax Cut Proposals," 979–80). David Stockman blames the Republicans for starting the bidding war (*The Triumph of Politics* [New York: Harper & Row, 1986], 267). His table at p. 268 charts the total cost of the bill.

60. "Reagan Makes Appeal to Voters for Tax Bill," *Washington Post*, July 28, 1981; "Republican Bill to Cost More, Hill Study Says," ibid., July 30, 1981; Ward Sinclair and Richard Lyons, "Tactics That Won," *National Journal*, August 1, 1981, 1371–76; *Congressional Quarterly Weekly Report*, August 1, 1981, 1377.

61. "Budget Fight Shows O'Neill's Fragile Grasp," *Congressional Quarterly Weekly Report*, May 9, 1981, 786; "Tip O'Neill on the Ropes," *Time*, May 18, 1981, 17.

62. "GOP Starting Media Blitz," *Congressional Quarterly Weekly Report*, July 25, 1981, 1325.

63. "The Campaign against Tip O'Neill," *Congressional Quarterly Weekly Report*, July 25, 1981, 1367.

64. "Senate Unanimously Rebuffs President on Social Security," *Washington Post*, May 21, 1981; "The Social Security Flap," *Congressional Quarterly Weekly Report*, May 23, 1981, 896.

65. Ronald Reagan to Thomas P. O'Neill, Jr., September 24, 1981.

66. *Congressional Record*, 97th Cong., 1st sess., September 25, 1981, H 6626.

67. Ibid.

68. Spenser Rich, "O'Neill Seeking Social Security Data by April 15," *Washington Post*, October 14, 1981.

69. "Remarks of the Speaker before the Democratic Caucus" (September 16, 1981, mimeographed).

70. Majority Leader Wright's four-point policy (forgiveness for past sins, leadership bills, pattern of voting on them, awards based on these votes) was not endorsed by Speaker O'Neill. O'Neill had no desire to adopt a formal party position on

loyalty matters. The policy was dropped as soon as it was announced, the later caucus retribution against Phil Gramm notwithstanding. In *Majority Leadership in the U.S. House*, 73–76, Sinclair takes the Steering and Policy Committee's role in policy development under O'Neill more seriously than I do here. She cites Wright's four-point statement as representing party policy, but this was not the view expressed to me by O'Neill's staff.

71. Thomas P. O'Neill, Jr., press conference, March 23, 1982 (transcript).
72. Thomas P. O'Neill, Jr., press conference, April 6, 1982 (transcript).
73. Thomas P. O'Neill, Jr., press conference, April 21, 1982 (transcript).
74. Thomas P. O'Neill, Jr., press conference, April 26, 1982 (transcript).
75. Thomas P. O'Neill, Jr., press conference, April 29, 1982 (transcript).
76. Ibid.
77. Helen Dewar, "House Overrides President, 301–117, on Spending Bill," *Washington Post*, September 10, 1982; Dennis Farney, "House Overrides Appropriations-Bill Veto by 301–117 as Reagan Coalition Dissolves," *Wall Street Journal*, September 10, 1982; "Senate Joins House in Overriding Veto," *Washington Post*, September 11, 1982; Lou Cannon, "President Loses a Battle, Gains a Campaign Issue," *Washington Post*, September 11, 1982.
78. "House Passes $1 Billion Democratic Jobs Bill," *Congressional Quarterly Weekly Report*, September 18, 1982, 2292.
79. James Wooten, "A Sea Change," *Playboy*, February 1982, 114.
80. *Congressional Quarterly Weekly Report*, December 11, 1982, 3031–33. The proposed change would have required the signatures of two-thirds of the members to bring a proposed constitutional amendment to the floor.
81. "Democratic Caucus Rewrites House Rules, and the GOP Groans," *Washington Post*, December 13, 1982.
82. Gramm resigned his seat in Congress and then won it back as a Republican in the special election that his resignation triggered. He later won reelection as a Republican from his conservative Texas district, was rewarded with a seat on the Budget Committee by the House Republicans, and was launched on a successful campaign for the U.S. Senate seat vacated by the retirement of Republican John Tower in 1984. See "Representative Gramm Resigns, Says He'll Both Fight and Switch for Seat," *Washington Post*, January 6, 1983; "Texans Ignore Party Labels," *Congressional Quarterly Weekly Report*, February 19, 1983, 373; "Gramm Switches, Fights—and Wins," *Newsweek*, February 21, 1983, 29.
83. "House Panel Seats Assigned, Democrats Tighten Control," *Congressional Quarterly Weekly Report*, January 8, 1983, 4–6.
84. "Democratic Unity," *Wall Street Journal*, January 14, 1983.
85. Dennis Farney and Andy Pastor, "In the House the Jockeying Grows Intense for Coveted Seats on Energy Committee," *Wall Street Journal*, January 3, 1983, 29.
86. "Rostenkowski Seeks More Influential Role," *Congressional Quarterly Weekly Report*, January 29, 1983, 192–95; "Rostenkowski's Ways and Means," *National Journal*, February 5, 1983, 287; "Rostenkowski Asks Tax Freeze," *Washington Post*, February 9, 1983; "Rostenkowski Seeks to Cancel Future Tax Cuts," *Wall Street Journal*, February 9, 1983.
87. "Rostenkowski Enrages O'Neill on Tax Stance," *Washington Post*, February 10, 1983.

88. Thomas P. O'Neill, Jr., press conference, February 10, 1983 (transcript).

89. "Pragmatism Is the Watchword as House Budget Committee Heads into 1984 Fiscal Storm," *Congressional Quarterly Weekly Report,* March 5, 1983, 459–63.

90. Richard E. Cohen, "What a Difference a Year—and an Election—Make in Producing a Budget," *National Journal,* April 2, 1983, 696–99.

91. "Democrats on House Panel Advance Own Budget Plan," *Congressional Quarterly Weekly Report,* March 19, 1983, 544.

92. *Congressional Quarterly Almanac,* 1983: 231–39.

93. "We're Unable to Act," *Time,* November 28, 1983, 18.

94. *Congressional Quarterly Weekly Report,* November 19, 1983, 2407.

95. "We're Unable to Act," 19.

96. Ibid., 18.

97. Murray Edelman's excellent exposition in *The Symbolic Uses of Politics* (Urbana: University of Illinois Press, 1964, 1985) introduces the concept of symbolic politics. To Edelman, symbolism is ordinarily used to solace the public while private interests dominate the policy process from within. Symbolism is thus divorced from policy making. However accurate that depiction may have been of American politics in the 1960s, the thesis requires modification today. There are significant areas of policy making in which the Edelman formula still operates; but on the big ticket items of the 1990s, including budget and tax policy, as well as major foreign policy issues, symbolic appeals were used to drive the policy process. Private interests could not overcome the force of symbolic appeals, and instead tried to enlist them in their own cause. An exploration of the role of symbolism in the policy process would lead to an enriched understanding of American politics today.

98. Juan Williams, "President, Speaker Exchange Verbal Barbs," *Washington Post,* May 20, 1983. Id., "Reagan, O'Neill Spar over Poverty, Health of Economy," *Washington Post,* August 7, 1983.

99. The losers, obviously, were the Senate Democrats and the House Republicans. Due to the smaller size and more open rules of the Senate, however, Democratic senators were often players. The more restrictive House rules left little opportunity for the Republicans to have an impact on policy, and they were often very frustrated as a result.

100. Thomas P. O'Neill, Jr., press conferences, March 15, April 26, and June 17, 1983 (transcripts).

101. U. S. Congress, *Joint Hearings before the Senate Select Committee on Secret Military Assistance to Iran and the Nicaranguan Opposition and the House Select Committee to Investigate Covert Arms Transactions with Iran,* testimony of Robert C. McFarlane, July 14, 1987 (Washington, D.C.: GPO, 1988), 272.

102. Thomas P. O'Neill, press conferences, September 12, 13, 20, 22, 26, 27, 28, and 29, 1983 (transcripts); Gerald F. Seib, "Reagan Wants Congress to Back Marines in Beirut," *Wall Street Journal,* September 14, 1983; "Reagan, O'Neill Compromise on Force in Lebanon," *Washington Post,* September 21, 1983; "Congress Crafts 'War Powers' Compromise," *Congressional Quarterly Weekly Report,* September 24, 1983, 1963.

103. Thomas P. O'Neill, Jr., press conference, October 24, 1983 (transcript); "Reappraisal," *Washington Post,* October 25, 1983; "O'Neill Stays the Course on the Blood-Soaked Lebanon Policy," ibid., October 25, 1983.

104. "Lebanon Policy Is Questioned as Support Wavers on Hill," *Congressional Quarterly Weekly Report*, January 7, 1984, 3-7.

105. "Reagan Lobbies a Restive Congress on Lebanon," *Congressional Quarterly Weekly Report*, January 28, 1984, 125.

106. *Congressional Quarterly Weekly Report*, February 4, 1984, 227.

107. "Reagan Writes an End Note for U.S. Troops off Lebanon," *Congressional Quarterly Weekly Report*, April 7, 1984, 769.

108. Thomas P. O'Neill, Jr., press conference, April 10, 1984 (transcript).

109. Thomas P. O'Neill, Jr., press conference, October 28, 1983 (transcript).

110. Thomas P. O'Neill, Jr., press conference, November 9, 1983 (transcript).

111. *Congressional Quarterly Almanac*, 1983: 82-H, 112-H; 1984: 54-H, 94-H; 1985: 22-H; 1986: 20-H, 54-H.

112. In January 1980, Carter led Reagan 62 percent to 33 percent; in January 1984, Reagan led Mondale 51 percent to 44 percent (George H. Gallup, Jr., *The Gallup Poll* [Wilmington: Scholarly Resources 1981], 5; id., *The Gallup Poll* [Wilmington: Scholarly Resources 1985], 3).

113. Thomas P. O'Neill, Jr., press conference, February 29, 1984 (transcript).

114. Thomas P. O'Neill, Jr., press conference, June 6, 1984 (transcript); "Hart Told to End Strife within Party," *Washington Post*, June 8, 1984.

115. "Democratic Panel Dissolves with Jackson Wishes Unmet," *Washington Post*, June 22, 1984.

116. "Ferraro Joins '84 Ticket by Acclamation," *Washington Post*, July 20, 1984.

117. Mark Shields, "Man behind the Woman," *Washington Post*, August 3, 1984; Linda E. Demkovich, "Fairness Issue Will Be Campaign Test of Reagan's Record on Budget Policies," *National Journal*, September 8, 1984, 1648-53.

118. At the end of each day's legislative business, the House entertains special orders, during which members may speak on any subject they wish. Special orders time is divided between the two parties, and by rule the minority party gets first claim. Usually the special order speeches and colloquies are given to an empty chamber. They often relate to some ceremonial matter, a testimonial, or some member's particular legislative interest. That the Republicans used special orders to attack the Democrats was an innovation due entirely to the presence of the C-SPAN coverage, which provided a way of reaching a larger audience. See "Live from Capitol Hill," *Washington Post*, September 6, 1979; Ronald Garay, *Congressional Television: A Legislative History* (Westport, Conn.: Greenwood Press, 1984); *Congressional Quarterly Almanac*, 1984: 206-8; *Congressional Record*, May 7, 1984, H3434; May 14, 1984, H3795; May 14, 1984, H3789-90; May 15, 1984, H3840. A member's words may be "taken down" on a motion by another member if, in the opinion of the chair, they violate the norm that members may not speak personal ill of other members on the floor.

119. Michael Barone and Grant Ujifusa, *The Almanac of American Politics, 1986* (Washington, D.C.: National Journal, 1985), lxiii-lxiv.

120. Richard E. Cohen, "Boll Weevils Lead Charge against Speaker," *National Journal*, November 17, 1984, 2191-92.

121. Margaret Shapiro, "O'Neill Faces New Pressure to Step Back," *Washington Post*, November 16, 1984; Cohen, "Boll Weevils Lead Charge against Speaker," 2191-92.

122. Shapiro, "O'Neill Faces New Pressure."

123. John F. Kennedy, *Profiles in Courage* (New York: Harper & Brothers, 1956), 186–210. On Norris's view of Cannon, see Richard Lowitt, *George W. Norris: The Making of a Progressive, 1861–1912* (Syracuse: Syracuse University Press, 1963), 142.

124. "House Committee Seats Filled; Assignments Delayed in Senate," *Congressional Quarterly Weekly Report*, January 26, 1985, 141–43.

125. "O'Neill Turns Conciliatory on Reagan," *Washington Post*, January 28, 1985.

126. These figures are derived from the unofficial transcripts of the speaker's press conferences provided to the author by staff. It is not known if transcripts of all press conferences are included, but a staff member was assigned to transcribe every press conference and few, if any, were probably omitted.

127. Hedrick Smith, *The Power Game: How Washington Works* (New York: Random House, 1988), ch. 14, discusses these two bills and the strategy of "reshaping" legislation.

128. "Senate's Initiative Leaves Democrats Frustrated at Leadership, Republicans," *Congressional Quarterly Weekly Report*, October 12, 1985, 2036–37.

129. CRS Issue Brief, "Sequestration Actions for FY89 under the Gramm-Rudman-Hollings Act" (Congressional Research Service, Library of Congress, Washington, D.C., January 2, 1989, mimeographed).

130. Barber B. Conable, Jr., *Congress and the Income Tax* (Norman: University of Oklahoma Press, 1989), makes the point about purchasing reform with bracket creep.

131. "Tax Action Gets Boost in House," *Washington Post*, February 25, 1985; "Rostenkowski Urges Support for Tax Reform," ibid., February 26, 1985; Jeffrey H. Birnbaum and Alan S. Murray, *Showdown at Gucci Gulch: Lawmakers Lobbyists and the Unlikely Triumph of Tax Reform* (New York: Random House, 1987), 100–103.

132. "Opportunity Knocks: Rostenkowski to Answer Reagan on Taxes," *Washington Post*, May 28, 1985; Steven V. Roberts, "A Most Important Man on Capitol Hill," *New York Times Magazine*, September 22, 1985, 44; "Tax Lawmakers Will Leave Finger-Prints on Any Overhaul of the Federal Code," *Congressional Quarterly Weekly Report*, June 1, 1985, 1038; "Rostenkowski: A Firm Grip on Ways and Means," ibid., June 6, 1985, 1316–19.

133. The first quotation is from Roberts, "A Most Important Man," 48; the second is from Thomas P. O'Neill, Jr., press conference, September 4, 1985 (transcript). See also Richard Cohen, "The Politics of Tax Reform," *National Journal*, September 21, 1985, 2170.

134. Randall W. Strahan, *Change in Congress: The House Committee on Ways and Means* (Charlotte: University of North Carolina Press, 1990) provides the best recent account of the Ways and Means Committee. See also Birnbaum and Murray, *Showdown at Gucci Gulch*, 117.

135. Roberts, "A Most Important Man."

136. Richard E. Cohen, "Tax Reform, Democratic Style," *National Journal*, November 30, 1985, 2719; "Ways and Means Finishes Tax Code Overhaul," *Congressional Quarterly Weekly Report*, November 30, 1985, 2483–97; "GOP Tax Alternative Put Aside," *Washington Post*, December 4, 1985.

137. "GOP Defeats Attempt to Consider Tax Bill," *Congressional Quarterly Weekly Report*, December 14, 1985, 2613–16. Under the standing rules of the House, bills come to the floor under open rules. The Rules Committee can, however,

report bills to the floor under rules that prevent all amendments (closed rules), or make in order only some (modified rules). The House must vote to approve or disapprove the rule governing a bill before it can consider the bill itself. The speaker controls the Rules Committee by nominating the members from his party. He can use his influence with the committee to produce rules favorable to his legislative ends. If a voting majority on the floor fundamentally opposes the bill or some aspect of it, it can defeat the rule and force the adoption of a new rule more favorable to its goals. Therefore, the speaker's power presupposes, rather than creates, a voting majority.

138. Richard E. Cohen, "Frustrated House GOP Demands Respect from White House," *National Journal,* December 21, 1985, 2898–2901. See also Timothy J. Conlan, Margaret T. Wrightson, and David R. Beam, *Taxing Choices: The Politics of Tax Reform* (Washington, D.C.: Congressional Quarterly Press, 1989), 125–29; Birnbaum and Murray, *Showdown at Gucci Gulch,* 158–59.

139. "GOP Defeats Attempts to Consider Tax Bill," *Congressional Quarterly Weekly Report,* December 14, 1985, 2613.

140. "House Reverses Self, Passes Major Tax Overhaul," *Congressional Quarterly Weekly Report,* December 21, 1985, 2705–11.

141. Birnbaum and Murray's *Showdown at Gucci Gulch* provides the best account of the passage of the tax reform bill of 1986.

142. Thomas P. O'Neill, Jr., press conferences, February 3, March 4, 22, and 29, April 30, May 6, 8, and 14, August 12, September 9, 16, and 17, 1986 (transcripts).

143. Thomas P. O'Neill, Jr., press conference, September 23, 1986 (transcript).

144. The concept of bipartisanship is relative. Speaker O'Neill and Budget Committee Chairman Bill Gray enjoyed poking fun at Ronald Reagan's conception of bipartisanship—all of the Republicans plus one Democrat. Yet when *Congressional Quarterly* labels as a partisan vote one on which a majority of one party votes against a majority of the other party, it is insensitive to the political dynamics of partisanship. For example, when the House rejected the rule on the tax reform bill in 1985, Speaker O'Neill demanded that President Reagan produce fifty Republican votes before agreeing to bring it up again—not a majority. With regard to the bills mentioned in the text, the budget resolution and the drug bill were each supported by a majority of Republicans and Democrats. The immigration bill and the trade bill drew only sixty-two and fifty-nine Republican votes respectively. Yet the trade bill was politically defined as a Democratic bill and the immigration bill was not. It seems that a bill is bipartisan in the politically relevant sense when it draws substantial votes from both sides of the aisle and is not used as an instrument for one party to club the other. See Thomas P. O'Neill, Jr., press conference, September 23, 1986 (transcript); *Congressional Quarterly Weekly Report,* November 15, 1986, 2901–3.

145. Edward Walsh, "The Man of the House Retires," *Washington Post,* October 19, 1986.

146. "Media, Power Shifts, Dominate O'Neill's House," *Congressional Quarterly Weekly Report,* September 13, 1986, 2131.

147. "They Call Him 'Mr. Speaker,'" *Houston Post,* December 7, 1986.

148. Paul West, "The Wright Stuff," *New Republic,* October 14, 1985, 23.

149. Carl Albert, interview with author, April 1987.

150. *Congressional Quarterly Almanac*, 1977: 7.

151. Roberts, "A Most Important Man," 50.

152. For Speaker Wright's use of the Rules Committee, see Roger Davidson, "The New Centralization on Capitol Hill," *Review of Politics* 50 (Summer 1988): 346–64; Sinclair, "Majority Party Leadership: A Reassessment"; Stanley Bach and Steven S. Smith, *Managing Uncertainty in the House of Representatives: Adaptation and Innovation in Special Rules* (Washington, D.C.: Brookings Institution, 1988). The use of special rules has much history behind it, as chapter 2's discussion of Reed and Cannon and chapter 3's discussion of caucus government by the Democrats indicates.

153. Richard E. Cohen, "Minority Blues," *National Journal*, May 9, 1987, 1156.

154. Jack W. Germond and Jules Witcover, "Wright's Tax Ideas Are Test of Reagan's Clout," *National Journal*, April 14, 1987, 640; "Wright Launches Push for Tax Rise Support," *Washington Post*, March 5, 1987; "Wright Presses Tax Hike Campaign," ibid., March 6, 1987; "Democrats Find Taxes Treacherous Territory," ibid., March 15, 1987; "Hill Finds Raising Taxes and Especially Unsavory Prospect This Year," ibid., May 28, 1987.

155. "Wright Ekes Out Tax Bill's Passage," *Washington Post*, October 30, 1987.

156. "House Chaos Provided a Day to Remember," *Washington Post*, October 31, 1987.

157. Janet Hook, "Bitterness Lingers from House Budget Votes," *Congressional Quarterly Weekly Report*, November 7, 1987, 2712–13.

158. James A. Barnes, "Partisanship," *National Journal*, November 7, 1987, 2825.

159. *Congressional Record*, 100th Cong., 2d sess., May 24, 1988, H3576–91. The partisan issue continued to fester. See Richard B. Cheney, "An Unruly House: A Republican View," *Public Opinion*, January/February 1989.

160. "Reagan Reports 'General' Accord on Latin Proposal," *New York Times*, August 6, 1987.

161. William Schneider, "Giving Peace Sort of a Chance in Nicaragua," *National Journal*, August 15, 1987, 2103.

162. "Wright Steers Middle Course on Contra Aid," *Congressional Quarterly Weekly Report*, September 19, 1987, 2255.

163. "New Contra Politics: Wright Dominant Force," *Congressional Quarterly Weekly Report*, October 31, 1987, 2661; Steven V. Roberts, "Reagan and Wright Caught Up in Feud," *New York Times*, November 15, 1987. In broadcast interviews immediately following the announcement of his resignation, Wright indicated his belief that his role in the Contra affair, more than any other act, turned the Republicans implacably against him.

164. "Wright Steers Middle Course on Contra Aid," 2255.

165. "Omnibus Trade Bill to Get a Second Chance," *Congressional Quarterly Weekly Report*, June 18, 1988, 1668. The plant-closing provision was later passed as a separate bill and President Reagan permitted it to become law without his signature. The bill had become an issue in the 1988 presidential campaign.

166. "Reagan Wins Concessions in Funding Bill," *Congressional Quarterly Weekly Report*, December 26, 1987, 3185.

167. "Pepper Bill Pits Politics against Process," *Congressional Quarterly Weekly Report*, June 4, 1988, 1491–93; *Congressional Quarterly Almanac*, 1987: 493–505.

168. *Congressional Quarterly Weekly Report*, June 18, 1988, 1647–50; September 17, 1988, 2585; October 1, 1988, 2699–2701.

169. "House-Passed Drug Bill Has Clear GOP Imprint," *Congressional Quarterly Weekly Report*, September 24, 1988, 2661–62.

170. Richard E. Cohen, "Quick-Starting Speaker," *National Journal*, May 30, 1987, 1409–13; id., "Full Speed Ahead," *National Journal*, January 30, 1988, 238–44; Janet Hook, "Jim Wright: Taking Big Risks to Amass Power," *Congressional Quarterly Weekly Report*, March 12, 1988, 623–26.

171. Compare Smith, "O'Neill's Legacy for the House" (cited in note 1 above) with "Speaker Jim Wright Takes Charge in the House," *Congressional Quarterly Weekly Report*, July 11, 1987, 1483. See also Sinclair, "Majority Party Leadership: A Reassessment," and Davidson, "New Centralization on Capitol Hill," 345–64.

172. Tom Kenworthy, "Panel Reaches No Conclusion on Wright Probe," *Washington Post*, June 3, 1988; Janet Hook, "Ethics Panel Gingerly Confronts Wright Case," *Congressional Quarterly Weekly Report*, June 4, 1988, 1498–1501; id., "Ethics Panel to Open Broad Inquiry on Wright," ibid., June 11, 1988, 1579; "Statement of House Speaker Jim Wright" (June 10, 1989, mimeographed).

173. Janet Hook, "Common Cause Seeks Inquiry into Speaker Wright's Finances," *Congressional Quarterly Weekly Report*, May 21, 1988, 1394; id., "Chronology of an Investigation," ibid., April 15, 1989, 795.

174. Peter Osterlund, "House Ethics: The Wright Stuff," *Christian Science Monitor*, May 31, 1988.

175. *Congressional Insight*, January 6, 1989, 1.

176. On the pay increase controversy, see Janet Hook, "Pay Raise is Killed, but the Headaches Persist," *Congressional Quarterly Weekly Report*, February 11, 1989, 262–63; ibid., "How Pay Raise Strategy Came Unraveled," ibid., February 11, 1989, 264–67. On Gingrich's election as House GOP whip, see id., "Gingrich's Selection as Whip Reflects GOP Discontent," ibid., March 25, 1989, 625.

177. House Committee on Standards of Official Conduct, 101st Cong., *Report of the Special Outside Counsel in the Matter of Speaker James C. Wright, Jr.* (Washington, D.C.: GPO, 1989), and *Statement of the Committee on Standards of Official Conduct in the Matter of Representatives James C. Wright* (Washington, D.C.: GPO, 1989). See also Richard Whittle, "Wright Accused of 69 Ethics Violations," *Dallas Morning News*, April 18, 1989; Tom Kenworthy, "House Committee Charges Wright with 69 Ethics-Rules Violations," *Washington Post*, April 18, 1989.

178. Tom Kenworthy, "Panel Drops Some Charges in Wright Ethics Inquiry," *Washington Post*, April 5, 1989.

179. Ken Ringle, "Memory and Anger: A Victim's Story," *Washington Post*, May 4, 1989; Charles R. Babcock, "Speaker Loses His Right-Hand Man," *Washington Post*, May 12, 1989; Dan Wright, "Top Wright Aide Quits Over Criminal Record," *Washington Post*, May 12, 1989.

180. "Eight Days in May," *Congressional Quarterly Weekly Report*, June 3, 1989, 1291. See also David Rogers, "House Panel Hears Heated Arguments to Drop, Keep Charges against Wright," *Wall Street Journal*, May 24, 1989.

181. Janet Hook, "Passion, Defiance, Tears: Jim Wright Bows Out," *Congressional Quarterly Weekly Report*, June 3, 1989, 1289.

182. John M. Barry's *The Ambition and the Power: The Fall of Jim Wright* (New York: Penguin Books, 1989) provides an inside account of Jim Wright's speakership. Barry makes an icon of Wright for his leadership in the 100th Congress, leaving him little choice but to defend Wright against the charges brought against him in the 101st. Barry, a good Hobbesian, sees the Wright saga as a story of ambition and power, but his interpretation lacks a theoretical context for explaining the Wright speakership as a permutation of the office in the democratic era.

183. Charles R. Babcock, "Money Has Big Role in Coehlo's Career," *Washington Post*, May 28, 1989; Jeff Gerth, "Coehlo Enriched Party without Gaining Riches," *New York Times*, May 28, 1989; Carol Matlack, "Coehlo's Road to Resignation Began with a Bid for Investment Advice," *National Journal*, June 3, 1989, 1350–51. On Coehlo's actions on behalf of savings and loans, see House Committee on Standards of Official Conduct, *Report of the Special Outside in the Matter of Speaker James C. Wright, Jr.*, 23. On Coehlo's role generally, see Brooks Jackson, *Honest Graft: Big Money and the American Political Process* (New York: Knopf, 1989).

184. Christopher Madison, "The Heir Presumptive," *National Journal*, April 29, 1989, 1034–38; Janet Hook, "The Turmoil and the Transition: Stage Set for New Speaker," *Congressional Quarterly Weekly Report*, May 27, 1989, 1225–26.

185. Tom Kenworthy and Dan Balz, "House Democrats Reeling from Blows: Gephardt Jumps into Majority Leader Race as Current Team Crumbles," *Washington Post*, May 28, 1989.

186. Janet Hook, "House to White House: How Tough a Trail," *Congressional Quarterly Weekly Report*, May 10, 1986, 1025–29.

187. Jeffrey H. Birnbaum, "Gephardt to be House Majority Leader; Gray Wins Third-Ranking Post of Whip," *Wall Street Journal*, June 15, 1989.

188. Janet Hook, "House's New Leadership Brings Next Generation to Power," *Congressional Quarterly Weekly Report*, June 10, 1989, 1376–83.

189. Most speakers have been in their sixties when first elected. In the twentieth century Henderson (59), Longworth (56), and Rayburn (58) attained the speakership when still under sixty; Rainey (77) and McCormack (71) were over seventy. Floor leaders have tended to be in their fifties. In the twentieth century only Mann, Snell, and Rhodes among Republicans and Rainey, Byrns, and Bankhead among Democrats were past sixty when first elected. Gephardt is the youngest Democratic floor leader since Claude Kitchen, who was forty-six when he succeeded Oscar Underwood in 1915. Charles Halleck became the youngest Republican floor leader in the twentieth century in 1947 at forty-six. The average prior service of twentieth-century speakers is 13.25 terms, and the model prior term of service is 13. Foley was elected speaker in his thirteenth term. The average prior service of twentieth-century floor leaders is 10 terms, with a mode of 8. Gephardt was elected majority leader in his seventh term; only McCormack, Clark, and Williams among Democrats and Halleck among Republicans had the same or less seniority when first elected floor leader. Gephardt should take caution from McCormack's experience, however. He

was elected Democratic floor leader in 1940 in his sixth term at forty-nine; he became speaker in his seventeenth term at seventy-one. Gingrich, elected speaker at age fifty-one, is the youngest speaker since Reed.

190. Harold Seidman and Robert Gilmour, *Politics, Position, and Power: From the Positive to the Regulatory State* (New York: Oxford University Press, 1986).

Chapter 6. The Republican Speakership

1. David Rohde, *Parties and Leaders in the Postreform House* (Chicago: University of Chicago Press, 1991).
2. Richard E. Cohen, "Foley's Honeymoon," *National Journal,* June 15, 1989, 1799–1801.
3. Janet Hook, "Rout of Democratic Leaders Reflects Fractured Party," *Congressional Quarterly Weekly Report,* September 30, 1984, 2529–31.
4. Christopher Madison, "Negotiating a Fiasco," *National Journal,* October 20, 1990, 2568.
5. Criticisms of Foley's leadership are reported in Christopher Madison, "Foley's Muted Call to Arms," *National Journal,* February 23, 1991, 479; Richard E. Cohen, "Foley's Balancing Act," ibid., June 15, 1991, 1396–98; id., "Faulting Foley," ibid., August 10, 1991; Tom Kenworthy, "A Highway Bill That Taxed the Speaker," *Washington Post National Weekly Edition,* August 12–18, 1991, 12; and Chuck Alston, "The Speaker and the Chairmen: A Taoist Approach to Power," *Congressional Quarterly Weekly Report,* November 2, 1991, 3177–78.
6. Thomas S. Foley, "Speaking for the House," in Ronald M. Peters, Jr., ed., *The Speaker: Leadership in the U.S. House of Representatives* (Washington, D.C.: CQ, Inc., 1995), 247–62.
7. Janet Hook, "The Bank Buck Stops with Foley," *Congressional Quarterly Weekly Report,* March 14, 1992, 600; David Rogers, "Angry House Democrats Divided by Scandal Speak of Mutiny and Turn Their Fury on Foley," *Wall Street Journal,* April 3, 1992; Richard E. Cohen, "Foley in Peril over House Bank Fiasco," *National Journal,* March 21, 1992, 711.
8. David S. Broder, "Congressional Sham, Public Cynicism," *Washington Post,* December 9, 1990, K7.
9. Ronald D. Elving, "Foley Helps Put the Brakes on Drive for Term Limits," *Congressional Quarterly Weekly Report,* November 9, 1991, 3261–63; Jack Germond and Jules Witcover, "The Speaker's Angry Constituents," *National Journal,* October 29, 1994, 2538; Richard E. Cohen, "Ominous Rumbling on Foley's Home Turf," ibid., October 1, 1994, 2294.
10. Clifford Klauss, "New Congressmen's Revolt Shows Early Signs of Fading," *New York Times,* November 24, 1992, A11.
11. Janet Hook, "Reforms Are Hard to Come By as 'Reform Month' Looms," *Congressional Quarterly Weekly Report,* October 2, 1993, 2613–18; id., "Congressional Reform Panel Winds Up Work in Discord," ibid., November 27, 1993, 3249–50; Eliza Newlin Carney, "Dead Ended," *National Journal,* July 23, 1994, 1733–37.
12. Bob Woodward, *The Agenda: Inside the Clinton White House* (New York: Simon & Schuster, 1994); Elizabeth Drew, *On the Edge: The Clinton Presidency* (New York: Simon & Schuster, 1994), 164–73.

13. Haynes Johnson and David S. Broder, *The System: The American Way of Politics at the Breaking Point* (New York: Little, Brown, 1996), 476–532; Dan Balz and Ronald Brownstein, *Storming the Gates: Protest Politics and the Republican Revolution* (New York: Little, Brown, 1996), 59–110.

14. Balz and Brownstein, *Storming the Gates,* 19–58.

15. The best recent treatment of House Republicans is William F. Connelly, Jr., and John J. Pitney, Jr., *Congress' Permanent Minority?* (Lanham, Md.: Littlefield Adams, 1994).

16. An excellent and concise account of the Republican reforms is found in C. Lawrence Evans and Walter J. Oleszek, *Congress under Fire: Reform Politics and the Republican Majority* (Boston: Houghton Mifflin, 1997).

17. Richard E. Cohen, "Team Gingrich," *National Journal,* January 14, 1995, 66–79; David S. Cloud, "Speaker Wants His Platform to Rival the Presidency," *Congressional Quarterly Weekly Report,* February 4, 1995, 331–35.

18. Evans and Oleszek, *Congress under Fire,* 89.

19. Richard E. Cohen, "The Role Players," *National Journal,* January 27, 1996, 164–78; Juliet Elperin and Amy Keller, "The Vision Thing Comes to House Committees," *Roll Call,* January 22, 1996, 1; Gabriel Kahn and Damon Chappie, "In House, Wielding Gavel Ain't What It Used to Be," ibid., 30. In each of these cases the speaker had solid support in the Republican conference and the senior members who were bypassed did not. Gingrich did not seek to deny a chairmanship to any senior member with an established constituency in the conference. Still, the speaker sent a strong message.

20. Newt Gingrich, "Leadership Task Forces: The 'Third Wave' Way to Consider Legislation," *Roll Call,* November 16, 1995, 5; Newt Gingrich, *To Renew America* (New York: Harper Collins, 1995), 122; Juliet Elperin, "House Bills Bypass Committee Process," *Roll Call,* March 18, 1996, 1.

21. The contextual perspective on legislative leadership is grounded in classical organization theory, which tended to make institutional leadership a dependent variable. See Joseph Cooper and David W. Brady, "Institutional Context and Leadership Style: The House from Cannon to Rayburn," *American Political Science Review* 75 (1981): 411–25; and David W. Rohde and Kenneth Shepsle, "Leaders and Followers in the House of Representatives: Reflections on Woodrow Wilson's *Congressional Government,*" *Congress and the Presidency* 14 (1987): 111–33. Yet contemporary management theory emphasizes the potentially transformative effect of organizational leadership. See W. Edwards Demming, *Out of the Crisis* (Cambridge: Massachusetts Institute of Technology, Center for Advanced Engineering Study, 1982); and Peter F. Drucker, *The Effective Executive* (New York: Harper & Row, 1967). Traditionally, legislative leadership has been regarded as inherently transactional. See James MacGregor Burns, *Leadership* (New York: Harper & Row, 1978), pt. 4. Yet there is evidence that due to demographic and cultural changes, legislative leadership is becoming more integrative. See Cindy S. Rosenthal, "Women's Ways of Political Leadership" (Ph.D. diss., University of Oklahoma, 1995); and Kenneth Thomas, "Conflict and Conflict Management," in Marvin Dunnette, ed., *The Handbook of Industrial Organizational Psychology* (Chicago: Rand McNally, 1975), 889–935.

22. Scot M. Faulkner and Lawrence D. Longley, "Changing the System: Institutional Change (and Inertia) in the U.S. House of Representatives" (paper

delivered at the Second Workshop of Parliamentary Scholars and Parliamentarians, Centre for Legislative Studies, University of Hull, August 3, 1996).

23. *Congressional Quarterly Weekly Report*, December 21, 1996, 3461.

24. For profiles of Newt Gingrich and his political world, see Nancy Gibbs and Karen Tumulty, "Master of the House," *Time*, December 25, 1995, 55–87; Connie Bruck, "The Politics of Perception," *New Yorker*, October 9, 1995, 50–77; and Gail Sheehy, "Newt's Revelations," *Vanity Fair*, September 1995, 147–55.

25. Robert Blake, *Disraeli* (London: Eyre & Spottiswoode, 1966), 759–66. The comparison of Gingrich and Disraeli is not simply a matter of historical analogy; Gingrich cites Disraeli as his model as a party builder (Newt Gingrich, interview with author, July 4, 1996).

26. Cohen, "Team Gingrich"; Fred Barnes, "The Executive," *New Republic*, May 22, 1995, 25–27.

27. James G. Gimpel, *Fulfilling the Contract: The First 100 Days* (Boston: Allyn & Bacon, 1996), 114–28.

28. Helen Dewar, "Update on the Contract: Promises Waiting to Be Kept," *Washington Post National Weekly Edition*, August 21–27, 1995, 14. In remarks to military officers at the Army's Training and Doctrine Command Center in 1995 Gingrich characterized the Contract as an exercise in the implementation of doctrine aimed at transforming the culture of the House Republicans along lines of military theory. According to this view, the Contract was less important as a body of legislation than as a vehicle for the implementation of a leadership regime. Although the speaker's military characterization of the Contract no doubt reflects accurately his perception of it, it seems unlikely that it was originally conceived by Republican members in this light. See Damon Chappie, "General Gingrich Ices the 104th Congress," *Roll Call*, September 30, 1996, 1; and id., "Gingrich Enlists Army, But Top Official Worried," ibid., October 3, 1996, 1.

29. Jason DeParle, "Newt's Fiercest Fight," *New York Times Magazine*, January 28, 1996, 35–37; Warren L. Nelson, "The Powerhouse," *Government Executive*, May 1996, 48–52.

30. Adam Clymer, "Special Counsel Will Investigate Ethics Case Affecting Gingrich," *New York Times*, December 7, 1995, 1; Jackie Koszczuk, "Democrats Push to Expand Gingrich Investigation," *Congressional Quarterly Weekly Report*, December 16, 1995, 3783–84.

31. David E. Rosenbaum, "A Murky Impasse: Data vs. Principle," *New York Times*, November 16, 1995, A14; Alan Murray, "Locking Horns: Partisan Intransigence May Keep Budget War Unresolved for Months," *Wall Street Journal*, November 17, 1995, A1.

32. Two extensive accounts of the budget war are Elizabeth Drew, *Showdown: The Struggle between the Gingrich Congress and the Clinton White House* (New York: Simon & Schuster, 1996); and David Maraniss and Michael Weisskopf, *"Tell Newt to Shut Up!"* (New York: Touchstone, 1996). On Clinton's vetoes, see Mark T. Kehoe, "Clinton Veto Tally Up to Eleven," *Congressional Quarterly Weekly Report*, January 6, 1996, 10.

33. Karen Tumulty, "Getting the Edge," *Time*, June 5, 1995, 23–25; George Hager, "To Deal or Not to Deal," *Congressional Quarterly Weekly Report*, October 14, 1995, 3120; David E. Rosenbaum, "House Passes Budget Bill, Bedrock of

G.O.P. Agenda; Much Bargaining Remains," *New York Times*, October 27, 1995, A1.

34. David Maraniss and Michael Weisskopf, "Gingrich Has An Epiphany: A Deal Is Impossible," *Washington Post National Weekly Edition*, February 3–11, 1996, 10–13.

35. Labor-union attack ads against Gingrich are reported in Peter T. Kilborn, "With New Militancy, Nation's Unions Hope to Drive Republicans from Congress," *New York Times*, February 19, 1996; Jonathan Weisman, "Republicans Battle Unions on Hill and on Airwaves," *Congressional Quarterly Weekly Report*, August 10, 1996, 2250–52; and Phil Kuntz, "GOP Launches Counterattack against Labor for Its Bid to Help Democrats Recapture Congress," *Wall Street Journal*, August 20, 1996, A12. Democratic attacks ads on Gingrich on Medicare are reported in Adam Clymer, "Both Political Parties Wage Medicare Debate on the Air," *New York Times*, August 16, 1995, A13; Tim Curran, "Seize Medicare Vote, DCCC Tells Recruits," *Roll Call*, October 16, 1995, 1; and Christopher Georges, "GOP Adopts Risky Strategy on Medicare, Taking Case for Cuts Openly to Voters to Blunt Attack Ads," *Wall Street Journal*, April 23, 1996, A24.

36. Morton M. Kondracke, "Health, Welfare Reform Prospects Are Boosting Divided Government," *Roll Call*, July 25, 1996, 8; Donna Casala, "In Senate Balancing Act, Lott Finds His Footing," *Congressional Quarterly Weekly Report*, July 27, 1996, 2091–94; Jackie Koszczuk and Donna Cassata, "From Revolution to Realism: The 104th Bids Farewell," ibid., October 5, 1996, 2832–39.

37. Janet Hook, "Gingrich Sees Less Militant Agenda for House GOP," *Los Angeles Times*, November 21, 1996, 1; David Rogers, "Gingrich, Accepting Speaker's Post, Sees 'Moral Obligation' to Work with Clinton," *Wall Street Journal*, November 21, 1996, A24.

38. Juliet Elperin, "Sound and Fury Prompts Faulkner Exit," *Roll Call*, November 25, 1996, 1; id., "New Top Administrator Cleans House," ibid., December 5, 1996, 1.

39. George Hager, "Budget Will Still Be the Issue to Test Moderates' Muscle," *Congressional Quarterly Weekly Report*, November 9, 1996, 3217–19; Jackie Koszczuk, "Members Move to Claim Center as Voters Demand Moderation," ibid., 3198–3207; Eliza Newlin Carney, "Coalescing Catches On: Can It Help?" *National Journal*, December 7, 1996, 2646, 2648; Dan Balz, "A Moderate Romance," *Washington Post National Weekly Edition*, December 9–15, 1996, 11.

40. "Gingrich Issues His Own Statement," *CNN AllPolitics*, December 21, 1996, http://www.allpolitics.com/news/9612/21/gingrich.statement/index. shtml.

41. Adam Clymer, "Gingrich Makes Appeal to Party; Moderate Urges Him to Step Down," *New York Times*, January 7, 1997, A1; Larry Margasak, "Gingrich Appeals for Loyalty," *Washington Post*, January 7, 1997, A1. As a part of the agreement by which Gingrich accepted the charges, the language of the charges was modified to suggest that both the violations of the IRS code and the false statements to the committee might have been unintentional. Later, after being reprimanded by the House, Gingrich contended that he had not intentionally done anything wrong and had never admitted that he had. Special Counsel James Cole's report suggested otherwise.

42. Adam Clymer, "G.O.P. Narrowly Re-Elects Gingrich as House Speaker, Despite Ethics Accusations," *New York Times,* January 8, 1997, A1. In December 1923 the Republicans, with a narrow 225-207 majority, could not gather 218 votes to reelect Speaker Gillett when a handful of progressives withheld their votes seeking concessions on House rules. Nicholas Longworth negotiated an agreement on the rules, and on the eighth ballot Gillette was elected with 215 votes, a majority of members casting votes for candidates by name. See the *Congressional Record,* December 3-4, 1923, H5-15.

43. The complete report of the Ethics Committee, along with supporting documentation, has been released to the public. The best published synopsis is in *Roll Call,* January 6, 1997. Reports of the final vote include Janet Hook, "House Approves Punishment of Gingrich, 392-28," *Los Angeles Times,* January 22, 1997, 1; John E. Yang, "House Reprimands, Fines Speaker," *Washington Post,* January 22, 1997, A1. Analyses of the documentation include Blaine Harden, "Ego and Ambition Mark Speaker's Writings," ibid.; and Glenn F. Bunting, "Gingrich PAC Used Charity to Route Gifts Papers Show," *Los Angeles Times,* January 22, 1997, 1.

44. Jackie Koszczuk, "Revolutionary Rhetoric Fades as GOP Softens Its Edges," *Congressional Quarterly Weekly Report,* November 23, 1996, 3299-3306; Richard E. Cohen, "The Era—or Aura—of Good Feelings," *National Journal,* November 23, 1996.

45. Jackie Koszczuk, "Unpopular, Yet Still Powerful, Gingrich Faces Critical Pass," *Congressional Quarterly Weekly Report,* September 14, 1996, 2573-79; Damon Chappie, "House Republicans Talk Peace, Study Up on 'War Games,'" *Roll Call,* December 2, 1996, 1; R. W. Apple, Jr., "Analysis: Gingrich Is Back But Subdued," *New York Times,* January 8, 1997, 1; Richard E. Cohen, "The Once and Future Newt Gingrich," *National Journal,*December 21, 1996, 2751.

46. Randall Strahan has developed an interesting theoretical framework that stresses leadership opportunities as moments in institutional time. See Randall Strahan, "Leadership in Institutional and Political Time: The Case of Newt Gingrich and the 104th Congress" (paper delivered at the annual meeting of the American Political Science Association, San Francisco, August 29–September 1, 1996).

47. United States Houses of Representatives, Committee on Standards of Official Conduct, 105th Cong., 1st sess., exhibit 42, House assigned number (HAN) 02103-01252.

Index